SPEECHES

SPEECHES

M. VISVESVARAYA

GYAN

Published by

Gyan Publishing House
5, Ansari Road
Daryaganj, New Delhi-110002
Phone: 011-47034999, 9811692060
E-mail: books@gyanbooks.com

Distribution Network
gyanbooks.com
India, USA, Canada, UK, Australia

ISBN: 978-93-7447-020-6 (PB)

First Published, 1917

2nd Impression 2026

Printed at: Gyan Press, Delhi.

SPEECHES
Author: M. VISVESVARAYA

SPEECHES

BY

SIR M. VISVESVARAYA, K.C.I.E.

DEWAN OF MYSORE

1910-11 to 1916-17

BANGALORE:
PRINTED AT THE GOVERNMENT PRESS
1917

PREFACE.

THESE speeches are collected and printed in one volume by direction of His Highness the Maharaja.

They are primarily intended for reference as a record of public functions. But they may also appeal to the large and growing body of public men and Government officials who are working to promote the welfare of the country.

One idea repeats itself in these speeches with insistent iteration, *viz.*, that the Mysore standards of earning and living are low, that this low efficiency is due to ignorance and lack of training, and that every subject of His Highness the Maharaja can render personal service to his country by encouraging education, effort and enterprise to the best of his power and opportunities.

M. V.

BANGALORE,
8th August 1917

TABLE OF CONTENTS.

SPEECHES BY

SIR M. VISVESVARAYA, K.C.I.E.

DEWAN OF MYSORE.

I. SPEECHES MADE BEFORE ASSUMPTION OF OFFICE OF DEWAN.

1910–1912.

ADDRESS TO MYSORE ENGINEERS.

[The Fourth Session of the Mysore Civil Engineers' Association was held in the Association rooms, Bangalore, on 14th November 1910. SIR (then Mr.) M. VISVESVARAYA, in opening the proceedings, delivered the following address :—] 14th Nov. 1910.

Gentlemen,—It gives me great pleasure to welcome you to the fourth session of the Civil Engineers' Association in Mysore. With the permission of Government, it has been possible to hold this session in Bangalore, in the current month, instead of as in past years during the busy season of the Dasara in the Capital City.

We meet here with a threefold object. First, we have to consider the working of the Association with a view to enhance its usefulness in the coming years. Secondly, the papers on professional subjects which some of you have prepared will be read and discussed. Thirdly, it is proposed to take the opportunity of your presence here to exchange views on some of the more pressing questions connected with the maintenance and management of public works in the districts.

These annual meetings, if good use is made of them, will afford a valuable opportunity, to every member, of coming into intimate contact and comparing notes with his brethren from all parts of the Province on matters connected with the everyday practice of his profession.

The Civil Engineers' Association in Mysore was started in the year 1907 under the guidance of Mr. W. McHutchin, M.I.C.E., the late Chief Engineer of this State, and his energetic Deputy, Captain Bernard Dawes, R.E., whose premature death we all deplore. I understand that the late Captain Dawes, Mr. C. M. Mahadeva Sastri and Mr. B. C. Srinivasiengar were among the principal promoters.

In these days of specialization it is not easy for everyone to purchase and possess for himself all the latest books and leading engineering periodicals, so necessary to keep abreast of progressive thought in the world. This Association provides the means of co-operative effort in this respect; and therefore in his own interests, it ought to be the solicitude of every engineer in the State to help in maintaining the Association at a high standard of efficiency.

At present the books of the Association are stored in one of the rooms of the Northern Circle Office. The members complain that the circulation of the professional papers is slow and irregular. We require new rooms, more engineering journals, many new books, and a small establishment. His Highness' Government have recently been approached in the matter of accommodation and for an annual grant for the purchase of professional periodicals. I have every hope that our appeal will meet with a generous response.

Address to Mysore Engineers.

When suitable rooms and the necessary establishment are provided, we should be able to take more interest in the working of the Association. The engineers who are at headquarters or who visit headquarters should have all the latest books available for consultation, particularly in those branches of engineering with which we are most concerned in this Province. Sooner or later, a section of the Library should be devoted to electrical and railway engineering for the use of officers and private gentlemen interested in the Cauvery Power Scheme and railways. Of the more valuable books and periodicals it may be necessary to buy and keep duplicate copies, one intended for circulation and the other to be always available for reference in the Library.

In order that the business of the Association may be conducted properly, we require not only your enthusiasm but also your powers of self-restraint in the observance of the rules. Papers or books circulated should be returned punctually within the time allowed, or in cases of delay, an additional fee should be recovered. I trust, before we separate, you will discuss all such questions and appoint a working committee of officers in whom you have confidence and place the business of the Association on a satisfactory footing.

Compared with the area and population of the State, we are responsible for a large and efficient system of public works, developed and perfected by successive British engineers. The prosperity of Mysore is practically what it is on account of its public works, chiefly irrigation tanks and channels, both ancient and modern.

In respect of buildings, either in number or variety, we are not behind other Provinces or Native States in this country. Our travellers' bungalows are more numerous and commodious than in any other part of India I know of.

There is also a good system of roads; even in the remotest parts of the Province, cultivators are able to carry their produce to the market in all seasons of the year.

We have a splendid system of tanks in the country which is a testimony alike to the precarious supply of fertilizing moisture and to the industry of the people. There are nearly 29,000 tanks, large and small, and 2,500 of these are what are called "major tanks" which bring in an annual revenue of over Rs. 300 each. So actively has the policy of tank construction been pursued in the past that in parts of the country like the Kolar District there is little or no room for new tanks. There is no Province in India—perhaps none in the world—in which so many tanks are found crowded into so small an area. From calculations made a few months ago, I found that the irrigation tanks represented a capital asset of over six crores—an asset which the present generation has inherited from its predecessors. The soil without being very fertile is well adapted for irrigation. But for these tanks in many parts of this dry plateau, there would be no population and no cultivation. The river channels exist in tracts not subject to severe drought. The tanks are also partly responsible for a portion of the dry crop cultivation, and the irrigation system including river channels is responsible, directly or indirectly, for more than half the land revenue of the State.

We have made very good progress in regard to town water supply. There are three large installations, which supply water to populations located at a considerable distance from their source, under the very competent management of Mr. V. Rangasawmy Iyengar, Executive Engineer. In the case of Bangalore, water is raised by pumping from a distance of over 14 miles. We have also here the largest Jewell Filter installation in India.

Address to Mysore Engineers.

One of the earliest drainage schemes carried out in India on the European model outside the Capital Cities was the small installation in the Fort at Mysore by Mr. Standish Lee. This gentleman is also responsible for the engineering work in connection with town-planning both at Bangalore and Mysore. It is true that the extensions in these places are largely the creation of Government; still, they stand out as examples of foresight and thoughtful construction, reflecting much credit both on the engineer and the administrators who developed them.

We have also in Mysore the pioneer electrical undertaking in India, *viz.*, the Cauvery Power Scheme, under the able supervision of my friend Mr. Gibbs. The scheme brings in a net revenue to the State of over Rs. 12 lakhs and indirectly helps Government to earn another 16 lakhs from royalty, and to maintain the largest gold mining industry in India. The output of gold at the Kolar Gold Fields is, as you know, over Rs. 300 lakhs a year.

Among ancient works, there are a few historic forts and some magnificent religious buildings of great artistic value. The famous temples at Halebid and Belur exhibit types of sculptural art perhaps unrivalled in the world.

I have already said that in respect of irrigation, we have made as good progress in the State as anywhere else in the world. We have one large lake newly constructed at Marikanave which is second only in capacity to the Assuan Reservoir, but our pride in the size of the lake is sobered by the fact that it only fills about one-sixth full annually although it bottles up a whole river draining 2,075 square miles of catchment.

Our tanks are numerous but the majority of them are of comparatively small size. They came into existence in days when the construction of larger ones was not understood. Although useful in ordinary seasons and in periods of moderate scarcity, they are liable to fail when they are most needed, as the experience of the famine of 1876-77 has shown. When such failures occur, the results are disastrous. As already remarked, the river channels exist in tracts not subject to frequent deficiency of rainfall. There is need therefore for a class of works not hitherto attempted in the State, *viz.*, storage works for collecting the surplus rainfall of the *malnad* regions for the fertilization of the dry *maidan* lands.

There is yet another point to be noticed with regard to irrigation. At present the irrigation under our tanks is managed by rule of thumb; the produce is not what it should be on account of bad seasons and the prevailing ignorance in water distribution. In some of the advanced countries like Italy, canals are constructed and maintained by Government or a company, and the control and distribution of water after it leaves the main canal is undertaken by societies or associations composed of the cultivators themselves. The latter employ private consulting engineers even as people engage lawyers. In this respect, I think we may with profit follow the lead of the Italians and gradually encourage people to maintain local irrigation works, first under the advice of a Government technical staff and eventually of engineers in private practice. As irrigation is the mainstay of the country and intimately associated with agriculture, it will have a valuable educative effect in self-help. Need I say that the more the people of individual localities look after their own affairs in this respect, the greater will be the productive power of the country and the less the responsibility of Government for relieving distress in times of famine?

The country is also in sore need of further railway development. At present, including the Bangalore-Madras line, which does not belong to the State, we have 462 miles of railways, or at the rate of one mile for every 11,990 persons residing in the State; in British India the rate is one mile for every 8,709 persons, in the United Kingdom, one for 1,809 persons, in the United States of America, one for 330 persons and in Canada, one for 234 persons. It is clear we want more railways very badly.

With the exception of the palaces and a few public edifices, there are no large buildings in our cities to compare with the high and magnificent buildings which adorn Bombay or Calcutta or any of the great commercial cities of Europe or America. In Europe, the construction of buildings higher than seven to nine stories is not permitted. In America, buildings styled "skyscrapers" are carried to enormous heights. The highest existing building of the latter class in the City of New York measures 715 feet above foundation level. The construction of another building of 62 stories and 900 feet high has been recently sanctioned. A single building of this class can accommodate the entire population of one of our small mofussil towns.

Town drainage is an expensive matter in Europe, and with our limited resources we cannot hope to attain the European standard for a long time to come. Deep underground sewers in Europe are kept so scrupulously clean and many of them so well lighted with electricity that people can walk through miles of them without discomfort.

In the matter of town-planning, there is a new awakening in the West. City, town and village extensions are planned beforehand with the same care, as to their requirements, as individual buildings, and there are associations in every important city in America for providing parks, widening roads, beautifying promenades and public places. All large cities—and many small ones too—are constantly undergoing renovation, alteration and improvement. Every large city, between Constantinople at one end and San Francisco at the other, seems to know what every other important city is doing in the way of improvement.

Year by year the death rate in Europe is going down, but on account of malaria, the loss of life in India, and in our own State in the *malnad*, is going on unchecked. Malaria is a preventable disease. The preventive measures, to be effective, require local initiative and co-operation which at present are not to be found in this country. In parts of Italy like the Roman Campagna and the districts of Ferrara, lagoons and malarial swamps have been drained and land below the level of the sea reclaimed and kept dry and made available for habitations and cultivation, by artificial pumping. In most places here, we only want a few ditches cut, but there is no organization to do even that. Malaria can be stamped out if only people took care to drain the pools, to level broken ground to an even slope, to cut ditches and lower the level of subsoil water where necessary some eight or ten feet below ground surface and remove undergrowth and decaying vegetation within (and for a furlong or two all round) inhabited areas. These are sovereign remedies, but in order to be effective, people must provide them by their own combined effort.

As remarked a few days ago in a very graceful speech by His Excellency the Governor of Madras, we reside in one of the most beautiful and picturesque provinces on the face of the earth. There are views witnessed here the like of which are to be found nowhere else in the world. Visitors to Japan, like our Sanitary Commissioner, will tell you how clean and attractive every place of interest is, and how neat and orderly every temple is maintained in that country. As in Japan, so in Mysore, almost every picturesque spot, be it on a hill top, glen or river bank, is utilized for building a temple, but people have neglected even to maintain what they have inherited. What a paradise this country would be, could we but educate our people to keep temples, bathing ghats, public buildings and open spaces clean and sanitary!

There is an unusual stir in the domain of technical engineering at the present time. New and startling developments are being noticed in many lands. In crowded cities, in the midst of congested population, railways are taken either overhead or deep underground. In Berlin and New York, rapid communication is maintained by overhead railways. The underground tube railways of London cross and recross the Thames below the river bed. Motor vehicles and wireless telegraphy have revolutionized the means of communication and a flying machine is about to emerge from its chrysalis stage.

From the contemplation of recent developments and ideals, let us return for a moment to our work-a-day conditions to consider the normal duties of the engineer in the districts.

One of the first duties of the engineer is to maintain an epitome of statistics, data and information pertaining to the district in general and to public works in particular. It is only by possessing correct information and comparing the works and resources of one district with those of another and the cost of maintenance of one year with that of previous years, that the engineer will get a true perspective view of his charge. In a recent printed official circular, I have indicated the main heads under which this information may be compiled, and I trust every Executive Engineer will check and perfect the details for his district with a view to enable us to issue a brief Manual of Public Works in due course.

Address to Mysore Engineers.

The bulk of the work in the districts is of a very ordinary character but it is not on that account to be despised. Many a young engineer may find no higher work to design or construct than a road culvert or a tank sluice. A dispensary or a dak bungalow may be his dream in architecture. But whatever the work, if the designs are to be proper and economical, a close study of local conditions and a correct knowledge of how similar work is best done elsewhere are very necessary. The young engineer may lay to heart the advice which Mr. Moberly Bell of the London *Times* gave on a similar occasion. "If your business," said he, "is only to sweep a crossing, remember that it is your duty to make that crossing the best swept in the world."

To ensure sound work, *specifications and rates* should be constantly revised and maintained up to date. The supervision of the subordinate officers and contractors should be close and effective; and a constant watch should be maintained on peculation and bad work.

There is a vast amount of work awaiting scientific treatment such as the observations of, and calculations for, discharges of rivers and tank weirs, the experiments for the duty of water as applied to irrigation, the testing of the strength and improving the quality of materials, etc. The investigation of projects both for new works and for the improvement of existing works is one of the most important duties of the district engineer.

Whether the work in the districts is to be maintained well or ill, whether the management is economical or the reverse, depends largely on the efficiency of the staff and particularly on the personal energy and foresight of the head of the district.

Before I close this brief address, perhaps you will allow me to make a passing reference to the drawbacks of the less efficient section of our engineers and subordinates and offer a few words of advice, particularly to the junior members of the profession.

Our defects have grown with us, with our tradition, environment and climate. The cold climate of Europe demands a high standard of activity as well as of comfort. Movement is necessary there even to keep oneself warm and there is stir and activity everywhere. An unmarried working man in Europe will want Rs. 30 for bare subsistence whereas the Indian labourer is content with Rs. 5 or less. There is similar disproportion in the working and earning capacity of the two races in every grade of life and in every sphere of activity, which in India is not enriched by preparation or organization. An Englishman, unless asleep, feels an invisible compulsion to be doing something, to consider time as of some importance. With us, according to custom and tradition, the charm of life consists in ease—ease from the absence of compulsion to do anything. In a French book recently translated by Sir William Meyer of Madras, the author* says: "If India possessed a more fertile soil and were better endowed with mineral wealth, she would still languish in poverty if the natives continued to work with the same apathetic indifference as at present. Slackness is the worst curse of the country. At first sight, everybody seems to be taking an active part in some common toil; as a matter of fact, several persons are looking on at the labour of one. As has been cynically remarked, out of five people who seem to be working, one is doing nothing, one is resting, one is looking on and another is helping the previous three. Everyone endeavours to escape his full toll of toil."

The Public Works Department is not altogether free from this taint of slackness. There are engineers who seem content to keep things going, to sign papers, answer

* M. J. Chailley's *L'Inde Britannique (Administrative Problems of India).*

enquiries for the day without a thought for the morrow. They avoid all work that is not compulsory, so long as they can do so without actually getting into trouble. Whether their duties be light or heavy, they are always in arrears. They do about, say, 75 per cent of what is expected of them and wait for calls for the remaining 25 per cent. When a man is transferred from one station to another within the few thousand square miles of this Province, I receive piteous appeals of inconvenience and hardship for a reconsideration of the order.

We are too much accustomed to soft conditions. The number of working hours is fewer here than in Europe. There are more Government holidays in this State than even in British India. Official employment is sought for because once a man gets into service, whether efficient or weak, wise or imprudent, he is practically sure of a competence for the rest of his life.

Closely associated with slackness is lack of initiative—the inclination to look for instructions from the top at every step. No original investigation will be possible unless every one thinks for himself. The remedy to this state of things is a resolve to work hard. No one is any the worse for hard work. "The more energy we put forth," said an eminent German to me, "and the more we use our intelligence, the greater the pleasure, provided we do not overdo it to the point of fatigue." With industry and by studying technical books and papers, even men of mediocre talent can excel. But unless people consider slackness a disgrace, there is no hope of improvement.

Every engineer should travel at least in British India to acquaint himself with the best practices of British engineers. The more enterprising men among you ought to visit England and other foreign countries to study the latest methods of engineering construction and administration.

Address to Mysore Engineers.

These are days of specialization; engineering is becoming a complex science. No man can be an expert in every branch of engineering, but every one while maintaining a general standard of efficiency in his daily work, can specialize in some subject suited to his experience and bias, and attain a high degree of proficiency in it. I trust the younger men of our service will choose early and specialize in some subject or other.

The other day one of the junior members of our service, who is undergoing practical training in England, wrote to me and said that he had applied and been recommended for a scholarship in aeronautics. I do not know whether he has succeeded but at least the attempt shows a spirit of enterprise worthy of all praise.

The resources of the State are meagre, the establishment limited and the responsibility of this department to maintain the public works in a state of efficiency is great.

Our works may be small in magnitude but the engineering characteristics of any given class of works are the same all the world over. We require the same training and knowledge as in any other country, in order to design with skill and execute with economy. We cannot afford to fall out of date either in our information or methods.

Gentlemen, I have nothing more to add. If I have referred to some of the drawbacks of our engineers, it is because without knowing our defects, without realizing proper standards, we cannot hope to improve. In other countries, men less gifted and with far less theoretical training than ourselves turn out more work and earn higher rates of remuneration, because they have a sort of mercantile activity and working power which our people lack. I would therefore say to the young engineer—"Study the business methods of our European fellow-engineers, cultivate system, give strict attention to detail, avoid both lack of confidence and over-confidence, and rely on yourself and your work for your material advancement. Remember character is more important than cleverness."

If the members present here to-day endeavour to inoculate every official and employee from top to bottom with similar ideals, the way is paved for a high degree of individual and aggregate excellence in the Department. I have ventured to give this advice because there is good material among our young men and I am anxious they should make proper use of their opportunities. I ask you to believe that the advice comes from one whose strongest sympathies are with efficiency and progress.

SPEECH AT THE SCHOOL FOR DEAF MUTES AND THE BLIND.

7th Jan. 1911.

[Presiding at the Decennial Celebration of the School for Deaf Mutes and the Blind at Mysore, on 7th January 1911, Sir M. Visvesvaraya made the following speech :—]

Gentlemen,—After the proceedings which we have all followed with great interest, it only remains for me to say a few words to congratulate the committee and the staff of the school on the efficient maintenance of the institution during the past year.

I have taken the place intended for another. You will all share my regret that Mr. Campbell, who was to have presided, is slightly indisposed and is unable to be present. Mr. Kantaraj Urs asked me at the Gymkhana, late last evening, to assist at this function. Although a hundred objections crowded to my mind soon afterwards, I could find no excuse at the moment and therefore accepted the honour. The Honorary Secretary, Mr. M. Srinivasa Rao, has just read a brief and lucid report. He has pointed out that according to the census of 1901, there are over a thousand children of school-going age, suffering from these physical defects in the Mysore Province of whom only 35 are being trained in this school. With the growth of years, no doubt there will be more schools of this class and a larger percentage of the infirm will be brought under the domain of training.

Judging from the report and the demonstrations, we have an efficient teaching staff under an enthusiastic expert teacher in the present headmaster. I understand the subjects taught at present are weaving, tape-weaving, rattan work, and music. Later on sewing, drawing, printing, manufacture of carpets, and other home industries might be added.

The articles manufactured in the school have earned high commendation at several exhibitions and I understand that some of the boys have evinced musical talent of a high order. The best testimony to the usefulness of the institution is the statement in the Secretary's report that several of the past students of the school are, at present, usefully employed and are earning an independent living.

The school owes its present position to the munificence of His Highness the Maharaja and the past and present Dewans of the State and to a small extent to the generosity of charitably disposed persons in Mysore. Great credit is due to the originator Mr. M. Srinivasa Rao for his enthusiasm and disinterested labours since its foundation.

You will agree that the committee and particularly Mr. Kantaraj Urs, the Chairman, and Mr. Srinivasa Rao are to be congratulated on the progress made so far.

Speech at the School for Deaf Mutes and the Blind.

Before closing, I wish to add a few remarks on the utility of such schools. The educational principle of the twentieth century is the education of all the people for the work of the people. In Western countries, the expenditure on education and technical training is considered a national investment. That is why most of the Western countries have resorted to compulsory education. By educating everyone at the proper age, the citizens are equipped with the capacity to earn an honest living. Similarly by seeking out weaklings like the deaf and dumb and giving them a training, they are made self-supporting and useful members of society.

In the city of New York, the Municipality gives education and books free for the use of students up to the B.A. standard. They firmly believe that the prosperity of the city as a whole depends on the education and skill and efficiency of the people.

Another Western principle of which this institution is an example is the utilization of charity for stimulating self-help. A rich or charitable man among us will feed or maintain a number of the weak and the decrepit as long as he can, and if he is asked about their future, what would happen when he is unable to render them further help, he will only reply that Providence will take care of them. The Western principle is quite different. Charity is used for encouraging self-reliance which is the more permanent form of assistance.

Wherever any large number of people remain without education, and the natural ability of the people goes unutilized, it is considered a reflection on Government and the community as a whole.

This institution helps to equip defectives with a certain amount of education and skill which enables them to earn an independent living instead of being a burden on society. The deaf and the blind have their lives brightened and their interests widened by the training they receive to the mutual benefit of themselves and the community. Although the school accommodates only less than three per cent of the deaf, dumb and blind boys in the country, it is gratifying that a beginning has been made. The school serves one of the higher purposes of civilization, and small though it is, its maintenance among us does credit to the philanthropy and public spirit of the leading men of this city.

SPEECH AT BANGALORE CENTRAL COLLEGE DAY MEETING.

[On March 16, 1912, the students, past and present, of the Bangalore Central College, celebrated the "Central College Day." A large and distinguished gathering was present. Sir M. Visvesvaraya, presiding at the public meeting held in connection with it, made the following speech :—] 16th Mar. 1912.

Mr. Tait, Ladies and Gentlemen,—I esteem it a privilege to take part in this function to-day. It is pleasant at all times to visit old scenes and meet old friends, and to-day we have the added pleasure of meeting so many *alumni* of the college and of calling ourselves "old boys."

There are several types of boys present to-day: from the old boys who have just left college to the grey-bearded boys who hold positions of responsibility in the official and public life of the State. There are also the boys

C

Speech at Bangalore Central College Day Meeting.

proper, namely, the students, the embryo citizens of the future. Boys, old or young, you are one and all delightful company, and in the name of the College Day Committee, I offer you all a cordial welcome.

My first thoughts on such an occasion naturally go to the time, now more than thirty years ago, when I was a student of this institution. In those days, the college, the high school and the middle school were all accommodated in the central building and under one Principal. The west wing had not been added; there were fewer out-buildings, no quarters for the Principal and no hostel for the boys. Small though it was, the old building accommodated not only all the college and school classes, but for some time an Engineering School as well.

The college has kept pace with the growth of this charming station. The main building has been extended; the south wing in which we are assembled was completed last year. An equally magnificent building to be added as a north wing was sanctioned by His Highness the Maharaja a few months ago on the recommendation of the Dewan, Mr. T. Ananda Rao, who has always favoured a liberal expenditure on education.

The number of students in the college, which was 72 in 1881, has risen to 238 in 1911. Only four or five students graduated in a year in my time. Now the number is over five and twenty. In the strength and capacity of the staff, in point of accommodation, in attendance and, as we have seen, in the number of graduates passed out, the college has developed and grown. Under Mr. Tait, as under Messrs. Waters and Cook, the institution continues to enjoy a high measure of public confidence, and we have every reason to be proud of our *Alma Mater*.

One of the pleasantest memories of my college days is my association with the first Principal of this college,

Speech at Bangalore Central College Day Meeting.

Mr. Charles Waters, who, to our great regret, passed away last year. By his sympathy and earnestness, Mr. Waters exercised much influence over the students of my time. He left this country in 1882, but I met him again twenty-six years later. I had the privilege of corresponding with him almost to the day of his death last year, and his letters have acted as an inspiration in my work all through life. I have no doubt there are many old boys of this college living who, like myself, remember with deep gratitude the personal interest Mr. Waters took in their careers for many years after he left this country.

The memory of this College Day brings into our recollection another loss we have sustained in the death of one of the most respected and distinguished of our old boys. I refer to the late Dewan Sir P. N. Krishnamurti. He was the first chairman of this function. To many of you, and particularly to the organizers of this gathering, this occasion will recall sad thoughts, for the inspiring speech which he made from this chair in 1909 must be still ringing in your ears.

From a Government of India review on education published last month, we gather that the total number of scholars, both male and female, who attended educational institutions in British India in 1910-11 was 6,345,582; the corresponding figure in the same year for Mysore was 138,153. Compared with the total population, the proportion of scholars attending educational institutions was 2·49 per cent for all India and 2·42 per cent for Mysore. The total expenditure on education in British India was Rs. 919 lakhs and in Mysore Rs. 19 lakhs. The cost, calculated per head of population, in British India was As. 4-6 and in Mysore As. 5-4. In the neighbouring Presidencies of Madras and Bombay the percentage of the population attending educational institutions was slightly better than in Mysore, namely, 2·97 and

3·20, and the expenditure per head of the entire population As. 5 and As. 7-4, respectively.

The following figures may be interesting as showing the progress of education in Mysore since 1881, the year I left college:—

	1880-81	1890-91	1900-01	1910-11
Total number of institutions, public and private.	2,000	3,410	4,009	4,267
Total number of pupils under instruction.	53,872	96,427	116,468	138,153
Total number of students in English Colleges.	132	330	364	438
Percentage of scholars to population of school-going age.	8·57	13·22	14·15	16·9
	Rs.	Rs.	Rs.	Rs.
Total expenditure on education...	3,91,028	6,39,737	10,98,170	18,79,133
Expenditure on English Colleges only.	26,371	49,832	1,15,181	1,36,673
	As.	As.	As.	As.
Total expenditure per head of population.	1 6	2 1	3 3	5 4

Although we have made some progress as compared with our past, the educational outlook of the country is far from satisfactory. The demands of our day in consequence of the rapid strides made by civilization are far greater than they were twenty or thirty years ago. Our efficiency as a country depends not on our better position compared with our past but on our progress in relation to the other civilized countries of the world, to the other members of the family of nations. For instance, the percentage of the entire population actually attending school is as high as twenty-one in some of the advanced countries. In Mysore it is less than two and a-half. The expenditure on education in advanced countries like the United States is as high as Rs. 12 per head. Our expenditure is less than As. 6 per head.

Speech at Bangalore Central College Day Meeting.

Progress in every country depends mainly on the education of its people. Without education, we are a nation of children. The difference between one man and another, apart from birth and social position, consists in the extent of knowledge, general and practical, acquired by him. We may safely assume that men in all countries within certain limits start with the same degree of intelligence. A civilized nation is distinguished from an uncivilized one by the extent of its acquired intelligence and skill.

The reason why, roughly speaking, the earning power of an average Englishman is more than twenty times that of an average Indian is the former's acquired capital, skill and working capacity. In the United Kingdom, about 95 per cent of the population can read and write; in America, in Canada, in Belgium and in Japan, 80 to 90 per cent or more. In Mysore, only six persons in every hundred can read and write. Even in Russia, which is considered the most backward of European countries, about 25 per cent of the entire population are literate. In only one Mysore village out of five is there a school. Only one boy out of four grows up educated and only one girl out of eighteen.

The causes of our low standard of living are obvious. The nearer we approach England and other foreign countries in respect of the proportion of educated people in the country, the greater will be our earning capacity and material progress.

To illustrate my meaning, I may mention that, fifty years ago, the Japanese had about the same proportion of educated people as Mysore. They have, by adopting compulsory education and other Western methods and by special encouragement and sacrifices, raised the proportion to nearly 90 per cent. In Mysore, however, we have made no appreciable progress.

Speech at Bangalore Central College Day Meeting.

To show how education, production and progress go hand in hand, the following comparison of Mysore with Canada, a country whose population is only about one-fourth larger than ours, may be found interesting :—

	Canada	Mysore
Number of Universities	18	Nil.
Number of people of school-going age attending school.	1,288,594	138,153
Percentage of educated people to the entire population.	Over 80	6
Number of miles of railway	24,731	411
	Rs.	Rs. a. p.
Value of manufactured produce per head ...	303	8 4 0

According to the Census of 1911, there were 7,081,869 persons in Canada and 5,705,359 in Mysore. The comparison I have just made shows how extraordinarily active, skilful and prosperous the Canadians are, compared with their brethren in Mysore. No wonder that the Governor-General of Canada was able to say in a public speech last year that the rate of progress in that country was amazing.

Practically the entire female population of the country grows up uneducated. The agriculturists who form the bulk of the people also go through life without education. Do we realize what a potent addition would be made to the life-force of our people if their intelligence were properly trained and put to active work? The present state of things can only be remedied by Government providing more funds, by cheapening education and making it compulsory, and by enlisting private effort and enterprise.

Education, as at present imparted, is deficient in quality. It does not provide for moral training. It does not correct defects of character, of tradition and of environment; nor does it equip people satisfactorily for the practical work of life according to modern standards.

Speech at Bangalore Central College Day Meeting.

The morals taught in our religious books are excellent, but the background is deceptive as it applies to the conditions of life in the country several thousand years ago, and, as a result, the Indian youth starts life with ideals which take no note of the realities of the struggle in the present-day world.

We are accustomed to one man rule. Among us, co-operative effort is utterly lacking. Our associations, councils, boards and committees, somehow, do not thrive. In such bodies, the faculty of disputation is unduly developed; that of decision and action is feeble or lacking.

As compared with Europe, our climate and traditions all predispose us to a life of inaction and ease. We are influenced either by religious sentiment, class patriotism or belief in *kismet*, whereas the activities of western nations rest on an economic basis. While they think and act in conformity with economic necessities, we expect to prosper without acquiring the scientific precision, the inventive faculty, the thoroughness, the discipline and restraints of modern civilization.

No one who has seen western countries can fail to be struck with the low standard of living and the extreme poverty of our people. In a country like ours, where the rainfall is uncertain, it will never do to place reliance on agriculture alone. Whether rain falls or fails, people must live. It is absolutely necessary that they should be taught to practise alternative occupations in order to tide over bad seasons. The State and the public are interested in seeing that every person, male or female, in the country, is doing some work and is maintained at least partly by his or her own exertions and that the number of drones is kept down at a minimum.

In the primary stages, every person should be taught to read, write and cipher; and if he is an agriculturist, as the majority of our people are, he should know the elements of practical agriculture besides one other elementary industry or trade to keep him usefully employed when field work is slack.

As regards secondary education, we want to equip the student with higher practical ability and less abstract knowledge than at present.

It is necessary to provide continuation schools to give training in agriculture, industries and commerce for all the boys and girls who are obliged to work for a living, before they are sixteen or eighteen years of age. In Europe a continuation school is intended to establish and extend the knowledge gained in the elementary school in such a manner that the scholar learns to appreciate the bearing of his acquired knowledge on the needs of life. Schools for teaching handiwork and domestic economy for girls should be provided on a liberal scale. In order to give the people a proper sense of proportion in the practical business of life, commercial and business education and training should be imparted in all grades of public instruction.

As regards moral training, I would prefer the Japanese system in which teachers are employed to teach the practical needs of life in schools. In teaching morals in a Japanese school, it is laid down that the special object is the cultivation of the conscience of children, the fostering of their moral sensibilities and the enforcement of the practical performance of human duties. It is provided that the spirit of loyalty and patriotism shall be specially awakened. The young student is also given advice regarding the social sanctions, sense of honour and his duties to the State. Teachers are enjoined to take pains to secure firm and lasting results. The student is asked to attach great importance to the value of time, punctuality, and discipline and he is given training and opportunities for independent thought and action leading to self-reliance.

Both in Japan and on the continent of Europe, conscription plays an important part in instilling habits of discipline as an introduction to life. I would also invite attention to the recent organization of what is known as the "Youth-care" movement in Germany. The function of "Youth-care," according to the official definition, is "to work towards the creation of a joyful, physically efficient, morally excellent youth, filled with a sense of solidarity, fear of God, love for the home and the fatherland." The idea is to start, in every district, organizations for supplying secular instruction, sport, religious and moral teaching. In England, the Boy Scout movement is doing something in the same direction.

As regards practical education, a few months ago, a Committee appointed by His Highness' Government, with which the late Mr. Weir was closely associated, drafted a scheme for developing technical and commercial education in the State. The draft scheme is printed and has been issued for the opinion and suggestions of representative officers and leading private gentlemen of the State. It deals with technical education from the lowest to the highest grade. It makes provision for commercial education. Agriculture was outside the scope of the Committee's work, but I hope this, the premier industry of the country, will not be overlooked when the technical education scheme comes to be seriously taken up by Government.

Under the orders of His Highness the Maharaja, a beginning has been made in the direction of the development of industries and commerce in the country, but, having regard to the magnitude of the work, progress must necessarily be slow. No great developments can be expected in a few years where decades would be insufficient. Industries and industrial and commercial education should, however, go hand in hand, and it is a matter of some satisfaction that a beginning has been made or is about to be made for developing both.

I will now say a few words about university education. We have all heard of the great movements in Northern India for the establishment of a Mahomedan University at Aligarh and a Hindu University at Benares. My interest in these movements is not for the reason that they are either Hindu or Mahomedan, but because we want more first class universities in the country.

You are aware that there has been a talk, for some time past, of starting a university in Mysore. It has the active support of one of the highest officers of the State, and I entirely agree with him. As was remarked by His Excellency the Viceroy in his recent speech on the Dacca University, "the more such universities are multiplied and distributed over India, the better it will be for the cause of Indian education and for the development of the moral character no less than of the intellectual ability of the students." There is one university, on an average, for every two and a-half millions of population in the United Kingdom and one for every three millions in Germany. The population of Canada is scarcely 25 per cent more than that of Mysore and yet that country has eighteen universities. I do not see why we should not have at least one university in Mysore. Ours may be an examining university at first and gradually developed into a teaching one, for which increasing facilities are being provided every year. I understand fears are entertained in some quarters that the graduates turned out here may not get recognition abroad. If a university is started, and if proper standards are maintained, the recognition is sure to come. But if we are to wait till we are assured of future recognition by other employers of labour, we may have to wait till the Greek Calends. The earlier years will be one of struggle. The students may desert the new university and go to Madras and Bombay, but that must be expected and faced. Speaking from some personal knowledge of the Canadian universities, I may say that we have professors in Mysore at least as good as could be found in the smaller universities of Canada, and I have no doubt of the success of the scheme if we are assured of the continued interest of the leading educationists in the State.

In the Bombay University, a Faculty of Commerce has just been established, and the Governor, Sir George Clarke, has done much during his tenure of office to encourage scientific education. His Excellency attaches great importance to the association of science with modern commerce and industry. Similarly, our university may make the imparting of technical and commercial education a speciality, for that is the most profitable form of education that you can impart to the rising generation nowadays. Combined with the Research Institute, which, I believe, will also shortly develop into a university, Bangalore may become a great centre of learning.

It is not in the glory of Bangalore as a seat of learning that we are interested. What intimately concerns us is the equipment of the city for developing the intellectual ability and executive power of our citizens and for the training it should afford to prepare future manufacturers, merchants, business men, economists, lawyers, sanitarians, engineers, statesmen, etc., for the country.

The educational system of the country should be closely adapted to local needs and resources, and it would be wrong to suppose that the present system is incapable of improvement or change.

It might interest you if, in passing, I mentioned a few

peculiarities in the educational methods and practices of Western countries and Japan.

In most of the civilized countries, including Japan, primary education is compulsory. In Belgium, where it is not so, and where education is in the hands of the clergy, even the smallest village has a school and the communes provide village lads with scholarships to enable them to attend industrial schools in the towns and cities.

Municipalities, Chambers of Commerce and other public bodies contribute a large part of the cost of special education. The Manchester Municipality contributes about 60 per cent of the cost of the School of Technology in that city.

There are four commercial Universities in Germany maintained chiefly by private individuals and manufacturers. The commercial High School of Berlin, founded in 1906 by the Association of Business men, is administered by a body of senior merchants of that city.

The Chambers of Commerce do the most towards the support of the continuation schools in Germany. By means of these schools, every mechanic and artisan is given opportunities of bettering his knowledge of his industry in his leisure hours.

Instruction, in manual work in wood and iron in Germany, and in agriculture in Italy, is given by itinerant teachers.

For Government officers, Court officials, etc., a knowledge of commercial matters and economic science is considered important. The London School of Economics and Political Science has classes for training Civil servants. In 1909, about 25 per cent of the candidates in that institution were in training for the Civil Service. The school has also classes for officers qualifying for administrative posts in the Army.

Similarly the commercial Universities in Germany give

a training to Court and administrative officials and Consular officers.

It is usual in Western countries and in Japan for teachers to take out boys for excursions to places of interest. At present a large batch of schoolboys from Australia have proceeded on a visit to America to get a glimpse of the New World.

Every civilized country sends out, at intervals, committees of investigation to study improved methods of education in advanced countries.

There are no fees charged and books are given free to students up to the B.A. standard in the schools of New York. A great many students in the University of Tokio carry on their studies with the aid of books lent by the University Library.

Free meals are provided to a large number of school children in London. In some of the States of America, boys are carried to schools at the public expense.

The point I want to emphasize to-day is this. Let there be no more vagueness of what we want and what we should prepare ourselves for. We may not strive for positions in the Army or the Navy or in occupations like aviation which require high scientific skill and daring. But in most other activities of the human race, there is no reason why we should not prepare ourselves to take a humble part. If this is to be so, it is the business of the wisest in the land to select those pursuits and occupations which give early promise of increased prosperity and to provide the people with the highest and best training needed for the purpose.

There will be no dearth of opportunities for trained men in this country, but there is a distinct dearth of education to qualify people for business occupations and a great lack of organization for multiplying such occupations.

Speech at Bangalore Central College Day Meeting.

What strikes an observer of Japanese life most is the homogeneity of the people and the practical unanimity of opinion both among leaders and common people as to the necessity of progress on modern lines. Japan has adopted the business ways and business ideals of prominent Western nations and has prospered. The Japanese are remorselessly logical and insist on practical efficiency at any cost. Their sudden rise is justly described as one of the marvels of the nineteenth century. India has practically stood still, because she has been suspicious of Western ideals and half-hearted in the practices of Western ways. The good work done by the British Rulers, themselves the foremost representatives of the world's most active civilization, has not had its full result for lack of co-operation and aspiration in the people. Progress on modern lines is a necessity. We cannot afford to ignore scientific discoveries which have almost vivified material nature. Past ideals were for past times. We must adapt ourselves to the ever-shifting conditions of existence or be content to be left behind in the race for material prosperity.

We see that, under the fuller and quicker civilization of the West, people are healthier, they live to a greater age and enjoy higher standards of comfort, and their intelligence and activities have a freer scope. There is an accumulation of transmitted skill and thought which is being further developed and applied to the reproduction of wealth and the improvement of material prosperity. To achieve any rapid progress in this direction, definite ideals and sustained effort are necessary. As remarked by one of the foremost English statesmen of our time, "Destiny is not a passive agent that lies in the lap of the gods, but is an active instrument that lies in your own hands to shape as you will."

Our leaders need to give close attention to the investigation of all the great problems of our time in so far as they affect this country. No great improvement can be effected without definite ideals and organization. "Investigate, educate and organize" should be our watchwords if we are to quicken the life pulse of the people and train them for a larger and fuller life.

One word more and I am done. As the highest seat of learning in the State, we look to this College, with its staff of able and zealous professors, to give the lead in educational activities.

Gentlemen, I now propose the toast of the Central College, coupling with it the name of its learned Principal, Mr. Tait.

ADDRESS TO MYSORE ENGINEERS.

[The Fifth Session of the Mysore Engineers' Association was held at the Association rooms on 22nd March 1912. Besides members, there was a large and distinguished audience present at the opening of the session. Sir M. Visvesvaraya, in opening the same, delivered the following address:—] 22nd Mar. 1912.

Gentlemen,—At the last session of this Association which was held in November 1910, it was your unanimous desire that future conferences should be convened in the month of January every year. But the visit of the principal officers of Government to Delhi on account of the Coronation Durbar and the tours which followed have led to the postponement of this year's function to the month of March.

As this is the busiest working season for the engineer

in the districts, we have arranged to finish the work of this session in two days and have thought it necessary to curtail the number of subjects and size of the papers. I have no doubt you will appreciate my own contribution to this economy by a reduction in the size of the Presidential Address this year.

Since we last met, two retired officers of this department who have rendered valuable service to the State in the past have passed away, *viz.*, Col. D. McNeil Campbell, R.E., and Mr. Standish Lee. Many of you no doubt have already heard the news with deep regret. The former was the Chief Engineer of this State for over six years and in that period he was closely associated with the construction of the Marikanave dam which was begun during his term of office in the ministry of Sir K. Sheshadri Iyer. He was also responsible for some of the work done in connection with the Cauvery Power Scheme in collaboration with Major A. J. DeLotbiniere, R.E.

Mr. Standish Lee was original in many ways. Under a sympathetic head like Sir K. Sheshadri Iyer, he was able to pave the way for the construction of several important water-supply and drainage schemes. He was perhaps the first engineer in India outside the Presidency cities to design and construct an underground pipe sewerage scheme and I believe he was also one of the first to start town-planning in this country.

The report which has just been read by our Honorary Secretary, Mr. K. Krishnaiengar, shows that since last year we have made some substantial progress in developing the work of this Association. Mr. Krishnaiengar has himself contributed largely to this progress. For the first time in its history, we have a building with furnished rooms made available for our use. We have also a collection of books, forming the nucleus of a Library, and a Reading Room supplied with some of the leading engineering periodicals of the world. The rooms are open to members at stated hours of the day, and both books and papers are issued regularly to mofussil members according to rules framed for the purpose.

In the coming year, we expect to be able to enlarge the Railway Branch of the Library. Before long I hope we may be able to induce the members of the Electrical Engineering Department to amalgamate their Library with ours with a view to the increased efficiency of both.

A constant watch should be maintained on foreign periodicals and catalogues in order to be able to select and order out the best books, periodicals and other publications from time to time. It is only in this way that the Association will come to possess the latest information and literature pertaining to activities in foreign countries in all branches of engineering in which we are interested.

There has been some progress during the past year in the development of large public works in the State. To begin with irrigation works first, I may mention that the Marikanave Reservoir system has been thoroughly investigated and proposals formulated for improving the productive power of that project. It is found impossible to irrigate the whole of the area commanded by the low level channels without ruining the fertility and the health of the tract. If the water is to be used profitably, a much larger area should be brought under command by extending the canal system. A high level canal has, therefore, been projected which, when sanctioned and completed, will involve an addition of about nine lakhs to the capital outlay. It will more than double the irrigated area and proportionately increase the revenue from the system. Government have been pleased to sanction the adoption of the Block System of Irrigation under the canals, and it is gratifying to learn that the cultivators

D

have accepted the principles of that system and are cordially co-operating in its introduction. Our aim in respect of this work is to increase its remunerative character by concentrating irrigation, as far as possible, on valuable crops, chiefly sugar-cane, and simultaneously endeavouring to improve the health of the tract. By reducing the area watered as well as by efficient drainage, sugar-cane can afford to pay a water rate up to about one-tenth to one-fifteenth of the gross produce per acre. By affording facilities for high-rated crops, we hope to be able to increase our revenue, and with it also the prosperity, of the tract. During the year, a valuable history of the project has been written by Mr. H. D. Rice, Executive Engineer, who was himself intimately associated with the work. I hope the good example set by him will be followed by others in the case of other similar works.

The principal event of engineering interest in the State during the year is the sanction accorded by the Government of His Highness the Maharaja to the construction of the Cauvery Reservoir dam. The dam is the first practical attempt to impound the waters of the Cauvery which for ages have been allowed to run to waste. The Cauvery Falls were harnessed about eleven years ago, and the dam now under construction will add further to the productive power of the valley in the shape of increased irrigation and power supply.

The dam is intended, as you are aware, to store 11,000 million cubic feet in the first stage and 37,500 million cubic feet in the final stage. There are between 4,000 and 5,000 work-people employed at present and the number will probably be doubled in the near future. The work is making satisfactory progress.

The irrigation works which form the life-blood of the country require special attention. Out of a total cultivable area of 8·57 million acres in the State, we have

854,000 acres or one-tenth under irrigation yielding a consolidated assessment of about Rs. 40½ lakhs. Of these, our minor irrigation tanks account for 315,896 acres, major irrigation tanks 424,149 acres, and river channels, mainly on the Cauvery, 114,300 acres.

Our predecessors in this department have done much to restore old tanks and build and extend new tanks and channels, and it is our turn now to continue and develop their good work. One important defect in the existing system is the haphazard manner in which the area of cultivation is regulated in reference to the capacity of a tank. The quantity of water required to irrigate an acre of rice, which is the principal irrigated crop in the country, depends on the rainfall, the nature of the soil and the character of the season. Irrigation under any tank has to take into account the storage capacity, the catchment area, the number and capacity of intercepted tanks in that area, the amount and distribution of rainfall, the retentive character or otherwise of the soil, the nature of the soil under irrigation, etc. That this question, requiring as it does the consideration of so many factors, should be left to be solved by rule of thumb by engineers and revenue officers is not satisfactory.

The *atchkat* or area under irrigation is often decided by the importunity of raiyats. They are always clamouring for extension. As it means increase of revenue to Government, there is ever a tendency to grant them. In the end, it means loss and often ruin to cultivators. Recently, I visited a tank under which people voluntarily surrendered the privilege of irrigation over an area of several hundred acres on some very plausible pretext. But minute enquiries showed that the majority of them did not care to continue the irrigation on account of the precarious nature of the supply and the losses they had suffered previously.

Address to Mysore Engineers.

Under the Cauvery channels again, the hot weather irrigation is a game of chance. No definite rules exist as to who is eligible for a second crop and who is excluded and in what part of the area under command a second crop should be cultivated. Some enterprising cultivators take out a crop of sugar-cane valued at several hundred rupees, while others have to be content with a crop of rice valued at Rs. 50 or less; and both pay the same water rate. There is no reason why an attempt should not be made to remedy these anomalies.

Sugar-cane and garden crops give the best return, and the growth of such crops wherever facilities exist should be specially encouraged. Irrigation cannot be said to have reached its high-water mark under a tank or a canal unless as large an area of sugar-cane is put down under it as the water facilities make it possible. An organized attempt must be made to develop sugar-cane cultivation for which, with the new storage in the Cauvery valley, there is now considerable scope. Our hope of making money from agriculture is chiefly through a large cultivation of commercial crops like sugar-cane, mulberry and garden crops.

Improvements seem desirable in these directions:—

(1) One or more representative tanks in each locality should be observed and studied for some years so that the data collected might be useful for revising the *atchkat* under other tanks in that area.

(2) The water supply to crops should be better regulated by measurement on a scientific basis as far as possible. This will lead to economies in the water used and a corresponding increase in the area irrigated.

(3) The cultivators should be trained in the economical regulation of water, and local enterprise should be encouraged with a view to ensure high-class cultivation and increased production of high-rated crops.

The silting and deterioration of *malnad* tanks is another matter which requires early investigation and attention.

Some of the methods and practices in regard to small buildings, treated as original works and repairs to existing ones, require readjustment and revision.

Annual repairs to buildings which are now carried out by fits and starts should be made more regular and systematic. New original works for all departments should be sanctioned from time to time according to a well-considered quinquennial or triennial programme. It is undesirable that increase or decrease of grants to buildings for any department should be a matter of accident and that it should depend on the apathy or energetic importunity of the head of the department.

The road problem is more to the front at present than ever before. The rapid increase of motor cars and automobiles has become the nightmare of the road engineer. Rich and influential people, who a decade back rarely went seven or eight miles beyond their residence, are now seen travelling in motor cars in the remotest parts of the State; and no nook or corner, no sharp turn or steep incline, no wash-out, hole or rut escapes their prying gaze. Complaints are now and then received on this account. I should not object to them if the funds available for repairs had increased in proportion to the refinement expected in the up-keep of the roads. We must, however, accept the situation, and that is why I have asked you to come prepared with your proposals and suggestions for concerted action in this respect for the future.

Every effort should be made to maintain a road in a state of efficiency by a judicious expenditure of the present grants. When this is impossible, special grants should be applied for, and only as a last resort should recommendations come for a permanent increase of grants.

A vigilant supervision should be maintained wherever a road begins to break up, and if pits or holes are formed in places which are not promptly attended to by the staff, every such case should be specially enquired into and the subordinate staff responsible brought to book.

Wherever special repairs are carried out, the officers concerned should be held responsible that the road surface is maintained in efficient order for at least five years. So long as complaints are not received, it is understood that the roads are kept in trafficable order. An Executive Engineer should consider it a discredit if serious defects on any road are brought to the notice of Government or of any superior officer without himself being aware of them. If a road is below the requisite standard, the fact should be reported at frequent intervals and the necessity of additional expenditure brought to the notice of the superior officers in proper time.

You may have noticed that His Highness' Government have decided to follow an active railway policy in future. They have also laid down the lines on which the extensions should proceed. Orders have been issued to commence the construction of the Chikballapur Light Railway. A survey for a light railway between Bowringpet and Kolar has just been completed and that for a line from Chikjajur to Chitaldrug begun. Although progress for various causes has been slow, there is every reason to hope for increased activity in this respect in the future.

Government have decided to open an Electric Tramway service in the Bangalore City. The Civil and Military Station authorities are also anxious to co-operate with us and to extend the service to the more crowded parts of the Cantonment limits.

In connection with the Cauvery Power extension works, we hope shortly to commence work on the Fourth Installation which will increase our power supply from a maximum of 13,000 h.p. at present to about 20,000 h.p. in the near future. The protection of the existing power and any future increase of same will depend on the completion of the reservoir recently begun.

It might be worth our while to investigate the water power resources of the Kadur and Shimoga Districts along the Western Ghats and to have rough schemes ready as demands for power supply are likely to arise in that region. The engineers responsible for public works in the districts concerned might note that they have an opportunity of doing some original work in this direction.

As regards water supply, there has been no lack of investigation and reports, but there is no money for providing new works as rapidly as they are needed. Towns, which till recently never knew what a piped water supply meant, are now clamouring for it. The ideals of Municipal conveniences have risen but not, in the same degree, the capacity or inclination of the people to pay for them. We have formulated schemes for the water supply of Chitaldrug, Davangere, Nanjangud and Seringapatam, all of which await provision of funds.

Coming next to drainage and sewerage, the largest scheme is that outlined for the Mysore City by the Chief Engineer and worked out in detail by Mr. D'Cruz, Executive Engineer, Mysore City Improvements Division. The scheme is at present awaiting the sanction of Government. A small drainage scheme for the town of Shimoga is under preparation by Mr. Bhore.

Recently, Government have asked us to investigate the question of a suitable hill station for the State to be used as a summer resort, and the subject is receiving attention.

Much has been done in the cities of Bangalore and Mysore in the direction of town planning in recent years.

During the past year, however, only a few minor improvements received attention in Bangalore and Shimoga, but more ought to be attempted hereafter. Our Sanitary Engineer is preparing a comprehensive plan of Bangalore on which all desirable improvements might be marked with the ultimate object of providing, gradually, some of the amenities of modern civilized cities as far as our resources permit.

Every city, town or village, is undergoing a process of change either on account of its situation, increased facilities of communication, increase or decrease of trade prosperity or other causes.

Alterations and improvements should be constantly going on. Roads, drainage, water supply, sanitation, parks, playgrounds and places of recreation should be improved or extended and adjusted to the needs of the population from time to time with due regard to modern standards and local resources and conditions. Every little improvement adds to the amenities of life.

Every village—an Indian village more than any other—requires attention in respect of the orderly alignment of houses and streets, of sanitation, temples, *chavadies*, plantations, wells, etc.

Many of our villages are in the lowest depths of squalor and degradation. It is a melancholy testimony to the decay of art in the country when the condition of the present day structures and villages are contrasted with the fine temples replete with art treasures, bathing ghats, *chattrams*, etc., found scattered throughout the country. The religious epics of the country contain descriptions of, and instructions in, town planning, although the very name of the art is unknown to the present generation.

The people of the Western cities now-a-days take a keen interest in the improvement of their towns. I may refer to one remarkable instance of the extent to which Western people are prepared to make sacrifices for such a purpose. In the year 1909, the leading citizens of the city of Chicago had collected a sum equivalent to about three lakhs and started an office with a staff of architects and were preparing designs at their own cost for the acceptance of the Municipality for execution.

Every visitor to Delhi must have been struck with the care and ability bestowed on planning the temporary camps during the recent Coronation Durbar.

We have all read in the papers that the planning of that city is now engaging the attention of the Imperial Government and that experts are preparing designs for the work. It is our hope that the new city may combine the conveniences and architectural features not only of the West but of both East and West. If the city of Delhi is to be a place of attraction to Indian Princes and Noblemen, as Washington is to the millionaires of America, some of the conveniences of Indian type which do not offend against Western taste might be introduced into the new Capital. Every Indian citizen is interested in the future metropolis of India. It would be an advantage if the preliminary designs are issued to the public for criticism and suggestions, before any scheme is adopted finally.

Last year I referred to certain defects of Indian engineers, their want of business habits and so forth, which, to my mind, detracted somewhat from their influence and market value as professional men. I would ask the junior members of this Association to endeavour to think out for themselves both the larger and the smaller problems connected with the public works of the country. I would say to them:—This will give you self-reliance and capacity for initiative. Taking the initiative does not mean, doing things according to your individual whims and fancies, or exceeding your powers, or incurring expenditure without authority. It only means that you should work in advance of what is to be done, and instead of waiting for others to move first, bring your best judgment into action. One project or work initiated and carried out by you is worth a dozen done under pressure. You should persistently urge on the attention of higher authorities whenever you are convinced that a thing is good and necessary, but you should be particular not to anticipate or exceed their orders except in extreme cases of necessity. Such cases must be so rare and must have such sound reasons at their back that, when they do happen, the superior officers should be able to acquiesce cheerfully in your decision.

Success depends very largely on your own capacity, integrity and keenness for work. If you get into the habit of giving your whole-hearted attention to the work entrusted to you, and if you are able to concentrate and absorb yourself in it, you may be sure others will not forget you. To men of capacity and intelligence, such application will often prove the "open sesame" to many a first class opportunity.

Then, there is the question of specialization. At the last session, we considered the need of special studies. No man can be a master of every subject, and if we are not to fritter away our energies, the comparatively small staff of engineers in the State cannot do better than concentrate attention, each on some one special subject. At the last year's Conference, many of you were good enough to promise to specialize in certain subjects which you named. I hope to-morrow when the question comes up for discussion, you will render a good account of the progress you have made during the past year and furnish to the Conference a list of what you propose to do in the coming one.

In the month of January last, the Dewan of Mysore

and I happened to visit a procelain factory in Calcutta. The manager, a young Bengali, educated in Japan, told us a pretty story concerning himself. When he first went to the Principal of the Tokio Industrial School, he was asked what he wished to learn. He replied that he wanted to study "pottery." "Young man," rejoined the Principal, "Pottery is a large subject and human life is only three score years and ten. How can you study all branches of pottery? Why will you not content yourself with one branch of the subject and make a thorough practical study of it?" The student took this advice and selected porcelain. He has worked steadily at that industry for six or seven years, and he is now the manager of a factory which is turning out very good procelain ware, perhaps the best yet produced in India.

Your own duties leave very little leisure for study, and what little time you can give would be most usefully spent on one or two subjects for which you may have an aptitude.

We might class the engineering subjects into, say, half a dozen groups, and all the members who choose any one particular subject might be made to correspond and work in unison. A senior officer, who is himself an expert in some degree, might undertake to help the junior members with advice and guidance in their special studies and furnish periodical reports of their progress to the managing committee of the Association.

Gentlemen, I will not detain you further. Many of you have worked hard and given proofs of your determination to succeed. The past year, though not eventful, has been on the whole one of fair progress within the State so far as the engineering profession is concerned.

Since November last, Government have been pleased to restore the direction staff which had been taken away just before I joined the department, and it is a matter of satisfaction to me personally that we shall be working in future under less stress and strain than it has been our lot within the past two years and a-half. There will be more time for you in the coming years for investigating new questions, for closer supervision of details and for perfecting the system of district administration generally.

Many important questions await investigation and solution, particularly in the direction of irrigation, railways, engineering, education and industries.

Through the thoughtful munificence of His Highness' Government, there are abundant opportunities for engineering work in the State at the present time. We start with bright hopes for the coming year,—hopes of finding interesting professional work for ourselves and of contributing our mite to the material prosperity of the country.

II. SPEECHES MADE AFTER ASSUMPTION OF OFFICE OF DEWAN.

1912–17.

REPLY TO AN ADDRESS BY THE MYSORE ENGINEERS' ASSOCIATION.

[An entertainment, organized by the Mysore Engineers' Association in honor of Sir M. Visvesvaraya, their retiring President, on his appointment as Dewan of Mysore, was given on the evening of 30th November 1912, in the Association premises, which were specially fitted up for the occasion. Mr. V. P. Madhava Rao, C.I.E., retired Dewan of Mysore, was in the chair. Besides the members of the Association, headed by Mr. Karpur Shrinivasrav and Mr. Krishniengar, were present the Hon'ble Col. Sir Hugh Daly, British Resident in Mysore, the members of Council and other high Officers of the Mysore Government, and many leading gentlemen, European and Indian, from the City and the Civil and Military Station of Bangalore. After the recitation of benedictory verses in Sanskrit, Telugu and Tamil, Mr. D. Sitharama Rao, retired Superintending Engineer, read the following address on behalf of the Association :— 30th Nov. 1912.

" We, the members of the Mysore Engineers' Association, beg leave to offer our humble and heartfelt congratulations on your elevation to the exalted office of the Dewan of Mysore. We are justly proud of this singular honour done to you, a very distinguished President of our Association. To those who are acquainted with your antecedents, your brilliant college and official career, your original work in the field of irrigation and sanitation, your wide knowledge of men and affairs, your extensive travels in foreign countries, and, above all, your many-sided activities during the past three years in Mysore, your

Reply to an address by the Mysore Engineers' Association.

appointment as Prime Minister of this State seems a fitting sequel and an honour highly deserved. You are the first head of a technical department who has been called upon to administer the affairs of the State, and this welcome departure from a time-honored custom we owe to His Highness, our beloved Maharaja, to whom we feel deeply grateful.

"To you, Sir, we are very highly indebted for the fostering care with which you have watched the progress of our Association. Need we say that your term of office as President of this Association has been a very eventful one. For we owe it to your initiative that the Association can boast of a suitable habitation and the nucleus of an up-to-date Library. It is your inspiration that encouraged many of our members to cheerfully come forward to specialise in various branches of engineering. The social aspect, given to our monthly and annual meetings, which is so much appreciated by all of us, will ever remain associated with your name. It is our earnest desire that you will be pleased to continue your kindly interest in the advancement of our Association and permit us to enlist your name as its Patron.

"That you may long continue as Dewan, that you may be blessed with health and strength and Heavenly Light to guide you in carrying on the onerous duties of your exalted position, that your tenure of office may be productive of manifold benefits to the people of this State, and that you may win higher honors and lasting fame, is the fervent and humble prayer of the members of the Mysore Engineers' Association." (Applause.)

Sir M. Visvesvaraya, who was cordially received, made the following reply :—]

Gentlemen,—I esteem it a privilege to receive the eloquent address which you have just read to me. It takes a far too generous estimate of my services to the Association. Although I cannot appropriate to myself all the kind things you have said, yet I value your greeting, because it comes from colleagues and fellow-workers who have borne the heat and burden of the day with me, and who have shared my hopes and disappointments in the work of the Public Works Department for the last three years.

This Association owes its origin to local effort under the sympathetic guidance of Mr. McHutchin and the late Captain Dawes. We are building on the activities inspired by our predecessors, and I am glad that in my time, with the sympathy and active support of the late Dewan, the Association has found a habitation. We have also been able to develop the library and reading room and organize frequent business and social gatherings. Thanks chiefly to the efforts of our genial Secretary, there has been a perceptible increase in the activities of the Association during the past two years.

We have at present a large variety of engineering works in progress within the State, *viz.*, irrigation schemes, architectural building projects, proposals for town improvement, important water-supply and drainage schemes, railway surveys and electricity works. No single engineer can be an expert in more than one, two or three of these great branches of engineering, and if the works are to be carried out and maintained efficiently and economically, we require specialists who are at the top, or very near the top of their profession. This is the reason why we have arranged to keep a number of engineers under training in each branch of engineering. The practitioner of to-day is the expert of to-morrow, and if we persevere in the arrangements made for specializing, we shall never lack men for maintaining our works in a high state of efficiency.

You have held some weekly, monthly and quarterly meetings and your Secretary has organized small social parties. They are all of great value in promoting good feeling and fellowship among members of the profession at headquarters. An engineer should not be content to regard himself merely as a tool to be worked in other men's interests, but he should take his share in the literary, social and public work of the country to the fullest extent of his ability and opportunities. These gatherings will be useful not only to bring all the active workers into close touch but also to help to attract waverers and obtain recruits for the Association.

I trust I shall not be appealing to you in vain if I ask you to increase your activities and to make every year of the Association more busy than the preceding one. If you do this, gentlemen, and gradually raise your importance and status, you cannot fail to obtain recognition. Any recommendations made by you, on your own initiative, will be listened to by Government with sympathy and respect. Government may also, of their own accord, consult you and avail themselves of your judgment and advice on important questions connected with the technical services of the State.

Perhaps a word or two here may not be out of place about the work of the department in which we are all so much interested. You are aware that a few days before I took charge of the office of Chief Engineer in 1909, extensive reductions in the department were ordered, the result of which was that, for quite two out of the three years of my service, I had to work without the full complement of staff that was given to my predecessors. This entailed a considerable amount of labour in which, I may take this opportunity to state, the officers of my staff bore their share with great patience and willingness. It was just a year ago that the original staff was restored to us but the restoration brought us no relief as it synchronized with considerable increase of work on account of the Cauvery Reservoir.

Our Public Works expenditure in the current year will be larger than in any previous one and yet, barring recruits in the lowest grades, we have got on without making any substantial increase to the establishment. I am not referring to the Railway Department, because although hitherto under the same Secretary as Public Works, it has always been treated as a separate organization. The percentage of establishment charges on our Public Works proper will probably be lower this year than it was in any previous one in the history of the department, and it will stand favourable comparison with corresponding results in British India.

As I have charge of the Public Works portfolio, I shall continue to be responsible, to some extent, for the work of the engineers in this State. And as stated already, I am looking forward in the years to come to a period of greater activity on your part and I hope to see that not only technical subjects but questions connected with business organization, character, courage, discipline, etc., in the practice of the profession, will come up for discussion at your meetings. Our engineers are accustomed to carrying out orders, but the training needed *to give orders* and to initiate measures has been defective. If an engineer merely carries out orders and executes other people's designs, his occupation will lack much of its stimulating interest and vitality. I have known several officers who are content with a low level of efficiency, not through lack of professional ability but chiefly through timidity or want of nerve. Another point I am never tired of impressing on the younger members of the profession is the necessity for working longer hours and doing everything on a system. Successful engineers everywhere work harder than we do. We should dismiss from our mind the idea that any great work can be accomplished, that any reputation in the profession can be made, without drill, discipline and iron labour.

Gentlemen, although my duties have been changed, my interest in the engineering profession, in which I have spent the best part of my life, will not cease. I notice that, in your address, you refer to yet higher honours and rewards for me. It will, I hope, not be regarded as an affectation of modesty on my part if I say that all I have wanted is opportunity for work and that thoughts of personal advancement have not influenced my actions in recent years. With the important duties now graciously entrusted to me by His Highness the Maharaja, I have all the scope for work that I may have ever longed for. I seek no further reward. The pleasure of working for a few years more, of serving my Sovereign and my country is enough for me. Their interests will be my constant thought, and their approbation, if I am able to secure it, will be my best reward. Gentlemen, I thank you.

REPLY TO BANGALORE CITIZENS' ADDRESSES.

12th Dec. 1912.

[Shortly after his appointment to the Dewanship of Mysore, Sir M. Visvesvaraya received Addresses from the citizens of Bangalore and from various public bodies, Associations and Communities in the State. The presentation of these took place on the 12th December 1912, at the Albert Victor Hall, Lal-Bagh. There was a large and distinguished gathering present on the occasion, including Mr. T. Ananda Rao, C.I.E., Sir M. Visvesvaraya's predecessor in the office of Dewan of Mysore. Mr. Harianna, a well known merchant of the City, read the citizens' address, which was as follows:—

"We, the citizens of Bangalore, beg to offer you our sincere and hearty congratulations on your appointment, by His Highness the Maharaja, to the exalted office of his Dewan and trusted adviser.

Reply to Bangalore Citizens' Addresses.

"Your long training in the British Indian Service in which you rose to a distinguished position by dint of merit, your close acquaintance and association with the liberal-minded and progressive communities in the Presidency of Bombay, your eminence as an expert in Irrigation and Sanitary Engineering, your added experience on questions connected with the moral and material well-being of peoples gained in the course of a long tour of study and observation in Europe, America and Japan, above all, your spotless character, devotion to duty and a desire to uplift the masses, encourage us to hope that you will bring the same high qualities, as have distinguished you in the past, to bear upon the discharge of the duties of the higher sphere to which you have been called.

"It is also a matter of satisfaction to us that you are a son of Mysore who, seeking his fortunes abroad at the outset of his career, has come back to the land of his birth in his mature years to give it the benefit of his enlightened and devoted service.

"We are proud to say that our beautiful city with its fine and unsurpassed climate has always held a prominent place as a sanitarium and a centre of trade and other useful activities. May we be permitted to hope that, during your beneficent Dewanship, measures will be devised to further develop trade and improve the economic condition of the masses and to give local self-government to the city in a real sense by placing our civic life on a broader basis?

"We need hardly point out that another matter deserving of your kind consideration is the improvement of our City by equipping it with all the modern conveniences and comforts of life, so as to make it worthy of its premier position in the State.

"In conclusion, we pray that God Almighty may grant you health, strength and long life to enable you to serve the people with justice and love."

Sir M. Visvesvaraya next received the other addresses, including those of the Arya Dharma Bodhini Sabha, the Central Mahomedan Association, the Vokkaligara Sangha, the Commercial Association, Bangalore City, and the representatives

Reply to Bangalore Citizens' Addresses.

of the Lingayet, Arya Vaisya, Jain, Devanga and Mahratta communities.

Sir M. Visvesvaraya, who, on rising, was given an ovation, in his joint reply to these addresses, said :—]

Mr. Ananda Rao, Citizens of Bangalore, Ladies and Gentlemen,—I thank you very heartily for the warmth and cordiality of your welcome and for the high honour you have done me in presenting these ten addresses, on behalf of the citizens of Bangalore and other important communities and public bodies, in the presence of this large and representative gathering.

As the addresses have all the same purpose and the same subjects are discussed in more than one of them, I trust you will allow me to return a collective reply.

Referring, first, to representations of a local or sectional character, I may mention that the necessity of improving the sanitation, trade facilities, and, if I may add, the beauty of the City of Bangalore, is engaging the attention of His Highness' Government. Much has been done already in the past, but a great deal more remains to be done, particularly in respect of improved drainage and communications. In Western countries, there is great activity displayed at present for making towns and villages more healthy and more convenient for business and residential purposes. Usually, all improvements are carried out at the expense of the townspeople themselves. In many cities I have known, associations of private citizens exist which spend their own money to prepare designs for civic improvements. When the designs are ready, they are handed over to the Municipality concerned for execution. I wonder if some such work cannot be done in Bangalore by the leaders and by the Municipal Commissioners. If private citizens take the lead, I believe some of the smart young engineers we have here may be induced to give their spare time to work out plans and estimates. His Highness' Government recognize that, in the peculiar position of Bangalore, a share of the cost of the improvements will have to be borne by Government for some time to come.

The Mahomedan Association, the Lingayet Education Fund Association, the Arya Vaisya Community, the Devanga Community and the Jain Community, ask for a larger representation for their communities in the public service. Some of you ask also for special representation on the public bodies and on the Municipalities. In several addresses, reference is made to the need of financial help for the education of your young men here and in foreign countries.

As regards the public service, every community must qualify itself by education. Public service will be efficient only if the best and the most highly-educated men are appointed to it. The best hope of the communities you represent lies therefore in competing among themselves in training a large number of eligible young men from each. The last request, *viz.*, the granting of financial help for educating young men in foreign countries, has the fullest sympathy of His Highness' Government. Some facilities have been afforded already and the question will receive further consideration in consultation with the experts and responsible heads of the departments. The Arya Dharma Bodhini Sabha may feel assured that as His Highness the Maharaja is a patron of Sanskrit learning, every reasonable facility will be given for the encouragement of Sanskrit literature.

Some of the more minor questions referred to in the addresses may perhaps be more appropriately dealt with if a special representation is made in each case to Government or the departments concerned.

I will now pass on to matters of more general interest.

Reply to Bangalore Citizens' Addresses.

The Vokkaligara Sangha, in their very eloquent address just read, put forward a formidable list of progressive measures for the consideration of His Highness' Government. I use the word "formidable" advisedly in relation to our limited capacity and opportunities. The addresses suggest the granting of liberal powers of interpellation and debate in the Representative Assembly, powers of interpellation and discussion of the budget in the Legislative Council, the broadening of the representative character of the latter, and the liberation of Municipalities and the Press from restrictive regulations and control.

It has been my privilege to visit and watch the discussions in some of the great Parliamentary Assemblies in session in different parts of the world. But they are all countries in which the great majority of the people is educated and is animated more or less by similar ideals and aspirations. The questions of constitutional privileges and wider franchise in Mysore bristle with difficulties, and I must confess to great hesitation in approaching them without thorough preliminary study. I can only promise, for the present, to give my best attention to the investigation of the questions raised.

Almost all the remaining subjects referred to in the addresses may be classed as economic. Some of you deplore, and rightly too, the ignorance of the masses, ask for free and compulsory primary education and the establishment of more schools, foreign scholarships, more extended technical education, an Agricultural College, etc. All these questions and more are under consideration and some substantial progress has been already made by the Education Committee under the guidance of my friend, Mr. H. V. Nanjundayya, the Senior Councillor, assisted by the officers of the Education Department. Additional funds have been allotted for the extension of primary education in the current year during Mr. Ananda Rao's term of office. A Bill for the introduction of compulsory education has already been published and practical proposals regarding technical education are before Government. If the leaders of the public wish for any further measures, the Committee will doubtless be glad to receive proposals of a constructive character, particularly if they are accompanied by suggestions for ways and means.

As regards agriculture, the staple industry of the State, there is also a large number of practical questions under investigation by the Agricultural Committee and the Agricultural Department.

Development of sugar-cane cultivation, sericulture, improvement of tanks, tapping subsoil water for perennial irrigation, development of village industries—all these come under the purview of the Agricultural Committee.

The most important need of the country, next to the spread of education, is the equipment of the agricultural population with a knowledge of the conditions of existence in the world and power of calculation in regard to their personal concerns. Another need is the encouragement of co-operative effort to enable the people to form themselves into associations for procuring manure and seed and for obtaining a market for their produce and other similar objects.

If we also teach them how to maintain their tanks and canals and administer the distribution of water on scientific lines, we shall have given them a valuable lesson in self-help. For, although we have less than one million acres under irrigation out of a total of six million acres cultivated in the State, the irrigated crops play an important part in the agricultural economy of the State. The aggregate value of the crops is probably more than one-half of that of the dry crops.

In several addresses, Gentlemen, attention is drawn

to the necessity of extension of railways, tramways, a central State-aided bank, practical training in industries, establishment of technical schools, development of industries and commerce. These subjects, in their preliminary stages, are receiving the attention of the Industries and Commerce Committee of the Economic Conference. Railway projects are being worked out by an able officer lent by the Government of India. The wide experience of Mr. Chatterton in industrial matters is being utilized for the promotion of manufactures and commerce and for training young men for industrial occupations. The question of a State-aided bank is under the active consideration of Government.

You will thus see, Gentlemen, that under the orders of His Highness the Maharaja, official and semi-popular agencies have been brought into existence for the study of questions connected with the progress and material prosperity of the people. When any measures are approved by the Committees and sanctioned by Government, there is a competent department or agency ready to give effect to them.

The investigations which have been set on foot will take into account conditions in British India and elsewhere and gradually reveal to us, in their true perspective, and, in the order of their urgency and importance, the material wants of the people and the best means of satisfying them with due regard to the resources at our disposal.

But, Gentlemen, we must not disguise from ourselves the fact that the circumstances of the country are not favourable to rapid progress.

In the first place, as stated in one of the addresses, lack of education is a stumbling block. Only 1 male person in every 9 is literate and 1 female in 77. In only one village out of five is there a school. The total literate population of both sexes is only 6 per cent as against 80 to 95 in progressive countries. Out of a population of 57 lakhs, our effective force of intelligent workers numbers less than 3½ lakhs.

In normal seasons, the cultivators have no steady occupation for nearly six months in the year. In a famine, the entire body of agriculturists go without work. And as prices rise simultaneously with lack of employment, the extent of misery caused on such occasions is appalling. You cannot have forgotten that in the famine of 1876-77, more than 20 persons in every 100 died of starvation.

The margin between comfort and destitution among our poorest classes is very narrow. There is a large number of agricultural labourers who are abnormally sensitive to the effect of drought and inferior harvests. Only at the beginning of the last monsoon, on account of late rains, some of the poorest people in the Kolar District were reduced to subsisting on the roots of the aloe plant. Gentlemen, you will allow this is a state of things which no civilized Government should tolerate.

Recently, a representation was received from the people of the Mysore City to the effect that distress prevailed there owing to a rise in prices. If the rise is due to temporary causes, such as congestion of railway traffic or the cornering of grain, Government might attempt relief, but prices have been going up for several years past as a result of improved communications and improved means of transport all over the world. "India," said an economist the other day, "is no longer an isolated country ploughing its own lonely furrow, but she has entered the international markets of the world. This is why the slightest change in other countries affects her industries and commerce vitally."

While prices have been steadily going up and the population continues to grow, there has been no marked increase in the occupations of the people or their earning capacity. On the other hand, the population dependent on agriculture in Mysore has increased during the last decade.

Distress due to a rise in prices is the result of larger and more powerful forces than the calamities of seasons and has to be combated by measures which require forethought and long preparation.

The remedies are clear. The intelligence of the people should be developed and their earning capacity and efficiency improved. Occupations should be multiplied and every one who has capacity for work must be made to work. The use of machinery should be rendered popular and more training given in science and in mechanical and industrial pursuits. Co-operative effort, whether in public or municipal administration, or in industries or trade, should be systematically encouraged.

The problem of education is most acute, and with regard to primary education, it should not be too late for any one up to the age of 35 to learn the three R's. Instead of only 3½ lakhs of literate people, there is no reason why we should not have five and thirty. I would appeal to every citizen in the State to make a special effort to encourage the education of both boys and girls by every means in his power, by sending more pupils to existing schools, by providing additional schools, by private tuition and by home classes.

Many of the progressive measures involve slow preparation, persevering effort and expenditure of money. The public on their side should study the true purpose and enter into the spirit of the measures and give their whole-hearted co-operation. There should be a free and frank interchange of views between all workers in the same field. The Government, the public and the Press should be actuated as far as possible by the same aims and motives and the same standards of judgment.

Reply to Bangalore Citizens' Addresses.

In all the addresses you have been pleased to read to me, you state what, in your opinion, His Highness' Government should do, or what I should do, but there is not one word said of what you yourselves are going to do, not one word even of offer of co-operation on your part. I can make no promise or response on such terms. If the public ask me what His Highness' Government is going to accomplish during my term of office, I will only say it will depend on what the people themselves may help to build up. Government will be what the people make it; it cannot be much in advance of the capacity of the people. I attach great importance to the co-operation of the leaders of the public, each in his legitimate sphere of activity. We have able officers, both European and Indian, in the service of the State, to help us, and if the people also give evidence of a disposition to move, to awaken from the lethargy of years and show capacity to undertake reforms and improvements, Government will be prepared to guide and direct their activities into healthy and profitable channels.

It only remains for me to reiterate my warmest thanks for the cordiality of your greeting and for the assurances of your confidence and good will in my favour. No persuasion is needed to strengthen my resolution to engage every faculty and effort in the promotion of interests committed to the keeping of Government.

Gentlemen, it will be my pleasing duty to convey to His Highness the Maharaja the sentiments of loyalty and respect to which you have so fittingly given expression in the addresses. His Highness watches over your interests with unceasing vigilance and solicitude, and I know His Highness' dearest wish is that the Government and the people should co-operate, on a basis of common ideals and aspirations, and work with mutual good will, confidence and hope for the future.

REPLY TO AN ADDRESS BY THE CITIZENS OF MYSORE.

7th Jan. 1913. [On the evening of the 7th January 1913, the citizens of Mysore assembled at the Rangacharlu Memorial Hall, Mysore, to present an Address of congratulation to Sir M. Visvesvaraya, on his elevation to the office of Dewan of Mysore. Nearly two thousand people, including several European ladies and gentlemen, were present on the occasion. After benedictory verses and music, Mr. M. L. Vardhamanayya, Secretary to the Reception Committee, read the Address in Kannada, which, *inter alia*, referred to Sir M. Visvesvaraya's work in Bombay and to his interest in the economic progress of his countrymen.

In reply to the Address, Sir M. Visvesvaraya said :—]

Gentlemen,—I have a few valued friends in the Mysore City, but it has not been my privilege to be associated with the citizens at large in any public work or function in the past. My obligation to you is, therefore, all the greater for the honour you have done me in presenting an address of congratulation on this occasion.

You, in this city, have already given expression to our sense of horror and detestation at the news of the recent dastardly attempt on the life of our popular and broad-minded Viceroy. His Excellency has been doing his duty with wisdom, caution and magnanimity, and the attempt on his life seems peculiarly wicked. It has aroused intense indignation in all parts of the country, and we fervently hope that His Excellency's recovery may be speedy and complete and that he may soon be able to resume the functions of his high office.

It is also my painful duty to refer to the sudden and premature death of my valued colleague, Mr. Dalvai Devaraj Urs. His brief career as a Councillor was marked by earnestness, sweet reasonableness and sturdy common sense. He has left many friends to mourn his loss,

Reply to an Address by the Citizens of Mysore.

particularly in this city, where he was well known and popular, and where the family name of Dalvai is held in great respect.

I believe on this occasion you will expect me to refer to some of the local matters in which you are directly interested. The city has undergone extensions in recent years; it possesses a good water supply derived from the Cauvery. Drainage works on a large scale on modern lines have been projected and are being carried out. Your streets are lighted by electricity from the Cauvery Power Scheme. The holding of annual Exhibitions under the orders of His Highness the Maharaja is much appreciated not only by you but by large numbers of His Highness' subjects who visit the capital for the Dasara from all parts of the State.

Quite recently, Government have sanctioned a sum of about Rs. 1,40,000 for the extension of the Jewell Filter plant with a view to improve the purity of your water supply. The construction of a new hospital block has been decided on. A Technical Institute, by amalgamating existing institutions, will shortly come into existence.

Gentlemen, you will thus see that Government are doing all they can for the improvement of the city; indeed, more than they have done for any other city or town in the State.

A great deal more yet remains to be done. The further extensions and orderly growth of the city, increase of occupations for the people, improvement of education, particularly female education, require attention. Mysore has produced a few girl graduates, but somehow the activities on behalf of female education appear to have slackened after they came up to a certain stage. Women need more practical education in house-keeping, domestic economy and practical arts. The existing institutions require to be improved in this respect. To further these and other similar objects, Government would like to see more private enterprise in evidence. We want the co-operation of all men of light and leading who love the city and who are prepared to work for its development.

Then there are also questions connected with the development of the district as a whole. Mysore is at present practically at one end of a single line of railway, and all traffic has to pass through Bangalore. If this city is to be allowed to thrive and come into prominence, there must be railway communications opened towards the north, south and west, at an early date. You are aware surveys and enquiries are in progress with an eye to future developments in this direction.

The construction of the first stage of the Kannambadi Reservoir will provide a large amount of storage for hot weather cultivation which should be profitably utilised for sugar-cane. If Government officials and the people co-operate from now, about 10,000 acres of sugar-cane can be brought under cultivation within the next five years. This will mean an addition of about 30 lakhs to the annual produce or income of the district. To bring this large industry into existence, a practical working scheme has to be prepared. I shall be glad to indicate the main lines of a scheme, but the working out of the details must be left to the local officers in consultation with the leading men interested in agriculture and trade.

There are numerous other questions which should engage your attention, such as extending the use of machinery, starting mills and small industries, developing forest products, etc., for all of which we require local initiative, enthusiasm and enterprise on the part of the people.

In addressing the citizens of Bangalore on the 12th of last month, I referred to certain public questions affecting the State as a whole. I alluded to the rise in prices and the changed conditions under which we live and work, as a result of the rapid growth of communications. I stated that though the conditions under which we live have radically changed, our ideals have not. The Hindu ideal is that this world is a preparation for the next and not a place to stay in and make oneself comfortable.

The nationality of Western countries, on the other hand, rests on an economic basis. Their activities, political, industrial and social, are subordinated to the resources at command, and they all aim at the creation of more wealth and increased comfort.

If we want to know in what direction to move, we must compare ourselves with, and be guided by the experience of, progressive countries. The comparison brings to light certain startling truths which I am never tired of repeating and which cannot be too often, or too strongly, impressed on the attention of our people.

The material progress of every country is always powerfully influenced by the condition of its education, and education in this State is at a very low ebb.

Ninety-four persons in every 100 of our people are illiterate. In progressive countries, the percentage of illiteracy does not usually exceed 10 or 15.

Seventy-two per cent of the population of Mysore depend on agriculture. In England, the number dependent on agriculture is very small, the entire population living under rural conditions being less than 22 per cent. No country, so largely dependent on agriculture, under conditions of such precarious rainfall as ours, can be called prosperous.

For nearly six months in the year on an average, the ordinary Mysore cultivator has no regular occupation.

The efficiency of our workmen is low. They lack manual training and discipline. It is computed that three Indian workmen are required to do the work of one labourer in progressive countries.

Reply to an Address by the Citizens of Mysore.

The earning power of a Mysorean is computed at about one-fifteenth of that of an average European, or less.

The prosperity of a country is measured by the number and magnitude of its industries and the volume of its trade. We have not awakened even to the necessity of maintaining correct statistics in this respect.

The annual correct death rate in Mysore is over 30 per 1,000; in Europe, it is 15 to 18. The average duration of the life of a Mysorean is less than 25 years. The same in America and Europe varies from 45 to 54.

It is necessary that these truths must soak into the minds of the people before they can seriously realise the need for exertion.

We must endeavour to improve the lot of the masses by encouraging self-help and private enterprise among them. The hope of the country lies in co-operation; in large numbers of people learning to act and work together. As by experience our people come to learn that in the multitude of counsellors there is wisdom and in union there is strength, the necessity of co-operative effort will come to be more and more appreciated.

I attach much importance to the investigation of public questions by associations or committees of intelligent people, because thereby many questions can be kept under investigation and many brains kept at work. On such associations or committees we must place picked men of ability, worth and self-sacrifice, men with a sure instinct for the essential who can seize an idea and tirelessly work at it till it becomes an accomplished fact.

I think every Taluk or Municipality should form a small committee to study its local deficiencies and wants and endeavour to supply them more largely by its own efforts. Four or five leading men, trusted by the local people, and working as a committee of progress, should be able to do much for a Taluk. A money grant may be made for their expenses or the Committee may be allowed to raise a local cess. The funds might be supplemented by voluntary contributions in various ways. One or two officials might be attached to the Committees for executive work. Each local Committee might be asked to send in a report every year (a report of two or three pages should suffice at the outset), with a few essential statistics showing the increase of population, increase in education, improvements in agriculture, additions to factories and joint-stock companies, growth in the value of manufactured goods or exported produce, number of minor tanks restored, increase in area irrigated, etc.

The whole State may be divided for this purpose into about 85 or 90 units including all Taluks and Municipalities. If in a period of, say, three years, are added a thousand people to the educated population of each taluk, a lakh of rupees to the value of exported or manufactured produce and four or five minor tanks to the total number of restored tanks, the gain to the whole State will be very appreciable. A little done every year will mean much in a few years. A little done for each locality will be much for the whole State. Although individual efficiency may be small, yet by co-operation and by large numbers working with definite objects and ideals, much effort can be put forth and much work done.

Under the scheme for co-operative effort I have described, questions of a provincial character may be investigated by the existing Representative Assembly, the Legislative Council and the Central Committees, or whatever modifications of these may be necessary. The purely district requirements may be attended to by the District Boards and Committees. The Taluk Boards and Committees may deal with smaller concerns or schemes of purely local interest.

The exact form of the organization and the methods

of election and nomination may be discussed and settled gradually, but the scheme outlined shows in what manner provincial and local activities may be co-ordinated so as to form an intelligent part of an intelligent whole.

Compared with progressive countries, our working efficiency is low, our earning power is small, our standard of living is poor, our people die early and the masses of the agricultural population are steeped in ignorance. It may not be possible to raise our standards to the level of progressive nations, it may not be desirable to reproduce their institutions here in their entirety, but, if we are to render a proper account of ourselves, the methods adopted and the successes attained by them should be ever kept before our eyes for study and emulation.

If any citizen of the State has any important proposal to advance, his best course will be to place it before one of the existing local bodies or Committees, and through it, endeavour to influence public opinion and Government. His Highness the Maharaja commands me to assure you, and through you the public of this State, that any constructive scheme of administrative or economic interest that may be put forward, provided it is conceived in the interests of large masses of the population and influentially supported, will receive the very earnest consideration of His Highness' Government.

OPENING OF THE LOCAL FUND DISPENSARY AT SAKLESPUR.

Mar. [Sir M. Visvesvaraya arrived at the newly constructed Local Fund Dispensary building, Saklespur, at 6 P.M., on 15th

Opening of the Local Fund Dispensary at Saklespur.

March 1913. A large and distinguished gathering, including most of the European and Indian planters of the neighbourhood and local officers, had assembled there. Dr. P. S. Achyuta Rao, Senior Surgeon and Sanitary Commissioner, and Dr. Asirvatham, District Medical and Sanitary Officer, received the Dewan. Mr. Graham Anderson, C.I.E., in opening the proceedings, made an eloquent speech, thanking the Government for their benevolence in sanctioning a building for the Dispensary. He was followed by Dr. Asirvatham, who requested the Dewan to formally declare the new building open.

In acceding to the request, Sir M. Visvesvaraya said :—]

Gentlemen,—I have just arrived at the last stage of a very pleasant and instructive tour through the *malnad* country commencing from its northern end in Shimoga. One finds in places like Ikkeri, Nagar, Hebbe, Jagar Valley and Mudgere unmistakable traces that an active and skilful people inhabited the country at no distant date. At any rate, two or three centuries ago, this part of the country seems to have been very thickly populated, perhaps more than the *maidan*. But the only indications now left of an active past are the ruins of old fortresses and irrigation works and a few exquisite stone carvings in deserted temples amidst a weak and declining population.

In a speech made in Bangalore in the month of January last, His Highness the Maharaja referred to the loss of population in the *malnad* which he said was a matter of great concern to his Government. It has been explained to me that the annual influx of population from the coast districts has diminished within the past ten years on account of the extension of railway from the south up to Mangalore, the development of fisheries along the west coast and to some extent the depression in the coffee industry. Whatever the cause, there is no reason to doubt that the flow of population from the coast districts has received a check.

Opening of the Local Fund Dispensary at Saklespur.

In the district of Shimoga, there are three pure *malnad* taluks and three semi-*malnad* ones; in Kadur two *malnad* taluks and two semi-*malnad* ones; and in the Hassan District only one *malnad* taluk and one semi-*malnad* taluk and sub-taluk.

It is noticed from the Census figures that in the purely *malnad* taluks of these three districts there was a fall in the population of 26,905 souls or 8·2 per cent in the decennium ending 1911. The fall in the semi-*malnad* taluks in the same period was 30,731 or 6·1 per cent. The total loss of population in the *malnad* area of these three districts has been 67,632 or nearly 7 per cent, as against an increase in population in the whole State of 4·8 per cent. The total decrease of population in the Kadur District has been 5·8 per cent, in the Shimoga District 2·8 per cent, while in the Hassan District, the bulk of which is *maidan*, there has been an increase of 2 per cent in spite of the heavy loss of 14 per cent in the Manjarabad Taluk.

There is no doubt that a large part of the population suffers from malaria as evidenced by the numerous cases of fever and of enlarged spleen and liver and the general anæmic condition of the people. From all accounts, mortality among infants seems to be appallingly large.

The cause seems to be the excessive growth of vegetation which is enveloping towns and villages and placing man at a disadvantage in his struggle for existence. The valleys are full of rotten leaves and every shower helps to wash down decaying vegetation and to pollute the streams. The Bhadra river, near its source, and other hill streams show this contamination in the very colour of their water.

The chief remedy is to clear vegetation all round habited areas, for a furlong or so round each hamlet, for half a mile or so round each village, and for a mile or

Opening of the Local Fund Dispensary at Saklespur.

more round each town. To my mind, it is necessary to keep the surroundings of towns and villages free from vegetation as it is from irrigation. Many towns in Italy have been reclaimed from malarial infection by clearing rank vegetation from their neighbourhood. The lantana, which has been encroaching in these parts, seems to deserve special attention as I learn that it favours malaria and is injurious alike to human and plant life.

Then there is the water supply difficulty. The rainfall in this region is very heavy, varying roughly from 80 to 150 inches, but it escapes rapidly down the hill slopes leaving little sub-soil storage behind. The country is parched up in the hot weather and except in deep valleys and other favourable situations it is difficult to get water by means of wells. The people must be taught to avoid the use of polluted supplies from streams and irrigated fields in which the country abounds. A persistent effort should be made to dig more wells and prevent the use of water which is not boiled or sterilized.

One grave feature of the present situation is the excessive mortality noticed among women in child-birth and among infants. On account of, perhaps, malarial poison in the system, women in child-birth require careful treatment. The state of pregnancy is justly regarded with great apprehension in this region. I understand, over a large area, women are subjected to barbarous treatment at this particularly critical period of their life. The mortality among infants before they are three years old may also be traced to malarial poison.

The immediate remedy that will suggest itself is to train a sufficient number of midwives from among the local population. A beginning should be made by importing more trained midwives for the present.

The great bulk of the labouring and agricultural population, at least in the northern and central *malnad*, is steeped in ignorance and superstition and is unenterprising. It is said that the enlarged spleen or liver, from which many people suffer, brings on a condition of torpor or languor which renders them indolent. A large number in Shimoga and Kadur Districts are bound to the sowcars from generation to generation and are hopelessly indebted. They live in houses which are too close to the paddy flats and too close to cattle sheds in which manure is allowed to collect and fester. They have not learnt to clothe themselves properly against the sudden variations of weather characteristic of this region, and so fall an easy prey to pneumonia. Their food is of the poorest and often unwholesome and, as stated already, the water they drink is poisoned by decayed vegetable matter. They have practically no education worth the name and therefore no training or preparation whatever to resist the deadly effects of the climate.

Such insanitary conditions are, however, not peculiar to Mysore. They are met with in several places along the Western Ghats. Many years ago, I had occasion to examine the river valleys in the Dongs in Khandesh with a view to develop irrigation. That was before the Tapti Valley Railway was constructed. The Dongs are similar to our *malnad* but inhabited by a wild race of Bhils who believe in evil spirits. The country is traversed by rivers and streams, the waters of which are so unwholesome that the principal ones bear such suggestive names as *Sarpini* (serpent), *Vinchini* (scorpion) and *Kalapani*. This is no exaggeration because the names are printed on the Topographical Survey maps of the Government of India. The waters of the streams were covered with a green scum and so injurious were they thought to be that some of the European officers who visited the area preferred to prepare their tea from soda water.

The present unsatisfactory condition of the *malnad*

seems to be due to the effect of malaria and the hopeless inability of the lower classes of the population to adapt themselves to their environment. Special measures seem necessary to equip the population with the powers of resistance necessary to withstand the climate and strengthen their sinews by the struggle against adverse circumstances. This can be done by spreading education among the children of the labouring and agricultural classes. Instruction should be given in the public schools on the distinctive characteristics of the *malnad* climate and the mode of life and habits best calculated to promote healthy existence in the tract. Sanitary principles should be taught to grown-up people by means of leaflets and peripatetic lectures equipped with lantern slides. The establishment of travelling dispensaries and free distribution of quinine have also been suggested. It may be necessary to open out new roads, construct steam tramways to provide rapid communication both with the *maidan* and the west coast and to start industries to utilise forest products.

There are, I am glad to say, many well-to-do European and Indian planters residing in the *malnad* and a large body of sowcars and landholders who may be expected to co-operate with Government in any scheme calculated to develop the tract.

As you may know, the policy of His Highness' Government is to help those who help themselves. If the leaders of the people wish to take an active part in the development of this tract, their advice and offers of help will be most welcome to us. The other day, both at Sagar and Tirthahalli, I was gratified to find there were people able and willing to raise funds, if necessary, for the extension of railways. There may be many persons who would be willing to teach sanitary principles and modern habits of life to the labouring classes if only they themselves knew how. Some of the young men of the locality should be sent abroad to receive training and equip themselves to be able to discharge such duties to their fellowmen.

If a carefully thought-out scheme of development is prepared to restore the necessary population and vitality to the *malnad*, it should be possible to finance it eventually by means of increased revenue from local sources, chiefly from forest products.

Many of you, perhaps, may not be aware that I was once a Sanitary officer and have had opportunities of advising in other places in regard to measures for the prevention of malaria. I was for a couple of years member of a Committee appointed to enquire into the causes of malaria in the city of Bombay. I have, however, no wish that the impressions I have formed should be taken as having any authority either from a sanitary or administrative point of view. They may be regarded in the light of suggestions thrown out to invite discussion. We all agree that the loss of population is a calamity and that the present drift should be checked. His Highness' Government are anxious to go to the root of the matter and do whatever may be possible within the limits permitted by their resources.

The mitigation of malaria is one of the problems which are now pressing to the front in the administration of British India. The telegrams in the past few days give the gratifying news that in the budget before the Imperial Legislative Council, large grants are being given to local administrations for this purpose. You will agree that the Mysore State should not lag behind in this respect.

The permanent remedies I have suggested have yet to be fully investigated, and they will take time to bear fruit, but immediate relief can be afforded to the suffering population to some extent by building and equipping more hospitals and employing more trained midwives. Government have been giving facilities in this respect for several years past and the building we have assembled to open to-day has been constructed in pursuance of that policy.

I desire to thank Mr. Graham Anderson for his generous appreciation of the efforts of His Highness' Government in sanctioning the construction of this building. As he very truly points out in his interesting speech, credit is particularly due to Col. Smyth and Mr. Asirvatham for pressing on the attention of Government the urgent need for a new building. Some credit is also due to the Public Works Officers who designed and constructed the building.

Gentlemen, I have much pleasure in declaring that this hospital building is now open and that it *is* dedicated to the relief of suffering among the townspeople of Saklespur and the surrounding country.

ADDRESS TO MYSORE ENGINEERS.

[The Sixth Session of the Mysore Engineers' Association opened at 12 noon, on Thursday, the 27th March 1913, in the Association Rooms, Bangalore. Besides the members who had come specially from the interior of the State for the occasion, there were a number of visitors. **27th Mar. 1913.**

Sir M. Visvesvaraya, who was a former President of the Association, in opening the proceedings of the session, said :—]

Gentlemen,—I have been invited to discharge quite a superfluous function. I am here to-day at the request of your Committee to open the Sixth Session of the Mysore Engineers' Association. Many of you have come at some sacrifice to attend this annual Conference, and it gives me no ordinary pleasure to meet you once more and offer you a cordial welcome.

During the past year the Association has had a home and a properly-equipped library and your Committee has, I believe, taken advantage of these facilities and been able to hold more meetings and put in more work than in any previous year.

I do not wish to dwell on this occasion on what has been done, but I should like to make a passing reference to some of the new questions which are pressing to the front for solution and with regard to which your services are in increasing demand. The management and repairs of roads is among the most important of these. The report by the Committee appointed last year may be discussed with advantage with an eye to practical action. I would lay special stress on the need for economy in the maintenance of roads and for greater personal attention on the part of our officers to the spreading and consolidation of road materials in the monsoon.

I notice that there is no paper on your Agenda on masonry dams. I presume the engineers have been too busy with construction work to find time to write a paper on the subject; but I trust this omission will be supplied at the next year's Conference. Railway work under the guidance of our Engineer-in-Chief is making rapid progress. I hope that, at the next Conference, we may have some papers from the Railway Engineers.

I am glad that town planning is receiving attention. I commend to your special attention the study of municipal engineering, water supply and drainage with a view to supply cheap but efficient designs suited to the character and capacity of the people. Many of our towns are so poor that a piped water supply and sewerage are entirely beyond their means.

As you may be aware, His Highness' Government are deeply concerned with the question of the mitigation or eradication of malaria in the *malnad*. I think one or two engineers would do well to study what I may term "Malarial Engineering," that is, the scientific treatment of malarial tracts as practised in British India and in western countries for the prevention of malaria.

The Public Works Department has already issued a report embodying proposals for the improvement of irrigation in the State. The report is printed and I would ask you to discuss the proposals in order to perfect the details for practical action. One of the proposals is to prepare for a large sugar-cane plantation under the Cauvery canals as soon as stored water is available for the purpose.

Another scheme which should be pushed through has reference to the experimental working of a few selected tanks and canals on scientific lines including the distribution of water by measurement. A third proposal is to teach the villagers to maintain and manage the minor tanks and to undertake the economical distribution of water by their own hands.

Some of these questions might be attended to by the people themselves if there were architects and engineers in private practice. Unfortunately, every person in this country who qualifies himself for a profession, continues to sit at the doorsteps of Government demanding an appointment. There should be room in Bangalore and Mysore for one or two private firms of builders to assist the public in constructing new houses in the extensions. An engineer who wants to start private practice would do well to associate himself with one of our efficient contractors in building work, of whom I am glad to say we have quite a large number. Similarly, in the restoration or construction of tanks and channels, there is much scope for private practitioners if proper facilities are provided. As I remarked on a former occasion, the smaller tanks are silting up and new tanks are not taking their place as rapidly as the old ones are deteriorating. The tanks were originally constructed by the residents in the neighbourhood who are also the fittest people to maintain them, being the parties most interested in their preservation. But Government have assumed the responsibility without counting the magnitude of the work to be done or its cost. It is now patent that no Government Department, however large or efficient, will be able to cope with the work, that is, with the maintenance of the enormous number of tanks with which the country is studded and on which the prosperity of our rural population is so largely dependent. As a preliminary step, this Association should do what it can to set up a few engineers in private practice and to induce the public to patronise them.

Before I close, I wish to add one word in favour of efficiency, for I know your strong points and your weaknesses. We are anxious that every Executive Engineer in charge of a district should give a specific portion of his time to important work and to supervision. He should be a man of more than ordinary industry and character. If he is not that and is merely a humdrummer, he will have to make room for one who has these essential qualifications. For, the District Engineer is the pivot of our Public Works administration. If he is active, every one under him will be active; if he is slack, the entire district establishment suffers from inertia. One supreme test of efficiency and character is to find a man doing his work with zeal and method whether any one is looking on or not, or whether the work itself is appreciated or not.

Address to Mysore Engineers.

Every one should receive his remuneration in proportion to his efficiency and according to the value of his services to the State. A high officer of Government said to me a few days ago that Government should recognise only one caste in dispensing official favours, namely, a caste comprising all the efficient and honest men in the service as opposed to those lacking in these qualities. People are born, they cannot choose their caste. But, into this new caste, every one may find admission, according to the measure of his ability, by hard work and straight dealing. The very attempt to keep it as a goal, and to rise to the new caste, will do good. It will make every timid man self-reliant, and even a dull man bright. I hope every one of the junior members present here will strive by study, by great industry and unswerving perseverance, to raise his reputation for efficiency and probity. No one who does this can fail to succeed or to raise the good name of the engineering service to which he belongs.

I have, within the past six weeks, received requests, from outside the State, for the loan of the services of four or five engineer officers. As we are very short-handed ourselves, it has not been possible to comply with the request. I mention this fact as it is an indication that there will be increasing opportunities in future for all competent members of the profession who wish to distinguish themselves.

Before you close your labours, I trust you will enable your President to communicate to Government particulars of any original work you may have accomplished during the past year and some details of your progress in the special studies which you solemnly undertook to prosecute at the last year's Conference. I have no doubt you will prepare, as in previous years, a programme of the special studies which the members propose to undertake in the coming year. His Highness' Government will be prepared to help the Association, should you require any further facilities to improve yourselves.

Gentlemen, much varied work is being done by you in the different parts of the State. Some of it is criticised, much of it goes unappreciated; but, on the whole, I believe that it is efficiently performed and is producing solid results.

SPEECH AT THE MYSORE LEGISLATIVE COUNCIL.

4th April 1913.

[Sir M. Visvesvaraya opened the proceedings of the Mysore Legislative Council on 4th April 1913, with the following remarks:—]

Gentlemen,—Before proceeding with the business of the day, I wish to address a few words of greeting on this the first occasion I meet you in this Council.

The members may well be proud of the work which the Council has accomplished during the six years of its existence. It began as a purely nominated body but has at present two elected members returned by the Representative Assembly. I understand it has to its credit nearly 30 enactments placed on the Statute Book whose object was either to help in the administration of the law or to promote the economic well-being of our people.

There is a considerable amount of legislative work awaiting handling, and if the Government and the representatives of the people work in a spirit of harmonious co-operation, this Council cannot fail to prove a potent instrument for good.

The future too is full of promise. I have been far too short a period in touch with the affairs of the State to be able to indicate on what lines the work of this Council should develop in future. But this much I can say, namely, that it will be the endeavour of His Highness' Government to utilise this Council and the Representative Assembly in an ever-increasing degree to ascertain the views, wishes and sentiments of His Highness' subjects on matters intimately affecting their welfare.

As stated already, two elected members are being nominated to the Council on the recommendation of the Representative Assembly. Including the latest appointment, we have now got a non-official majority in the Council. You require no greater proof to show the confidence His Highness the Maharaja places in the wisdom and loyalty of the leading public men of the country.

I trust that, as in the past, our discussions will continue to be conducted in a spirit of mutual concession and toleration and that I may rely on the sympathy and support of the members in our efforts to carry through useful legislation, and in maintaining the dignity of our proceedings.

ADDRESS TO THE MYSORE ECONOMIC CONFERENCE.

[The Fourth Session of the Mysore Economic Conference, a body created for the consideration of proposals affecting the economic improvement of the people, was held at the Public Offices, Mysore, on the 11th June 1913. 11th June 1913.

Address to the Mysore Economic Conference.

In opening the proceedings of the Conference, Sir M. Visvesvaraya, in his capacity as President of the Conference, delivered the following address :—]

Gentlemen,—It is my privilege, by direction of His Highness the Maharaja, to welcome you to the Fourth Session of the Mysore Economic Conference. The discussions and investigations by the Conference and its Committees have revealed many needs of the country which must be supplied sooner or later, and some of its resources which might be utilized for the promotion of its material prosperity. Investigations both into general questions as well as particular subjects are in progress, and the more time and ability are brought to bear on them, the more definite will be the conclusions which the Committees and the Heads of Departments will be able to recommend for adoption by the Government and the people.

The great bulk of our people are uneducated and agriculture is their chief occupation. They have no industries or trade, on modern lines, worth mentioning. No country so largely dependent as ours on agriculture can be said to be prosperous. The margin between the ordinary standard of living and destitution among our people is very narrow. At the first sign of scarcity which is usually occasioned in this country by a failure of rain, the poorest of our people are plunged into a state of distress and, in a severe famine such as happened in 1877 in Mysore, large numbers of them are liable to die of starvation.

On account of the rapid growth of communications, the whole world is becoming one country and the prices of the necessaries of life and commodities are becoming more and more uniform. Those people will be able to live in health and comfort that have capacity to buy them, capacity derived from disciplined activity, trained skill and superior knowledge of the affairs of the world.

Address to the Mysore Economic Conference.

Every European country believes that activity, brains, science and thoroughness are necessary for ensuring a high standard of living; and the Government and leaders of those countries are untiring in their efforts to equip the people with the necessary skill and energy. Such countries are prospering and are yearly adding to their stores of wealth.

It will avail us little to know how much better we are now than we were twenty or thirty years ago unless our present standards of working and earning are appreciable by comparison with progressive countries.

I wish to repeat here some of the comparative statistics to bring the difference home to you. The figures bear repetition not only by me here but from mouth to mouth, by young and old, through the length and breadth of His Highness' Territories. They ought to give food for serious thought and rouse the most sluggish temperament among us to action. Some of the statistics are necessarily approximate, but they will be found to be sufficiently accurate for purposes of a general comparison.

Taking education first, out of 57 lakhs of people in Mysore, only 3½ lakhs can read and write, that is, only 6 persons out of every 100. The corresponding ratio in advanced countries is 85 to 95 persons in every 100.

In the United States of America, the expenditure incurred on education amounts to about Rs. 14 per head of population; in Mysore, it is less than six annas per head.

In the most progressive countries again, nearly one-fifth of the total population are at school. The proportion in Mysore is one-fiftieth.

Although we have a population of nearly six millions, we have no Universities in Mysore. In Canada, with a population scarcely 25 per cent more than in Mysore, there are 20 Universities; in the United Kingdom, there are 20 Universities for a population of 45 millions and in Germany 21 Universities for a population of 65 millions.

As regards newspapers and periodicals, there is, according to published statistics, one paper on an average for every 18,799 persons in the United Kingdom, one for every 4,077 persons in the United States of America. In the Mysore State, the total number of papers and periodicals of all kinds, several of them of very little value, is 36, which gives one periodical on an average for every 158,482 persons.

Formerly, only 5 to 10 per cent of the population in every country received what may be termed liberal education. It was not then considered necessary to give any training to persons engaged in agriculture, industries or manual labour. But the civilized countries have now discovered that education is necessary for all manual occupations and industries, and that the higher the standard of education and science applied to industrial callings, the greater the wealth produced.

The more advanced countries accumulate wealth by their devotion to industries and commerce, on which large numbers of people are engaged. The value of manufactured produce in the United Kingdom is Rs. 326 per head or about 30 times that produced in Mysore.

In the United Kingdom, only about one-eighth of the people are engaged in agriculture, in Germany one-sixth, in Japan three-fifths, while in Mysore, nearly three-fourths of the population are so dependent. In recent years, the number dependent on agriculture has swollen by the addition to its ranks of unskilled artisans who lost their industries on account of the fierce competition with the manufactured products of Western countries.

The calculated earning power of an average Mysorean is about Rs. 30 per head per annum, whereas an average European earns about Rs. 400 per head and an average Englishman Rs. 600 to 700.

The correct annual death rate in Mysore is, I believe, about 30 per 1,000, whereas in some of the most advanced countries, it is as low as 15 to 18. The average life of a Mysorean is estimated at 25 years, while that of an American or a European is between 45 and 55 years.

The comparative study and investigation of questions, which we have begun, cannot fail to help in spreading sound ideas on economic subjects among the people and gradually reveal to them causes of their inferior position as compared with progressive countries and indicate the spheres of work in which they might profitably engage themselves in future.

Hitherto, the thinking work was left chiefly to Government officials. In future, it will be shared by both officials and non-officials. Eventually, the work should be transferred largely to non-officials.

The activities connected with economic improvements should be shared both by high and low so that every one may be made to think and act according to his capacity and opportunities and every one may take his part, to the best of his ability, in the work of the economic development of the country. All persons interested in any particular industry or commercial question, no matter in what part of the country they may reside, should be made to think and work in unison as far as possible.

When the great majority of the people fall in with such a scheme of development, we will be gradually creating well-informed and able men and experts in every branch of activity, and raising the level of business capacity and earning power in the country.

The Conference has been started by His Highness' Government to provide facilities in these directions. The work of the Conference is developing gradually ; but like

G 2

all such institutions, progress must be slow as people have to be trained to new ideas. It will be seen from the reports of the Committees that the Bank scheme is now taking shape, the Compulsory Education Bill has been introduced into the Legislative Council, large grants have been given for primary education, a Department of Industries and Commerce has been brought into existence, a few installations for the manufacture of jaggery and other industrial experiments have been started and a substantial move made in connection with technical and commercial education. The rules of the Conference have been revised to simplify and facilitate the work of the Committees.

The activities and expenditure of this Conference fall mainly under three heads, *viz.*,

(1) Education,
(2) Agriculture, and
(3) Industries and Commerce.

For the investigation and propaganda work to be done by the Committees and the staff, the expenditure to be incurred annually will be less than 1½ lakhs. All the other expenditure incurred will be for the actual work of the three Government Departments concerned.

We are making provision for a large increase of expenditure under education but it will not be so large as it might be. I may mention that, in the neighbouring Presidency of Madras, the amount provided for education was 45 lakhs two or three years ago. This year it has been increased to over 81 lakhs. We have not been able here to provide for an increase in the same liberal proportion. But I do hope that the public will make further sources of revenue available for pushing on educational work in the State.

In the Agricultural Department, the expenditure will be increased from Rs. 79,000 to a little over 1½ lakh. But the provision is very inadequate compared to the needs of the case. For about the same population, in the Dominion of Canada, over 30 lakhs were spent in 1909-10 through the Department of Agriculture to help the farmers of that country.

The expenditure provided for the Department of Industries and Commerce is Rs. 1,25,000. We have not yet perfected our arrangements for giving loans and advances to industrial and business concerns likely to profit by them.

The resources of Government are inadequate and we must therefore look to the co-operation of the people to supplement the efforts of Government to make provision for all the progressive measures considered necessary.

In our warm climate we have not got the same incentive to exertion and we may never be able to attain the same level of prosperity as Western people, but no organized effort on our part in the directions indicated will go unrewarded in reducing the great distance, economically speaking, which at present separates us from them.

If the intelligence of our people is kept undeveloped, their skill untrained, their activities unstimulated, the average standards of working and living will remain low, and the country will continue to be populated, as at present, by ignorant, unskilled and indolent masses who, in times of scarcity or stress, will be unable to help themselves. Safety therefore lies in educating the people and equipping them with skill and science and keeping them active. This is what His Highness' Government have in view in introducing the various measures for improving the economic efficiency of our people.

OPENING OF HARIHAR PUMPING INSTALLATION.

11th Aug. 1913.

[At the invitation of Mr. Balappa, son of Mr. Bhimappa Bondaday, Sir M. Visvesvaraya consented to open the new pumping installation erected by him at Harihar. The Dewan arrived at Davangere station on the 11th August 1913, and on alighting was met by the leading officials and non-officials of the district, including a large concourse of people from the surrounding villages who had been attracted to the place by the visit of the Dewan. The party motored in the evening to Harihar where the Dewan formally inaugurated the pumping plant amidst great rejoicings. There was a large number of people present, many having come from Dharwar, Hubli, Ranibennur, Davangere and Bangalore. In a Kannada address, Mr. Balappa requested the Dewan to formally open the installation. In the course of this address Mr. Balappa said that at first he did not desire to consult the Government officials, but as complications and difficulties arose in installing the plant, he had to seek Government aid and now he was more than satisfied and prayed for permission to express his and his father's indebtedness and gratitude to His Highness the Maharaja's Government for having successfully installed the pump and plant.

Mr. A. Chatterton and Mr. M. Chengiah Chetty spoke, at the conclusion of which Sir M. Visvesvaraya, in declaring the installation open, said :—]

Gentlemen,—I am here to-day at the suggestion of my friend Mr. Chatterton, to mark the appreciation of His Highness' Government of the enterprise shown by Mr. Bhimappa Bondaday in putting up this interesting pumping installation. The river Tungabhadra has its source in our *Malnad* country and, as its supply is abundant and unfailing even during the hot weather, there is much prospective benefit to look for in these parts by the use of its water for irrigation. A project has been prepared for an irrigation canal system on the Bhadra river

Opening of Harihar Pumping Installation.

but it will be some time before we can find money to carry it through. In the meanwhile, we must welcome every effort—particularly private effort like this—to utilise the waters of the river for the extension of high class cultivation in this region.

From the account you have just heard, we gather that the object of this installation is to irrigate about 70 acres of land. The owner ordered the machinery after first obtaining designs and specifications from Mr. Chatterton, but when difficulties arose in the course of its erection, he had recourse once again to the technical skill of the Director of Industries and his staff. Mr. Chatterton's experience and reputation in this respect, as many of you may know, is unique. What he does not know about pumps is probably not worth knowing. Mr. Chatterton has erected numerous plants in the Madras Presidency and is, without question, the leading authority in India on the subject of pumping installations. I am also pleased at the words of appreciation with which Mr. Chatterton refers to the work of his Assistant, Mr. Sitaramachar.

This pump will be worked by an oil engine. Oil is the favourite fuel at present for small installations, but dependence on imported fuel should be avoided as far as possible, because then the commercial success of our large irrigation installations will be at the mercy of high prices and foreign markets. Steam engines, too, are not economical for operating small pumps. One remedy seems to be to extend the use of suction gas engines like the one working in the Banglore Tannery. It should be possible, at no distant date, to manufacture the requisite supply of charcoal from the redundant wood supply of our dense *Malnad* forests. The manufacture and transport facilities should be on a sufficiently extensive scale, to enable us to obtain the fuel at a moderate cost. The question is receiving the attention of our Director of Industries and Commerce.

Another prospective source of power supply is the generation of energy at our waterfalls and conveying the same by wire to distant plains to work pumps for lifting water for the irrigation of private farms. We already use the power from the Cauvery falls for mining, lighting, mills, factories, looms, etc. The energy can also be applied for agricultural operations, for lifting water for saw mills and threshing machines, for crushing cane, for pulling paddy, for ginning cotton and extracting oil. You can drive your ploughs, heat your water and cook your rice by electric power. There are several waterfalls in our beautiful country, which are inviting to be harnessed and which, with the aid of storage, can be made to generate a steady supply of energy to be placed at the service of our rayiats in a hundred ways. In this connection, I may remind the good people of the Chitaldrug District that there is energy now lying unused at the Marikanave dam, and Government will be only too ready to develop the energy if sufficient demand arose in the neighbourhood to make it worth their while.

You know our tanks are used chiefly for rice cultivation and they run dry, after the rice crop is watered, for four to eight months. Behind and below the earthen dam of every large tank, there are abundant stores of subsoil water which could be utilised to enable sugar-cane, or mulberry or garden crops dependent on the tank to tide over the drought in the hot weather.

An acre of rice crop gives produce worth Rs. 40 or Rs. 50, but I have known that, on some of the canals under my own supervision in the past, an acre of sugarcane yielded a gross income of more than Rs. 1,000. Few people can hope to get rich by growing ragi or rice, but most cultivators in Mysore get their spare cash for luxuries by growing sugar-cane in small plots. They maintain the crop by primitive water lifts worked by bullocks or men by laborious methods. There is abundant subsoil water below the tanks and there is an inexhaustible market for jaggery and it only wants enterprise in our larger cultivators, and co-operation in the smaller men, to benefit by the use of pumps operated by power machinery.

Our raiyat, though industrious and docile, is ignorant, very ignorant, but that is his misfortune rather than his fault. He wants light and leading and more of sympathy than contemptuous neglect. He must be taught to feel that if he depends more on himself and stiffens his backbone instead of seeking redress, for all sorts of grievances under the sun, by making long-winded petitions to Government, he will be raising his position and the self-respect of the agricultural country as a whole. By self-help, he will gain far more than he can ever hope to do by trusting to outside help. The cultivator should be taught to change his conservative methods of work and to make the most of every legitimate opportunity. This will come gradually by the extension of mass education; and His Highness' Government, following the lead of the Government of India, are straining every effort to foster education, including agricultural and manual training. The newspapers, like the *Vokkaligar Patrika*, the *Sadhvi* and the *Vrittanta Patrika* might do much if they opened their columns generously for disseminating information calculated to help the upbuilding and the bettering of agriculture throughout the country. Through their aid, the raiyats in all parts of the State should be able to consult one another by correspondence, in which all kinds of questions pertaining to the improvements of the farm and the home can be asked and answered.

Next to education, the raiyat should acquire a capacity for co-operation and organization. Instead of indulging in factions and hereditary feuds, which in some villages of the *malnad* are transmitted from generation to generation, he should be taught to co-operate and work with his fellowmen. The hard truth should be hammered into him that, it is only by mutual help and co-operation, the moral tone and capacity of the entire population can be raised. Everyone should be made to realise that by quarrelling with his neighbour, he lowers his neighbour's capacity, his neighbour's wealth, and, not infrequently, even the neighbour's means of livelihood as well as his own. There should be co-operative associations for the purchase of seed, of agricultural implements, agricultural machinery and manure, and for providing markets for agricultural produce and for developing rural industries and other similar objects. In Western countries, the principle of co-operation is carried to such an extent that co-operative picnics are organised and educational excursion trains run to enable large bodies of cultivators to visit places of interest for the study of new methods of agriculture. If the cultivators are taught what co-operation and organization can do for them, they will no longer remain helpless dependents or petitioners, and Government will be relieved of the embarrassing positions in which they find themselves placed in times of scarcity or famine. There are more tanks in Mysore in comparison to the area of our State than anywhere else in India, or, perhaps, in any other part of the globe. People now-a-days, expect His Highness' Government to undertake the repairs of even small tanks and channels. Our forefathers could not have brought so many tanks into existence if they had not depended on co-operative effort. The growth of the principle of co-operation will improve the earning capacity of our rural population. I am glad to be able to say that, by the exertions of our enthusiastic Registrar, the movement of co-operative societies is making good progress, although a great deal more yet remains to be done. It should be our aim and hope that an intelligent farmer who cultivates a large area and takes part in local trade should have the same opportunity of rising to positions of influence as any person of his education among members of the liberal professions in our towns and cities.

Another chief handicap is the powerful influence of tradition, indifference to change and belief in fatalism. The sooner he is weaned from these influences, the more activity will the raiyat show and the better will it be for him and for the country. In a rapidly changing world, with prices rising and competition growing keener every day, he cannot afford to sit still or drift into stagnation. As an example of the enormous losses which people suffer by their conservatism, I may mention the condition of the silk industry in Mysore. The supply of cocoons is defective because diseased eggs are being allowed to hatch. Some three months ago I asked a European traveller, who called on me, to favour me with his views on the present condition of the silk industry in Mysore. He very obligingly made enquiries on the spot and reported to me that the hope of any improvement only depended on teaching better methods to the raiyat. He wrote : "I can see that these Indians (meaning the Mysore raiyats), although repeatedly disappointed by the disastrous effects of diseases caused simply by the absolute absence of hygienic principles, keep on trying their luck, year after year, and bend their head to what they call the 'will of God' instead of calling it the 'consequences of their folly.'" He went on to remark that the important point, *viz.*, the effect that increased attention, common sense and cleanliness had upon the crop, reared in the farm entirely escaped his attention. The fatalism of despair, which has taken so strong a hold of the cultivator in the rural areas, is a great stumbling block in the way of rapid progress. Our efforts should be to stimulate a spirit of enquiry and activity. If the cultivator learns to think and enquire, he will become alert to fresh ideas and eager to take to improvements and will acquire gradually the power and the capacity for adapting himself to the rapidly changing conditions of our time.

This is a small private installation and its success, in a commercial sense, although assured under good management, has yet to be tested. But it is to be welcomed because it is a new venture. It is something out of the rut of traditional agriculture. It conveys a lesson to the richer cultivators among us of what science can do for them. Above all it is an example of initiative, of perseverance, of enterprise on which the owner Mr. Bhimappa and his son deserve our hearty congratulations.

His Highness the Maharaja, who watches such projects with enthusiastic interest, has commanded me to convey his good wishes for the success of this undertaking and his hope that Mr. Bhimappa's example may find many imitators.

Gentlemen, I now declare this pumping installation open. I earnestly hope that it may bring prosperity to the owner and serve as an inspiring example of self-help and enterprise to people in this neighbourhood.

MYSORE DASARA EXHIBITION.

3rd Oct. 1913. [The formal opening of the seventh Mysore Dasara Industrial and Agricultural Exhibition was held at the Exhibition grounds, on 3rd October 1913, before a large and distinguished

Mysore Dasara Exhibition.

audience. Dewan Sir M. Visvesvaraya, who performed the ceremony, received on address of welcome from the Exhibition Committee. The Address was read by Mr. G. H. Krumbiegel, Secretary to the Committee.

In reply to the Address, Sir M. Visvesvaraya said :—]

Ladies and Gentlemen,—I have no doubt every one of us present here will wish that this exhibition had been opened by His Highness the Yuvaraja who, as Mr. Krumbiegel has told you, has in previous years honored us by performing this ceremony. He was to have arrived last week, but owing to the accident of a few days' delay in his return, the duty of assisting at the function this year has devolved upon me.

In this connection, many of you will be pleased to hear that we have received telegraphic news that the Yuvaraja landed in Bombay at about 8 o'clock this morning.

As an example of the interest taken by the Yuvaraja in industrial concerns, I may mention to you that the very first thing he did on landing in Europe was to send us samples of clay from Marseilles, as he knew we were interested in starting a tile manufactory in Mysore.

The Mysore Dasara Industrial and Agricultural Exhibition was sanctioned by His Highness the Maharaja in 1907 with a view to promote agriculture and the arts and industries of the State. It has now become an annual event, due to the personal interest taken by His Highness, and is one of the attractions of the Dasara. It receives exhibits from all parts of India. The number of visitors has steadily increased from year to year. I notice that the number who witnessed the Exhibition last year was double that in 1910. The Exhibition is much prized by His Highness because it provides instruction and amusement to his subjects who come for the Dasara from all parts of the State.

Government have not been slow to lead and give

generous assistance towards objects which this Exhibition has in view. We have recently started a Department of Agriculture and a Department of Industries and Commerce. We have also Committees, both Central and District, for promoting agricultural and industrial enterprises in the State. An advance in developing industrial and agricultural education has been made by the establishment of the Chamarajendra Technical Institute in Mysore, an Agricultural School near Bangalore and also Mechanical Engineering and Commercial Schools in the latter city. Exhibitions like these are a fitting corollary to these measures.

I hope it may be possible later on to add a permanent hall of industrial and agricultural machinery in connection with the Chamarajendra Technical Institute to give opportunities to persons interested in machinery and plant to come to Mysore to observe, study and see them worked at all times of the year.

Mr. Krumbeigel brings to notice that the number of local exhibitors this year is small. This is probably because the objects and uses of the Exhibition are not fully brought to the notice of the people in the districts and interest is not kept alive. There should be a network of organization for bringing the labours and interests of all people, who are likely to profit by the Exhibition, to bear on the year's work. The District Committees should be able to enlist for this work the co-operation of all persons who can give their money or personal service, or send exhibits.

Our thanks are due to Mr. Krumbiegel for undertaking this work, by command of His Highness the Maharaja, in addition to his regular duties, and for the high standard aimed at by him in the arrangement of the exhibits and the thoroughness with which the work is done every year.

As regards this year's exhibits, Mr. Krumbiegel has refrained from revealing what good things we may expect to see presently. I am sure there will be much in the Exhibition to interest every visitor and appeal to every taste. He has prepared us for a little disappointment in one or two matters; but I hope that, by the time the distribution of prizes comes off, he may be able to give a better account and be in a position to assure us that, taken as a whole, this year's Exhibition has been a greater success than any of its predecessors. He complains of the paucity of exhibits in the Machinery section, but, at the same time, he is good enough to hint that there may be compensations, and that the Ladies' section is likely to elicit admiration. But I do not wish to keep you in surmise when it is so easy for us to enter the building and see things for ourselves.

Ladies and Gentlemen, I have great pleasure in declaring the Seventh Mysore Dasara Exhibition open.

ADDRESS TO DASARA REPRESENTATIVE ASSEMBLY.

[The thirtieth session of the Dasara Representative Assembly was held at the Public Offices, Mysore, on the 11th October 1913. Besides the representatives from the different parts of the State, there were present on the occasion the Hon'ble Sir Hugh Daly, K.C.I.E., British Resident in Mysore, and a large number of European ladies and gentlemen. 11th Oct. 1913.

Dewan Sir M. Visvesvaraya, in welcoming the members, delivered the following Address:—]

Gentlemen,—I esteem it a privilege, by command of His Highness the Maharaja, to welcome you to the thirtieth session of the Dasara Representative Assembly and to place before you, in accordance with precedent, an account of the more important events of the administration of the past official year, as well as a forecast of the measures contemplated in the current and coming years.

The south-west monsoon this year was weak and there was no rain worth mentioning in the months of July and August. Considerable apprehension was felt during the time the drought lasted and prices had begun to go up. But a welcome change occurred in September and the ragi crop which was in peril has been partly saved. The rainfall in the last and the current months has been favourable, and although this year may not be considered a prosperous one, there is so far no cause for apprehending distress.

Proceeding to the principal events of the past year's administration, I will take up the subject of finances. first. It may be discussed under two heads, *viz.*, the revised estimates for 1912-13 and the budget for 1913-14. These estimates, together with the statement explaining the salient features of the financial position, were published in the *Mysore Gazette Extraordinary*, dated the 6th August last, and have been before you for the past two months.

As the early rains had failed and sowings had been postponed in consequence in several parts of the State, the estimate for 1912-13 was a cautious one. The favorable change in the seasonal conditions that followed improved the prospects and the result is reflected in the revised estimate for the year. The revenue for 1912-13 stands, according to the revised estimate, at Rs. 272·92 lakhs and the expenditure at Rs. 248·68 lakhs. You will therefore see that instead of there being a considerable excess of expenditure over receipts as anticipated at budget time in 1912, there is a substantial surplus of 24·24 lakhs.

Address to Dasara Representative Assembly.

Analysed into ordinary and extraordinary, the figures for revenue and expenditure stand thus :—

	Lakhs		Lakhs
Gross Revenue—1912-13 ...	272·92	Gross Expenditure—1912-13 ...	248·68
Deduct Extraordinary Revenue—		Deduct Extraordinary Expenditure—	
(1) Mining	19·20	(1) Cauvery Reservoir ...	17·50
(2) Cauvery Power Scheme	14·25	(2) Cauvery Power Scheme	·60
(3) Water-supply to the Mines	2·29	(3) Railway construction...	·80
		(4) Tramways ...	·10
	35·74		19·00
Net Ordinary Revenue ...	237·18	Net Ordinary Expenditure...	229·68
		Surplus on the Ordinary Account ...	7·50
Total ...	237·18	Total ...	237·18

There are certain revenues of the State which cannot be reckoned as permanent and these have been shown in the above table as amounting to 35·74 lakhs. Also certain items of expenditure have to be considered as extraordinary, because they are incurred on capital account works and may therefore be treated as an addition to the State assets. The net ordinary revenue and the ordinary expenditure show that there was a surplus of 7·50 lakhs on the ordinary account.

It must, however, be mentioned that these satisfactory results are due to the exceptionally favourable feature of the year's transactions in connection with sandalwood sales, railway earnings, land revenue collections and excise contracts.

The last financial year may be said to be a very prosperous one. The transactions have, on the whole, resulted in a net addition of 16·74 lakhs to the reserves which, including this addition, stood at 192·11 lakhs on 1st July 1913.

The budget estimates for 1913-14, framed on the expectation of a normal year, provide for a gross revenue of 257·17 lakhs and a gross expenditure of 313·55 lakhs.

Address to Dasara Representative Assembly.

Analysed into ordinary and extraordinary, the figures stand thus:—

	Lakhs
Gross Budgetted Revenue	257·17
Deduct—	
(1) Mining Revenue ...	19·00
(2) Cauvery Power Scheme	14·25
(3) Water-supply to the Mines ...	2·29
	35·54
Net Ordinary Revenue ...	221·63
Deficit on the Ordinary Account ...	26·82
Total ...	248·45

	Lakhs
Gross Budgetted Expenditure ...	313·55
Deduct Extraordinary Capital Expenditure—	
(1) Cauvery Reservoir ...	30·40
(2) Cauvery Power Scheme Fourth Installation ...	13·05
(3) Railway construction...	15·00
(4) Tramways ...	6·65
	65·10
Net Ordinary Expenditure...	248·45
Total ...	248·45

The ordinary estimated revenue and expenditure of the year are 221·63 lakhs and 248·45 lakhs respectively, showing a deficit of 26·82 lakhs. This expenditure is due to special non-recurring grants to certain important departments like Public Works, Education, Agriculture and Industries. Most of these grants will, from their very nature, not be repeated. So the deficit need occasion no anxiety. The special adventitious revenue amounted to 35·54 lakhs and the special capital expenditure to 65·10 lakhs, showing an excess expenditure of 29·56 lakhs. The total excess of these two accounts comes to 56·38 lakhs which will be met from the reserve in hand of 192·11 lakhs already mentioned. Government have adequate funds, either in cash or in the shape of temporary investments, for meeting this extraordinary expenditure and it will not be necessary to draw upon the permanent investments for the purpose.

As will be explained in the sequel, certain departments which either produce revenue or which urgently needed development, like the Forest, Police, the Taluk Establishments and Account, have been reorganized recently with a view to improve their earning power or efficiency, as the case may be. A careful financial forecast of the

State for the three years commencing from 1913-14 was prepared and the situation during the triennium, as it would be, on the basis of expenditure as it stood in the year 1912-13, was fully discussed and provision was made for additions to the recurring expenditure to the extent of 5 lakhs during the triennium beginning with 1913-14. A non-recurring expenditure to the extent of 18 lakhs for the same period of three years was also approved by Government. This expenditure includes a recurring annual grant of Rs. 4·10 lakhs and a non-recurring grant for three years of Rs. 7·50 lakhs on education.

In last year's Address you were informed that the Government of India had been pleased to deal in a liberal and generous spirit with the question of the surplus revenues of the Civil and Military Station, Bangalore. The matter is still under the consideration of the Government of India with regard to the exact amount to be refunded to the State and the mode of calculating the surplus to be paid in future, and their final reply is awaited.

With regard to the Account Department, it is only necessary to refer here to one or two important measures sanctioned by Government. In accordance with the views repeatedly urged in this Assembly, greater facilities have been afforded to the general public for the investment of their savings by doing away with the annual limit of Rs. 2,000 and the aggregate limit of Rs. 5,000 for deposits in the Saving Banks, with effect from October last, and providing for the receipt of deposits without any limitation as to amount.

With a view to increase the efficiency of the Comptroller's Office and to provide for the increase of work caused by the creation of new departments and the development of existing ones, Government have recently strengthened the gazetted and ministerial staff of the department. A special feature of the reorganization scheme is the creation of the office of a Deputy Comptroller who will have direct charge of the Railway and Public Works Accounts under the supervision of the Comptroller. This measure has become absolutely necessary for a stricter control of the contemplated large expenditure of about 65 lakhs on Public Works and Railways in the current year and a similar large expenditure likely to be incurred in the coming years.

The rules for regulating the recruitment of officers to the Mysore Civil Service were revised in January last, which also provided for the holding of a competitive examination for the selection of officers. The first examination under these revised rules will be held next month and 19 candidates have been approved for admission.

Coming to the subject of land revenue, the past year cannot be said to have commenced under very good auspices as the rainfall in April, May and June had been somewhat deficient, particularly in the Bangalore, Kolar, Tumkur and Mysore Districts. But heavy rains fell over the State in July and all tanks received a good supply. Both the south-west and north-east monsoons were favourable. The average total rainfall was 46·08 inches and exceeded that of the previous year by 12·76 inches, and that of the last 42 years by 8·97 inches. The rains were abundant and well distributed.

Ragi was more extensively cultivated and its outturn was better than in the previous year. Sugar-cane and cholum yielded a good crop. The outturn of paddy was also satisfactory except in the districts of Bangalore and Tumkur, where the crop suffered to some extent by disease. A marked preference to grow cotton in place of food crops was noticed in some parts of the Chitaldrug District, where the area under cotton increased by 52,387 acres during the year. In spite of the favourable rainfall and better outturn of crops, there was no improvement in the prices of food grains which continued to rule high.

For various reasons such as increase of work in many directions, the necessity for greater efficiency in taluk administration, and a steady rise in the price of food grains, the scale of salaries fixed for the Taluk Office establishment so far back as the year 1897 was considered unsuitable to the conditions of the present day. The scale has accordingly been revised and provision has been made for a general increase of pay at an additional recurring expenditure of about Rs. 44,000 per annum. It is hoped that this will result in attracting to the Taluk Offices a better class of recruits and increasing the efficiency of the taluk administration generally.

Steps are being taken to publish a Taluk Manual for regulating the work of the Taluk Offices and defining the duties and responsibilities of taluk officials, their relations to the public, and rules for their personal conduct.

The gross receipts of the Excise Department during the year amounted to Rs. 50,94,310 against Rs. 45,45,518 in the previous year, showing an increase of Rs. 5,48,792, nearly half the increase being due to the increased shop rental derived during the auction sales and the remainder to increased consumption during the year. The gross revenue for the year under report is the highest on record since the beginning of Excise administration, and the increase in revenue is accompanied by a corresponding increase in consumption under all heads. Taking all aspects of the question into consideration, the increase is not altogether a matter for congratulation, although it doubtless means that illicit use was kept down at a minimum and the Department was efficiently administered during the year.

Steady progress was made in the work of the Forest Department. The total revenue realized under all heads was about Rs. 33,02,920, which is a record figure. This large increase was mainly due to the unusually high rates secured for sandalwood, the total realizations from which amounted to Rs. 22,92,419.

The executive establishment of the department was reorganized at an additional cost of Rs. 65,514 and it is hoped that this will result in enhanced efficiency of the service.

The Forest Department is managed efficiently enough at present, but it is necessary that it should, in future years, devote special attention to the investigation of the commercial value of all the forest products, and it may also be necessary to employ expert establishment in order to increase the revenue from this source to the fullest extent that the local conditions admit of and may be permissible under scientific management. It cannot be considered satisfactory that fuel for local consumption and sleepers for railways should be imported from outside while a redundance of such material is rotting in our forests for lack of enterprise and adequate efforts among the local population. A scientific examination is likely to bring to light the existence of much material of great commercial value, which might, if properly worked and developed, provide new occupations to the people and bring additional revenue to Government.

The orders of Government in regard to the improvement of the position and prospects of the members of the Judicial service referred to in Mr. Ananda Row's Address of last year were brought into effect in November 1912.

The Additional Munsiff's Court, established at Chikballapur in February 1911, was made permanent, but to promote public convenience it was removed to Dodballapur at the close of the year, with jurisdiction over the taluks of Dodballapur, Nelamangala and Goribidnur. The territorial jurisdiction of the Principal and Additional

Munsiffs' Courts (now styled the First and Second Munsiffs' Courts) at Bangalore and of the Chikballapur Munsiff's Court was in consequence readjusted so as to secure a more equitable distribution of work among the three courts.

The Bench of Honorary Magistrates inaugurated in the year 1909 in each of the Cities of Bangalore and Mysore as an experimental measure, having been found to be successful, was made permanent. A temporary additional Sessions Court was established in Mysore in March 1913 to try the case of rioting which occurred in Kannegal in the Chamrajnagar Taluk. More activity was shown by the department during the year in the inspection of subordinate courts in the State than in previous years.

There has been a perceptible improvement in the investigation and detection of crime in the Police Department. The question of the reorganization of the Police Department, which was brought forward by the Dasara Representative Assembly on several occasions, has received due consideration, and you will be glad to learn that His Highness has been pleased to sanction a scheme for a revision of the several branches of this important department. The revised scheme involves an additional annual expenditure of Rs. 75,000 and its chief feature is the provision of better pay for the constabulary. The constables serving in the Cities of Bangalore and Mysore will hereafter draw Rs. 11, 10, 9 and 8 in lieu of their present pay of Rs. 9, 8 and 7. The scheme also provides for an increase of Re. 1 per head to the constables of the District and Railway Police, the strengthening of the Inspectorate and the Investigation Centre Staff, and a suitable improvement of the organization and equipment of the headquarter Training School to meet modern requirements.

Address to Dasara Representative Assembly.

The prospects of the Police force having been improved, it is hoped there will be no difficulty in securing capable recruits in future. The adoption of a scheme for the further improvement of the discipline and *morale* of the force and for more systematic and efficient inspections throughout the State is also under contemplation.

The standard of discipline and efficiency of the Military Forces of the State continued to be maintained as usual and the administration of the department was satisfactory. It is under contemplation to reorganize the Infantry Barr Forces so as to improve the pay and prospects of the officers and men with a view to secure greater efficiency.

The scheme for reorganizing the Transport Pony Corps into a Bullock Train under the registration system did not prove satisfactory, many cases having come to notice in which the owners had sold or replaced registered bullocks without permission. It has, therefore, since been decided to dispense with the registration of cattle and re-mount the corps wholly with Amrut Mahal bullocks which are now available. It is proposed to utilise the services of the corps in ordinary times in procuring fodder for itself and the mounted corps and other departments of the State, and thus save some transit and cutting charges.

The Medical Department has continued to do good work during the year.

The construction of the new building for the Ophthalmic Hospital, named after His Excellency Lord Minto, was completed during the year at a cost of nearly 2¾ lakhs of rupees and was formally opened for the use of the public by His Highness the Maharaja in January last. Being equipped with the most modern appliances and provided with an expert staff having, at its head, a Superintendent and an Assistant both trained in England, the institution will no doubt prove a great boon to the suffering population.

Address to Dasara Representative Assembly.

Proposals for providing suitable buildings for the Public Health Institute, which is to include the Vaccine Institute, are under the consideration of Government.

The subject of depopulation in the *malnad* also received considerable attention during the year. Recently a special officer was deputed to investigate the question and a sum of one lakh of rupees has been provided in the current year's budget to give effect to such of the suggestions as appear to the Government to be of immediate practical value in ameliorating the condition of the *malnad* population.

A few complaints having been received in regard to the purity of the lymph used for vaccination, a Committee has been appointed consisting of the Sanitary Commissioner and two other high Medical Officers to conduct an inquiry into the question in detail.

The work of the Economic Conference has been further developed and the action taken on the recommendations of the Conference is separately described under the different departments concerned. The constitution and working of the Conference has now been consolidated and placed on a satisfactory basis. A full-time officer has been appointed as Secretary to the Conference and also Secretary to Government, in order to co-ordinate the work of the Committees of the Conference and the departments of Government concerned. Several uncertainties in the matter of the constitution and work of the Conference which hitherto existed have now been removed and the Conference has started on a new career of useful work. Every effort will be made to enlist the support and co-operation of all classes, official and non-official, to promote the objects which the Conference has in view.

I may now proceed to enumerate the more important measures in which practical action has been taken. The scheme for the establishment of a State-aided Bank, in regard to which the Conference took the initiative in 1911, has now taken practical shape and the Bank has opened business from the 2nd of this month. The imposition of income-tax, with a view to strengthen the financial position of the State and also to make the burden of taxation more equitable by bringing under contribution those among the richer classes who at present contribute much less than their due share to the State revenue, is engaging the attention of Government. Substantial progress has been made in the extension of primary education, and a bill for introducing compulsory education was passed last month in the Legislative Council. Investigations are in active progress for the development of sericulture, the manufacture of jaggery by improved methods and the erection of pumping machinery for irrigation. The establishment, of a weaving factory with all the latest improvements, of a tile factory at Mysore, of pharmaceutical works, of oil-mills to deal with oil-seeds and particularly with cotton-seed, and of an industrial depôt in Bangalore, are other matters which have engaged or are engaging the attention of the Conference. Apart from this record of work, the Conference is making the people think, investigate, organise and initiate measures of progress in a variety of matters.

The resolutions carried at the fourth session of the Conference in June last have already been published, as also the report of the work done by the three Central Committees. I may take the opportunity here to observe that the responsibility of the members of the Central Committees and, in some measure, of those of the District Committees, is very great. Government expect that when any gentleman consents to serve on these Committees he agrees *ipso facto* to take an active interest in, and to contribute to, the constructive work of the Committees during the time he remains a member.

Address to Dasara Representative Assembly.

The year was one of more than usual activity in educational matters. Dealing first with the ordinary progress of education, the number of public and private institutions increased by 90 and the attendance by 7,226. The percentage of boys at school to the male population of school-age rose from 30·1 to 31·3 and that of girls at school to the female population of school-age from 6·2 to 6·8. The number of pupils under instruction in comparison with the population of the State gives a percentage of 2·9. A great deal more remains to be done to spread primary education in the State. A special grant of two lakhs and a half—one lakh for opening new Primary Schools and improving the existing ones, and a lakh and a half for the construction of Village School buildings—was sanctioned during the year, and a similar special grant of two lakhs and a half has been sanctioned in connection with the current year's budget. The Government have no doubt that the Department of Education is fully alive to the responsibility resting upon it for giving practical effect to the various important schemes that are being sanctioned from time to time.

With regard to higher education, further arrangements were in progress to complete the equipment and the staff required for the two First Grade Colleges to adapt them to the new University Regulations. The Central College was affiliated in Branch II (B), Chemistry, of the B.A. Pass Course. The Chemical Laboratory building is now very nearly complete and provides ample accommodation for the classes concerned.

Government have under consideration the question of opening Honors Courses for both the First Grade Colleges in certain branches in the near future.

A comprehensive scheme of elementary and advanced technical and commercial education has been approved by Government and it consists in the main of the establishment of the Chamarajendra Technical Institute at Mysore, and a Commercial and a Mechanical Engineering School at Bangalore. The present Engineering School and the Industrial School at Mysore will be combined to form the nucleus of the new Chamarajendra Technical Institute, which will be located in the spacious building specially constructed for it. The institute will consist of five sections, *viz.*, the Engineering section, the Industries and Crafts section, the Fine Arts section, the Commercial School section and the Workshop.

The Commercial School at Bangalore provides for an elementary course in commercial subjects in English and Kannada for one year and a secondary course in English for two years. Arrangements will also be made for the delivery of lectures of an advanced character by specialists on commercial subjects, economic science, statistics, public administration, banking and other allied subjects.

The Mechanical Engineering School will undertake to teach the management and care of steam and oil-engines, erection of machinery, working of mills, electric work, driving motor cars and other subjects. A new building is under construction for this school, but for the present it is located in the Sheshadri Memorial Hall. The school has been placed under the supervision of an Assistant Engineer of the Public Works Department who has had special training in electrical engineering at the Faraday House, England.

Responsible committees have been appointed to administer the internal affairs of the above-named institutions and subsidiary rules have been framed for their efficient working. Facilities will be provided in these institutions for the training of men already engaged in professional or other work. The main object of Government in starting these institutions is to create an incentive to manual work in the younger generation and to enable them in after life to earn their livelihood by some independent profession.

The opening of a printing class in connection with the Commercial School is under consideration. The instruction imparted will be free and of an elementary character for the present. Government will be prepared to enlarge the scope of its usefulness and provide for higher instruction in the several branches of the art of typography, if the facilities now provided are appreciated and freely taken advantage of by the public.

Lessons according to the prescribed curriculum are being regularly given under the scheme of religious and moral instruction introduced in November 1908. After nearly five years' experience, it is still difficult to say what real advancement has been made and whether any of the desired results have been achieved. In Colleges and High Schools where the teaching of the subject is in the hands of capable teachers the lessons are instructive, but in other schools, want of trained teachers to handle the subjects and the paucity of suitable text-books have made the teaching to lack interest and to become more or less stereotyped. The question has to be further discussed as to whether in the long run it is not wiser to leave this branch of education to the parents and communities concerned.

In view of the growing educational activities of the State and the need that is felt to ensure that the increased grants given are utilized to the best advantage, the appointment of a Deputy Inspector-General of Education has been sanctioned. This officer will be entrusted with the direct charge of Vernacular education, both elementary and secondary, in the State.

The Department of Industries and Commerce was established in January last and it now deals with the work carried on till then by the Special Adviser for

Industries and Commerce. The special function of the department will be to devise and elaborate schemes for immediate practical action, to conduct investigations likely to lead to such action and to collect statistics and serve as a bureau for industrial information. The work of the department during the year may be conveniently described under three main heads, *viz.*, experimental industries carried on at the expense of Government, industrial work for private individuals carried on at their own cost, and general industrial inquiries, including the preparation of statistical information regarding the trade and commerce of the State.

With a view to afford facilities to persons engaged in industries to obtain capital for the purchase of machinery and of raw material, Government have recently sanctioned rules for the grant of *takavi* loans similar to those in force for loans given for agricultural improvements.

Government have recently engaged the services of an expert on sericulture from Italy for developing this important industry in the State. It is computed that in some of the past years, the State exported silk valued at over a crore of rupees.

An Agricultural School has recently been opened in Bangalore and at present fourteen students are attending it. As soon as possible, short courses in the vernacular for agriculturists will be introduced and in this way it is hoped to reach large numbers of the raiyat population. The course in the school is arranged to be as practical as possible. The major portion of the students' time will be occupied in practical farm work, only the principles of elementary sciences being taught to enable the students to understand agricultural processes. Practical training will also be given in the construction and repair of implements and machines, elementary carpentry, blacksmithing and the working of oil engines.

Address to Dasara Representative Assembly.

The past year witnessed satisfactory progress in the Co-operative movement in the State. The number of societies rose from 208 to 343, one society having been wound up and 136 societies registered during the year. The membership of these institutions increased from 13,148 to 24,536, the working capital from Rs. 6,75,312 to Rs. 12,89,338, and the reserve fund from Rs. 18,833 to Rs. 30,600. This expansion has been general throughout the State, except in the Kadur and Chitaldrug Districts, where the conditions necessary for the spread of the movement are not sufficiently favourable and progress has been rather slow.

The total expenditure on public works from all sources including Local Funds amounted to about Rs. 51 lakhs during the year against 44½ lakhs in the preceding year, and the average of 45½ lakhs during the past ten years. Of this amount Rs. 23½ lakhs were spent on irrigation works, and 27½ lakhs on Civil Works and Military buildings.

The most important irrigation work in hand during the year was the construction of the first stage of a dam across the river Cauvery at Kannambadi which was started in November 1911. Excluding the electrical power scheme, the work is estimated to cost about Rs. 91 lakhs. The operations of the year were chiefly confined to the excavation of foundation in the river bed, which gave no inconsiderable trouble owing to the presence of water and springs and the existence of a deep mica vein close to the south bank. Nevertheless, almost the whole of the excavation for the dam in the river bed portion was completed and the foundations laid. The question of payment of compensation for lands coming under submersion and the re-settlement of the displaced population on fresh lands engaged the anxious attention of both the Revenue and the Public Works authorities during the year, and a scheme of land compensation in lieu of money compensation has been devised after a careful study of the whole question. An expenditure of Rs. 16½ lakhs was incurred during the year, which brought the total outlay on the work to Rs. 23½ lakhs up to end of June 1913.

In regard to the second stage of the Reservoir project contemplated by the Durbar, the Government of India have recently appointed a Court of Arbitration presided over by Sir Harry Griffin, Judge of the High Court of Allahabad, assisted by the Hon'ble Mr. Nethersole, Inspector-General of Irrigation in India, as Assessor. The proceedings of the Court commenced on the 18th July last. After framing the issues, the Court adjourned its sittings to the latter part of this month.

Rules under the Tank Panchayet Regulation have been framed and will shortly be introduced into three or four representative villages in each district with a view to observe their operation in practice. Proposals for the re-organization of the establishment under the Minor Tank Restoration Scheme are under consideration.

Steps have been taken for controlling the distribution of water below selected tanks in the districts. Proposals in this behalf for the Sowlanga and Sulekere tanks in the Shimoga District have been matured and those for the rest are in different stages of development.

The question of the constitution of an Irrigation Division is before Government. It is proposed to entrust to this division the work of the development of the sugarcane cultivation under the channels fed by the Cauvery Reservoir, the scientific distribution and control of irrigation below selected tanks, the collection of hydraulic data as regards rainfall, run-off and flood discharges and the completion of tank maps and registers.

Chief among the miscellaneous public improvements

may be mentioned the erection of a Jewell Filter and a subsidiary pumping plant for improving the water-supply of Mysore City. The power and plant-house is approaching completion and the machinery of the Jewell Filter is being fitted up.

The fourth installation of the Cauvery Power Scheme was started, and orders for a major portion of material and plant required for the scheme were placed with foreign firms. Final location of the tramway line for the City of Bangalore and the construction of a car-barn and generating station are approaching completion.

In consequence of the growth of work in the Railway Department, a separate Railway Secretariat was constituted with the Engineer-in-Chief, State Railway Construction Department, as *ex-officio* Secretary, and his Personal Assistant as Under-Secretary.

The gross receipts on all the open lines of the State amounted to Rs. 36,93,226, which is an increase of Rs. 4,40,477 over those of the previous year. The expenses on all the State lines during the year amounted to Rs. 21,05,637 as against Rs. 19,15,764 during 1911-12.

The total net earnings aggregated Rs. 15,87,519 or 6·24 per cent on the entire capital of Rs. 2,54,22,488. The interest on the English loan of Rs. 1,63,82,801 amounted to Rs. 7,17,377 during the year. Deducting this from the net earnings, the sum credited to the State was Rs. 8,70,212.

Although the railway receipts have improved to a certain extent within the past few years, the net result of the railway transactions has, on the whole, been one of considerable loss to the State. Taking into consideration only the interest charges paid by the State, the total loss from the open lines up to date is estimated at about 55 lakhs.

The Railway Construction Department was engaged

during the year under review in revising old projects and preparing new ones. The sanction of the Railway Board has been applied for, for the construction of the following lines:—

(1) A line from Mysore to Arsikere *via* Yedatore, Hole-Narsipur and Hassan. The alternative chord line from Mysore to Konehalli has been given up. The final location survey is being proceeded with and construction work will be started immediately sanction is received.

(2) A line between Bangalore and Hosur. A re-survey of the line is being made.

(3) A Forest Tramway from Tarikere to Yedahalli for which preliminary investigations were carried out during the year. A communication has just been received conveying sanction to this project.

An estimate was prepared for the Chikjajur-Chitaldrug line on the meter gauge during the year and submitted to the Government of India for sanction. Estimates have also been prepared for a line of railway from Kolar to Chikballapur *via* Srinivaspur, Chintamani and Sidlaghatta connecting the Bangalore-Chikballapur and Bowringpet-Kolar Railways now under construction. The question of financing these lines is under the consideration of Government. The estimates prepared for a line between Hassan and Mangalore by Messrs. Gilchrist and Groves were examined with a view to revise and bring them up to date.

The Bowringpet-Kolar Railway is approaching completion and is expected to be open to traffic next month.

At the request of the Bangalore-Chikballapur Light Railway Company, the construction of that line has been undertaken by Government on behalf of the Company and the work is making satisfactory progress.

The publication of a Geological map of the State, to embody on a uniform and comprehensive plan the essential features of the survey work so far completed, was sanctioned during the year.

I may refer here to a very unfortunate accident which recently occurred at the Kolar Gold Fields and which resulted in the death of 42 persons on the 21st August last. In view of the magnitude of the accident, Government appointed a Committee on which there was also a Judge of the Chief Court to enquire into the matter. The report of the Committee has been received and is under consideration.

An enquiry into the conditions of the Muzrai institutions in the State and the submission of a comprehensive report regarding their administration, reorganisation and improvement have been ordered by Government and a Committee appointed therefor have entered upon their work.

As the condition of the private printing presses throughout the State appeared capable of much improvement and to stand in need of expert assistance and advice, the Superintendent of the Government Press has been asked to visit such presses, on application, and help them with his advice.

As the Deputy Commissioners of Bangalore and Mysore had, for some time past, found themselves unable to devote the required amount of attention to the affairs of the two city municipalities in consequence of their multifarious duties, Government relieved them of their duties as *ex-officio* Councillors and Presidents of the Municipal Councils towards the latter part of the year. As the time was considered opportune for appointing a non-official President for the Bangalore City Municipality, Rajasabha Bhushana Dewan Bahadur Mr. K. P. Puttanna Chetty, Retired Councillor, was appointed President of the Bangalore City Municipal Council from 1st February 1913. An officer of the Public Works

Department was appointed as whole-time President of the Municipal Council and Chairman of the Board of Trustees in the Mysore City as a tentative measure.

Indications of co-operative effort are visible in connection with the work of the Economic Conference, although the District Committees have only just begun to apply themselves seriously to constructive work.

In another sphere there have been signs of progress. I refer to the active administration of municipal affairs by honorary workers. As stated elsewhere, Rajasabha Bhushana Dewan Bahadur Mr. K. P. Puttanna Chetty has taken up the office of President of the Bangalore City Municipality and Messrs. Seshadri Iyengar, S. Malhar Rao and C. Vasudeva Rao, of that of Vice-President of the head-quarter municipalities of Tumkur, Kolar and Chikmagalur. The disinterested public work of Mr. K. P. Puttanna Chetty, both in connection with our premier municipality in the State and with other public undertakings since February last, has elicited warm admiration.

The progress of the co-operative movement is due to the disinterested labours of several of our public men headed by Rajamantra Pravina Mr. C. Srinivasiengar and Mr. D. Appu Rao.

Several wealthy citizens have shown commendable liberality in building public schools and hostels to meet the educational requirements of the people.

His Highness' Government highly appreciate all these indications of public spirit and they hope that the public will also encourage such acts by showing their appreciation of disinterested labours wherever they may be found.

Having now given a retrospect of the principal events of the year's administration, I shall proceed to place before you a brief statement of the measures in progress and under contemplation.

Address to Dasara Representative Assembly.

Government have embarked on an active railway policy. They are desirous, if possible, of extending the railway line from Nanjangud in the Mysore District to join the South Indian Railway on one side or the other of the Nilgiris. The question of linking up Arsikere on the Bangalore-Harihar line with the port of Mangalore is also under consideration. In regard to both these lines, Government are prepared to construct the portions of the railway within State limits, and both the questions are at present under correspondence with the Government of India.

The construction of minor feeder lines within the State will be actively proceeded with in the order of their urgency and importance.

The construction of productive public works is proceeding as rapidly as circumstances permit. A forward policy in this respect is subject to two essential limitations, *viz.*, (1) that the investment in each case should be remunerative and constitute a fresh asset, and (2) that, under no conceivable circumstances, should the finances of the State suffer embarrassment.

The Kannambadi Reservoir is being pushed on with the connected works. The main object of the reservoir, as you are aware, is to provide irrigation for perennial crops for which hitherto there has been no satisfactory provision in that valley and to protect the supply of electric power. That reservoir, if completed on the scale already designed, will store some of the water which is now going to waste into the sea, and along with the canals to be completed will prove a large protective work which will materially minimise the evil effects of famine. The reservoir will also contribute to the extension of the cultivation of high-class perennial crops which will be fully protected.

The Fourth Installation of the Cauvery Power Supply

Scheme is well in hand, and we have just concluded an agreement with the Kolar Mining Companies, under which protection will be afforded to the existing power supply by the storage in the Kannambadi Reservoir, and the Mining Companies will also obtain additional power supply. You may be aware that mining is now carried on in places at a depth measuring nearly one mile below ground surface. The arrangement now come to will enable the Mining Companies to work the mines at greater depths with profit and will also bring in additional revenue to Government. We have recently reduced the rates for electric power in the City of Bangalore with a view to encouraging power consumption for industrial purposes, and Government will be prepared to further increase the power supply to the cities of Bangalore and Mysore, should demand arise for more.

Special arrangements are being made at present on an experimental scale for the better supervision of the major irrigation tanks and channels with a view to the scientific control and distribution of water and the more extended cultivation of sugar-cane and other commercial crops.

The improvement of minor irrigation works, about which repesentations have been made so often in this Assembly, awaits the completion of the necessary village organization for developing the works with Government help. It is the hope of His Highness' Government to deal effectively with this problem of minor tanks in the coming years.

The town-planning schemes for Bangalore and Mysore, the water-supply and drainage projects for numerous towns in the State require systematic development, and some of these are receiving attention.

The newly started Industries and Commerce Department will be given every facility to assist private industries and enterprises.

Address to Dasara Representative Assembly.

The Agricultural Department has been strengthened by the appointment of a Director and the arrangements necessary for developing its activities and operations to promote the agricultural interests of the State are receiving attention.

Great importance will hereafter be attached to the development of the co-operative movement with a view to extend the co-operative principle to many forms of business in villages and to rural transactions generally.

A new Village Courts Act has just been passed; the establishment of Village Panchayets for the management of village sanitation, irrigation and other functions of the village communities will receive the earliest consideration of Government.

As described already, orders will issue shortly regarding the practical measures proposed for reducing the unhealthiness and arresting the decline of population in the *malnad*.

Following the example of the Government of India, larger grants are being given and much attention is being paid to the development of education within the State. A Scheme for establishing a University for Mysore is engaging the attention of His Highness' Government.

The above are measures in regard to which we see our way clear. There are numerous other matters under investigation or in various stages of development or study.

It may also probably interest you if I give here a short retrospect of the progress which the country has made since 1881 during the 30 years ended 1910-11. As every one of you may be aware, the Rendition of the country took place on the 25th March 1881, after a very successful administration by the British Commission for half a century. Owing, however, to the terrible effects of the great famine of 1876-78,—the severest through which the State has passed during the past fifty years,—the beneficial effects of the British administration were not visible to their fullest advantage in 1881. In the words of Dewan Rangacharlu, that famine "cost the State 160 lakhs of rupees, involved the Government in a debt of 80 lakhs and withal deprived the province of a million of its population and crippled its resources for years to come."

The population of the State, which in 1871 numbered 5,055,402 souls, fell to 4,186,188 in 1881 on account of the famine of 1876-78 and rose to 5,806,193 in 1911, or an increase of 15 per cent over that of 1871.

The town population which in 1881 was computed at 13 per cent of the total population fell to 11 per cent in 1911, probably for want of sufficient occupation for the people in the towns.

The population dependent on agriculture which in 1881 was 33 lakhs rose to 42 lakhs in 1911.

As regards agriculture, the occupied area, excluding coffee, amounted to 4,213,505 acres in 1881-82 and 7,438,463 acres in 1911-12. The increase is 79 per cent. The growth of agriculture since the Rendition has been extensive but not intensive.

The total revenue of the State which amounted to about 50 lakhs at the beginning of the last century was 101 lakhs in 1880-81 and it rose to 247 lakhs in 1910-11 including what is known as "fortuitous revenue" from the Gold Mines. Land Revenue has increased from 69 to 106½ lakhs, Excise from 10 to 43·69 lakhs, and Forest from 7 to 21 lakhs.

The expenditure also has more than doubled, *viz.*, from 101 lakhs in 1880-81 to 223 lakhs in 1910-11. The charges against land revenue have increased from 14 to

21 lakhs, excise from a small sum of Rs. 18,000 to over 3 lakhs, forest from 2 lakhs to nearly 7 lakhs, law and justice including jails from 6 to 8½ lakhs, education (from provincial revenues) from 1·50 to 10·53 lakhs, medical from 1·63 to 7·20 lakhs and public works from 10 to 30 lakhs.

The railways which were only 50 miles in 1880-81 rose to 411 miles in 1910-11 and the capital outlay on them in the same period from 25 to 250 lakhs.

The mileage of provincial roads has nearly doubled since the Rendition.

Among other public works may be mentioned the extension of channel irrigation in the Cauvery and Kapini valleys, restoration and repairs to numerous tanks and the construction of two great public works, *viz.*, the Cauvery Power Scheme and the Marikanave reservoir. The cities of Bangalore and Mysore were extended and improved.

The expenditure on education from all sources rose from Rs. 3,91,028 in 1880-81 to Rs. 18,79,135 in 1910-11; the cost of education per head from Re. 0-1-6 to Re. 0-5-4. The school-going population has increased from 53,872 in 1880-81 to 1,38,153 in 1910-11 or nearly three times.

A few industries, small and large, including the gold mines of Kolar and the manganese mines of Shimoga and a few cotton and other mills have come into existence. But most of these are unconnected with local enterprise and, in themselves, afford no evidence of the progress of the people either in technical knowledge or co-operative spirit.

The above retrospect shows that the high standard of efficiency reached in the days of the British Commission has been maintained unimpaired, while, at the same time, a steady and substantial progress has been made in every department of the State. It shows, too, that the administration has been carried on with close loyalty to the principles followed by the previous British administration, that the slender surpluses have been carefully husbanded from year to year, and utilized in the construction of productive public works and the country has perceptibly advanced in material prosperity. The Government and the people have been brought into closer touch by the association of the people in local and municipal administration and in the Representative Assembly and the Legislative Council.

Since this Assembly came into existence, the wants of the people are better known to the officials and the intentions of Government better understood by the people.

The question of improving the efficiency of the services has been receiving the anxious consideration of His Highness' Government. The latest measure for such improvement, as you are aware, is the sanction accorded by His Highness the Maharaja to the revival of the Mysore Civil Service Examination scheme, under which the best local young men have a chance of competing for appointments in the State service. His Highness' Government have also recently strengthened the staff and improved the prospects of officials in some of the departments which either yield revenue or have felt themselves starved for some time.

Measures are under contemplation to arrange for a system of "efficiency audit" with a view to provide for more frequent and systematic inspections, to improve the office manuals and standing orders, and to ensure that the rules and orders in force are properly worked, or if not workable, promptly modified; that beneficent activities of every kind receive stimulus, that serious irregularities receive prompt attention; that, in short, waste of power and slackness of execution in the different departments of Government are controlled and minimised.

Efficiency must be maintained if the Government is to get value for the money which it is spending on its establishments. In a country like ours where the system of Government departments is maintained on the European model and the staff employed to work them have not fully adopted European business habits, an "efficiency audit" is as much a necessity as a "financial audit."

A few words here about measures for improving the capacity of the people may not be out of place.

It is not difficult nowadays to construct public works, railways, tramways or other works, because skilled agencies can be imported for the purpose. Foreign capital can be obtained if we are able to guarantee a fair return on the outlay. It is also easy to man the public service with the best talent available in India or, for that matter, of the world, because there is an abundance of such talent seeking employment. The help of outside agencies which, while benefiting themselves, are also likely to benefit us, should be welcomed. But large enterprises carried out entirely with outside help will not increase the capacity of our people or raise the status of the country. And, unless in the fiscal and geographical area known as Mysore, the intelligence of the people, the natural resources and the available capital act and re-act on one another, and with cumulative effect, the country cannot be said to be making any permanent progress.

There are certain features in our present condition which necessitate anxious watchfulness on our part. The country has no doubt progressed within the past 30 years. People are better housed, better clothed and normally better fed, and the average standard of living has also risen; but the advance in these directions is due to the general progress of the Indian continent, as a whole, rather than to any organized activity or design on our part.

Only one person in every sixteen is able to read and write. The cultivators are not fully occupied even in normal seasons; in years of scarcity, for months at a time, they are left without occupation and without hope. Three-fourths of our population are dependent on agriculture and the great bulk of them live in villages without activities or aspirations outside their individual households. Our land-owners are small men, our business is conducted by small traders and artisans, each working singly for himself. The lessons of co-operation and organization have not permeated even the top strata of society.

The first Dewan since the Rendition, with the experiences of the famine of 1876-78 fresh before him, drew attention to a similar state of things then. In his address to this Assembly in 1881, Mr. Rangacharlu strongly urged the need for industries and industrial development, remarking "that no country can prosper unless its agricultural and manufacturing industries were equally fostered."

He was also of opinion that "when all the world around is making marvellous progress, the 200 millions of people in this country cannot much longer continue in their long sleep, simply following the traditions of their ancestors of 2,000 years ago and earning a miserable subsistence, ready to be crushed on the first occurrence of a famine or other calamity."

These words are as true to-day as they were when they were uttered thirty years ago and, unless a change is attempted, they will continue to be true thirty years hence.

"It is not Governments or forms of Government," remarked His Highness the Maharaja in a speech delivered so far back as 1903, "that have made the great industrial nations but the spirit of the people and the energy of one and all working to a common end."

Following the lead of His Highness, we must develop the life and capacity of our people by encouraging in them self-help, power of initiative, courage to change, courage to create new things, spirit of co-operation and a capacity for organization.

Reasonable scope for the co-operative effort of the people in the State is provided for, however imperfectly it may be at present, by the organization known as the Economic Conference; and no one who has witnessed the educational activities, the roar of industry and the keen competition in trade, that is going on in the advanced countries of the West, can fail to sympathise and co-operate with the objects of that movement.

The organization is intended to stimulate co-operative enterprise in cities and towns and gradually among the rural population ; but since nine-tenths of the people live in villages, it appears to me that a special effort is necessary to stimulate economic activity in rural areas.

The village forms a convenient unit for purposes of economic effort, for taking stock of progress at the beginning and end of the year. If each village shows a little improvement, from year to year, the collective result will be large. No village should be considered as maintaining a fair standard of enlightenment which does not keep 5 to 10 per cent of its population under education. No village should fail to subscribe to one or two well-conducted vernacular newspapers to keep itself informed of what is going on in the outside world. Every village family should be induced to keep in reserve grain or money sufficient to tide over a famine of two years. No cultivator's family should be without a subsidiary occupation to provide the members with the means of livelihood when agricultural operations are slack, or are stopped during scarcity or famine. Every village should show some public improvement or other as the result of the collective effort of its inhabitants at the end of each year.

The villages may be called upon to publish once a year a few essential statistics of their economic growth. And as the great bulk of our population live in villages, any effective organization to improve village efficiency cannot fail to make a potent addition to the life force of the people and the productive power of the country.

There is one important message which I am commanded by His Highness the Maharaja to announce to this Assembly and which I may refer to at this stage. The Representative Assembly was brought into existence in 1881, that is, in the very first year after the Rendition. While there are representatives on it of the highest ability and intelligence, the Assembly is, in the main, composed of representatives from the districts and the taluks. At present, it meets once a year and, considering the size and resources of our State, it is too large a body to meet oftener. No practical scheme has yet been put forward to show in what direction and in what manner the usefulness of this Assembly can be enhanced. It may be advantageous, at this session, to consider questions pertaining to the composition of the Assembly, the methods of electing members thereto, its functions and the system of transacting business. If the members discuss these questions and make known their views, the same will be submitted to His Highness for his gracious consideration.

His Highness has decided to increase the number of representatives from this Assembly on the Legislative Council from two to four and also to nominate eight representatives from it on the Economic Conference.

As you are doubtless aware, our Legislative Council is based on the model of the British Indian Act of 1861; but, as that Act has been revised twice since that year, His Highness thinks that the representative character of our Council might be safely improved so that it may be nearer the standard of the Councils in British India.

The local Legislative Council consists of 15 to 18 members at present. This number will be increased to 24 in future. Of these, four will be nominated, as already stated, on the recommendation of this Assembly, four by territorial representation from the districts, ten will be officials and six nominated members. There will thus be eight elected representatives of the people instead of two, the present number. It is necessary that the members nominated on the recommendation of this Assembly or of the districts should possess a sufficient knowledge of the English language to be able to take part in the proceedings of the Legislative Council.

His Highness has been pleased to accord to the Council, but with definite limitations in the early stages, the privileges of Budget discussion and interpellation. The limitations are necessary because our resources and establishment are limited and the time of the officials is already much taken up by the periodical functions.

The interpellations will not exceed twelve questions at each session, and the nature of the questions to be admitted will depend, among other considerations, on the measure of support accorded to them by the members.

Suitable rules will be framed for the purpose after the Legislative Council Regulation is amended.

These changes, which His Highness the Maharaja has been graciously pleased to sanction, will enable the representatives of His Highness' subjects to be associated in the Councils of the administration and bring their influence to bear, for all good ends, on the policy and activities of Government.

I need not repeat here that on His Highness the Maharaja rests the ultimate responsibility for the good government of the country; and he trusts he may rely on the loyalty, wisdom and public spirit of his subjects, that the privileges now accorded to them will be exercised with caution and moderation for the promotion of the good government of the country and the permanent well-being of his subjects.

One of the most hopeful signs of awakening and progress of the country is the example set to us by the visit of His Highness the Yuvaraja to Europe. The Yuvaraja, who has been travelling abroad for the past six months with a staff of three officers and a young gentleman of the Ursu community, has just been welcomed home with great warmth and enthusiasm. In his travels in Europe, the Yuvaraja spent a life of ceaseless toil, visiting numerous institutions and studying the varied activities of the countries he passed through. From all sources we learn that he met with a cordial reception wherever he went and he has come back to us, leaving pleasant memories of his visit behind him, rich with experiences and an ardent desire to help in the uplift of the people. The people of Mysore are naturally proud of a prince who has shown such unusual enterprise at his age in travelling both East and West in search of knowledge and culture. They greatly appreciate the courtesy extended to him by the leading public men of England, and by some of the cities like Glasgow and Dublin which he visited.

The example of foreign travel set by a member of the Ruling House of Mysore will, it is hoped, be largely followed in future by His Highness' subjects with highly beneficial results.

Before closing this Address, His Highness commands me to announce to you formally the pleasing news that, next month, he will have the privilege of welcoming into our State His Excellency Lord Hardinge, the Viceroy and Governor-General of India. I have no doubt that the news will be hailed with rejoicings in all parts of the State and that His Highness' illustrious guest will be received with the loyalty and respect due to the representative of His Most Gracious Majesty the King-Emperor. Our pleasure in welcoming Their Excellencies Lord and Lady Hardinge will doubtless be doubly sincere on account of the admiration which we all feel, in common with the rest of India, for the policy of good-will and high purpose pursued by His Excellency, since his advent, towards the Native States and the people of this country.

REPLY TO DASARA ADDRESSES.

[At the thirtieth session of the Mysore Dasara Representative Assembly, held at the Public Offices, Mysore, on 11th October 1913, Dewan Sir M. Visvesvaraya received addresses from the representatives of the Kolar Gold Field Mining Board, the Central Mahomedan Association, the Sadananda Vardhini 11th Oct. 1913.

Sabha of Melkote, the Lingayet Education Fund Association, and the members for the Tumkur District and for the Taluks of Nagamangala and Malur.

Sir M. Visvesvaraya made a collective reply as follows :—]

Gentlemen,—I desire to express my sincere thanks to you for the addresses you have now presented to me and for the appreciative terms in which you have referred to the administration of the State.

The addresses contain references to several subjects of local interest and importance, but as the contents of these addresses came to my notice for the first time only yesterday morning, and as most of the questions raised in them find a place among the representations which we shall take up for detailed consideration during the rest of our session, I shall not detain you with any but the briefest observations regarding them.

As regards the proposal to give power to the Superintendent of Police to deal with undesirable persons in the Kolar Gold Field mining area, I may state that a Bill has been prepared to amend the provisions of the Mysore Mines Regulation and is now before the Legislative Council.

The suggestion for amending the existing law by providing for the summary trial of cases of unlawful possession of mining material of less than Rs. 50 in value, will be carefully examined, and before coming to a decision in the matter, Government will give due weight to the representations of the Mining Board.

The remaining requests of the Mining Board are already under consideration in the respective departments of Government. They all involve more or less additional expenditure and will receive attention in the order of their urgency and importance.

The request of the representatives of Koppa for the extension of railway service to that town will be noted for consideration. I have already announced that sanction has been received for the construction of a 2-feet gauge tramway from Tarikere to Yedahalli.

In some of the addresses reference is made to the paucity of representatives of special communities in the public service, in the Legislative Council and other bodies. I may assure you that Government are fully alive to the need for giving reasonable facilities to encourage backward classes. But I must remind you that, owing to the growing complexity of modern administration, a higher standard of average attainment and capacity for the public service has now to be insisted on than was necessary a decade or two ago. The only way you can help your respective communities, to gain admission into Government service, is by educating your young men.

Some of the addresses now read come from bodies like the Lingayet Education Fund Association and the Central Mahomedan Association, which are all associations composed of members of important sections of the people whose main object is to spread secular education among the communities concerned. His Highness' Government greatly appreciate the efforts that are being made by these bodies to ameliorate the condition of their respective communities.

As you are aware, there is a vast field for work of this character among all classes and sections of the people, and Government will always be glad to help organizations formed with the object of promoting education and the moral and material welfare of the people.

I may refer here to only one or two spheres of work which eminently deserve the attention of the members of this Assembly and the true natural leaders of the people. In my address I have drawn attention pointedly to the condition of our villages and the vast possibilities of improvement before them, if only an organized effort is made for the purpose. Any movement intended to reach the remotest villages and the individual residents therein should be necessarily carried out largely by private agencies. There must be many people in the taluks capable of developing into unselfish leaders. If such men will rise and take the occasion by the hand, they have a noble opportunity of advancing the best interests of the rural population.

It gave me great pleasure to listen to the graceful reference in so many addresses to the return of His Highness the Yuvaraja from his European tour.

In conclusion, may I assure you, gentlemen, that it will be my pleasing duty to place before His Highness the Maharaja the sentiments of deep loyalty and devotion contained in your addresses.

SPEECH AT THE MYSORE LEGISLATIVE COUNCIL.

3rd Feb. 1914.

[A meeting of the Mysore Legislative Council was held at the Public Offices, Bangalore, on 3rd February 1914, at 12 noon, when a large number of official and non-official members were present. Sir M. Visvesvaraya, President of the Council, occupied the chair. The principal business before the Council referred to the Bill to amend the Mysore Legislative Council Regulation I of 1907, in view of the recent enlargement of the Council and the grant of the powers of interpellation and discussion on the State Budget. Mr. S. R. Balakrishna Rao, an elected member, urged that the privilege of moving resolutions on administrative matters should also be conferred

Speech at the Mysore Legislative Council.

on the Council. He was supported by the bulk of the elected members, but after discussion, he dropped the proposal.

In winding up the proceedings of the Council, Sir M. Visvesvaraya said :—]

Gentlemen,—As this is the last occasion on which we meet under the old constitution, I feel a word or two from me, before we separate, may not be out of place.

As you are aware, His Highness the Maharaja graciously decided, in October last, to increase the strength of this Council, to improve its representative character and enlarge its duties and functions.

The Legislative Council was brought into existence nearly seven years ago with the object, as was stated at the time, of ascertaining the wants, feelings and aspirations of the people in the enactment of Laws and Regulations. Mr. Balakrishna Rao seemed dissatisfied that the power of moving resolutions was not conceded. Considering the Council itself came into existence so recently, you will agree that, with the instalment of reform now conceded, the development of the Council may be regarded as fairly rapid. In future the Council will be concerned not only with the work of legislation but also with matters connected with general administration as well as the preparation of the budget.

The work of the administration is growing in volume and complexity. As we begin to enquire more and more minutely into the lives of the people, and to study what is being done in the various departments of State and public life in British India and abroad, we cannot fail to be struck with the inadequacy of our efforts to cope with the needs of the country. If we are not to lose ground, the more important needs at least must receive our unremitting attention.

For this purpose, His Highness' Government wish to come into closer contact with the interests which they are charged to promote and they desire more intimate co-operation with the leaders of the people.

There are numerous public activities claiming attention, some official, some semi-official and others which may be described as non-official and unconnected with legitimate Governmental activities. We want workers for all the three classes of activities. Persons who have the aptitude and will to take part in these activities might associate themselves with the Committee or Department of Government concerned. And to deal with activities which do not fall within the sphere of work of Government, that is, questions connected with social and moral progress, I have no doubt there is enough public spirit in the country to bring a separate organization into existence. It is our interest and ambition slowly and gradually to enlist into the service of the country every person who has resource, ability or enthusiasm for public work.

I need not repeat here that any expression of views on public questions based on a thorough preliminary study, from persons of ability or worth, working disinterestedly for the welfare of the people, will be always welcome.

With the aid of this Council and other agencies, His Highness' Government look forward to a period of active work for the amelioration of the condition of the people, and they have every hope that in such work they will receive public sympathy and co-operation in an ever-increasing degree in the years to come.

REPLY TO NANJANGUD MUNICIPALITY.

[In the course of an official tour, Sir M. Visvesvaraya received, on 28th February 1914, an address of welcome from the Nanjangud Municipality. 28th Feb. 1914.

In replying to the address, Sir M. Visvesvaraya said :—]

Gentlemen,—Before commencing my tour, I had requested the Deputy Commissioner to discourage public addresses, as far as possible, as I thought that the same object would be more effectively served by public meetings and informal discussions with the people, such as we had in the *cutcherry* here on Thursday morning. As you intended to do me a good turn and had prepared and printed this address before I arrived here, I have no wish to seem discourteous. It gives me much pleasure to accept the address both on account of your friendly sentiments and the important interests which you represent. For, Nanjangud is not only a renowned place of pilgrimage, but is also a centre of intelligence and prosperity in this part of His Highness' territories.

I share your gratification that the new water-supply scheme has been sanctioned. The Chief Engineer, who was here three days ago, has assured me that preparations are well in hand to start work.

I am glad that in respect of this scheme you have practised the principle of self-help which you rightly commend in your address. Should you approach the drainage question also in the same spirit, I have no doubt His Highness' Government will be prepared to meet you half way.

Since coming here, I have made the acquaintance of your non-official Vice-President, and I feel that you have every reason to be satisfied with him and that I may congratulate both you and him on his appointment. He is a young gentleman of position and education, who has not lost the fresh keen sense of public duty and ambition, with which every young man starts life on leaving his University.

You very rightly say that the town harbours some epidemic or other—cholera, plague or malaria—from one end of the year to the other. I am not surprised that this is so; for the town is close to the canal, the river water which is used for drinking purposes is polluted, the sewage mostly sinks into the sub-soil, and the Gundal river has become a huge latrine up to its junction with the main river. Added to all this you have large numbers of people streaming in and out, by rail or by road, bringing in disease or carrying disease with them. The defenceless condition of the town in a sanitary sense is a permanent invitation to epidemics of every description.

The new water-supply will probably put a stop to cholera but the panacea to other evils is efficient drainage and sanitation. The drainage problem is more difficult of solution as the works needed will be costly. One important work at least, namely, a masonry intercepting drain along the river bank to carry off all the liquid refuse from the town must be carried out without delay. Until you have sufficient money to construct branch mains and pipe drains you must be content with an intercepting sewer into which should be emptied all liquid refuse as rapidly as may be feasible. This may be done either by hand or by means of rough drains at first, and eventually by pipe drains and branch sewers. The ultimate aim of a sound sewerage scheme is to carry away automatically, within an hour or two after its admission into the drains, both solid fæces and liquid refuse to a point outside the town where it could do no harm. This is, perhaps, an impractical ideal in the present state of your resources, but the nearer you approach to it the healthier will be the town. You must commence with a comprehensive scheme from the outset and every step you take should lead to the completion of that scheme and be furthering its intentions.

If I may make a suggestion, I should put a wall or fence on both sides of the Gundal river for some distance and arrange to police the main river front against indiscriminate use of the bed and banks by the pilgrims. But policing alone will not avail unless you first provide a large number of decent latrines, and keep them very clean, and not in the repulsive condition one often sees them in and which is so abhorrent to caste people.

There are few countries, except perhaps China, where insanitation, penury and filth are associated with places of religious worship as in India. Nanjangud is perhaps no exception to this. Is it too much to ask the Dharmadarsis of the temple to arrange that every pilgrim washes his feet at the entrance and wipes them dry with a towel and that suitable receptacles are kept in the interior of the temple for depositing fruit and decaying matter, which pilgrims may want to throw away or may carelessly drop in their passage through the corridors? Cleanliness is next to godliness. The interior should be kept scrupulously clean at all times and no one after a walk through the streets should be permitted to approach the shrine with unclean feet. The effort to introduce reforms like this may cause a little inconvenience at first but, after a few months' experience, every right-minded person will appreciate their true value and cheerfully acquiesce in them.

I am here to-day at the close of a very interesting tour. My time was spent in close contact with the people, in long and frequent conversations with all classes, from the Municipal Councillor in the town to the peasant in the village hut. The study of the condition of the poorer classes is one of fascinating, if, at times somewhat melancholy, interest.

The main wants of the people are education, pure water and more occupation. The people of these parts are fully employed during the four monsoon months. They find work but for half the time in the cold weather and perhaps one-fourth of the time in the hot weather. It was only yesterday that village after village made this confession in the presence of our District officers. Women have no defined occupation outside their ordinary domestic duties except in assisting the men in their field work for a couple of months. Taking men and women together, it seems to me that the rural population of these parts make use of their time and energy only to the extent of about 50 per cent of their present capacity or marketable value. If, to this, be added the fact that nine-tenths of the people live in villages and more than 95 per cent of them are illiterate and unskilled, you will agree that the preventable waste of productive energy in the country is little short of appalling. The absence of steady occupation for many months in the year has demoralised the people, developed in them habits of slackness and weakened the spirit of self-reliance.

The great difficulty in the way of rapid provision of facilities for education and water-supply is the number of sects and subjects, Hindu and Mahomedan, high caste and low caste, "left-hand" class and "right-hand" class, and so on, into which the community is divided. The Mahomedans want separate schools and a separate organization even to a separate Inspectress of Schools. In some places, the Thoreyas are not allowed to attend the common school. The Panchamas are not allowed to associate with the Thoreyas. None of these communities will drink out of the same well, or allow their children to drink out of the same fountain of learning. If one good well were built in the village it might serve all. One large school might accommodate all classes and creeds and all grades of education under one roof. Most villages can afford to construct one such well and provide for one such school if they clubbed all their resources for the attempt. But, as matters stand, the resources are frittered away and none of the communities get a good well, or an efficiently managed school, because there is not enough money to go round for all.

I have travelled through many villages outside India, both East and West. There is no country I can recall in which artificial differences are carried to this ridiculous extreme. I hope the new Village Committees, if they do nothing else, will open the eyes of the people and gradually bring home to them the folly of so much division, and the uselessness of attempting to attain, by class or individual action, what is only successfully accomplished in every country by communal effort.

There are, however, streaks of light in the horizon. The demand for education has grown in volume and intensity to an extent which may be termed phenomenal. This view is vouched for and acquiesced in by the Deputy Commissioner and by the District officers and the staff officers who accompanied me. In many villages people have begun to employ their own teachers, perhaps after ineffectually waiting long enough for Government help. Enquiries showed that, in some of the taluks, there were more indigenous schools supported by the people than Primary schools maintained by Government. The Panchamas and the Parivars all ask for schools. The few educated Panchamas have an appearance of refinement about them very different from the hunted looks of their illiterate brethren. Two or three days ago, the barbers of Nanjangud petitioned for a school for themselves. All classes are clamouring for education and this is the first healthy sign of progress I can report from these parts. Many villagers who asked for schools were told by the Circle Inspector and myself that they would have to pay half the cost including maintenance. To my surprise, the majority of the villagers agreed to go even so far. This, to my mind, is a remarkable proof of the awakening of the people. I have His Highness' commands, and I have the full sympathy of my colleagues in Council, when I say that the Government on their part are prepared to strain their resources to the utmost, if necessary, in order to meet this prime want in the rural economy of the State.

Gentlemen, it will be my pleasing duty to report to His Highness the Maharaja the conditions I have witnessed, and to submit the representations I have received in town and village, from thousands of His Highness' loving subjects.

In respect of Nanjangud, you have made this duty doubly pleasant to me because you ask me to convey to His Highness an expression of gratitude for favours already received, and of your genuine loyalty to His Highness' throne and person.

SPEECH AT THE MYSORE LEGISLATIVE COUNCIL.

14th April 1914.

[A meeting of the Mysore Legislative Council was held at the Public Offices, Bangalore, at 12 noon, on the 14th April 1914. It was the first meeting of the Council since its enlargement under Regulation I of 1907.

In opening the proceedings of the Council, Dewan Sir M. Visvesvaraya addressed the assembled members thus:—]

Gentlemen,—This is an occasion of some importance in the life of this Council, since we meet here for the

Speech at the Mysore Legislative Council.

first time with our constitution improved and functions enlarged, under the new Regulation graciously sanctioned by His Highness the Maharaja.

From this day forward, you will exercise the privilege of interpellation and your opportunities for *discussion and criticism* are also enlarged. In other directions also, have opportunities been afforded to the leaders of the people to associate themselves in public work with Government in district, town and village. The discussions should be pursued in every case with an eye to determination and action. Investigation and discussion, if persevered in, cannot fail to lead to practical measures for improving the lot of our people.

There is nothing in the criticism that we get in this country as compared with other advanced countries that any one can take exception to. The only difference perhaps is that criticism is directed more against new measures than against stagnation and that the volume of constructive work done in the country, as compared to the amount of criticism levelled against it, is disproportionately small.

In a semi-developed country like ours, we need for the public service every brain that can devise and every hand that can execute measures to foster progress. We should do nothing to discourage effort and action ; otherwise the energy and driving power which the country sorely needs may dry up at its very source.

Later on, when the volume of constructive work grows, when the country has produced more thinkers and workers and when driving power becomes the rule and passivity the exception, criticism on the Western party model might become helpful and stimulating.

Till then, I pray you not to carry criticism beyond the point where its constructive value ceases.

Gentlemen, our meetings will be more frequent in

future and our deliberations will carry more weight on account of the increased representative character of this Assembly.

I am voicing the feelings of my colleagues and myself when I say that it gives us great pleasure to welcome so many representatives of the public and that we esteem it a privilege to be associated with them in the work of this Council.

ADDRESS TO THE MYSORE ECONOMIC CONFERENCE.

3rd June 1914. [The fifth session of the Mysore Economic Conference was held at the Public Offices, Mysore, on the 3rd June 1914 and the following days. There were, besides the members of the Conference, a large number of visitors. In opening the proceedings of the Conference, Sir M. Visvesvaraya said :—]

Gentlemen,—To-day we complete the third year of our activities, and, on behalf of His Highness' Government, I welcome you to the fifth session of the Economic Conference. Since we last met, the strength of the Conference, excluding the President and Vice-Presidents, has been increased from 42 to 48 members. His Highness the Maharaja, with His Highness' characteristic liberality and trust in his people, has been pleased to order the introduction of the elective principle in nominating non-official members to the Conference. Sixteen, or one-third of the total number, have accordingly been elected, eight being returned by the districts and eight by the members of the Dasara Representative Assembly.

The reports placed before you will show that fair

Address to the Mysore Economic Conference.

progress has been made in all the three branches of Conference work.

Increasing facilities are being given for developing primary and technical education. A scheme for developing female education in the State and another for the establishment of public libraries in Bangalore and Mysore are under the consideration of Government. A few lectures were delivered by recognized experts in subjects relating to the Conference work. In connection with the project for a University in Mysore, information is being collected regarding the conditions under which the smaller Universities are working in the British Colonies and foreign countries. The questions connected with education will receive increasing attention in future, as Government are convinced that activities in this direction are of the highest importance from an economic point of view.

During the year, the Department of Agriculture was reorganized and the scope of its work considerably enlarged. Questions affecting the agricultural population, such as the creation of large farms, improvement of tanks, extension of sugar-cane cultivation, etc., are engaging attention and enquiries into the economic condition of the raiyat are being pursued. Rules have been sanctioned for the grant of loans for dairy farming. Two experts have been appointed, a central silk farm has been started, and a silk association formed, to develop sericulture. Young students are being trained in sericulture and horticulture and arrangements are being made to distribute disease-free eggs to cultivators engaged in the silk industry. The question of educating the adult population in the rural areas in the three R's, and of spreading correct ideas of business among them, is receiving attention, with a view to enabling the cultivators to maintain farm accounts and calculate their income and losses. The co-operative movement is making satisfactory progress.

Turning to industries and commerce, you are aware that a department came into existence at the beginning of last year. Eleven pumping installations and five or six saw and other mills have been started and efforts are being made, by the grant of *takavi* loans and other means, to make the use of machinery popular. Instruction in weaving is given in the Government weaving factory in Bangalore and other outstations. Demonstration parties have been organized to popularise fly-shuttle weaving. The three sugar-cane crushing plants established are reported to be working successfully. Recommendations have been made by the Committee regarding the establishment of a wood distillation plant, and, at its instance, the starting of a chromo-lithographic press has been sanctioned. Experts were appointed and investigations pursued regarding the possibilities of the manufacture of tiles, porcelain, matches, paper, coir-matting, etc. A report on the Industrial Survey, prepared by the special officer appointed for the purpose, has just been issued. The Bank of Mysore, which came into operation eight months ago through the efforts of this Conference, is at present carrying on transactions to the value of over Rs. 23 lakhs.

Besides the newly-formed standing committee, there are three central and eight district committees working since 1911, and 29 taluk progress committees have been formed up to date. Several important questions which have been under deliberation and investigation by the committees are slowly taking practical shape.

The work of a committee falls chiefly under three heads. In the *first* place, it has to collect local information and statistics on all subjects engaging its attention. Some of this information, if carefully compiled, may be of sufficient value to be printed and issued for the use of the people. Similarly, corresponding information has to be collected from foreign countries and spread among the local population. *Secondly*, the economic needs and wants of the area concerned should be examined, and a list of the more important ones prepared in the order of their urgency and importance. The list should be periodically revised and kept up-to-date. The investigation of each item should be pursued until a remedy is found or a decision come to. The *third* important work is to put forward practical working schemes for meeting wants and effecting improvements, and, after the same are approved, to suggest measures to execute them and to watch progress. The committee might also take up any other connected questions for study and investigation.

Government have already decided that important schemes prepared by the committees may be transferred to Government Departments for execution or necessary action. In special cases, the execution of schemes may be entrusted to the Chairman and the Secretary, or even to individual members of a committee, under proper sanction.

The subjects taken up by a committee should be distributed among individual members for study and investigation. Every member should be a working partner of the committee and give his experience, ability, money or enthusiasm to the work. The results of investigation by individual members may be brought up, in the rough, from time to time, to get the advice and general approval of the committee. When the results and recommendations are ready, it will be the business of every other member to study them. After discussion, the committee may decide whether the proposals placed before it are sound and fit to be recommended for adoption;

if not, it might ask the member concerned to revise them till it is satisfied. In this way, every member will have the results of his work examined and adopted by the committee as a whole and he will also have an opportunity of assisting in the approval of the work of other members in the same manner. The recommendations and resolutions will represent the matured opinion of at least the majority of the members forming the committee.

When any member of the Conference or of the general public has thoroughly mastered a subject and is convinced that improvements are necessary or that any existing defect requires to be remedied, he should not rest content until a way is found. That is the first beginning of improvement. I am glad to say that there were several instances, in recent months, of officers and private gentlemen exhibiting a marked degree of enthusiasm in the promotion of practical schemes. Collecting and spreading information on any subject, careful study, discussion, investigation, etc., if zealously pursued, cannot fail to lead to the growth of sound ideas and yield practical results.

No committee will lack work if the members bear these essential considerations in mind and endeavour to give effect to the instructions already issued by Government.

During the past year, several new rules and orders were issued to consolidate the work of the committees. The organization is in a stage of growth and development and such defects as there are will disappear only with time and patience. These defects are due to the novelty of the attempt itself, the time it takes for members to thoroughly understand the object and character of the work entrusted to them, and the difficulty in getting a trained staff.

Address to the Mysore Economic Conference.

It is impossible, in the early stages of any large movement, to avoid defects. Better mistakes and defects with movement and progress, than perfect system and order in a state of stagnation.

It is some small gain that officials and non-officials have now begun to sit and work together and investigate jointly for the first time problems connected with the permanent prosperity of the country. It must be some satisfaction also that a large number of people are kept thinking, working and investigating economic problems.

In the course of the discussions which commence to-day, opportunities will be afforded to members to ask questions and suggest improvements with a view to perfecting the organization, and all important suggestions will receive the best consideration of the Conference and Government.

There can be no two opinions as to the necessity of strengthening our economic position in Mysore. The chief reason why we should do so is the poverty of our people, their low standard of living, their low level of earning and achievement, the sufferings they endure in times of drought and the risk of loss of life to which they are exposed in a severe famine. The second reason is the inordinate rise in prices and the rapidly-changing conditions of business and trade due to the growth of communications. A third reason is that large resources hitherto unutilized lie idle, which we might turn to good account for the betterment of the people.

I shall quote a few figures to show how Mysore compares with two of the most prosperous British Colonies, namely, Canada and Australia. The former has a population of 7 millions, the latter 5, and Mysore represents the mean of the two, or 6 millions. One would expect that, having regard to the similarity of population, there would be some resemblance between the conditions in Mysore and the two Colonies, but the figures I am quoting show that, compared to them, Mysore is nowhere in the race for economic progress.

	Canada	Australia	Mysore
1. Population	7,206,000	5,083,000	5,705,000
2. Education—			
No. of Universities ...	20	6	Nil.
No. of Newspapers ...	(not known)	1,200	36
Percentage of literates to total population.	Between 80 and 90		6
Percentage of pupils at school to total population.	18·6	14 7	2
3. Revenue (£ millions) ...	41	21	1·8
Expenditure (£ millions) ...	38	17	2·1
4. No. of Post Offices ...	13,859	8,225	485
No. of Telegraph Offices ...	624	4,180	49
5. No. of miles of railway open	28,035	18,653	422
6. Average earnings per head per annum (approximate)	From Rs. 400 to 700.		Rs. 30
7. Death rate per 1,000 of population.	15·12	10·5	Nearly 30
8. Trade per head (£) ...	28-8-1	30-18-8	1-0-4

The figures have been obtained from the best sources within my reach and are believed to be approximately correct.

A few days ago, we all read a telegram in the papers, according to which Lord Denman, the Governor-General of Australia, remarked that "he doubted whether there were 5,000,000 people anywhere in the world who were so prosperous as the Australians." Earl Grey, the late Governor-General of Canada, stated last year that "the prosperity of that Dominion was amazing."

These facts and figures must serve as an eye-opener to the people of Mysore. I refer to them here not because I have any hopes of our reaching the level of prosperity of the two Colonies, but because it will do us good to know what organization and human endeavour are capable of achieving under favourable conditions.

The nationality of our people rests on a religious and fatalistic basis, not on an economic basis, as in the West.

There are still people among us who believe that the golden age was in the past, the world is on the down-grade and the old-world conditions might yet be reproduced some day. The Hindu ideal of life is that this world is a preparation for the next and not a place to stay in and make ourselves comfortable. We are devoted to past ideals, although, out of necessity or from prospect of personal gain, we have partly taken to Western methods of work and business. There is a yearning for the old ideals and a half-hearted acquiescence in the new and, on the whole, the genius of the people is for standing still.

If we are to follow in the wake of other countries in the pursuit of material prosperity, we must give up aimless activities and bring our ideals into line with the standards of the West, namely, to spread education in all grades, multiply occupations and increase production and wealth. All other activities should conform themselves to the economic ideal.

I have been asked whether economic activities should absorb our attention to the exclusion of all others and whether some attention should not be devoted to civic and social progress. I agree that something should be done to stimulate work in every direction, and I shall proceed to make a few observations to show how the other professions and activities in the State might be stimulated. There has been a frittering away of energy in various directions in the past, because it has not been utilized with sufficient concentration and in a manner calculated to produce the largest results.

All the activities and professions in the country may be defined and classed under, say, six divisions in a village, twelve in a town and up to eighteen in a city. Nearly all the activities in a town and village are also practised in a city, although the extent to which they are practised may vary.

Taking a town, say, of about 10,000 inhabitants, for example, the activities and professions may be classified into a dozen divisions as under:—

1. Education,
2. Agriculture,
3. Industries and manufactures,
4. Trade and commerce, co-operative and joint-stock enterprise,
5. Town-planning and improvements, water-supply, drainage and house-building,
6. Municipal Government and sanitation,
7. Physical exercise and recreation,
8. Business training, neatness, economy and public morals,
9. Religion and art,
10. Social activities and improvements,
11. Miscellaneous activities and professions not falling under any of the above heads, and
12. Any other activities peculiar to the locality.

The first four heads come under the purview of this Conference and we are gradually doing what may be needed to help to train the people. As regards all other activities, with the exception perhaps of those connected with religion, a central committee may be formed in each town and it may appoint some one, an individual or a sub-committee, to the charge of each class of work and hold itself responsible to see that the work of that profession is progressing, that people engaged in it are active and are able to help themselves.

In a village, the following six divisions of activities and professions might be enough:—

1. Agriculture,
2. Subsidiary occupations,
3. Education,
4. Industries, manufactures and trade,

Address to the Mysore Economic Conference.

5. Village communal work including settlement of disputes, and
6. Village administration.

The classification into 6, 12 and 18 is quite arbitrary, but it is necessary to indicate even an approximate arbitrary number for the sake of definiteness.

In every city, town and village, as already stated, a central committee or association should be responsible for providing agencies to keep all these organizations moving and in efficient working order.

The work to be done by the individual or sub-committee in charge of each activity or profession will be to bring together all the people interested in the work and make them act in unison, collect information and statistics, obtain useful information from abroad and spread the same locally, hold public and committee meetings and conferences, issue bulletins, leaflets and newspaper articles, collect funds and do everything in its power to arouse the people interested in that particular activity or profession, and make them think, move and act together and endeavour to raise their standard of work to the highest level attainable.

Besides the local activities in each residential area, there should be an agency to guide and advise the individuals or committees engaged in the same profession or class of activity throughout the State. This guidance may be entrusted to an association or committee of leaders in the capital of the State or in some important town. The central authority will do for the whole State what each responsible individual or sub-committee does for the town. For each profession or class of activity, there will thus be a local agency to promote its objects and a central agency to guide and co-ordinate work throughout the State. There will come into operation local and radial forces to stimulate progress in each profession or activity, and the interlacing of the efforts which will follow cannot fail to raise the standards of work, or earning capacity, or both, of the people participating in the activities.

Progress, if it is to be sustained, should be many-sided; but, in the present state of the country, economic progress with which we are concerned demands our chief attention. It is for the representatives of the people to develop other activities, and I feel persuaded that if an organization such as I have outlined is brought into existence, every important activity and profession in the country will receive its due share of attention; there will be both co-operation and differentiation and every person engaged in any profession or business will be kept thinking, working and moving according to the best of his capacity and opportunities.

There is waste going on in the business life of our people in many ways—waste both of resources and of opportunities. There is waste of energy due to insufficient occupation, because agriculture gives full employment for only six or seven months in the year. There is waste due to illiteracy, because ninety-four persons out of every hundred are uneducated. There is waste through ignorance of the ways of the civilized people, because we fail to utilize their accumulated asset of wisdom and experience. Waste is also going on through our imperfect acquaintance with the commonplaces of civilization and lack of correct business ideals and business standards in daily life. Mental energy is wasted in caste disputes and village factions. Capital is wasted because money is hoarded instead of being made available for productive purposes. There is waste of health because, although leading moral lives normally, men and women grow prematurely old for want of pride of person and attention to the elementary laws of health.

The largest waste of all is the lack of capacity for co-operation, the difficulty of ensuring harmony, sympathy and oneness of feeling, in matters affecting the larger interests of the State.

The work of this Conference, which is to induce people to think ahead and work ahead and economise human energy, may be described as a war against waste. Our people should realize that if they have to get on now-a-days, they must give up indefinite ideals and lazy thinking and subordinate all activities and accomplishments to certain well-defined needs of material progress. They have to take more pains over their work, toil longer hours and submit to the discipline and restraints of civilization. That will enable them to find continuous employment, raise standards of comfort, live longer and healthier lives, increase production and share in the world's activities and pleasures of eventful living.

SPEECH AT THE MYSORE ECONOMIC CONFERENCE.

[The fifth session of the Mysore Economic Conference finished its deliberations on 10th June 1914. In winding up the proceedings of the Conference, Sir M. Visvesvaraya made the following speech :—] 10th June 1914.

Gentlemen,—The work of the session is over, and I would bespeak your indulgence while I make a few observations before closing the proceedings. I have no doubt I am voicing the sentiments of the entire assembly when I say how very much we value the presence of His Highness the Yuvaraja at these meetings. His Highness has been attending early and late and evincing the keenest interest in our proceedings, and we have every hope that he will take an active part in the economic work of the State in the near future. No one who has watched His Highness' activities since his return from Europe will fail to recognise that we have in him a leader of great promise for all useful and progressive movements in the country. I must congratulate the assembly on the high level of the discussions and the spirit of conciliation, restraint and good temper with which the several subjects were handled by the speakers.

Turning to the questions discussed, I agree that the development of Kannada literature is a laudable object, but a semi-official Association like ours cannot undertake to enter into relations with people outside the State. Such work should be left to private individuals or Associations. The publication of a Children's Magazine is an excellent proposal, and I hope it will receive the early attention of the Education Committee. As regards the question of extending normal schools, Mr. Shama Rao has explained the progress already made, and how much attention is being given to the subject at present. With regard to technical education some of you may be aware that we have a very complete scheme to act upon, but our real difficulty at present is to find competent men to give effect to it. If we obtain the services of one or two good Professors we can make more rapid progress.

As stated by Mr. Nanjundayya, we are negotiating with experts to obtain the services of suitable men. It is true we have an ambitious educational programme, and we are only too well aware of the imperfections in the existing arrangements, but, happily, we have also a very enthusiastic and level-headed officer at the head of the Department, who enjoys the full confidence of His Highness' Government. We are endeavouring to deal with new problems on one side and to remove existing defects on the other. We are advancing in new directions, and you may be sure we have not omitted the precautions needed to consolidate the base of our operations.

The development of instruction in agriculture, which is our basic industry, is proceeding satisfactorily under the able guidance of the head of the Department, Dr. Coleman. He is popular with the cultivators and is showing increasing interest and co-operation in the work of the Agricultural Committee. In respect of sericulture, we have made a distinct advance, though what is being done is of the nature of spade work, and we have as yet no appreciable practical results to place before you. As regards the proposition connected with minor tanks, I fear that, if the people throw off what little responsibility they now have for the maintenance and restoration of these tanks, things are bound to go from bad to worse. Tanks are to agriculture what education is to the general prosperity of the State. I have repeatedly urged that they can be satisfactorily maintained and improved only by the people of the villages concerned, who originally constructed them, and any attempt to transfer the maintenance to Government may lead to further delay. What people should ask for is a contribution, subsidy or other concession from Government, rather than the transfer of their responsibility to a Government establishment, which may never be equal to the task. Even if we convert all our graduates into engineers and employ them on the work they will not be able to do justice to it.

There has been cordial co-operation between the Industries and Commerce Committee and the head of that Department during the year, which has enabled the Committee to do much useful work. The question of the formation of industrial suburbs in our towns and cities is one of some importance, and the evils of allowing things to drift have been clearly brought to your notice by Mr. K. P. Puttanna Chetty and other gentlemen. The question of rates for electric power is a small one and you may rely on the Committee and the Government doing all they can to meet the wishes of the people.

The proposal to appoint a Central Committee of Cooperation, as approved by you at yesterday's meeting, is an important one, but it has yet to receive the sanction of Government. The publication of a periodical in English and Kanarese for spreading economic literature is one of those proposals on which practical action is overdue. Private enterprise should take up the work and, failing this, the Committees may step in. It is not desirable to have any journals conducted under official control. The Committees might help if a private syndicate comes forward with definite practical proposals. The railway project from Kadur to Chikmagalur deserves encouragement, but its consideration has had to be postponed for want of establishment at present. I hope in the meanwhile, the District Boards will collect as much capital as they can for carrying out the project.

As regards the general work of the Conference, I would suggest that the provisional programmes of the Central and District Committees be revised and made more definite in the course of the next few weeks, before they are finally adopted for guidance. The Committees might take stock of their progress once in three months, so that none of the important items on the programme may be lost sight of. No member who is prevented from doing any real work, either for want of time or opportunities, should remain on any committee. Every citizen of the State should give a portion of his time, money or enthusiasm for public work, no matter how small and what form it may take, and every member of a committee should study and specialize in one or more subjects, until

Speech at the Mysore Economic Conference.

a practical result or decision is reached. No person who takes up new subjects suited to his education and capacity need think that he is wasting his time in the attempt.

I was gratified to notice that the Conference, which includes so many elected members, gave a solid vote in favour of increased expenditure on the objects of the Conference. In view of the adverse comments regarding the expenditure on the Conference work, I trust the answers given to questions put by the members will show that the expenditure is properly controlled. The objection to an outlay of 1½ or 2 lakhs on this work will apply with equal cogency to half a lakh or to any expenditure, however small. Taking the size of the country, the population and the magnitude of the interests affected into consideration, an expenditure of 2 or 3 lakhs in giving a business education to the people of the State cannot be considered excessive. It must be remembered that the provision is of a temporary character and can be easily stopped at short notice. We spend 18 to 20 lakhs on the education of children and it could not be considered an extravagance to lay out 2 or 3 lakhs more in training the "older boys." Having regard to what is being done in this respect in other countries, the State outlay, if anything, seems very inadequate.

As pratically the entire proceedings of this session have been thrown open to the public, a word or two of explanation may not be out of place as to why we did not wish to admit the public into our deliberations till now. The Press takes a too generous view of our activities, and we often get credit for many things we do not deserve. We may be raising expectations, some of which at least may not be realized. But the main reason is that discussions of details of commercial projects and business concerns are likely to be objected to by the persons who furnish them. One important advantage of open discussions, however, is that the public will be able to follow the proceedings and to that extent understand the need for closer co-operation and sustained activity.

Three years ago, when, under his His Highness the Maharaja's gracious orders, this Conference was brought into existence, there was much comment, and an amount of excitement and disapproval in certain quarters bordering on unrest. I am glad to see that the unrest has disappeared. As people become familiar with our objects and methods, the unrest is giving place to acquiescence and active enthusiasm. The enthusiasm exhibited for the work by officers and non-official gentlemen alike is worthy of all praise. The Secretaries of the Conference have had very hard work, and in spite of the unkind remarks about the travelling allowance, no one who has followed their work can fail to admit that they have been doing material service to the Committees and the public. They do not travel of their own accord, but always, with the knowledge of the chairman. Many non-official gentlemen have been doing excellent work. It would be invidious to mention names, but the work done by Mr. Puttanna Chetty and gentlemen like Mr. C. Srinivasa Rao, Mr. Abdul Quddus and Mr. H. V. Rangasawmy cannot be passed over without notice. The brunt of the work, however, has fallen on the Deputy Commissioners and in some measure on the Assistant Commissioners and Amildars. Many of these officers have been keen on rousing the population and have done much valuable work. The more I come into contact with them, the greater has been my feeling of regard for them and appreciation of their worth and services.

We are fortunate in having able officers at the head of the three Departments with which the Conference Committees are intimately associated. The greatest need now is increased co-operation from the leaders and the public, and the master word is work. The time has arrived for increasing the quality and output of work in every grade of life according to the capacity and the opportunities of the individual. The average citizen should learn to work methodically, work longer hours, work in harmony with others and make sacrifices for the public cause. A determined effort should be made to reduce the number of the uneducated and the unemployed in the country. There are a thousand and one matters which require study and specialization; a thousand details have to be perfected, and we want tens of thousands of brains to attend to the work. I earnestly hope that those who have not taken an active interest in the Conference work till now will take kindly to it in future, and that those who are already enthusiastic will redouble their efforts in the coming year.

SPEECH AT THE MYSORE LEGISLATIVE COUNCIL.

[The Mysore Legislative Council met at the Public Offices, Bangalore, on the 7th July 1914, for the discussion, for the first time in its history, of the State Budget for 1914-15. In bringing to a close an interesting debate on the same, Sir M. Visvesvaraya, as President in Council, made the following speech:—] 7th July 1914.

Gentlemen,—The discussions have continued to a late hour and I find that my colleagues have taken out of my mouth many of the explanations that I intended to give with reference to the observations of non-official members. My remarks will therefore be very brief. This is the first Budget discussion that has taken place since His Highness was pleased to accord new privileges to the Council, and I wish to congratulate the members on the excellent use they have made of the week's time that has passed since we last met, on the high level at which the debate has been maintained, and on the moderation, ability and business acumen displayed in the discussions.

I also wish to associate myself with the other members in congratulating Mr. Chakravarti on his able and lucid exposition of the State Budget.

The principal features of the Budget are an increase of revenue under forests and excise and a substantial increase of expenditure under education, and on establishment and equipment for a number of departments which hitherto considered themselves starved. The most prominent feature is the large and unprecedented provision of over 95 lakhs on railway, irrigation and other capital account works. We received 30 lakhs last year and we expect the balance of 13 lakhs to be paid to us this year from the surplus revenues of the Civil and Military Station. We are grateful to the Government of India for recognizing the claim of the Mysore Durbar to the surplus revenues and paying the arrears due to us. We are deeply interested in the prosperity of the Civil and Military Station and we have in the past done what we could to help them in connection with their water-supply and lighting. We look forward to closer identity of interests and to greater mutual co-operation hereafter.

Foremost among the projects in progress for developing the material prosperity of the State is the Cauvery Reservoir works at Kannambadi. These works are intended to store the waters of the Cauvery which would otherwise run to waste into the sea. The construction of foundations in the river bed is now over and the works are making very fair progress.

As regards railways, the Mysore-Arsikere Railway is under construction and the proposed lines from Nanjangud to Erode and Hassan to Mangalore are under correspondence with the Government of India. An incorrect report has got abroad and also found its way into the papers that railway construction is making slow progress. I do not know of any period in the history of railway construction in Mysore when work was pushed through more vigorously than at present.

As regards forests, the revenue has increased of late years and I consider that it is capable of further increase. We have appointed two special officers to inspect the forests and investigate the prospect of utilizing forest produce for industrial purposes. Many parts of our forests are yet untouched by the hand of man and the revenue is capable of further expansion to a material extent without injury to any of them. In this connection, I wish to refer to the retirement of Mr. Muthannah a week ago from the position of Conservator of Forests in Mysore, which he held for over twelve years with conspicuous ability and distinction. Possessing European business habits, an untiring activity and a keen love of his profession, Mr. Muthannah effected many solid reforms in the department which have brought increased revenue to Government and enhanced the value of the forests as a State property.

Besides projects for material improvement, we are interesting ourselves in improving our people. We have doubled the expenditure on education during the past four or five years; in doing this we are only following the example of the Government of India. The expenditure on the Agricultural Department has been doubled, investigations in sericulture begun, and a new department of

Industries and Commerce formed with a view to create new occupations for the people. Our policy is to give instruction to children in schools and develop practical business capacity in the people through the agency of committees.

We at present derive an appreciable revenue of over 30 lakhs from past State enterprises and the mining industry and we are adding to our permanent assets by investing our savings and current surpluses on new works. We have also the satisfaction of being able to construct railways and irrigation works without borrowing, although it would be quite legitimate to borrow for such objects. We have endeavoured to improve the efficiency of five or six departments by strengthening the establishments and making non-recurring grants. We have inaugurated special schemes of economic and social improvements in the interests of the village population and the *malnad* area.

As regards education, Mr. Shama Rao has already informed you that we are providing funds and making arrangements to double the school-going population within the next three years. Only a few days ago, His Highness was pleased to sanction an additional grant of 3¼ lakhs, for the further development of primary education.

A beginning has been made also in the direction of making the State balances available for the use of the public for promoting local industry and trade through the agency of the Bank of Mysore.

We are satisfied that our finances are prosperous, our credit is good and our resources are spent in the best interests of the people. But there is a dark side to the picture. Although we are better than our past, the condition of the people cannot be said to be satisfactory.

Some weeks ago at another similar meeting, I compared the conditions in Mysore with those in Canada and Australia because the population of those colonies was about the same as Mysore. As we are discussing our financial position, it may interest you to know that the Colony of Australia has ten times the revenue of Mysore, and Canada about twenty times.

Our difficulties in this country are an erratic monsoon and an ignorant population. The last year's monsoon was unsatisfactory, this year's has been late. People have to be content with a low level of comfort and a low standard of living, which, in the case of the poorer classes, is liable to change into destitution at the first sign of scarcity.

The chief remedy to this state of things, so far as the agricultural population is concerned, is to arrange for storage of water. Over 70 per cent of the people in the State are dependent on agriculture for their food supply and cultivation is rendered precarious by the fitful character of the monsoon. If water which would otherwise go to waste is collected and stored in large reservoirs, it will be available for growing crops throughout the year. Such works will provide occupation to the people in all seasons and are the best form of protection against famine that we can provide in this country.

A great deal has been said on minor tanks. The difficulties in developing these tanks lie deeper than the public or their leaders imagine. That they are of paramount importance to the people there can be no two opinions. But whoever finds the money, the tanks should be constructed, repaired and supervised by the people of the locality and not by a centralised Government agency. The tanks are silting up and new ones are not taking their place as fast as the existing tanks are deteriorating. The salvation lies in teaching the people to put forth local effort to repair or restore old tanks and construct new ones. Government will be prepared to pay a portion of the cost wherever necessary.

A second remedy is the multiplication of occupations besides agriculture from which people can make a living during portions of the year when agricultural work is slack.

A third remedy is to give education and business training to people, to enable them to understand how they might improve their present lot and raise their standard of living, effort and achievement.

It is now getting late and I do not wish to traverse any of the points already explained by previous speakers. I would only refer to the criticisms about the Economic Conference and say that, in doing what we have attempted, we are guided by the example of more civilised States and the lessons derived from the past history of such States. We are unable to show results while the schemes are yet developing. We cannot pull up a plant by the roots to demonstrate that the roots are growing. For achieving any important results, many years of preparation are necessary and I trust that, in respect of our activities in this direction, we may confidently bespeak the patience and support of the people during such preparation.

For the purpose of economic development, we intend to spend about three lakhs a year for a period of five years. We are doing very much less than what the country needs and the occasion demands and if we are not proceeding fast, it is because we want to take the people with us without which no improvement can be said to be permanent.

Government confidently look to you, and the leaders of the people generally, not only to advise them and co-operate with them, but also to correctly interpret Government measures, intentions and policy to the people.

Any discordant note at this time, however much it may be justified in more advanced countries, will only confirm our conservative population in their old ways and make the task of improvement difficult. The finances will improve with the improvement in the earning power and the tax-bearing capacity of the people. In order to improve this capacity, the public and their leaders should respond to measures initiated in their interest, and every one should join in endeavouring to develop among our people the virtues of industry, thrift, self-help and co-operation.

In conclusion, I may assure you, Gentlemen, that all suggestions of value made in the course of these discussions will be noted and Government will give their best consideration to them.

ADDRESS TO DASARA REPRESENTATIVE ASSEMBLY.

[On the 30th September 1914, the thirty-first session of the Mysore Dasara Representative Assembly was held at the public offices, Mysore. Dewan Sir M. Visvesvaraya occupied the chair as President. Besides the Hon'ble Sir Hugh Daly, K.C.I.E., British Resident in Mysore, there were present on the occasion a large number of persons, European and Indian. In welcoming the representative members, Sir Visvesvaraya delivered the following address :—]

30th Sept. 1914.

Gentlemen,—I rise, in obedience to the command laid upon me by His Highness the Maharaja, to welcome you to this, the thirty-first session of the Dasara Representative Assembly, and to place before you an account of the past year's administration of the State and of the measures projected or in operation to promote the well-being of His Highness' subjects.

The thought which is uppermost in our minds at the present moment is the great war which is convulsing Europe from end to end and the effects of which, on account of the growth of communications, are felt over the entire habited portion of the world. India, as forming part of the British Empire, is intimately concerned in the war. That we are able to go on with our ordinary routine duties at such a time without undue anxiety or excitement, we owe to the great sea-power of the Empire and the normal orderliness of British methods of administration. The war has brought the subjects of His Majesty in the Indian Empire nearer to the Throne, and at no time were the harmony of feeling and the solidarity of interests between the rulers and the ruled, between the Paramount Power and the Feudatory States, felt to be closer than they are at the present time.

As a Feudatory State, we have endeavoured to do our part. His Highness the Maharaja has placed his troops and the entire resources of the State unreservedly at the disposal of the Imperial Government. His Highness has also contributed a sum of rupees fifty lakhs towards the cost of the Indian Expeditionary Force which is now fighting the Empire's battle on the Continent.

In conveying this offer in a letter, dated 20th August 1914, to His Excellency the Viceroy, His Highness said:—

"This is a time at which the Feudatory States and all the subjects of the British Empire should stand shoulder to shoulder for her defence, and I desire to assure Your Excellency, in all sincerity, of the devotion and loyalty of my people and our readiness to make every sacrifice to protect our common interests."

Address to Dasara Representative Assembly.

His Excellency the Viceroy concluded a highly appreciative message in these words :—

"For the moment, I will only add that the thought that you, my friend, have shown such splendid patriotism at a time like this fills my heart with a warm glow of pleasure."

It would be superfluous to say before this Assembly that the action taken by His Highness has met with universal acclaim in every corner of the State.

The subject which next claims our attention is the state of the season. The rainfall of last year was scanty and ill-distributed. It began late and ended early. In the five monsoon months of June to October, the total rainfall amounted to 19·38 inches in Bangalore, against an average of 27·09 inches, and to 29·25 inches for the whole State, or 10·32 inches short of the average. The heavy fall of the south-west monsoon did not commence till late in September and that of the north-east monsoon carried us only into the earlier part of October. The rainfall of these two months did much good, but the effect was partly marred by the abrupt termination of the north-east monsoon in the first week of October.

The result was a shrinkage of area under the ragi crop and some increase in that under gram. The yield of neither crop was good. The tanks failed to get the usual supply of water and the outturn of paddy in the *maidan* tract was adversely affected. In the important paddy-growing areas of the *malnad* and the Mysore District, however, the paddy crop was by no means unsatisfactory. A large number of cattle have died and many have lost condition for want of fodder.

The current monsoon also began badly. The usual *mungar* rains were not very abundant nor well distributed. In the months of June and July, the rainfall amounted to 2·59 and 13·33 inches, respectively, including the fall in the *malnad* parts, against an average of 4·51 and 10·25 inches; but in the *maidan* areas, the corresponding figures were 0·72 and 2·58 inches against an average of 2·22 and 3·61 inches respectively. The situation was partly relieved by the favourable rains of August, but the crops in many parts are yet young and the rainfall in the next few weeks must determine the character of our harvests at the end of the season.

As a result of the rapid communications and the changing conditions of the outer world, prices have been going up in recent years and the precarious rainfall of the past two successive seasons has raised them to famine rates. This is causing much hardship to the poorer officials, artisans and labouring classes. The cultivators have been getting very good prices for their crops, which have enabled them to pay their revenue with ease; but in areas in which the crops suffered more than ordinary damage, the raiyats have had very little left to sell.

Government have done all in their power to meet the situation. Tank beds have been ordered to be given out for cultivation; funds have been sanctioned for sinking drinking water wells; State forests have been thrown open to free grazing; arrangements have been made for procuring and supplying fodder; and a large amount of money—in fact, all that the Revenue Officers asked for—has been made available for granting loans and advances.

Steps have been taken to have the village programmes re-examined with a view to ascertaining whether the works included in them are sufficient and well distributed. With many village works ready to hand and the unusually large number of public works and railways, some of great magnitude, in progress in different parts of the State, we are peculiarly well circumstanced in the matter of providing work to persons in need of employment.

During the year, His Highness the Maharaja had the

privilege of welcoming His Excellency the Viceroy in our midst. The tour lasted from the 3rd to the 21st November 1913, and it included Gersoppa Falls, Mysore, the Kheddas, Bangalore, and the Kolar Gold Fields. The visit cannot be referred to without recalling the memory of Her Excellency Lady Hardinge who accompanied the Viceroy and who, to our great sorrow, is now no more. I have no doubt I am voicing the sentiments of the entire Assembly when I say that our respectful sympathies are with His Excellency Lord Hardinge in his great bereavement, and it is our earnest hope that His Excellency may have strength to continue the administration of this great Empire with the same conspicuous sympathy and success that have characterised it till now.

Another event of outstanding importance was the generous act of the British Government in sanctioning the substitution, in place of the Instrument of Transfer of 1881, of a new Treaty for Mysore, indicating the high esteem in which His Highness the Maharaja is held by the British Government. The change was welcomed by all classes of people, and was regarded as a signal proof of the sympathy and generosity which has always marked the policy of the Supreme Government towards this State. In this connection, I cannot do better than quote the sentiments to which His Excellency the Viceroy gave expression on the 6th November 1913, when he made this historic announcement in the City of Mysore :—

"I have now the pleasant duty of making an announcement, which it is as gratifying to me to deliver, as I trust it will be to Your Highness to receive. Some four months ago Your Highness wrote me a letter in which you took exception to certain features in the Instrument of Transfer of 1881, under which the Government of Mysore was restored to Your Highness' father, and you urged that the document should be revised both in substance and in form, in such a manner as to indicate more appropriately the relation subsisting between the British Government and the State of Mysore. After a very careful consideration of the question, I have decided, with the concurrence of His Majesty's Secretary of State for India, to substitute for the Instrument of Transfer a new Treaty which will place the relations between us on a footing more in consonance with Your Highness' actual position among the Feudatory Chiefs in India. His Majesty's Government, in accepting my proposal, have observed that Your Highness' views on this question were stated with much force and moderation and that they derive additional weight from the high character and reputation which Your Highness has always borne. With this observation I desire to associate myself in the very fullest degree, and I look on it as a particularly happy circumstance, that it should have fallen to my lot to convey to Your Highness on this auspicious occasion so striking a proof of the esteem and regard in which you are held by those responsible for the Government of this great Empire."

The reforms in the Legislative Council, which His Highness the Maharaja was pleased to sanction and which were announced to you last year, have been fully given effect to. They included the nomination of four elected members from this Assembly and four from the districts, and the grant of the privileges of interpellation and discussion of the budget.

The reformed Council met three times during the year and the State Budget of the current year was placed before them for discussion in June last with an explanatory statement by the Financial Secretary. The discussion took place on the 7th July and was participated in by nearly all the non-official members present.

The number of members on the Executive Council has

been increased from two to three, in consequence of the appointment of His Highness the Yuvaraja as an Extraordinary Member. The Yuvaraja, as you are aware, worked for some time as Military Secretary to His Highness the Maharaja, but the post offered too limited a field for his abilities, and His Highness therefore decided, after the Yuvaraja's return from the European tour, that he should be appointed as an Extraordinary Member of the Council. The Yuvaraja has now held that high office for about eight months, and though it is not for me to appraise his work, I cannot refrain from expressing the admiration of a colleague for the soundness of judgment and the breadth and freshness of view that he brings to bear on questions which come before him.

I will now refer briefly to the operations of the Departments of Government, one by one, beginning with the Financial Department.

As you are aware, the financial statement of His Highness' Government for the year 1914-15 was for the first time discussed in the Legislative Council in July last.

The revenue for the year 1913-14, according to the revised estimates, stood at Rs. 317·30 lakhs and the expenditure at Rs. 237·23 lakhs, showing a net surplus of Rs. 80·07 lakhs. Omitting Rs. 30 lakhs received on account of surplus revenues of the Civil and Military Station, the year's transactions showed a surplus of Rs. 50·07 lakhs made up as under :—

Increase of revenue in excess of budget figures	30·13	lakhs
Savings in ordinary expenditure	11·22	,,
Estimated surplus in the original budget ...	8·72	,,
Total ...	50·07	lakhs

Special grants aggregating Rs. 65·10 lakhs had also been made for important capital works, *viz.*, the Cauvery Reservoir Works, extension of the Cauvery Power Scheme, new Railways and Bangalore Tramways. Of these grants, the Departments were able to utilise to the extent of Rs. 37·68 lakhs. The principal reasons for the lapses are the postponement of the payment of compensation in connection with the Cauvery Reservoir Scheme and unavoidable delays in maturing schemes and ordering out materials for the other projected works.

Turning now to the budget estimates for the current official year (1914-15), which have been based on the expectation of a normal year, the gross revenue is estimated at Rs. 285·09 lakhs and the gross expenditure at Rs. 258·63 lakhs. Analysed into ordinary and extraordinary, the figures stand thus :—

RECEIPTS.	Lakhs.	EXPENDITURE.	Lakhs	Lakhs.
Gross Revenue ...	Rs. 285·09	Gross expenditure ...		Rs. 358·63
Deduct arrears of surplus revenues of Civil and Military Station ...	12·00	Deduct special grants for capital account works.		
		1 Cauvery Reservoir works ...	37·50	
		2 Cauvery Power Scheme extension	5·67	
		3 Electric Tramways	6·00	
		4 State Railways construction ...	36·00	
		5 Capital for subsidised Railways	10·00	95·17
Net ordinary receipts ...	273·09	Net ordinary expenditure		263·46
		Surplus in the ordinary account		9·63
	273·09			273·09

A study of the assets and liabilities of the State, as they stood on the 1st July 1914, will show that notwithstanding the heavy outlay on capital account works, the financial position may be regarded as entirely satisfactory.

It was noticed last year that the claim of the Mysore Government for the surplus revenues of the Bangalore Assigned Tract had received the generous recognition of the Government of India. After a careful scrutiny, the amount payable to the State to the end of the year 1911-12 was fixed at a little over Rs. 39 lakhs, of which a substantial instalment, *viz.*, Rs. 30 lakhs, was paid during the year.

The closing balance at the credit of the depositors in the Savings Banks on the last day of the year 1913-14 was Rs. 73,01,284 against Rs. 74,99,274 on the last day of the previous year, excluding interest in either case. The withdrawals in the year 1913-14 were in excess of deposits by nearly 2 lakhs, a result which is said to be partly due to depositors having transferred their funds from the Savings Banks to the Bank of Mysore.

The increase in the Gazetted and ministerial staff of the Account Department, referred to last year, took effect during the year under review.

In view of the large public works and railway projects in progress and the consequent increase in accounts work, the appointments of a Deputy Comptroller and of a Chief Superintendent for the Public Works and Railway Branch of the Department, were sanctioned.

The Mysore Civil Service Examination was held in November and December last under the revised rules of January 1913, and three of the successful candidates were appointed Assistant Commissioners, on probation.

Orders were passed during the year revising the scale of the revenue establishment of the Deputy Commissioners' Offices.

The Village Improvement Scheme came into operation about four months before the close of the year, and the results achieved will be explained in a future section of this Address.

I remarked last year that the receipts under excise revenue during the year 1912-13 had reached a record figure, but those of the year 1913-14 have proved even higher, being Rs. 55,28,281 or Rs. 4,33,971 in excess of the previous year. Nearly half of this was obtained from shop rental and the remainder from increased consumption. The increase occurred in respect of all dutiable articles except foreign liquor. The consumption of the cheaper kinds of this liquor is gradually on the decrease and liquors manufactured in the Central Distillery, Bangalore, are becoming more popular.

The total forest revenue realised during the year was also a record figure. It amounted to Rs. 32,71,336 and about two-thirds of this were obtained from the sale of 2,158 tons of sandalwood. The expenditure under conservancy and the establishment of the department was Rs. 7,45,476.

Two forest officers have been placed on special duty to survey the forest resources of the State and to investigate the possibility of utilising them for industrial purposes. These officers completed, by the close of the year, the exploration of the Ghaut Forests in the Shimoga District and of the forests near the head waters of the Tunga and in the Jager valley in the Kadur District. One of them also assisted the experts engaged by Government to investigate the possibility of starting the manufacture of pencils and matches in the State. These officers have submitted their detailed reports which are now under the consideration of Government.

The Khedda operations organized on the occasion of the visit of His Excellency the Viceroy to the State, in November last, were successfully conducted, and in spite of heavy casualties among the captured elephants, resulted in a net gain of Rs. 52,585 to the State.

A gratifying reform was made during the year in the Stamp Department by the issue of stamps bearing the portrait of His Highness the Maharaja.

The Stamp Manufactory, which till now had been located in a part of the Public Office Buildings, was removed to the new premises contiguous to the Government Press, where the new machines purchased during the year have been installed.

One notable event in connection with the judicial administration of the State was the Judicial Conference held at Mysore in June last for the purpose of discussing questions of importance relating to the administration of justice. The Conference, which was presided over by Rajamantrapravina Mr. H. V. Nanjundayya, C.I.E., First Member of Council, was the first of its kind and included among its members, experienced Judicial Officers and Advocates, besides several prominent gentlemen representing the general public. The resolutions passed and the recommendations made will be duly considered by Government.

The services of Sir Leslie C. Miller, till recently a Judge of the Madras High Court, have been secured to fill the office of Chief Judge of our Chief Court, rendered vacant by the death of Rao Bahadur Mr. P. S. Krishna Rao.

The proposals for improving the strength and prospects of the staff of the Police Department, outlined in my Address last year, have been given effect to and the total strength of the permanent force as improved was 862 officers and 5,161 men on the 30th June 1914. The jurisdiction over the Kolar Gold Fields Railway has been temporarily restored to the State and the necessary Police staff entertained for one year.

The discipline and efficiency of the Military Department were maintained at the usual high level and the health of the troops was good.

In my Address last year, I informed you that it was under contemplation to improve the pay and prospects of the Barr forces. A scheme involving an additional expenditure of Rs. 26,000 a year was recently sanctioned and is being given effect to.

Address to Dasara Representative Assembly.

I stated in my Address last year that a Committee had been appointed in July 1913 to enquire into certain complaints about the purity of the vaccine lymph used in the State. The Committee, after careful investigation, came to the conclusion that the Mysore lymph was free from harmful impurities and that, in point of potency, it compared very favourably with lymph manufactured elsewhere in India. They, however, considered that it was desirable to further reduce the extraneous, though harmless, organisms contained in the lymph and have made certain recommendations which have met with the approval of Government.

The Maternity Hospital at Robertsonpet will be shortly opened. The quarters for the staff have not yet been built, but the hospital work will be carried on by securing temporary accommodation for the present.

The Malnad Improvement Scheme, undertaken during the year for the sanitary and economic improvement of the *malnad*, will be referred to at a later stage of this Address.

The several committees of the Economic Conference and the departments connected with them were strengthened during the past official year, and special efforts were made to systematize the work of the Conference and make it more practical. At the commencement of the year, the constitution of the Conference and its Committees was modified slightly and their functions defined more clearly. As announced in my Address last October, 16 seats on the Conference were thrown open for election, 8 by the members of this Assembly and 8 by the district electorates, and these elected representatives took part in the session of the Conference in June last. As the Deputy Inspector-General of Education, who was the *ex-officio* Secretary to the Education Committee, had heavy duties to discharge, a whole-time officer has been appointed to look after the work of the Education Committee. The Standing Committee, whose chief function is to co-ordinate the work of the three Central Committees, met on two occasions during the year to consider sêveral important questions. The work of the District Committees has been placed on a more satisfactory basis by the formation of Sub-Committees corresponding to the three Central Committees.

The work of the Conference has developed to a material extent and the progress made will be referred to later on.

The number of public institutions increased from 2,725 to 3,001 or by 276 and their attendance from 131,539 to 158,334, or by 26,795. The number of private institutions also increased from 1,843 to 2,133 and their strength from 24,901 to 29,396. The increase in the number and strength of public institutions was chiefly due to the large number of primary schools for boys and girls opened during the year. The number of industrial and other technical institutions rose from 28 to 35. The total number of public and private institutions was 5,134 with a strength of 187,730 pupils as against 4,568 institutions with a strength of 156,440 pupils in the previous year. The total number of institutions, public and private, thus increased by 566 and their strength by 31,290. Of the total number of pupils, 154,319 were boys and 33,411 were girls, as against 129,009 boys and 27,431 girls in the year 1912-13. The percentage of boys at school to the male population of school-age rose from 29·8 to 35 and that of girls at school to the female population of school-age from 6·4 to 7·7, the percentage of boys and girls under instruction to the total population of school-age being 21·4 as against 18·0 in the previous year.

The Central College at Bangalore was affiliated to the Madras University in the Chemistry Branch of the B.A. Pass course and in the Physics Branch of the Honours course, but the institution of the Honours course in Chemistry had to be postponed for want of an Assistant Professor with European training. An Honours course in History and Economics was opened in the Maharaja's College at Mysore. The institution of these courses rendered some outlay necessary upon equipment and additional staff.

Other improvements were also made in Collegiate education, but the energies of the department were chiefly devoted to the development of elementary education. A special grant of one lakh of rupees was made for the expansion of village schools and a lakh and a half for the construction of school buildings. Sanction was also given to the opening of 1,000 schools under the grant-in-aid rules. The principle is that the villagers should supplement the grant given by Government by contributions in money or kind so that no teacher may have to serve on less than Rs. 10 a month.

A scheme of compulsory education has been sanctioned and will for the present be tried in 15 selected centres. Rules have been framed, funds provided, and all the requisite preliminary arrangements completed.

The expansion of primary and secondary education has created a need for a large supply of trained teachers and for a higher standard of training than has hitherto been available in the State. In order to provide for this, a scheme for re-modelling the Training Schools and increasing their number has been approved. Its principal features are the conversion of the Normal School at Mysore into a Training College by the addition of a training class for graduate teachers, the re-modelling of the Training Schools at Shimoga and Kolar and the immediate opening of a new Training School at Tumkur. The result of these changes will be that 440 teachers will in future be trained every year as against 254 at present.

Address to Dasara Representative Assembly.

The various arrangements for providing technical and commercial education sketched in my Address last year have been given effect to. A Mechanical Engineering School and a Commercial School have been opened in Bangalore and the new Chamarajendra Technical Institute has been formed in Mysore by the amalgamation of two existing institutions. All these institutions are reported to have done excellent work during the year. Arrangements have been made for opening additional sections in the Mechanical Engineering School for training industrial teachers, railway permanent way inspectors, engine drivers and telegraph signallers.

A printing class will be held tentatively for a year in a part of the Government Press building, where instruction will be given in composing, proof reading and printing.

Female education has also continued to advance. The number of public institutions for girls increased to 397 during the year from 360, the number in the previous year. Orders have been passed for the reorganization of the Maharani's College at Mysore and the Girls' Schools in the district headquarters with a view to enlarge their usefulness. A hostel will be attached to the College, and the present Widows' Home in Mysore will be taken over under Government management and will form an *annexe* to the College. The Government Girls' School, Bangalore, and the Empress Girls' School, Tumkur, will be raised to the High School standard by the opening of Kannada Upper Secondary classes. English Lower Secondary classes will be added to these schools as well as to the Aryabalika Patasala and the Chamarajpet Girls' School, Bangalore. Provision for English instruction will be made in the Malleswaram Girls' School, Bangalore, and the Girls' Schools at Kolar, Chikmagalur, Chitaldrug, Shimoga and Hassan. The reorganization provides for instruction in industrial and domestic arts in addition to education of a literary character. An Inspectress of Hindustani Girls' Schools has also been temporarily engaged.

Among other important measures introduced may be mentioned the appointment of a Deputy Inspector-General of Education to be in direct charge of Vernacular education and the revision of the grades of Educational officers and Head Masters and teachers in High and Anglo-Vernacular Schools so as to fix the number of appointments in each grade, to prevent overlapping of scales, to facilitate selection on the ground of merit, to allow interchange between the tutorial and inspecting staff and to make the pay of the teachers in Anglo-Vernacular Schools attractive. The benefits of the State Life Insurance have been thrown open to the teachers of aided institutions on certain conditions.

An Educational Exhibition was held at Mysore during the last Dasara and was largely attended. A similar Exhibition held in the Government High School at Bangalore in the latter part of December was also very popular.

It had been felt for some time past that if the Agricultural Department was to do any effective work in the way of improving the staple industry of the country, a considerable addition to its staff was necessary. The Department was accordingly re-organized during the year and the results are beginning to be apparent. The new arrangements could be brought into effect only four months before the close of the year, but even in this short period, it was found possible to inaugurate a large amount of new work, demonstration in particular, which had hitherto of necessity, been confined to a comparatively few places and which has now been extended to every district in the State.

In my Address last year, I mentioned that an Agricultural School had been opened at Bangalore for giving practical instruction in agriculture. The school has now completed the first year of its existence and has on its rolls 15 new students and 14 in the second year of their studies. A short course, which lasted a week, was held in connection with cultivating operations for the benefit of raiyats and landholders, and was attended by about a hundred of them. In the present year, it is hoped to have a regular series of such short courses, and buildings are being erected for the accommodation of persons coming to attend them.

The rules for regulating the grant of *takavi* loans for industrial purposes referred to in my Address last year, have been amplified so as to provide for the sale of machinery on a hire-purchase system as an alternative to *takavi* loans. *Takavi* and other loans, amounting to nearly one lakh of rupees, were granted during the year.

Twenty-six installations involving an expenditure of Rs. 1,44,000 had been completed and 13 were in hand at the close of the year.

As a result of the successful working of the pumping stations at Harihar and Hansvadi, a number of pumping plants for irrigation are expected to be established shortly on the banks of the Tungabhadra and its two main branches.

Several bulletins were issued during the year embodying the results of departmental enquiries which related, among other subjects, to the sugar industry in Mysore, the use of oil engine and suction gas plants, and the cultivation of sisal-hemp. The statistics of rail-borne trade hitherto received not being quite satisfactory, arrangements have been made with the Madras and Southern Mahratta Railway Company to obtain quarterly statements in detail of the imports and exports carried into and out of the Mysore State by rail.

The Co-operative movement made considerable progress

during the year. It is satisfactory to note that the movement is now extending to the *malnad* districts, where it had hitherto made little headway. While credit societies continue to maintain their popularity and usefulness, other forms of co-operation are coming to be gradually adopted. There are societies undertaking, for instance, the irrigation of land, the purchase of raw materials and the sale of commodities on the co-operative principle.

During the year under review, the number of societies rose from 343 to 530, the membership from 24,538 to 40,479, the working capital from Rs. 12,89,338 to Rs. 21,47,340, the total transactions from Rs. 59,52,081 to Rs. 96,28,523, the profits from Rs. 1,29,981 to Rs. 2,30,224 and the reserve fund from Rs. 30,600 to Rs. 56,240. The Central Bank at Bangalore is in a flourishing condition and has lent a sum of Rs. 2,65,000 to 57 societies. It continues to be the main source of capital to the rural societies. Three of the Unions have supplied capital to the extent of about Rs. 25,000 and one is contemplating to finance its affiliated societies to the extent of Rs. 20,000. As almost all the capital required was thus raised either locally or from the institutions mentioned above, it was not considered necessary to make any grants out of the funds placed at the disposal of the Registrar by the Government and from the Privy Purse of His Highness the Maharaja.

The third Provincial Co-operative Conference was held at Mysore last October and was opened by His Highness the Yuvaraja and presided over by Dewan Bahadur Rajasabhabhushana Mr. K. P. Puttanna Chetty. Smaller and less formal but equally useful conferences were held at ten other places and owed their initiative and success mostly to local effort and organization guided by the Registrar of Co-operative Societies.

Address to Dasara Representative Assembly.

The total expenditure on public works from all sources, including Local Funds, amounted to about Rs. 59¼ lakhs during the year against Rs. 51 lakhs in the preceding year. Of this amount, Rs. 29½ lakhs were spent on irrigation works and Rs. 29¾ lakhs on civil works and military buildings.

The construction of the Cauvery Reservoir at Kannambadi is progressing satisfactorily. The difficult portion of the work in the river-bed and the banks was completed during the year and the masonry rose to a height of 44 feet above the bed on the south bank and to 36 feet on the north bank. Water is now stored to a height of 8 feet at the gap in the centre of the dam. Arrangements are being made for the construction of turbine sluices in the dam with a view to instal a power station at the reservoir itself, from which energy may be supplied to the Belagola Pumping Station, Mysore, and other places in that neighbourhood.

In order to provide the owners of submerged wet lands with lands in exchange, Government have, besides adopting other necessary measures, sanctioned the execution of four channel projects, two of which have already been put in hand and the remaining two will be started during the course of this year.

A scheme has also been devised for the expansion of irrigation generally under the reservoir and for affording facilities for growing high-rated crops like sugar-cane, turmeric, mulberry, etc.

With a view to develop irrigation on a scientific basis, the formation of a new Irrigation Division has been sanctioned tentatively for three years, at an annual outlay of Rs. 30,000. The work assigned to the Division was explained in the last year's Address.

The Block System of Irrigation under the Marikanave Reservoir, which was brought into force from the 1st July

1913, is being carefully worked. The colonisation of the canal area and the improvement of sanitation and means of communication of the canal villages are receiving attention.

Panchayets have been constituted for 25 villages under the Tank Panchayet Regulation.

The fourth installation of the Cauvery Hydro-Electric Power Scheme had well advanced by the close of the year and is expected to be completed before July 1915. Reduced rates for electric power were introduced during the year with a view to encouraging its use for domestic and industrial purposes. The estimates framed for the scheme of Electric Tramways for Bangalore required revision, and the new works had to be held in abeyance. The work will be resumed as soon as an understanding is reached with the Civil and Military Station as regards their share of the estimate.

Up to 1900, the total length of railway lines open in the State was 410 miles and the capital outlay Rs. 223 lakhs. The length remained stationary till 1911.

The programme of Railway development sanctioned in Government Proceedings No. 224-30—Ry. F. 124-11-12, dated the 13th November 1911, provided for an addition of 259½ miles to the existing length at an aggregate outlay of Rs. 130 lakhs.

A State Railway Department was organised in 1912. Surveys and preliminary investigations in connection with the lines in the approved programme were vigorously prosecuted. The selection of the necessary staff, the investigation of the several alternative lines for some of the suggested projects and the necessity of submitting the final project estimates for the approval of the Railway Board naturally took up considerable time. Regular construction operations could not be started for a year or more from the date of organization of the department.

Estimates amounting to Rs. 110 lakhs for opening out

259 miles of different gauges have been brought on the sanctioned list. A project for a line from Bangalore to Hosur, estimated to cost Rs. 12·72 lakhs for 30·69 miles, is pending with the Railway Board. Projects for another 146 miles, estimated to cost Rs. 94 lakhs, are ready and are awaiting the settlement of the question of ways and means and conditions of construction and working. Arrangements are in progress for undertaking surveys for the Shimoga feeder railways and tramways to Hebbe and Kakankote.

Negotiations are in progress regarding three more lines intended to connect our system of railways with important places in the surrounding districts of British India, *viz.*, a line from Nanjangud to Erode, another from Hassan to Mangalore and a third from Mysore to the Coorg frontier ending for the present at Virarajendrapet along the left bank of the Cauvery. His Highness' Government attach much importance to the early construction of all these lines and particularly of the first named link.

The work on the Mysore-Arsikere Railway was commenced during November 1913 and is being pushed on vigorously. The section of the Tarikere-Yedahalli Tramway between Tarikere and Lakvalli has been opened for traffic, but work on the section beyond Lakvalli is delayed owing to the prevalence of plague in that locality. The works required in connection with the Bangalore-Chikballapur Light Railway between Bangalore and Yelahanka, have to be carried out by the Madras and Southern Mahratta Railway Company and estimates are under preparation. The section between Yelahanka and Devanhalli has just been opened for goods traffic. The rest of the work may be completed by the end of December 1914. Sanction of the Government of India was received very recently to the Kolar-Chikballapur Railway project and arrangements are being made to start work on that line. The project for the Chikjajur-Chitaldrug Railway has also been sanctioned by the Government of India and the question of financing the same as well as the Kadur-Chikmagalur and Chikmagalur-Hassan lines is under consideration.

Arrangements are being made to have properly equipped Loco, Traffic, Ways and Works Departments for working the State lines.

Further capital outlay is being incurred on the State open lines worked by the Madras and Southern Mahratta Railway Company, the total outlay to the end of 1913-14 being Rs. 2,56,00,000. Till the year 1907-08, the net earnings to the State from these lines were insufficient to meet interest charges, and the net result of working up to that year was a deficit of about Rs. 65 lakhs. Since 1907-08, however, the earnings have improved and the deficit has been reduced to about Rs. 50 lakhs.

Coming to the Department of Mines and Geology, the output of gold during 1913-14 was 559,640 ounces of an approximate value of Rs. 3,22,83,047 which shows a decrease of Rs. 95,897, compared with 561,270 ounces of the value of Rs. 3,23,78,944 in 1912-13. The total royalty realised was approximately Rs. 18,91,486 against Rs. 18,99,971 in 1912-13.

The shortage of water in the Cauvery during the months of May and June necessitated a serious reduction in the power supply to the Field, which retarded development work, but did not materially affect the output of gold. The outlook of the Field remains very much the same as during the previous year. The work undertaken last year at the Woolagiri Mine in the Mysore District was brought to a close in August 1913 as the developments were not promising. Work at the Siddarahalli Mine in the Kadur District has been suspended for want of funds.

In accordance with the decision of Government arrived

Address to Dasara Representative Assembly.

at last year, steps have been taken for the preparation and publication of a Geological Map of Mysore showing the general results of survey work. Separate maps on a larger scale and with detailed information will also be published for the more important areas likely to contain mineral deposits.

This is one of the important departments of Government which require reorganization and proposals to that end are under consideration.

The receipts under Municipal funds during the year amounted to about Rs. 10,97,000 and the expenditure to about Rs. 10,01,000, of which a sum of Rs. 2,87,000 was spent on Public Works, Rs. 2,31,000 on conservancy and the balance under other heads.

The question of financing the water-supply scheme of Davangere town, which is estimated to cost over 2 lakhs of rupees, was satisfactorily settled during the year, and Government have sanctioned a contribution of Rs. 30,000 towards the project and undertaken to execute the work without making any charge on account of establishment or tools and plant. Government have also sanctioned the grant of one-half of the cost of installing Jewell Filters for the Chitaldrug water-supply, and of carrying out certain improvements urgently required for the Kolar and Shimoga water works. A scheme of water-supply for the town of Dodballapur is under consideration, and it is noteworthy that the townspeople of that place have come forward with offers of subscriptions to the extent of Rs. 18,000 towards the cost of the project, of which a sum of Rs. 11,000 has been actually paid.

The construction of the underground sewerage and outfall works in Mysore was continued during the year. Sixty-nine properties were acquired at a cost of Rs. 50,677 and the total expenditure incurred by the Mysore City Improvement Trust Board amounted to Rs. 2,93,000.

Address to Dasara Representative Assembly.

In order to investigate the needs of the Bangalore City in the direction of improvements and future expansion, a Committee consisting of Engineer and other officers and leading non-official gentlemen has been appointed with Rajasabhabhushana Dewan Bahadur Mr. K. P. Puttanna Chetty as Chairman. The Committee met several times and have submitted a rough scheme of improvements to be carried out in the next three years. For preliminary operations in this connection, Government have placed a grant of Rs. 20,000 at the disposal of the Committee.

The receipts under the head of Local Funds General amounted to Rs. 2,23,000, and including the opening balance of Rs. 2,56,901 the total income was Rs. 4,79,901. The expenditure amounted to Rs. 1,70,700 and the year thus closed with a balance of Rs. 3,09,201.

The income under all heads of District Funds during the year 1913-14 was approximately Rs. 9,28,387 which, together with the opening balance of Rs. 6,56,497, amounted to Rs. 15,84,884. The total expenditure was nearly Rs.11,42,674, thus leaving a balance of Rs. 4,42,210 at the close of the year. A sum of Rs. 4,77,750 was spent on Public Works, Rs. 2,60,924 on Public Health, Safety and Convenience, and Rs. 3,02,603 on Railway construction. All the Local Boards in the Shimoga District were reconstituted during the year, and the Local Boards Regulation, II of 1902, was amended so as to empower the District Boards to levy a Railway Cess with the approval of Government.

A Committee consisting of Dewan Bahadur Mr. C. Srikantesvara Aiyar, Inspector-General of Police, and Mr. G. Aravamudu Iyengar, Muzrai Superintendent, was appointed to investigate the working of the Muzrai Department and report upon the various reforms and improvements needed in the administration of the Muzrai institutions. The Committee have sent up a detailed report on the several points referred to them for investigation. The report is now under the consideration of Government.

The new Muzrai Regulation came into operation from 1st January 1914.

The outturn of work in the Government Central Press was slightly less than in the previous year and the expenditure for the year amounted to Rs. 1,05,485 against Rs. 1,06,266 in the year previous. The reduction of output and expenditure was due to the transfer of a portion of the work to the Branch Press at Mysore and to the fact that on the whole a less quantity of printing was called for from the several departments and some printing was also done in private presses. The question of further reducing, if possible, the work done in the Government Press, is engaging attention.

The number of books and periodicals registered during the year was 117 as against 128 in the previous year.

The Government Gardens were satisfactorily maintained throughout the year and improvements effected to most of them.

Arrangements have been made for revising the *Mysore Gazetteer*, prepared by Mr. Rice, with a view to bringing it up to date. Praktanavimarsa Vichakshana Mr. R. A. Narasimhachar has been entrusted with this work in addition to his other duties as Officer in charge of the Archæological Researches. A definite programme of work for this department for the next three years is under the consideration of Government.

Having dealt with the chief events of the administration during the year, it may not be out of place to recapitulate some of the larger measures undertaken in the State for developing its economic resources.

Seven projects of this description seem to deserve notice,

Address to Dasara Representative Assembly.

all of which, save one, are making rapid progress. These are :—

(1) Construction and working of railways,
(2) Construction of a reservoir on the Cauvery river at Kannambadi,
(3) Further development of the Cauvery Power Scheme,
(4) Construction and repair of minor tanks,
(5) Malnad Improvement Scheme,
(6) Village Improvement Scheme, and
(7) Operations of the Economic Conference.

You may be aware that, between 1900 and 1911, that is, for nearly 12 years, there was a complete stoppage of railway activity in the State and the railway mileage in Mysore, compared to the population, fell short of that in British India. Since 1911, a persistent effort has been made to develop railway construction and as a result we have work going on, at present, on about 130 miles of railway.

The Kolar-Bowringpet Railway, the first new line completed since railway construction was resumed, was opened by His Highness the Maharaja in December last.

It is gratifying to note that the people in the districts are beginning to invest money in railway enterprises.

We want a length of about 1,000 miles of railway for adequately opening out our districts and to give an impetus to the agricultural and commercial prosperity of the State. The Railway service, when the lines are in operation, is also intended to provide profitable employment to the people of the State. The outlay already incurred is Rs. 256 lakhs and the programme of 1,000 miles when completed will bring the total expenditure to about 500 lakhs.

The question of utilizing the surplus waters of the Cauvery river within the Mysore State has formed the subject of a somewhat protracted controversy between this State and the neighbouring Presidency of Madras for the past three or four years, and last year the Government of India decided to refer the matter to a strong Committee of Arbitration for enquiry. The Committee conducted their investigations for nearly ten months and, in May last, submitted their award to the Government of India. His Highness' Government and the very large population interested in the development of the Cauvery valley within our State are confident of the justice of their claims and they anxiously await the decision of the Government of India on this momentous issue.

The Kannambadi Reservoir Project has for its object the storage of the surplus waters of the Cauvery river,—surplus which normally runs to waste into the sea. The present supply of the river channels is precarious. With an assured supply from the reservoir, the way will be paved for the cultivation of high class perennial crops not hitherto grown in that valley. Arrangements are being made to cultivate, with the aid of the storage, about 10,000 acres of sugar-cane under the existing and new channels.

A scheme for re-settling the population which will be drowned out by the new reservoir is being successfully dealt with by our officers.

The construction of the reservoir will enable Government to protect the power supply, which at present is somewhat precarious during the hot weather months, and to increase the same from about 11,000 H.P. to about 18,000 H.P. It is expected that the necessary works will be completed before July next, and if there is sufficient demand for additional power thereafter, further developments will follow.

It will be one of the duties of the Electrical Department to develop permanent markets for our power supply by extending its use for industrial purposes in the cities of Bangalore and Mysore.

The question of minor tanks has engaged our active attention during the year. Government have strengthened the Maramat establishment required in the districts at an additional cost of Rs. 42,312 and the grant for the restoration of minor tanks now stands at Rs. 2,00,000. Government are prepared to further increase the grant, if necessary.

A scheme is under consideration to encourage the people of the village or villages interested in a tank to carry out the work of restoration or repairs by their own efforts with aid from Government, in the shape of grants, remissions of assessment or other concessions. This is one of the measures in which the people's co-operation with Government in the years to come will be attended with the most beneficial results.

I stated last year that His Highness' Government intended to take active measures for the re-population, and the sanitary and economic improvement of the *malnad* portions of the three districts, namely, Shimoga, Kadur and Hassan. A scheme drawn up for the purpose was brought into operation in February last. To give an opportunity to the leading people of the districts to participate in the work, non-officials have been associated with the officials and local committees have been appointed, one for each district, as well as a central committee to control the operations, and they are provided with funds and an adequate staff. The measures in progress during the few months in which the scheme was in operation during the year comprise—removing rank vegetation, improving the supply of drinking water, shifting insanitary villages, popularising the use of quinine, spreading the benefits of vaccination and imparting to the people a knowledge of the rules of personal and domestic hygiene. A malarial survey with laboratory investigation has been commenced in order to identify the species of mosquito responsible for the spread of the disease. An experienced officer of the Medical Department was placed on special duty for a short time to formulate the lines of such a survey and investigation and to suggest improvements in the registration of vital statistics. Arrangements are in progress for increasing the number of vaccinators, midwives and compounders, and the question of providing additional dispensaries both of the stationary and travelling types and the necessary maternity hospitals is under active consideration.

Attempts are also being made to attract settlers to the *malnad*. Government have recognised that the problem of the *malnad* is partly economic in character and in this view have sanctioned measures for encouraging education, for multiplying occupations by developing local industries chiefly connected with forest produce, for opening up the country by increasing communications and for promoting co-operative enterprise.

Numerous details have yet to be perfected. Until the people are awakened to a sense of their own responsibility, progress will largely depend on the activity and enthusiasm which the Government officers entrusted with the operations may bring to bear on this work.

The Village Improvement Scheme, which I foreshadowed in my Address last year, was put in hand in the latter part of the year and it has made satisfactory progress in the few months it has been in operation. The following figures, taken from the most recent report, will indicate the results attained :—

Number of villages for which Committees have been formed out of a total number of 16,740 in the State	11,923
Number of Village Committees started ...	7,440

Address to Dasara Representative Assembly.

Number of villages in which people have agreed to devote half a day's labour once a week for communal benefit ...	6,126
Number of villages (in five districts) which have started libraries or subscribed for newspapers	55

Considering that the seasonal conditions last year were somewhat unfavourable and the outlook in the current year up to the present has not been very satisfactory, the extent of popular support given to the scheme is extremely gratifying.

Under the sanctioned scheme, the Government contribution towards the cost of works started by the Village Improvement Committees was fixed at one-third of the total cost: but in view of the attendant difficulties in carrying out the scheme in its initial stages, the Government contribution was increased to one-half for the year under review as well as for the current year.

The Village Improvement Committees undertook, during the period, work of permanent utility involving an estimated outlay of Rs. 1,25,000, of which the Government share amounted to Rs. 59,000. The balance of Rs. 66,000 was contributed by the villagers concerned either in cash or labour.

The Revenue Commissioner states that signs are not wanting to indicate the popularity of the scheme. It owes its rapid introduction to the enthusiasm and interest taken by our District Revenue officers. If wisely directed, its operations should be the means of spreading enlightenment among the people and stimulating co-operative action for improving the prosperity and conveniences of our villages. Nature has so liberally endowed our country with beautiful scenery and natural facilities of every kind that if only the people made the attempt, many a village might be transformed from a congregation of irregularly disposed huts—separated by ill-kept and insanitary spaces—into well-ordered, cleanly and attractive places of human abode.

The changes in the constitution and functions of the Economic Conference have been dealt with already.

The object of the Conference is, as you are aware, to improve education and develop agriculture and industries and commerce. On account of the low level of activity and achievement in this respect in the past, it is the prime duty of the State and the leaders of the people to help to guide the public to improve their economic condition. His Highness' Government spend about 2¼ lakhs a year at present, or less than 1 per cent of our revenues for the purpose of spreading sound ideas and preparing the people to participate in economic progress. Government are prepared to spend up to Rs. 3 lakhs per annum, if necessary, for a period of five years.

The work of the Conference is mainly carried on by the three Central Committees and the District Committees. These Committees have been investigating a large number of subjects of economic interest, which are in various stages of progress. Much spade work has been done in collecting useful information which is a necessary preliminary to the preparation of practical schemes. Some of the recommendations made by the committees have been sanctioned by Government and several others are under their consideration.

Amidst much generous enthusiasm, there have not been wanting criticisms of some of the measures in progress. Government are doing what they consider to be demanded in the true interests of the country and likely to satisfy the best informed opinion on each subject. If, in respect of any of these measures, at least half a dozen members of this Assembly meet and formulate their difficulties and objections, and ask for information, every endeavour will be made to meet their wishes. If alternative proposals of a constructive character are put forward, Government will not be slow to give the suggestions their best consideration.

Chief among the subjects dealt with by the Education Committee were the establishment of Public Libraries in Bangalore and Mysore, the improvement of Industrial Schools, the organization of physical education, the employment of itinerant teachers and lecturers, etc., the education of adults and the encouragement of literature in Kannada to make it a suitable vehicle for the spread of general and scientific knowledge among the masses of the population.

The Agricultural Committee took up during the year the question of the improvement of sericulture. This industry provides profitable occupation to people in 22 taluks of the State. The services of Signor Washington Mari, an experienced Italian expert, were secured for a year and a Central Sericultural Farm was opened at Channapatna, where he conducted several trials and experiments. In the first six months of this year, 51,000 cocoons of several varieties were raised and about half the number were sold to the raiyats. The experiments carried out in rearing the Mysore, Bengal and Italian worms and cross-breeds have yielded useful indications as to the directions in which the future development of the industry may be attempted.

A scheme is in preparation to build, in different localities, model rearing houses which will also serve as small seed stations for the present. A number of students have been trained in improved methods of sericulture and the staff of Assistant Inspectors has been increased in number and posted to several of the sericultural taluks. Steps have been taken to introduce sericulture into parts of the State where it was not in existence before.

A Silk Association has been formed at Channapatna,

consisting of people connected with all branches of the silk industry, with a view to spread knowledge of the new methods among the rural population. The Association is yet young but I hope that it will soon become a useful medium for bringing the people under the influence of our expert agency.

Considerable attention has been paid to horticulture and a survey of fruit areas has been undertaken to ascertain the possibilities of fruit culture in the State.

The feasibility of dairy farming has been investigated and encouragement is being given for the development of the industry by private enterprise.

The Committee has issued a number of bulletins containing useful information, both in English and Kannada, and has tried to reach a large circle of readers interested in scientific methods of agriculture.

The Industries and Commerce Committee considered the question of starting various industries, such as wood distillation, manufacture of cotton seed oil, pharmaceutical preparations, cultivation of sisal-hemp, cocoanut fibre, glass, matches, etc. Some of the enquiries have assumed a practical shape. The opening of a factory for the manufacture of pencils and the possibility of starting tile factories on a large scale in the Mysore District and the *malnad*, are under investigation by experts. An Industrial Depôt for the exhibition and sale of articles of local manufacture has been opened in Bangalore and is reported to be working satisfactorily.

The results of the investigation into the industrial condition of Mysore by Mr. V. S. Sambasiva Iyer, who was deputed for the purpose, have recently been published. His report brings together a large mass of information connected with the economic development of the country and also contains various useful suggestions for improving existing industries and starting new ones.

Address to Dasara Representative Assembly.

One of the important advances made in the direction of commercial development is the starting of the Bank of Mysore, which commenced work in October 1913. Through its instrumentality, a sum of about Rs. 30 lakhs is under circulation and very satisfactory banking facilities have been provided by the agencies established in various parts of the State.

The District Committees have also drawn up definite programmes of work and are engaged in investigating several questions of economic interest with special reference to the local areas concerned.

As the work connected with the Economic Conference has expanded, District Officers are finding it difficult to devote adequate attention to it without special assistance. Government have, therefore, recently sanctioned the appointment of a Superintendent or Organiser for each district, whose duty it will be to help the Deputy Commissioner and the District Committee in spreading information, stimulating local enterprise and helping people in organizing practical schemes with the co-operation of experts employed in the several departments. The Superintendents will be in touch with the various authorities concerned and will serve as a medium for co-ordinating the activities of the Central and District Committees.

Forty-seven Taluk Progress Committees have been formed to develop economic work in the taluks and it is expected that, in the course of the next few months, similar committees will be formed in all the remaining taluks.

It has been decided to issue at an early date a monthly journal in connection with the work of the Economic Conference, in English and Kannada, which will serve to bring into closer touch all persons interested and all agencies engaged in the work of the economic progress of the State.

In another place of this Address, I have referred to the

formation of Village Improvement Committees. It is the hope of Government that all these organizations, beginning from the central body and spreading among a large number of towns and villages, will work in unison and form the necessary agency for developing economic schemes, for ascertaining important local wants, for spreading information among a large portion of the people of the State and for organizing and directing into profitable channels whatever intelligence, energy, capital or enterprise may be available in the country.

I will next say a few words about measures taken for improving the working of the administrative machinery.

In last year's address, I mentioned that the question of improving the efficiency of the several branches of the public service had been receiving the special attention of Government and that it was proposed to introduce a system of administrative scrutiny and check described as "efficiency audit."

The system has been in full working order for the past two or three months. The establishment employed is temporary and consists of a Gazetted officer and a few clerks who form a branch of the General and Revenue Secretariat.

The officer is engaged in examining the standing orders and office manuals with a view to promote system and regularity in the transaction of public business and co-ordination of work between the various departments. He will help in the reorganization of Government departments which may require attention, in the inspection of individual offices when necessary and in taking stock of progress made on the special programmes laid down from time to time.

The system of Local Self-Government in the State dealing with the functions and responsibilities of Local

Boards and Municipalities is undergoing a thorough investigation. A committee of Government officers and non-official gentlemen, with Mr. M. Kantaraj Urs, C.S.I., Second Member of Council, as Chairman, which has been considering the subject for some time past, has just concluded its deliberations.

In every department of Government and public work, a large number of new questions arise from time to time requiring study and investigation and the Departmental heads often find themselves unable to give continuous attention to them. A list of subjects connected with the organization and development of the department is maintained, and a few selected subjects are taken up from time to time for investigation and report, with the help of Government officers and, when necessary, also of non-official gentlemen who may be interested in, or who may have made a special study of, the subjects. Several subjects have been dealt with in this way, and our sincere thanks are due to the gentlemen who have co-operated with Government and given their services for the work.

A stricter system of recruitment, based mainly on merit and capacity, should be introduced in all branches of the service after making reasonable allowance for the claims of special classes of tax-payers hitherto imperfectly represented in the public service. There is no reason why we should be content with men of ordinary calibre when we can get the pick of the talent available in the country for the same salaries.

The selection for promotion should be based on approved service and merit and for this purpose, correct records of conduct and qualifications should be maintained in greater detail than at present. If we are to encourage officers who are self-reliant and resourceful, it will be necessary to give special promotions to men of outstanding capacity and worth.

Address to Dasara Representative Assembly.

Government propose to issue shortly suitable rules to regulate the conduct and responsibility of officers of the various services of the State.

A new departure, during the year, was the tours of inspection undertaken by Members of Government under a revised system, resulting in a considerable amount of inspection work done by them. Out of a total of 68 taluks and 9 sub-taluks in the State, the two Members and myself have, between us, inspected 52 taluks and 5 sub-taluks. These inspections will be continued in the coming year also, and an endeavour will be made to sec that they lead to permanent results, and that the more important wants and grievances in each taluk are catalogued and constantly kept in view, both by the official and non-official classes, till the wants are supplied and the grievances redressed.

At present, there is a lack of information regarding essential facts pertaining to the administration in general and to the resources and needs of the people in particular in each district, city and important town. A beginning has been made to supply these wants by the preparation of hand-books for districts and guide-books for the municipal towns. Mr. K. R. Srinivasiengar, M.A., till recently Secretary to Government in the General and Revenue Departments, has been entrusted with the preparation of a statistical atlas and abstract. He is also compiling the district hand-books with the aid of the Deputy Commissioners of the districts concerned.

Mr. K. P. Puttanna Chetty, President of the Bangalore City Municipality, has issued a useful and neatly got-up hand-book for the Bangalore City, and the Municipal Councils of a few other towns have undertaken to publish smaller guide-books.

A hand-book for the Tumkur District has been published by Mr. B. J. Kumaraswamy Naik, Deputy

Commissioner, and another for the Kolar District, prepared by Mr. B. Ramaswamayya, is in the press.

The preparation of a Manual for regulating the work of the Taluk offices and defining the duties and responsibilities of the Taluk officials has been taken in hand. Mr. K. Srinivasa Rao, retired Deputy Commissioner, who has had considerable experience as a Revenue officer, has set an example of public spirit by undertaking to do the work in an honorary capacity. He has also completed the compilation of a Village Manual. A District Office Manual will be compiled for the guidance of officials as soon as the Taluk and Village Manuals are printed and issued.

I will now conclude with a few general observations on the present situation in Mysore and our hopes and fears for the future, from the standpoint of the prosperity of His Highness' subjects.

I have referred to the short rainfall and scarcity of food and fodder both last year and now. Bad seasons are increasingly frequent in this State. The methods of cultivation are primitive in large areas of the country and the application of science to farming is little known. Even in good seasons, the ordinary agriculturist goes without sufficient occupation for four to six months in the year. Many artisan and professional classes have had to abandon their special avocations through stress of competition and fall back on agriculture. The village tanks are getting silted and shallow, and they usually dry up a few months after the monsoon is over, with the result that scarcity of water for men and cattle is of common occurrence in the rural areas.

Our agricultural population is very ignorant. The power of initiative, co-operation and organised activity for public or private enterprises, which is so sedulously fostered in other countries, is utterly lacking in this State.

In my Address of last year, I devoted a section to the subject of the efficiency of the people. I have already explained what Government have done or are doing in order to develop the economic resources of the State and to improve the machinery of the Administration. As regards the improvement of the people, Government are doing all they can, by liberal expenditure on education and in other ways, to encourage industrial and commercial enterprise among the people.

In this connection, I believe it is permissible to ask—What are the people doing to help themselves? To what extent will they exert themselves for a more active participation in the civic and industrial life of the country? These questions will be repeated with growing persistency in the coming years and you must see to it that your response is hearty and increasingly unanimous.

The spirit of enquiry should be cultivated by our people and they should study what science has done for promoting human enterprise in foreign lands and practise the lessons deduced from such comparison.

Changes are going on unnoticed in the practical life of the people and many good and useful habits and practices of the past are disappearing. It behoves us to single out the more useful methods and practices, both our own and those of foreign countries at the present time, and familiarise the public with them, till they come to be accepted as standards in the daily life of our people.

Proposals are being discussed with a view to encourage the people to keep under study and observation every important activity in the country—municipal, economic, social and moral—with a view to the constant improvement of the standards of work and living of the persons engaged in them.

Address to Dasara Representative Assembly.

The object aimed at is to appoint some person or persons to be responsible for every profession or activity as practised in each city, town and village; to collect funds and stimulate work with a view gradually to improve the material and moral condition of the people in every profession and grade of society.

A beginning in this direction is being made in Bangalore under the leadership of our esteemed countryman, Dewan Bahadur Rajasabhabhushana Mr. K. P. Puttanna Chetty and, if voluntary effort is forthcoming, there is no reason why the City of Mysore should not follow the example of Bangalore and why other smaller towns should not take up this good work in their turn.

Government recognise that it is a part of their duty to help the people to improve their condition and equip them for the struggle for existence. The time has gone by when Government officers could afford to be content with collecting taxes, maintaining order and dispensing justice.

I am told on the authority of competent observers that there is a distinct improvement in the civic life of Bangalore City, and that Municipal Councillors and leading private gentlemen are giving their time and work ungrudgingly to municipal affairs and questions of public interest.

There are evidences of public spirit and increasing harmony between Government officers and the people in the districts, and I can speak from personal knowledge that our village population are making large sacrifices for promoting education.

When I outlined the Village Improvement Scheme in my address last year, some sixty members from your body offered help and co-operation to inaugurate that movement. I now see that that help has been given without stint. If in respect of all new undertakings, officials and non-officials are animated by the same ideals and work in unison, the beneficial results will be very marked. I earnestly hope that, in the coming year, our officers may look forward to increasing co-operation from you and from the general public whom you represent.

The recent growth of communications has been bringing us closer to the populations of the world. It is an advantage to come into closer contact with people more civilised than ourselves, if we can profit by their example. But we must recognise that this close association has also brought us increased responsibilities. It has brought us into the vortex of the struggle for existence and the first warning we have received is a rise in prices. Where formerly the economic effects of local enterprises were determined by local conditions, we are now called upon, without adequate training or skill and with our primitive implements, to take our place in international competition. In the face of the increasing severity of the struggle, our spirit of content, our indifference to science and material progress are a growing peril. Hard times will be coming if we are not more adaptive, and it is our duty to see that the awakening did not come too late.

REPLY TO DASARA ADDRESSES.

[At the thirty-first session of the Dasara Representative Assembly, held at the Public Offices, Mysore, on 30th September 1914, Dewan Sir M. Visvesvaraya received addresses from the representatives of the Kolar Gold Fields Mining Board, the South Mysore Planters' Association, the Central Mahomedan Association, the Vokkaligara Sangha, the Nanjangud Municipal Council, the Kadur District Board, and the Representative Assembly. 30th Sept. 1914.

Reply to Dasara Addresses.

Sir M. Visvesvaraya replied to these addresses collectively as follows:—]

Gentlemen,—On behalf of His Highness' Government, it gives me great pleasure to receive the several addresses you have just presented. As some of them were handed in only within the last twenty-four hours, I am sure you will not expect me to do more than give a collective reply.

In one of the addresses, you have stated that many an important event has occurred during the year. That is true, but as most of these have been referred to in the address just delivered, you will agree that further reference to the same would be superfluous.

I have already alluded to the war. I have no doubt it will be extremely gratifying to His Highness to learn that the payment of a war contribution is received with such magnificent enthusiasm by the leading representative bodies of the State. Having done what little we could, we can only hope and pray that the war may come to a speedy and successful termination in the true interests of humanity and of international law and order.

You have raised several questions and referred to various Government measures, to many of them with approval, to some with misgivings. The constant aim of His Highness' Government is to further the best interests of all communities in an impartial spirit and to raise the standards of work and earning power of the members of every community, so that, as far as possible, their normal prosperity may be independent of the ordinary vicissitudes of the seasons.

As regards reforms in the Legislative Council, certain privileges were given to you by His Highness last year, because he judged that the time had arrived for a forward move, and I have no doubt that any further reforms needed to improve the usefulness of the Representative Assembly will come in good time. I shall gladly submit all your representations in this matter for His Highness' gracious consideration.

With reference to the Cauvery Reservoir project, it is gratifying to find that the suspense in which we have remained for the past three years is about to end. In this connection, I have reason to commend the patience and good sense of our people in refraining from embarrassing Government by making frequent representations while the enquiry was in progress.

I have already referred at some length to the railway policy of Government and the questions concerning new lines which are engaging our attention. The two important lines we require at present are the through route to Erode and the Hassan-Mangalore Railway, or any alternative line to connect Mysore with the west coast. It does seem rather anomalous that, while the flow of our trade is mainly towards the west, we should have direct railway connection only with the east coast. These questions are under correspondence with the Government of India.

The suggestion by the representative of the Nanjangud Municipality that a Municipal Conference may be held periodically to discuss matters of municipal interest appears to me to be a very wise one, particularly when we are endeavouring in so many ways to develop "town planning." We must look to the public spirit of the members of the various Municipal Councils of the State to take the initiative in this respect.

Government regret that the supply of electric power ran short at the Kolar Gold Field during the hot weather months on account of natural causes; but I am sure that the Mining Board will be the first to acknowledge that His Highness' Government have done everything in their power to minimise inconvenience and loss. Government are glad that the transfer of the police jurisdiction on the Kolar Gold Field Railway is much appreciated by the Mining Board, and they hope that the Maternity Hospital at the Field will be opened without further delay.

As regards the roads, the Public Works Department has been handicapped by the fitful rainfall both last year and this season; but efforts are being made to maintain every road in as efficient a condition as its importance demands. The question of the introduction of the Pest Act raised by the representative of the South Mysore Planters' Association is under investigation. The representations of the Mahomedan community as regards their education will receive our earnest attention.

Regarding the Malnad Improvement Scheme and the analogy of Italy referred to in the address from the Kadur District, I may mention that the scientific investigation of the problem is not lost sight of. As I was once a sanitary officer myself and have had the advantage of visiting the interior of Italy, with the special object of studying the attempts there made to combat malaria, you may rest assured that the experience of that country is not being overlooked.

The address of the members of the Representative Assembly, which was last read, deals with the larger questions of policy and progressive measures needed in our State and I may say at once that Government are in general sympathy with the representations therein made.

It will give me very great pleasure to submit to His Highness the Maharaja the sentiments of deep attachment to His Highness' Throne and person conveyed in the addresses. We, who work daily with His Highness, know how constantly your interests, your progress, your prosperity are in his thoughts. I note with great pleasure the reference you have made to the enlightened interest which His Highness the Yuvaraja is taking in public affairs and the practical sympathy he is showing for the well-being of the country in so many directions.

It only remains for me, on behalf of my colleagues and myself, to return our sincere acknowledgments for the appreciative manner in which you have spoken of the year's administration. And, Gentlemen, I also thank you for the many kind things you have said about me.

SPEECH AT THE DASARA REPRESENTATIVE ASSEMBLY.

[The thirty-first session of the Dasara Representative Assembly came to a close on Wednesday, the 7th October 1914. In bringing to a close the proceedings of the session, Dewan Sir M. Visvesvaraya made the following speech:—] 7th Oct. 1914.

Gentlemen,—It will give me great pleasure to convey to His Highness the Maharaja the sentiments of devotion and loyalty to which you have given such eloquent expression. It will give me no less pleasure to convey your loyal greetings to His Highness the Yuvaraja. I thank you also for the kind words of appreciation with which you have spoken of the administration, but you must allow me to add that the Members of Council, Heads of Departments and the Deputy Commissioners, are sharers in the fullest measure of any credit that may be due for good work done during the year.

We have had a full week's session including the opening day. Many important subjects have been discussed and much valuable information has been placed before Government. I have no doubt we will all carry with us pleasant memories of the session, but I earnestly hope you will forget the frequent appeals I had to make to you in order to curtail the discussions. As I was anxious that no subjects should be passed over, either on account of the absence of the proposer or other causes, I have had to observe a time limit in regard to individual subjects. Had I not done so, perhaps, we might have lost much valuable time in unimportant discussions and been compelled in the end to hurry through or abandon a large number of subjects.

Chief among the important subjects brought up for discussion was the modification of the Press Act. I believe you are as well aware as I am that the present is not an opportune moment to take up such a question.

The suggested further reforms in the Representative Assembly have already been referred to in my reply to the addresses. There are now three Assemblies in the country on which elected representatives of the people have found seats and at which you could press your wants. If you continue to use your existing privileges for the permanent good of the State, I have no doubt all needful privileges will come to you in good time.

Turning to the subject of survey settlement in alienated villages, I may remark that, if two-thirds or three-fourths of the number of *Vrittidars* consent, it may be possible to introduce the survey settlement compulsorily. I have already, on behalf of His Highness' Government, promised the appointment of a committee of enquiry on which persons qualified to represent both the *inamdars* and their tenants might be represented.

The member from Tiptur asked for the formation of a Chamber of Commerce. I agree that such an institution is very much needed in the country. It is, however, a matter in which the initiative should come from the leading tradesmen of Bangalore, Mysore and other commercial centres. Government will of course be prepared to give every facility.

Speech at the Dasara Representative Assembly.

As regards Mahomedan education, Government have given and are prepared to give all reasonable facilities, but in its own interests, the Mahomedan community should acquire a working knowledge of the language of the State and endeavour to work in unison with other communities within it.

The question of a University for Mysore is engaging our earnest attention. We may expect to come to a decision in three or four months' time.

The claim of the *inamdars* to toddy revenue is also engaging our attention and I hope a satisfactory settlement will soon be reached.

As regards public works, I may promise that the tank and channel projects in the Suvarnavati and the Lokapavani valleys will receive attention in the coming year. The interests of the Bhadra project will not be forgotten.

The question of extending to the public the benefits of State Life Insurance is in the capable hands of our Comptroller, Mr. Chakravarti. If we do not meet with any great difficulties, he will doubtless see the scheme put through with all expedition.

As regards Local and Municipal Boards, I have already said in the course of the discussions that a committee, which included several non-official gentlemen, has just concluded its deliberations after an exhaustive examination of the whole question.

It seems to me that the funds of the Kalasa temple may be partly invested on local railways and partly expended on the town and temple of Kalasa. A small sum might also be utilised for encouraging the study of Sanskrit.

It seems desirable that all the subjects concerning a taluk should be catalogued and, if possible, District Conferences held to consider progress not less often than once in six months. It will give an opportunity for the settlement of many local subjects by the officers and the people immediately concerned. This idea will be further worked out in consultation with the Deputy Commissioners who seem willing to undertake the responsibility.

As regards the Village Improvement Scheme, I am glad to observe that the promises you gave last year have been so handsomely fulfilled. For the present, I am not inclined to support penal or coercive measures if the people fail to comply with the provisions of the scheme. It seems sufficient if lists of defaulters are sent to the Amildars and, if necessary, also posted in the village *chavadi*.

It is a matter for special satisfaction that the Deputy Commissioners and the Revenue officers are taking such an enthusiastic interest in the scheme. If the leaders and the people maintain their interest in this good work, it may not be long before we shall have many model villages in the country.

Dewan Bahadur Mr. K. P. Puttanna Chetty has met and addressed many leading members of this Assembly in the matter of the regulation of the professional and other activities in city, town and village. The object is to bring all activities and professions in the country under some sort of regulation, control and stimulating influence, chiefly to encourage co-operative effort and to standardise some of the more beneficent practices and habits and promote business life in the country. The great defect of the present day population is lack of capacity for concerted action.

It is a matter for great satisfaction to His Highness' Government that you have come forward with a request for the levy of income-tax, and your promise of co-operation in regard to minor tanks is creditable to your public spirit and encouraging to Government. Such acts on your side will increase mutual confidence and stimulate work in many directions in which the co-operation of the people with Government is so necessary. His Highness the Maharaja has commanded me to announce that he is prepared to sanction the proposals in connection with the minor tanks which were placed before you the other day.

The Government of India have been giving us their sympathy and help by lending us their officers and in other ways. His Highness the Maharaja is anxious that earnest efforts should be put forth to regulate and develop all beneficent activities in the State and stimulate every co-operative effort calculated to increase the intelligence, skill, refinement and earning power of his people.

I hope that all classes of people in the country whether Europeans, Hindus or Mahomedans, will work in unison and actively participate in this good work and fulfil these cherished wishes of His Highness the Maharaja.

SPEECH AT THE MYSORE LEGISLATIVE COUNCIL.

[A meeting of the Mysore Legislative Council was held at the Public Offices, Bangalore, on 21st November 1914. Sir M. Visvesvaraya, President of the Council, was in the chair. Being the first meeting of the Council after the outbreak of the great war, there was a large attendance of members and visitors. **21st Nov. 1914.**

Dewan Sir M. Visvesvaraya, in opening the proceedings, said:—]

Gentlemen,—We meet here for the first time after the outbreak of the great war in Europe, and I have no doubt it is the wish of every member of this Council that we should give expression to the feeling of deep loyalty and attachment to the British Empire which animates His Highness' Government and subjects in this grave crisis.

The war has affected us as it has affected every other country in the world. Imports and exports have fallen, prices rule high, money is somewhat scarce and business is slack. But these are trivial inconveniences when we consider the magnitude of the issues involved and the sacrifices which the Empire, as a whole, is making.

His Highness the Maharaja, with the loyalty characteristic of his House, has identified himself wholeheartedly with all the measures needed for carrying on the war and the preservation of peace in India.

It is a matter of pride to us that His Highness has made a contribution both in men and money—small, it is true, but a contribution all the same—towards the prosecution of the war. We are grateful that His Highness' troops have been given an opportunity of fighting side by side with those of His Majesty the King Emperor.

The people of this State are watching the war news with feverish anxiety. Evidences of this are to be found in the phenomenal increase in the circulation of newspapers in the State. And ever since the outbreak of hostilities with Turkey, telegrams and letters have been pouring in from the Mahomedan population in many parts of the State giving expression to their dissatisfaction at the attitude of Turkey and to their unfailing loyalty and devotion to the British Government.

His Highness' subjects have abiding faith in the value of the British connection and retain grateful recollections of the justice and fair play which have characterised the British attitude to our State in the past. It is no wonder that they are animated by a feeling of intense sympathy for the British cause.

Speech at the Gokhale Condolence Meeting.

There is, as you see, Gentlemen, a deep and widespread desire throughout India to help the British Government. The extraordinary unanimity of opinion in this respect and the profound peace which prevails both in British and Feudatory India are a striking testimony to the faith of the people in the permanent beneficence of British rule. This satisfactory outlook is also, in no small measure, due to the confidence of the public in the sympathy and sagacity of the eminent statesman who is at the head of the Indian administration at the present time.

SPEECH AT THE GOKHALE CONDOLENCE MEETING.

[A meeting to express sympathy with the members of the family of the late Hon'ble Mr. G. K. Gokhale, Member, Imperial Legislative Council, was held on 25th February 1915, at Government High School, Bangalore. Mr. Karpur Shrinivasarav, Chief Engineer, was in the chair. The hall was crowded to its utmost holding capacity and the proceedings lasted for more than three hours. Dewan Sir M. Visvesvaraya, who was specially present on the occasion, made the following speech in proposing the principal proposition put before the meeting:—] 25th Feb. 1915.

Mr. Chairman and Gentlemen,—We meet to-day to give public expression to the profound regret we all feel at the premature death of a great and distinguished countryman. It is very appropriate that Mr. Karpur Shrinivasarav, who was a school-friend of the Hon'ble Mr. Gokhale, should preside at this meeting. Having known Mr. Gokhale for over five and twenty years, I felt I should attend this condolence meeting, and associate myself closely with your chairman and the people of this City in paying our tribute of respect and admiration to the memory of the departed patriot. During my residence of about fifteen years as an official in the city of Poona, I was privileged to come into constant contact with Mr. Gokhale in social and civic life and to count upon him as a valued personal friend. In the early nineties of the last century, we met in a club almost daily. We took part —he and a few friends and myself—in starting the present Deccan Club in the historic Hira Bagh town-hall at Poona. The late Mr. Ranade and Mr. Gokhale were members of the first Managing Committee of that Club, of which I was one of the first Secretaries. In his paper, the *Sudharak*, Mr. Gokhale extolled the idea of a club and helped it in other ways; and for nearly ten years thereafter, he was a constant visitor, often spending three or four hours daily within the walls of that institution. Later, about the year 1902 and onwards, Mr. Gokhale was a member and afterwards Honorary President of the City Municipality of Poona, and my official duties brought me in contact with him in formulating a drainage scheme for that City.

In the obituary notices which have been appearing in the papers and in public speeches within the past three or four days, the great services rendered by Mr. Gokhale to the country have been appropriately eulogised. Mr. Gokhale was a strenuous worker; he had a massive intellect and great powers of concentration. From early life, he had trained his powers of discussion and debate to a wonderful pitch of efficiency. It was as a debater and a speaker of incomparable grace and forcefulness that he excelled. He stood head and shoulders above the men of his time in this respect. Whether in the Bombay Legislative Council or in the Imperial Council, he stood an easy first as a debater; and it was, as you may all know, as a critic of great force and ability that he came into prominence. He had a balanced intellect and studied both sides of a subject too well to take extreme views. He placed healthy and decisive limitations to his ambition. He often repeated the saying of Mr. Ranade that his work might be regarded merely as *dèbris* in the foundations of a future edifice which other hands may rear. He was content with this and he needed no higher recognition in his time.

Unfortunately, he suffered like many great Indians of our time, from an insidious disease and for years he told me he could not sleep for more than four to six hours of a night. It was this disease, I believe, that has actually shortened his life. He always thought that his great work was the example he set to the student population, many of whom from all parts of India frequently wrote and applied to him for advice and help. You all know that Mr. Gokhale regarded the late Mr. Ranade as his *guru*, and I wish in this connection to be permitted to refer to an incident which, I believe, is also referred to in one of the biographies of Mr. Ranade. On one occasion in Bombay as I was leaving his house after dinner, Mr. Ranade walked up with me to the outer landing. A friend of his, Mr. Modak, who had been ailing for a long time, was his guest. Pointing to the guest's room, Mr. Ranade remarked, "Do you know that there is a friend of mine in that room who is suffering from a disease from which all India suffers,—namely, paralysis?" In the opinion of both Mr. Ranade and that of his distinguished disciple, there was too little of activity and too little of work done or attempted by the people of this country. If there is any lesson which these two great men have left for us, it is their hard work, their capacity for taking trouble, their strong will-power and determined previous preparation for great events. In the midst of the prevailing lassitude and languor, these two strenuous workers have left behind them enduring examples to the rising generation. Mr. Gokhale had a magnetic personality and by the thoroughness of his work and his great grasp of the subjects he handled, he inspired faith and confidence in his judgment and had acquired a remarkable hold over the affections of his countrymen. Latterly, he had established world-wide interests and acquired an international reputation. Indians in every country were proud to point to him as an example of their countrymen who could rise to the level of the best in any land. It is the death of such a man that we mourn to-day. Some of us mourn the loss of a personal friend; some the loss of a gifted leader and worker; and the Empire as a whole mourns the loss of a great citizen and statesman who by his services has earned imperishable renown and left an enduring mark on the public life of this country. It may be long before we see his like again.

REPLY TO CHANNAPATNA ADDRESSES.

20th Mar. 1915. [While on a visit to Channapatna, on 20th March 1915, Dewan Sir M. Visvesvaraya received addresses of welcome from the inhabitants of the place. In his joint reply to them, Sir M. Visvesvaraya said:—]

Gentlemen,—I have listened with much pleasure to the several addresses you have presented in which reference is made to the measures engaging the attention of His Highness' Government and also to the more important local wants of this town.

Reply to Channapatna Addresses.

The improvement of sericulture is a subject of outstanding importance to this part of the country. You are aware that Government have taken active steps in the matter, and I am also glad that an influential association has been formed under the guidance of public spirited citizens like Mr. Abdul Quddus to promote the industry. I hope your efforts to bring a tile factory into existence may meet with speedy success.

Many of the addresses were brought to my notice so late that I have not had time to read them. The several requests made, including the one for a pure water-supply, will all be enquired into and receive the attention they deserve. I shall go into the details in the course of our discussions in this meeting. The addresses give evidence of a spirit of enterprise, activity and self-help in your midst which is very gratifying to me. You have among you a large and enterprising Mahomedan population and wealthy merchants, both Hindu and Mahomedan; there are several capable leaders and the taluk is not lacking in resources.

Your town seems marked out for industrial and commercial activity. I earnestly hope you may be able to concentrate your attention on the development of silk and a few other paying industries which would bring money and profitable employment to the people of the town and taluk.

It will give me great pleasure to convey your sentiments of loyalty and gratitude to His Highness the Maharaja who watches over your interests with ceaseless vigilance and loving care. I also greatly appreciate your courteous reference to His Highness the Yuvaraja's deep interest in your welfare and his varied activities to promote the prosperity of this State.

Gentlemen, I shall carry very pleasant reminiscences of my visit to your prosperous and enterprising town. I am glad I have had so many proofs of your activity and I thank you for the warmth and cordiality of your welcome.

ADDRESS TO MYSORE ENGINEERS.

26th Mar. 1915. [The eighth session of the Mysore Engineers' Association was held in the Association rooms on 26th March 1915. Dewan Sir M. Visvesvaraya, in opening the session, delivered the following address :–]

Gentlemen,—I have been honoured by your President with a request to attend this meeting and address a few words of greeting to the members, at the opening of this, the eighth session of the Mysore Engineers' Association.

The words I have to say will be few and they will be chiefly from a layman's point of view. I claim no authority on the ground of being an Engineer, because some of you may have come to think by this time that my knowledge of engineering is getting rusted by disuse. At any rate, you may justly say that I am too much preoccupied in non-professional work to be considered an earnest professional man. I may, however, assure you that I am in close association with the technical departments of Government and that the work of the engineer occupies an important place in my daily work and thoughts.

Taking all the departments of engineering together, I believe, we are spending in the current year no less than 120 lakhs or nearly the equivalent of one-half of the normal revenues of the State. There can be no doubt that, in the constructive work of the administration, the engineer's work occupies no inconsiderable share at the present time.

Address to Mysore Engineers.

The Association serves a very useful purpose. It brings together engineers working in all parts of the State and gives them an opportunity of exchanging views and improving their professional knowledge by collective effort. The engineers of the State of all denominations have begun to work together for this common object.

With regard to the regular work of the Association, the committees and executive officials are showing some activity but there is room for more. There should be more life in the weekly and periodical meetings, more order and regularity in the circulation of books and papers. In every grade of the engineer's service, we should insist on the observance of greater punctuality and better business ways, so that our officers, high and low, may keep themselves always in advance of what is to be done and faithfully fulfil their engagements with regard to whatever they agree to do.

The younger members of the profession should endeavour to broaden their outlook and improve their professional skill by study, travel, and observation. His Highness' Government are doing what they can to encourage foreign travel for this purpose.

I should like to see among our young engineers more capacity for initiative and willingness to undertake continuous work. It might be useful if the President made inquiries and prepared a list of men who have done original work and shown a capacity for initiative in this direction during the past year.

We have all classes of engineering work going on in the State—railways, irrigation works, roads, architectural buildings, town planning, water-supply, drainage, electrical engineering and the installation and management of machinery. We hope soon to make a beginning in mining engineering. It is not possible in a small State like ours to have separate Associations to promote all these objects severally, and so, this single Association will have to provide for the wants of all. You will recognise how very necessary it is to maintain this Association at as high a level of efficiency as may be feasible. Every branch of the profession should have a corresponding place, or section, in the business organization of the Association; every single section must have its separate collection of books and models, its supply of technical journals and its own bulletins; and the work of each section should be entrusted to a special sub-committee with an Assistant or Joint Secretary.

I wonder if the proposal would appeal to the members of the appointment of a small committee of, say, three persons, who would make it their business to keep themselves well posted with the rules and programmes and with information regarding the latest engineering works and progressive thought in British India and other parts of the world. The chief business of the committee should be to keep reminding the executive officials and members, of course in a respectful manner, of the work expected of them on appointed dates and offering suggestions regarding the subjects to be discussed, papers to be read and important developments requiring attention.

Such a committee may become a nuisance at the start, because it is sure to pose as a critic until it gains more experience for itself. Officers of the Association and members will also resent advice. Offence will be given and taken at the outset; but after some experience, the committee is sure to come to be recognised as an aid to the efficient working of the organisation. I mention this because the work of the Association is growing and is sure to grow, and greater checks and counter-checks are necessary to ensure its smooth working and enhance its usefulness.

Address to Mysore Engineers.

I am glad to notice from the agenda paper that you have been able to secure the co-operation of Mr. Chatterton and Mr. Bell for this year's conference and that they are going to read papers on subjects connected with their professional work, of which they are, without question, the ablest exponents.

Such co-operation will be a sure source of strength to the Association and I have no doubt will be widely appreciated. All branches of the engineering service will gain by working together and fraternising in this way.

In the coming year, railways, large irrigation works and electrical works are expected to occupy much of our attention. New workshops have to be started and existing ones improved. One of the most serious questions of our time is the rapid silting up of our reservoirs, which are not being replaced or improved at a rate approaching anything like the rapidity of their decay. More systematic efforts should be made to train local contractors in all kinds of engineering work for which some of them have shown great aptitude. This will help us in course of time to reduce Government establishments. A class of *maistries* should be trained in towns and villages to carry on the artizan or mechanic's work of the engineer. There is room for the services of two or three private firms of surveyors and architects within the State in connection with town extension schemes and even for the humble work of tank restoration and repairs. Great is the need for effort on the part of this Association to induce a sufficient number of engineers to specialise in the various branches of engineering. The subjects should be arranged in the order of their importance for the State and distributed among a large body of young men who will be the votaries, and who may one day hope to become experts, in the branches of the profession concerned. Some spade work has been done in this respect in previous years, but it is not enough. Such work might in future be entrusted to the Efficiency Committee already referred to, which might meet at least once a quarter, to take stock of promises and performances.

I have every hope that in the coming year you will put in as much energy and hard work as you can to cope with the heavy responsibilities entrusted to you, and to promote the interests of His Highness' subjects, in whose midst and for whose benefit you are working.

Gentlemen, with these remarks, I wish you godspeed in your deliberations.

OPENING OF THE BANGALORE EXHIBITION.

29th Mar. 1915. [On 29th March 1915, Dewan Sir M. Visvesvaraya opened the Bangalore City Municipal Exhibition. It was the first Exhibition of its kind held by the Bangalore City Municipality. A large and representative gathering had assembled on the occasion. Sir M. Visvesvaraya was, on arrival, received by the members of the City Municipality, headed by Rajasabhabhushana Dewan Bahadur K. P. Puttanna Chetty, Honorary President, and presented with an address of welcome, which was read by the Honorary President.

Sir M. Visvesvaraya in reply said :—]

Sir Hugh Daly, Ladies and Gentlemen.—The address which Mr. Puttanna Chetty has just read sets forth clearly the origin and objects of the Municipal Exhibition which we are assembled to witness to-day.

Many people will, perhaps, wonder why such an important function is organised at the height of the summer season. It has been explained that large numbers of

Opening of the Bangalore Exhibition.

people are expected to visit the city to witness the "Karaga" festival and the Municipality wanted to provide amusement to the visitors and utilise the occasion for promoting the trade of the city by exhibitions and demonstrations. This exhibition is calculated to bring together the visitors and the business men of the city and of the Civil and Military Station of Bangalore. It will also provide recreation and amusement to the residents of both areas.

The exhibition serves a threefold object. The Municipality merely wanted the permission of Government to hold the exhibition and they have not asked for any Government aid. It is gratifying to learn that the undertaking will prove a success financially and that the net proceeds will be handed over to the City Branch of the St. John Ambulance Association. Having regard to the colossal sacrifices which the Empire as a whole is making, such efforts, small or large, to provide relief and conveniences to the sick and the wounded, should receive the enthusiastic support of every loyal citizen. You will agree that no worthier object could have been thought of.

Perhaps I should not omit to say a word or two about the character of the amusements provided, having regard to the public comment on the subject within the past few days. I learn that the Municipality have dropped one of the three amusements referred to. As regards the remaining two, all I can say is that the representation came late and Government did not wish to embarrass the Municipality after the latter had made their plans. I understand these amusements were invariably permitted in former fêtes at this very site. The considerations raised by certain worthy members of the public have our sincere sympathy, and if they are good enough to favour us with practical suggestions and give instances of similar fêtes managed elsewhere without these accessories, their views will receive the earnest attention of the City Municipal Council and all concerned.

It only remains for me to congratulate Mr. Puttanna Chetty and the several earnest workers associated with him on their taking the initiative in this matter and also on their resolve to make this exhibition an annual event.

The time has come when large undertakings have to be attempted by the collective effort of large numbers of people. The country is in need of such service and every citizen should give a portion of his time, money or resources to public work according to his opportunities. He owes it to the community and the State. The community benefits by such work and the giver also indirectly. It is the willingness and capacity to work in this way, for indirect results and distant objects, that differentiate an advanced community from one whose organising powers are still primitive.

Mr. Puttanna Chetty held high office and, by his labours in civic and industrial matters since his retirement, he has set a noble example of unselfish work which is much valued both by Government and the people and is destined to leave a lasting mark on the public life of Mysore.

I hope all the anticipations which the organisers of this exhibition have in view may be realised and their efforts may result in a handsome surplus which is needed for a very worthy cause.

With these remarks, ladies and gentlemen, I have much pleasure in declaring the Bangalore City Municipal Exhibition open.

SPEECH AT THE MYSORE AGRICULTURAL SCHOOL.

[On 16th April 1915, the distribution of prizes to the students of the Mysore Agricultural School took place. There was a large and representative gathering present on the occasion. Dewan Sir M. Visvesvaraya occupied the chair. The reading of the report of the school and the distribution of prizes being over, Sir M. Visvesvaraya made the following speech :—] 16th April 1915.

Gentlemen,—This is the first time that the students of the Mysore Agricultural School pass out of the institution into the larger school of life, and Dr. Coleman honoured me by asking me more than once that I should be present at this function.

I am glad of the opportunity he has given me to get into closer touch with the good work that the school has been doing in the first two years of its existence. I congratulate the authorities of the institution on the results achieved, and I trust, that, as the usefulness of the institution and the improvements recently sanctioned by Government for the convenience of the students become better known, the school will attract the pick of the young men of the country.

Mr. Yegnanarayana Iyer has alluded in his report to the complaint nowadays that the most intelligent and capable of our young men avoid the professions, particularly the agricultural profession, to seek Government appointments. It is gratifying to learn on Dr. Coleman's authority that a considerable number of the passed students who are leaving the school to-day intend to go back to their land instead of taking up Government service.

Although our agriculturist is endowed with much natural intelligence and shrewdness and does all that is necessary to get a fair crop from out of our precarious rainfall, the fact remains that he is still very conservative and very ignorant.

Half the trouble is due to his slack ways. He works in the monsoon and a part of the cold weather; then he has no regular employment for four months during which he lapses into habits of idleness. Want of continuous employment has a demoralising effect in other ways also on his working efficiency as a producer.

There is an immense amount of work awaiting handling in the rural areas for people interested in agriculture, and it is to the batch of young students now sent out from the school and to similar recruits to be trained hereafter that Government look for the proper development of agriculture in the State on rational and scientific lines. With the knowledge of science that they possess, they should be able to grow two blades of grass where an uneducated raiyat is growing one. Their responsibilities extend not merely to the improvement of their own lands but to spreading in their neighbourhood the knowledge they have acquired and gradually increasing the number of those whom this institution may claim as its clientele. In this way, the institution should, in course of time, become the living centre of all agricultural progress in Mysore.

Through pressure of economic causes, too many people have taken to the soil in recent years. I may remark with due deference to Dr. Coleman's views that agriculture alone can never make a people rich and prosperous. But for a fair number of young men trained in the profession who are prepared to work hard on modern scientific lines there are careers open even in this State. I may mention the case of Mr. Oorgahalli Krishnaiengar who is an educated gentleman and a resident of this district and who is earning from agriculture an income which many an official might envy.

Speech at the Mysore Agricultural School.

His Highness' Government have endeavoured to encourage a class of gentlemen farmers by offering land in large blocks for cultivation. Through lack of capital and experience people have not yet come forward in large numbers to avail themselves of the privilege. If a few succeed, I believe it will not be long before a great many educated young men will want to take advantage of the facilities placed at their disposal.

The life of an agriculturist in the *maidan* areas is a perpetual struggle against the uncertainties of the seasons. In the *malnad* districts of Shimoga and Kadur, on the other hand, there are extensive areas of cultivable soil in a region in which the rainfall is practically unfailing. The climate is considered unhealthy because the lower classes of the people neglect the most elementary precautions to protect themselves against the evils of impure water, swampy land and excess of decaying vegetation. In the same region, persons, who take the necessary precaution as regards food and clothing and adapt themselves to their surroundings, have assured me that they consider the climate to be perfect.

Given the will and the perseverence to take up land, clear rank vegetation, build small tanks and toil patiently for 8 or 10 years for results, many prosperous farms might be built up in the *malnad* area in which our middle class young men, and large numbers of other cultivators besides, would find lucrative employment.

Dr. Coleman made a special study of agricultural education in his last visit to Europe and America and, as many of you may be aware, has written a book on the subject. It must be a great satisfaction to him to see his principles applied to practice and to witness to-day the first batch of students go forth from the school on which he has spent so much enthusiasm and ability. We are looking forward to further developments not only in the training of leaders in agriculture but also in teaching business habits and scientific methods of agriculture to large masses of our ordinary cultivators in Mysore.

I have visited the institution at Hebbal while the students were at work and can speak from some personal knowledge of the excellence of the practical training they have received. In my walks towards Hebbal, I have often met batches of these students and exchanged the time of day with them. I have also occasionally conversed with some about their work and prospects. The boys seem altogether a fine lot. They are well equipped and may be depended upon to give a good account of themselves.

It would be interesting to maintain in the school a record of the future careers of these boys. I hope when they go back to the soil, the young men will continue to practise the business ways they have learnt at school, that they will work regular hours, continue to improve their skill and capacity as they advance in age, and retain, to the last, the strength of character, and high ideals with which, I believe, many of them are starting life to-day.

Dr. Coleman has given them all the advice that they need, and I will now convey to the boys in your name, as well as my own, our congratulations on the prizes and certificates they have won and the assurance that our best wishes accompany them in their future career.

ADDRESS TO THE MYSORE ECONOMIC CONFERENCE.

[The sixth session of the Mysore Economic Conference was held in the Public Offices, Mysore, on 21st June 1915, Dewan Sir M. Visvesvaraya was in the chair. Besides the members, there was a large and distinguished gathering present on the occasion. Special seats had been provided on the daïs for visitors from foreign States. In opening the session, Sir M. Visvesvaraya delivered the following Address:—]

21st June 1915.

Gentlemen,—It is my privilege to welcome you to the sixth session of the Mysore Economic Conference which to-day completes its fourth year of existence. I venture to think that we may look back with a fair amount of satisfaction on the work which we have been able to accomplish during the period. With the ground prepared and the way paved in so many directions, we may confidently hope that the work of the immediate future will be better still. The ideas and methods of work of our organization, though foreign to the tradition and genius of our people, are steadily spreading and you will agree that there are, at the present moment, in many parts of the State, gratifying indications of a spirit of enquiry and a desire for economic betterment. I trust our deliberations at this session may enable us to further improve the organization and enlist the co-operation of a wider public.

Economic work such as we have undertaken is a matter of slow growth, and progress largely depends on the degree of response from the public. A friend, who recently returned from America, tells me that, some twenty years ago, the Agricultural Department of the States started a scheme for imparting practical instruction to farmers by sending demonstration trains to

Address to the Mysore Economic Conference.

villages, and large sums of money were expended on the project. For the first ten years or so, nobody could see any good from it, but they now find that it is bearing fruit and that the agricultural population has benefited enormously by the scheme.

In 1896, a number of Irish Members of the British Parliament, under the Chairmanship of Mr. (now Sir) Horace Plunkett, prepared a programme for the industrial regeneration of Ireland and the Committee concluded a very able and practical report with the following observation which I think may be appropriately quoted here as applicable to the conditions in Mysore :—

"The work which we have outlined must largely be "a work of time. Conditions and habits which have been "the growth of generations cannot be transformed in a "day. Nor can striking results be expected to follow "immediately upon the adoption even of the best con-"sidered schemes. Those who undertake such reforms "must be prepared to meet many difficulties and much "discouragement; but it would be a grievous mistake if "we were, therefore, to allow ourselves to be overcome "by obstacles which have been successfully confronted "elsewhere, or to lose faith in the capacity of our people "ultimately to reach the goal which has been gained by "other countries not more fortunately circumstanced "than Ireland."

The detailed reports of the work done during the year just ended will be presently placed before you by the respective Chairmen of Committees. I shall merely refer here to a few salient points.

The Agricultural Committee was chiefly concerned with the development of sericulture during the year. The scope of work at the Channapatna Sericultural Farm has been widened and the farm is now able to supply disease-free eggs. Steps are being taken to train raiyats in sericultural tracts in the methods of rearing cocoons inaugurated by Signor Mari. Four new sericultural stations have been opened recently for experimental purposes and rules have been sanctioned for the grant of loans for starting agricultural and dairy farms.

The Agricultural Department was engaged in the work of demonstration in popularising improved methods of cultivation, the distribution of seed and farm implements and the supply of oil cake for sugar-cane. The Hebbal Agricultural School sent out during the year a batch of students fully trained for the first time.

The Education Department has started about 1,050 additional aided schools and brought compulsory education into operation in fifteen selected centres. The Education Committee is developing an organization for preparing books in the Vernacular. Under the auspices of the Committee, a Kannada Literary Conference was held in Bangalore. The Committee have opened public libraries in the cities of Bangalore and Mysore and have a scheme ready for extending the same to smaller towns and rural areas. An educational survey of the State is also engaging attention.

A special feature of the year, from an educational point of view, was the increasing demand for schools in rural areas and the gift of many school buildings by private persons.

The University Scheme has been further developed but several important details have yet to be settled before the matter is carried to the stage of practical action. It is proposed to locate the new University in the city of Mysore.

Substantial progress has been made in regard to the introduction of machinery into the State. During the past three years, about sixty installations of power-driven machinery have been set up, of which the majority consist of pumping plants for lift irrigation; the others are for rice-hulling, cotton-ginning, oil-pressing, etc. The machinery for crushing sugar-cane and boiling the juice has worked successfully during the year. A model tile factory is in course of erection at Tirthahalli. Hand-loom weaving also received attention and over 280 additional fly-shuttle looms were brought into use during the year.

A number of schemes were taken up by the Industries and Commerce Committee for investigation and experiment, chief of which are sandalwood oil distillation, charcoal manufacture, manufacture of paper pulp and soap and the establishment of a cotton mill. The enquiries pursued by the Committee in regard to some of the industries show that the prospects of their establishment in the State are quite fair and that the labours of the Committee depend for practical fruition upon their obtaining financial co-operation from the public. I have no doubt the members of the Conference will use their influence in enlisting the needed co-operation. The work in connection with the floating of a Cotton Seed Oil Company with a capital of Rs. 3 lakhs is reported to be nearing completion. A Special Officer has been appointed to investigate and report on "Home Industries" in the cities of Bangalore and Mysore. The question of affording facilities to travellers in the interior is receiving attention and proposals for extending State Life Insurance and for giving a trial to the Village Savings Banks, prepared by the Industries and Commerce Committee, are before Government. A few joint-stock enterprises have been started but progress in this direction continues to be slow.

One of the first fruits of our work has been the establishment of the Bank of Mysore which is already benefiting the public. Seven branches have been started in the districts and the total value of the bank's transactions has risen to Rs. 40 lakhs. At a time of financial stringency due to the war, the new bank has rendered invaluable service to the trade of the Bangalore City and the whole State.

The District Committees have been giving attention to various minor items of work connected with the starting of implement depôts, agricultural associations, exhibitions, cattle shows, maintenance of night schools and carpentry classes, besides giving active help in other directions to the officers of Government Departments with regard to economic activities.

There were formed during the year fifty-eight Taluk Progress Committees, four Town Progress Committees and one City Progress Committee. The rules regarding the constitution and functions of the Progress Committees were suitably revised during the year to make their future work more effective.

Summing up the year's work, it might be said that sericulture is making steady progress. There has been satisfactory development in the field of education. In connection with the introduction of machinery and preparation of practical working schemes, there has been a fair amount of activity in the Industries and Commerce Department although progress was somewhat marred by the altered conditions brought on by the war, difficulties in obtaining suitable machinery and the tightness of the money market. But it is believed that the schemes already prepared and the results of experiments carried out will come in handy when the conditions again improve as soon as the war is over.

There has been an appreciable expansion of economic activity through the appointment of District Superintendents, the publication of the Economic Journal and the formation of a large number of Progress Committees already mentioned. The expanded work has yet to be consolidated and perfected and this work is well in hand.

In my last year's address, I spoke at some length on the all important question of the work of our committees. The work of the Conference, between one session and the next, practically means the work of the committees and that work is well or ill done according or not as the committees address themselves seriously to their duties. In choosing members of committees, regard should be had, not only to their ability, but also to their aptitude and enthusiasm for economic work. They should continue to be members only so long as they can afford the necessary time to study the subjects and aid their fellow members on the committee.

The system of transacting work through committees is somewhat foreign to our officers and leading public men but they are getting used to it. Till recently, the majority of the members were reported to be content with criticism. There was no previous preparation or study. The Chairman and Secretary usually did the major portion of the work and the members attended meetings to scrutinize and sit in judgment, ready to make an onslaught on the smallest new idea that might show its head. This attitude accounts chiefly for the poverty of the results complained of but it is a passing phase and should not discourage us. I earnestly appeal to the members to become working partners on the committees and constitute themselves both as workers and advisers; workers as regards subjects which fall to their share, and advisers or judges as regards subjects worked up by their fellow members. If business is transacted in this spirit, of which indications are not wanting, members cannot fail to do credit to their position.

Another important matter which should receive attention in this connection is that the committees should commence work at the beginning of the year with carefully thought out programmes. The Secretary to the Conference and other officers are prepared to give the committees every help and guidance in this respect. An effort is being made to prepare statements of essentials of work to be accomplished in the whole State, in the three branches of Conference activities, as far as such work is capable of being expressed in concrete figures. From these statements, the local committees and officers might select whatever work they might feel competent to undertake during the coming year.

The committees already started are semi-official bodies, but every town in the State may have one or more private associations in addition, depending on the capacity and public spirit that may exist in the locality.

There are at present within the State several independent associations and societies for promoting agriculture, trade and education, but they seem to work leisurely and without reference to activities in the same field by other agencies. It should be our ambition to induce them to co-operate and work under one common organization.

One of the essential duties of this Conference is to aid and encourage the growth of production in the country, both farm produce and manufactured products. Some of you may have read in a recent issue of the Mysore Economic Journal a rough estimate of the value of agricultural produce in the whole State. The calculations put the total amount of the farm produce of the country at about 14 crores for a population of 59 lakhs. This gives a gross income of Rs. 24 per head. The produce of our manufactures and other professional occupations is valued at about 4 crores more, thus making a total production in the State of 18 crores or Rs. 31 per head. The corresponding rate of production in European countries is estimated at between Rs. 300 and 600 per head.

Address to the Mysore Economic Conference.

We are not dealing with exact figures but with approximations. The figures may be capable of modification after more detailed enquiry but they are sufficiently near the mark to bring home to us the extraordinarily low level of production in this State.

The output per head in our country is roughly between one-twentieth and one-tenth of the corresponding production per head in European countries. The most casual thinker will see from this that an improvement is necessary and possible. If we increase the present output by, say, 50 per cent, the total will rise from 18 crores to 27 crores and the average earning power of the individual citizen from Rs. 31 to Rs. 46. If the average income increases to this extent, our people will be able to command greater comforts, and a very considerable improvement will have taken place in the standard of living. Where the difference is so great as ten to twenty times, an attempt to increase our present earnings by one-half does not look very ambitious. However unimportant it might appear as compared with progressive countries, an increase of production to the extent indicated, if effected within the next ten or fifteen years, will mark a great advance in our economic prosperity. It will be a result of which we might be justly proud.

An addition of 9 crores to the production of the country might be attempted somewhat in the following manner:—

	Crores.
By extending the area under cultivation and by intensive cultivation and improvements in existing methods of cultivation	1
By extending irrigation	2
By development of industries and commerce ...	3
By improving the earning power of the people by equipping them with knowledge, skill and business habits...	2
By all other means	1

Address to the Mysore Economic Conference.

It is unusual to particularise in this way, but I know of no other way to put the idea in an easily intelligible form to show what our activities might mean for the country, if rightly conceived and wisely directed.

If we proceed on the lines attempted elsewhere under similar conditions and follow the principles and practices which govern production in European countries and in the Colonies, I apprehend no difficulty in achieving these results. They are well within our reach.

Our State is mainly agricultural. A purely agricultural country which sells grain and raw material will always remain poor. If you manufacture an agricultural plough or a threshing machine within the State, you will get the machine you want and you will help to retain the money which you would otherwise send out of the country. If from your forest materials, you manufacture chairs, tables, benches and drawing-room furniture, you will make a great deal more money than if you sell firewood.

Agriculture and manufactures should therefore go hand in hand. An atmosphere congenial to the growth of industrial and commercial activities should be gradually created. Travelling facilities should receive special attention. Railways and roads should be extended and cart-tracks between villages efficiently maintained. There should be no town or village without a hotel or inn run on modern business lines. Our town population, which is less than one-tenth of the total population, is inadequate for industrial needs and should be increased at least to one-fifth. Town extensions should be laid out and sites for industrial suburbs and factories kept ready for new-comers. There should be a museum in every town for agricultural and commercial products as well as for demonstrating industrial machinery and plant. A library, a reading room and a bureau of information are also indispensable. There should be no town without half a dozen industries and no village without one or more rural industries.

The chief aim of the Economic Conference is to prevent waste and increase production. There is nothing in this aim which could be regarded as at all ambitious or impracticable. The figures I have given show that we do not aspire to reaching the European standards of production. We are nowhere in the race. With aims so unpretentious, there is no thought of supplanting the spiritual ideals of the country. The increase of production I refer to is a measure of supreme necessity. The present margin between the standard of living and destitution is, in the best of seasons, too small to maintain bare decencies of life, and the risks to which our people are exposed in a severe famine are too serious to be trifled with.

Moreover, the economic strain in the country is a growing, not a diminishing, evil. The population of the world is increasing rapidly. The struggle for existence is growing keener. Facilities of communication are multiplying and prices of foodstuffs have gone up since 1900 in many parts of the world from 15 to 50 per cent. In these days of growing hurry and strenuous toil, the idle and the inefficient are already finding it hard to maintain existence. The attempt to improve matters, you will thus see, has not come a day too soon.

His Highness the Maharaja has been anxious to give reasonable scope for the progressive instincts of his people and to provide them with every opportunity to improve themselves. It is with this object that His Highness was pleased to inaugurate this Conference. It wants to train the people, improve their present lot in life and assist them to build up their future prosperity. It wants to increase our schools, improve farms, build factories and develop our trade. It puts hope in us of better times for our people. So I commend its work, bespeaking for it the support of all true well-wishers of Mysore.

SPEECH AT THE MYSORE ECONOMIC CONFERENCE.

[The sixth session of the Mysore Economic Conference came to a close on the 26th June 1915, after sitting for five days and debating some two hundred propositions placed before it. In winding up the proceedings of the Conference, Dewan Sir M. Visvesvaraya made the following speech :—] **26th June 1915.**

Gentlemen,—It is usual for the President to pass in review the principal results of the session but, as it is already late, my observations will be very brief. Many of the subjects have been fully discussed but some have had to be dealt with rather cursorily. I am sorry several eloquent and interesting speeches had to be interrupted for want of time. I hope members will not, on that account, carry away with them any unpleasant memories of our debates. The subjects which were not discussed have been noted and will be referred to the committees concerned, who will take all necessary action and submit suitable recommendations to the Standing Committee or to Government.

I believe the general opinion is that the level of the discussions at the session has been satisfactory. It was high last year, but I think it was even higher this year. Members seem to have carefully thought out the subjects dealt with by them and the earnestness and enthusiasm they showed and the amount of information they gave were highly gratifying. It would be invidious to mention names, but perhaps I might be permitted to single out a few. Mr. Chatterton, Mr. Chakravarti, Dr. Coleman, Mr. K. R. Srinivasiengar, Mr. Venkatakrishnaiya, Mr. Chengiah Chetty and Mr. M. A. Narayana Iyengar took a leading part in the discussions. They dealt with their subjects, some with great eloquence, some with ability, and all with full information. We have learnt from Mr. Chatterton how to give and take criticism in perfect good humour.

It is a matter for satisfaction that the proposition which was moved with a view to change the constitution of the Conference in some essential particulars was vetoed by the almost unanimous vote of the members of the Conference. Probably, four years ago, the result might have been the very reverse. There were many doubters amongst the people then, but familiarity with the work of the Conference has converted them into enthusiasts. The doubters have become ardent supporters. Every year will add large numbers to our following. This shows that the members have approached the subjects with an open mind, and it is also a testimony to the soundness of the principles underlying our organization.

In reviewing the discussions of the past few days, I will confine my remarks to four main heads, namely, Education, Agriculture, Industries and Commerce and General Organisation. The question of the development of industrial schools has been discussed, including industrial education of boys and girls. Vocational training on a large scale for the masses is a question of outstanding importance at the present moment. Instruction should be imparted in all three grades, namely, higher, middle and lower. The highest must be for graduates, the middle of the class imparted in the Chamarajendra Technical Institute and the Mechanical Engineering School; and we want training in arts and crafts for the vast majority of the poorer classes and agriculturists. Business habits should be instilled into our labouring classes. Small books on business habits should be published and taught in the Elementary and Lower Secondary Schools. A system of lectures has been started in Bangalore and Mysore on finance, banking and commercial topics. It was only to-day that I heard that the people of Shimoga have started through the influence of Mr. Matthan and the leaders of the people, a weekly newspaper in Kanarese. I think it is necessary that every district should have one such paper. We must have two more dailies, one in Bangalore and the other in Mysore, to spread education. There is already a daily newspaper in Bangalore which is doing very good work but we want at least a Vernacular daily in Bangalore and an English daily in Mysore.

The question of grants for libraries in towns has been discussed. Perhaps, if half the initial cost is provided by the people of the area concerned and they are willing to bear three-fourths of the working expenses, it may be possible to consider proposals for aid from Government.

The question of helping poor students was discussed by Mr. Karpur Shrinivasrav. It is a very important matter but the work could only be undertaken by a private organization. Deserving students should also learn to do some work whereby to support themselves while under education. Both these courses may be possible. One important point which I should particularly like to draw attention to is the unequal distribution of schools in the State. They are not distributed on any definite principles based on area or population. We must prepare a map for each taluk showing groups of villages which have schools and those which have none. I think a proper distribution of schools is a matter requiring immediate attention and our energetic Inspector-General of Education will, I have no doubt, give his attention to the subject in the coming year: We have circulated a statement which has to be filled in order to form a correct estimate of the requirements of every taluk and city. We must see to it that in every town at least fifteen per cent of the population attend educational institutions and in every village at least seven to ten per cent do so. The Progress Committees or the leading men in every taluk should hold themselves responsible to keep a sufficient number of young men under instruction in colleges, within or outside the State, so that two or three graduates may come from that taluk every year.

As regards Agriculture, I would invite the special attention of the members to the study of rough estimates of farm produce placed before you. It would be very satisfactory if each taluk and district worked out the estimates for itself until a complete census of production for the whole State is available.

Sericulture is making some progress but the helmsman is away on account of the war. The work is now in the hands of Mr. K. Subba Rao who is carrying it on, on the lines initiated by Signor Mari. He may come back or we may get another expert very soon. But in the meantime we must continue the work as best we can under the guidance of one of our own officers.

Mr. Puttanna Chetty was good enough to suggest that fruit culture may be further developed. I think more apples and plantains were grown in Bangalore twenty years ago than now. It is necessary to increase their output in the coming years under scientific advice. Many a raiyat may place a half or a quarter of an acre of his land under fruit trees.

Speech at the Mysore Economic Conference.

As regards agricultural education, we have to see that more Mysore men are maintained in Agricultural Colleges outside the State. The work of the Farm at Hebbal has been a success and that work has to be further developed. The training of the raiyats in improved methods of cultivation is a very important matter, and at least ten raiyats from each taluk should be trained every year; and I have no doubt that Dr. Coleman will, with his usual enthusiasm, give special attention to this matter.

The question of paucity of labour should be thoroughly investigated. Men, women and children, all, must work. Manual labour should not be treated with contempt. For the Kannambadi works we have imported thousands of labourers, about 8,000 I think, while our own labourers are working in foreign lands. Last month while I was at Newara Eliya in Ceylon, I met cultivators from Thagadur in Nanjangud Taluk. Their wages after all are not appreciably higher than what they would get here. We have got plenty of labour in our own country but there is no organization to develop or exploit it. As regards subsidiary occupations, cattle breeding, carpentry and smithing, are important and there are ten or twelve other industries entered in the statement. Our agriculturists are not fully employed for four to six months in the year because there is no organization to teach them to do any better. The rural industries may be developed by local co-operative effort. People should learn to take full advantage of the opportunities placed before them. As to agricultural co-operation I am afraid Mr. M. A. Narayana Iyengar is somewhat disappointed because the Central Committee for co-operation he wanted has not been sanctioned. It would cost about twenty or twenty-five thousand rupees a year. But sooner or later it must come. I think that the agricultural associations may also take up some co-operative work.

Speech at the Mysore Economic Conference.

Under Industries and Commerce, the question of weaving, referred to by Mr. Puttanna Chetty, is the most important. It is the oldest industry and maintains the largest industrial population of the country. But it is languishing for lack of organization. A sub-committee should investigate in the coming year how to provide the necessary organization to supply capital and other facilities to the weavers.

On the subject of Land and Industrial Bank, the members gave some very interesting information. Our hands are full at present with the Mysore Bank and the large number of the co-operative credit societies which the Registrar has brought into existence. A Land Bank is also necessary and, sooner or later, one must be started. The Committee will doubtless investigate the question in the coming year with a view to practical action. We also want to make a beginning to induce graduates and undergraduates to take to industrial and commercial occupations. We send two or three persons at present for higher education in this connection. That is not enough. Arrangements should be made by the Committee to help the people to study the subjects themselves by supplying books and other conveniences to those anxious to undergo training locally.

The question of the manufacture of iron and steel has been under investigation but the report of the expert has not yet been received.

The establishment of a cotton and silk mill at Mysore is receiving attention and a syndicate has been formed to frame a working scheme. When the railway between Mysore and Arsikere is opened next year, cotton can be imported into Mysore as cheaply as into Bangalore.

There was a suggestion that some merchants might be sent abroad for purposes of study. This is an attractive proposal, but Government do not wish to find the whole money required. If there is sufficient enterprise forthcoming, they will consider what aid is deserved and may be given.

One other important question is the formation of large associations of private persons for each of the objects at present served by the Conference. We may have a Chamber of Commerce for the whole State, a Manufacturers' Association, an Agricultural Association and an Educational Association with head-quarters at Bangalore or Mysore and branches in every town where there are sufficient number of men willing and able to maintain them. These may exist side by side with the semi-official bodies and each of these may serve to stimulate the activities of the other. We have some associations and societies at present but most of them are effete institutions. Some have already disappeared and the remainder are in a moribund condition. The permanent staff of these associations might be maintained from fees collected from among merchants and industrial classes. To ensure continuity of work, however, the staff may be treated as members of Government Service. I throw out this suggestion for your consideration in the coming year.

As in the case of agriculture, a census of production of manufactured products in the State should be taken. It will be some time before the statistics are all correct; but a commencement might be made by filling up the statements already placed before you.

I wish to add a few words as regards the responsibility for our work in the coming year. The programme should be made as definite as possible. There should be more co-operation between all the agencies concerned, *viz.*, the various officers and the Central, District and Taluk Committees and as large a number of the people of the districts as possible should be induced to participate in the work of the Conference. The work of the Committees should again be subdivided among sub-committees and some of their practical schemes may be entrusted to individual members or syndicates. The smallest town and the remotest hamlet of the State should have a share in the work of the Conference.

The object of the Conference is to increase the prosperity of the people and everybody who can afford it should devote some time to such public work. By doing public work, you benefit your neighbours and the country and indirectly yourself. If, as a result of your efforts, the business of a local area is increased, there will be an increase of profitable occupation to all the inhabitants of that area. You will also share yourself, sooner or later, in the general rise of prosperity.

It is important that the technical departments of the State should closely associate themselves with the Committees. Practical schemes prepared by the departments should be sent to the Committees for opinion and *vice versa*. The Committees should be given every opportunity of obtaining full information of the work that is being done in the departments. The Industries and Commerce Committee is working in the closest harmony with the Department of Industries. There is also growing harmony between the Education Committee and the Inspector-General of Education. I have no doubt that the Agricultural Department and the Agricultural Committee will also set an example in this respect.

It is proposed to hold the monthly meeting of all the three Committees on one and the same day. Perhaps the last Saturday of the month may be found suitable. A brief sitting of the Standing Committee might precede the meetings of the three Central Committees. This will enable the members of all the three Committees to exchange views, to promote co-operation and smoothen all obstacles in the way of rapid progress.

Speech at the Mysore Economic Conference.

Government are prepared to render State aid to the extent such aid is given in other countries. It may be rendered in various ways, by experimenting and starting industries and, when successful, handing them over to private bodies; by guaranteeing interest for a term of years on private capital invested in new or infant industries; by granting *takavi* loans according to orders already passed; by granting subsidies to enable companies to declare a dividend in the first few years; by giving bounties to stimulate production; by starting workshops for experimental work and training artizans as suggested by Mr. Chatterton; by providing experts at Government cost; by employing foreign skilled workmen to instruct the people in minor industries; by providing expert advice in forming joint-stock companies; by purchasing articles required for Government use from local manufacturers as far as possible; by collecting and publishing correct statistics and circulating foreign publications containing useful information; by spreading knowledge of machinery and commercial information by means of exhibitions, conferences, etc.; by carrying on as State concerns some of the larger industries such as the manufacture of iron and steel, sandalwood oil, etc., and by exempting new industries from octroi duties and other taxes for a term of years. Had it not been for this terrible war we might have made much more rapid progress. The times are out of joint, machinery is hard to procure and the money market is tight. But we hope that with the close of the war better times will come both for the Empire and ourselves.

You will be glad to hear that His Highness' Government have made all reasonable financial provision for State aid required. His Highness the Maharaja has been pleased to authorise me to announce that a sum of Rs. 5 lakhs per annum will be available for the next five years for loans and encouragement of industries generally. His Highness has also been very particular that funds should be provided for education to the fullest extent permitted by our resources. As I was leaving Ootacamund to attend a Council meeting at Bangalore for the preparation of our budget for the coming year, His Highness said to me, "Be sure you do not stint money for education." And, as a result, the budget provision for education has been advanced by about three lakhs.

Gentlemen, we have already discussed the work to be done in the coming year. We have prepared programmes, formed Committees and voted funds. All that is now needed is a willingness on the part of the Committees to put in their best work, and a determination on the part of the people to take full advantage of the opportunities provided for their benefit.

SPEECH AT THE MYSORE LEGISLATIVE COUNCIL.

27th July 1915.

[The Mysore Legislative Council met at the Public Offices, Bangalore, on 27th July 1915, to discuss the State Budget. In bringing the debate to a close, Sir M. Visvesvaraya, as President of the Council, made the following speech :—]

Gentlemen,—This is the second time that the State Budget has come up for consideration at this Council and many of the members have taken great pains to study our finances. The level of the discussions has been high and non-official members have made some valuable contribution to the debate.

By a previous order of Government, a change of procedure in regard to Budget discussion was introduced from yesterday with a view to enable non-official members to obtain explanations of Budget figures. We were anxious that members should understand clearly the intentions and policy of Government so that they might make their observations with all available figures and data before them. The result of the discussions, to my mind, has been that members have brought to notice some important needs of the people; they have given us plenty of criticism but they had no practical suggestions to make as regards the composition or construction of the Budget. All the representations of a practical character as regards the people's needs have been noted and will receive the careful consideration of Government in due course.

The event which is overshadowing everything else at the present time is the great war which is devastating Europe. The war has also affected our Budget but it is with peculiar gratification that I noticed the warmth and enthusiasm with which member after member spoke of His Highness' modest contribution in men and money towards the prosecution of the war.

My colleague and Mr. Shama Rao have between them fully dealt with the questions relating to education. The proposal for a University for Mysore is receiving our earnest attention and I hope it may not be long before a decision is reached. The question of a College for Shimoga will also be considered at the same time.

Government have not yet decided whether or not to proceed with the Tramway scheme for Bangalore till the war is over.

The criticisms on the excise policy of the Government have been effectively answered by my other colleague and the Excise Commissioner. The greater portion of the increase of excise revenue is doubtless due to the very large concentration of imported labour on the important public works and railways now under construction.

The grants to the cities of Bangalore and Mysore amount to less than five lakhs and I think there is nothing unusual in such expenditure. These cities are visited by large numbers of people from the districts and they set the example to smaller towns. Every citizen of Mysore should learn to take a pride in our capital cities. You will notice we have also made provision in the Budget for small grants for water supply and town planning for mofussil towns. Government are willing to give more money if required for urgent works; but the projects take a long time to mature and the Municipalities themselves are, in many cases, in an impecunious condition, some being unable even to maintain the works when constructed.

In a financial sense, our railway enterprises in the past have not proved altogether satisfactory, and Government are taking needful measures to make future lines remunerative as far as possible. It is, therefore, with this object that an Advisory Committee has been formed and a few officials have been appointed.

A Committee is required because no single officer will find time to study all the details and develop proposals to meet the present and future needs of the State. We hope to get all these questions settled with the generous help of the Government of India.

On my return here yesterday, my attention was drawn to the proceedings of the South Mysore Planters' Association in which reference is made to the abandonment of the proposed Arsikere-Mangalore Railway project. It is true that at one time we were prepared to start work, but subsequent enquiries undertaken in the public interest brought to light various objections and difficulties. For one thing we received a definite statement that the Madras Government were not going to spend money to improve the Mangalore harbour which, as you know, is closed to shipping for three or four months in the year and that, for the present, the development of the Cochin harbour was receiving all their attention.

The construction of a railway down the Manjarabad Ghat will be very expensive and the Durbar fear that the railway will not prove a remunerative enterprise if it is to end in a port which is not open to shipping throughout the year. The permanent interests of the State require a better port. I have no doubt any alternative line to the coast which we may construct will also benefit the planters.

The special features of the year's budget are an equilibrium between revenue and expenditure, temporary diminution of our forest revenue on account of the war, a fresh source of revenue due to the Cauvery Reservoir under construction and increased grants to meet local wants in rural areas.

I think it would be more correct if the railway capital expenditure of four lakhs on open lines is taken out of the ordinary budget and added to our railway capital account. I have no doubt the Financial Department will approve of this course. I also think that a separate account should be rendered of all important capital account works and an abstract of such assets published with the State Budget. Such accounts are necessary to enable the Government and the people to watch the revenue results of commercial enterprises undertaken by the State.

I am glad that the official members have taken part in the debate. Mr. P. Raghavendra Rao made a very effective reply on questions of excise policy. Mr. M. Shama Rao, with his usual lucidity, has answered all the questions concerning his department. My colleagues and Mr. Chakravarti have between them fully dealt with the remaining questions raised in the debate. The brunt of the work has fallen on Mr. Chakravarti, and I have no doubt you will all appreciate the thoroughness and ability with which he has dealt with the criticisms. My colleagues and myself, who know how closely he watches the financial interests of the State, have much reason to appreciate the enthusiasm with which he is animated when he comes to defend the policy of Government.

Some members took a very gloomy view of the condition of our finances. They spoke of the present "crisis," "embarrassing situation," and so forth. The circumstances, in my opinion, do not warrant any such assumption. If you go closely into the question you will find that the truth is very different. *Our financial position to-day is stronger than it ever was in the history of the State except during the past two years.* The change in these two years is due to our investments on large productive works.

The cash balance between 1904 and 1909 was between 43 and 86 lakhs; but now it amounts to over 160 lakhs. This is *in addition* to over two crores of money remaining with us in the shape of investments from the public and otherwise.

What is really required is that we should maintain our credit at a high level. This should be done not by resorting to the primitive method of hoarding but by judicious investments, by borrowing for productive purposes, by a scrupulous discharge of all our financial obligations and by taking steps to see that large sums of money are kept in circulation in the country.

Before I conclude I wish to say a few words to show how our resources are being utilized for the benefit of the people.

Speech at the Mysore Legislative Council.

We are creating new assets in the shape of irrigation and electricity works and railways which will add permanently to the wealth of the people and the future non-tax revenues of the State.

We are increasing expenditure on education. Our State expenditure on education has practically doubled within the past few years, due chiefly to the anxious concern and generous sympathies of His Highness the Maharaja for his people.

We are also spending small sums on various local improvements in rural areas, such as water supply, tank improvements, etc.

Some small expenditure is also being incurred in developing industries and trade. Without more attention to these on our part, believe me, there will never be any large circulation of money or wealth worth mentioning in the country.

These are the directions in which we are utilizing our small resources.

The opposite view has also been put forward by certain members, namely, that we should reduce establishments and cut down expenditure in various directions. One member categorically mentioned a number of things which we may not do. All I can say is that if such views come to be translated into practice, it would mean stagnation and decay. Nothing would be pleasanter for an ease-loving Government than to stop all activities and content themselves with collecting revenues and dispensing justice. But that is not the modern view of Government. The question resolves itself into this: Is our programme to be one of activity and life, or of stagnation and decay? And happily there is no uncertainty as to which of these will find favour with the great majority of the members of this Council.

There have been whispers and alarms expressed by

various speakers about increasing expenditure. One member thought that he had established a climax of extravagance by pointing out that expenditure on a certain item had increased by 29 per cent in the course of ten years. Many other members also referred to the increase of expenditure in the same strain.

Now, gentlemen, I do not see why you should treat an increase of revenue and expenditure as if it were a calamity. If you look squarely into facts, you will find that in every civilized country, it is generally a sign of activity and prosperity. Increase of expenditure usually means increase of activities, increase of production and increase of earning power. If you study the figures of foreign countries you will see that, in the United Kingdom, the public expenditure has gone up in the past twenty years by 140 per cent; in that unfortunate country, Belgium, it has gone up by 120 per cent; in the colony of Canada by 300 per cent; in Japan by as much as 660 per cent; whereas during the same period the increase of expenditure in Mysore has been only 60 per cent. To my mind, if there is to be any criticism, you must blame us for going slow. We have advocated increased expenditure, of course on the assumption that we shall have a vigilant Government to supervise the expenditure, and an appreciative public anxious to profit by the opportunities placed before them. If these conditions did not exist, I agree that safety lies in maintaining the *status quo*.

Increased taxation and expenditure would become a burden and a calamity if Government lacked business capacity and people lacked business activities. The situation is being very closely watched. If in four or five years it is found that the people are apathetic and indifferent to the opportunities placed before them by His Highness' Government, we will at once reduce expenditure. As has been pointed out to you by the Financial

Secretary, we have kept a large portion of our development expenditure on a temporary basis with this object.

But Government have faith in the people. We must develop our organization. Progress depends on our making effective arrangements so that every individual citizen—whether official or non-official—does what he can to improve himself and those who come under his influence, and co-operate in the country's progress by contributing his share of duty and self-sacrifice. I earnestly hope that such co-operation from all ranks of the people and all communities may be forthcoming in an ever increasing degree in future.

ADDRESS TO DASARA REPRESENTATIVE ASSEMBLY.

[The thirty-second session of the Dasara Representative Assembly opened at the Public Offices, Mysore, on 19th October 1915. There was a large gathering present on the occasion, including the Hon'ble Sir Hugh Daly, K.C.I.E., British Resident in Mysore. Sir M. Visvesvaraya, in opening the proceedings of the session, delivered the following address:—] 19th Oct. 1915.

Gentlemen,—By command of His Highness the Maharaja, it is my pleasing duty to welcome you to the thirty-second session of the Dasara Representative Assembly, and to address you, in accordance with precedent, upon the past year's administration of the State and on the more important measures which will engage the attention of His Highness' Government in the current and coming years.

Address to Dasara Representative Assembly.

To us, as to the rest of the civilised world, the great European war continues to be an object of supreme concern. The destruction of treasures of art, historic buildings and ships, means the loss, in the course of a few months, of the fruits of generations of skilled human labour. The distressing events that are happening and the barbarous methods of the enemy have served to emphasise the moral significance of the struggle and have won for the Allies the sympathy and respect of the entire civilised world. The end is not, perhaps, as yet in sight, but the thoroughness and determination with which the allied nations are organising their resources, make it certain that their final victory cannot be far distant.

Since we last met, His Highness' offer of our troops for the war has been accepted and our Imperial Service Regiment left Bangalore for active service on the 13th October 1914 under the command of Col. J. Desaraj Urs, C.I.E., M.V.O. Its members, from all accounts received, have been behaving in a manner of which their countrymen may well be proud. The strength of the Depôt at Bangalore has been temporarily raised to replace casualties in the field. Government have also undertaken to train some remounts belonging to the Imperial Government.

Having regard to the magnitude of the operations, the help we can give is, after all, very little, but that little has been, and will continue to be given, without stint to the fullest measure of our limited resources.

The war has affected our finances and trade in various directions and a period of tension is upon us. Prices of food grains continue to rule high and machinery and materials for manufacture are difficult to procure. During the current year also, we shall probably have to forego a substantial portion of our sandalwood revenue. All this will doubtless change when the war is over, and we may hope that when progress is resumed, it will be at a pace which the interruption will only have served to accelerate.

The seasonal prospects were not very reassuring when we met here last Dasara. The *mungar* rains of April and May 1914 had been scanty and ill-distributed, and the south-west monsoon had proved unsatisfactory. Some difficulty was felt for drinking water, fodder had become scarce, particularly in the districts of Bangalore, Kolar, Mysore and Hassan, and anxiety was felt regarding the state of the crops. But these conditions did not, fortunately, last long, and the end of the monsoon brought us ample rains which largely made up for the deficiencies in the earlier part of the year. Some of the crops, such as sugar-cane and horse-gram, gave a good yield, and there was no reduction in the acreage under dry crops generally, though the outturn was not satisfactory. Judged in the bulk, the results of the year's operations cannot be said to have been very unfavourable.

The current monsoon began very well. The *mungar* rains were satisfactory over the greater part of the State. There was a break in the month of August and part of September but the heavy showers we have had within the past six weeks have served to ease the situation. Although we still want more rain, the prospects of the season, so far as present indications go, seem to be on the whole satisfactory.

Before proceeding to a description of the work of the departments, I shall refer to a few subjects of general administrative interest.

First and foremost I may be permitted to refer to the distinction of G.C.I.E. conferred by His Majesty the King-Emperor on Sir Sri Narasimharaja Wadiyar Bahadur, the Yuvaraja of Mysore. I have no doubt you will all join me in offering our respectful congratulations to the Yuvaraja on the distinction he has so worthily earned and on the important part he is taking in the administration of the State as Extraordinary Member of Council.

The session of the Representative Assembly last year extended over seven days, namely, from 1st to 7th October. Two hundred and ninety-two subjects were discussed of which 149 have been finally dealt with. The number of subjects still under consideration is 143 or, including those pending from previous years, 216.

It is the wish of His Highness the Maharaja that the elected representatives of the people in this Assembly should become more closely acquainted with the objects and plans of Government by a discussion of the State budget, and I shall be glad if you will suggest how this wish might be most conveniently given effect to.

The budget will have been passed at the beginning of the official year, but the suggestions of the members may be utilised in framing the following year's budget. If any of the suggestions be such as could be adopted without interfering with the integrity of the budget, Government may be able to give immediate effect to the same. At all events they will have an opportunity of gauging, and bringing the budget in line with, the reasonable wishes of the representatives of the people as far as possible.

The Legislative Council met four times and considered nine bills, including three pending from the previous year. With a view to render budget discussions more informing and useful, a preliminary meeting was held in July of this year, at which members were afforded an opportunity of obtaining information before they met for formal discussion.

You may remember that, at the last session of this Assembly, the members asked, among other things, for the grant, to the non-official members of the Legislative

Council, of the privilege of asking supplementary questions in connection with the powers of interpellation which they now enjoy. You will be glad to learn that His Highness the Maharaja has been graciously pleased to grant the request subject to the same rules as are applicable to Legislative Councils in British India. A member, who has asked a question, may put a supplementary one for the purpose of further elucidating any matter of fact regarding which a request for information was made in his original question. Detailed rules in the matter will issue in due course.

A few changes of importance have been made in regard to the Government Secretariats. For facility of work, five Secretariats with distinct functions have been constituted. The Military Secretary to His Highness the Maharaja has ceased to perform Secretariat functions in respect of the Departments under his executive control, and the State Geologist, who is now designated Director of Mines and Geology, has been afforded similar relief. The office of the Engineer-in-Chief for Railways has been separated from the Railway Secretariat. Measures are under contemplation for ensuring a greater degree of uniformity than exists at present in the methods of work followed in the different Secretariats.

Turning now to the finances of the State, the revenue for the year 1914-15, according to the revised estimates stood at Rs. 278·14 lakhs and the ordinary expenditure at Rs. 254·15 lakhs, showing a surplus in the ordinary account of Rs. 23·99 lakhs. Including extraordinary expenditure and the capital outlay on new railway and irrigation works amounting to Rs. 86·96 lakhs, the total expenditure came to Rs. 393·11 lakhs or Rs. 114·97 lakhs in excess of the year's revenue. In the budget the net outgoings had been estimated at Rs. 73·54 lakhs. The situation was thus less favourable than what was anticipated by Rs. 41·43 lakhs. The circumstances which brought about this result were the payment of a contribution of Rs. 52 lakhs to the Imperial War Funds, and a fall in the revenue to the extent of about Rs. 6·95 lakhs, due mainly to a set back in the sandalwood revenue, counterbalanced by savings in expenditure to the extent of Rs. 17·52 lakhs.

The State budget for the current year was presented to the Legislative Council on the 28th June 1915, and was discussed by that body on the 27th July following. The estimates as finally approved provide for a gross revenue of Rs. 274·02 lakhs and a gross ordinary expenditure of Rs. 273·70 lakhs. The total expenditure of the year amounts to Rs. 340·05 lakhs, including special grants on account of the following large public works:—

	Lakhs. Rs.
Cauvery Reservoir and allied works ...	25·00
Capital outlay on State railways and steam tramways	26·35
Subsidised or aided railways ...	7·00
Bangalore electric tramways ...	6·00
Cauvery Power Scheme—IV Installation	2·00
Total ...	66·35

The year's budget shows practically an equilibrium between receipts and ordinary expenditure. This is due to an anticipated decline of Rs. 15 lakhs in the sandalwood revenue, as a result of the war conditions and to the continuance of the provision made for certain special items of expenditure for the economic and social improvement of the people, amounting to roughly Rs. 11 lakhs. The present circumstances are of an unusual character and cannot obviously last long or recur with frequency, and it is not considered prudent to interrupt the continued operation of measures for the welfare of the people. Taking the experience of the past four years, during which the ordinary account showed a favourable balance amounting (in round figures) to Rs. 19, 52, 40, and 24 lakhs, respectively, it is not too sanguine to expect a surplus of at least 20 lakhs in normal years in future.

During the past four years, Government have spent nearly a crore and a half rupees on large productive public works, *viz.*, railways, the Cauvery Reservoir and additions to the hydro-electric works known as the Cauvery Power Scheme. These works will eventually yield a susbstantial return on the outlay incurred and will prove assets of great permanent value to the State. It is a matter for satisfaction that we have been able to carry out, from accumulated balances and current savings, works of this magnitude and character which, in other countries, would ordinarily be constructed from borrowed funds.

But our present method of financing has its limitations. The Government balance which was roughly Rs. 120 lakhs at the end of June last, according to the statement of assets and liabilities hereto appended, will, it is expected, be reduced to about Rs. 53 lakhs by the end of the official year. As this balance does not admit of further reduction, we have to consider whether the construction of new works of a productive character should be deferred till sufficient funds accumulate, or whether recourse should be had to borrowing.

Our policy will always be to maintain an annual surplus of, say, Rs. 10 to 20 lakhs, and, so far as we can see at present, it is unlikely that we shall ever have to borrow for current expenses.

If we borrow at all, it will be to create property, to

build up assets which will bring dividends, and increase the non-tax revenues of the State. Productive works of this kind, chiefly railways and irrigation works, are constructed exclusively out of loan funds in British India. We have to consider if it will not be expedient in this State also to employ loan funds more largely than we have done in recent years for the execution of such works. To construct the works from loan funds would be quite in accordance with approved principles of public finance and the practice of civilised countries. If financed solely from current savings, works of this class cannot be carried out rapidly. Besides, it is unfair to the present generation that they should be made to pay for assets the benefits of which will accrue, even in a large measure, to their successors.

Up to the end of last year Government have invested on productive railway, irrigation and other works not less than Rs. 504 lakhs. Towards this outlay, loan funds provided Rs. 200 lakhs; that is, Rs. 180 lakhs for railway construction and Rs. 20 lakhs for the Cauvery Power Scheme. For the repayment, sinking funds have been created from current revenues and the balance to the credit of these funds on 1st July 1915, stood at about Rs. 90 lakhs and Rs. 12 lakhs respectively. Government have thus got in their railway, irrigation and power supply works, unencumbered assets worth Rs. 406 lakhs created out of current revenue. Of this amount, assets worth Rs. 150 lakhs have been built up, as already stated, within the past three or four years.

If we should decide to borrow, as we well may in view of the considerations above set forth, we may either raise a loan from the public or draw upon the deposits with Government, which at present amount to over Rs. 2 crores. The latter course will mean that instead of investing the deposits in foreign banks, or in Government of India securities, we will be utilising a safe portion of them on productive works within the country itself, to the great advantage of both the people and Government.

But the question is not free from difficulties, not the least of which is the sinister association attached to borrowing in the popular mind. His Highness' Government are giving careful consideration to the matter, and you may rely upon it that the decision taken will be in conformity with the permanent interests of the State and the best informed opinion on the subject.

The gazetted staff of the Account Department was strengthened by the addition of two officers for the growing work in the Public Works and Railway Branches. The appointment of a Commercial Auditor was sanctioned for the audit of commercial concerns in which Government are interested and also of Government concerns in which accounts are kept on a commercial basis.

In spite of the war, the Bank of Mysore had a satisfactory year. The deposits of the public with the Bank rose from about Rs. 6,90,000 on the 1st July 1914, to over Rs. 20,32,000 on the 1st July 1915. The total transactions which amounted to Rs. 26 lakhs on 1st July 1914, stood at over Rs. 41 lakhs on 1st July 1915, and a net profit of Rs. 1,10,000 was realised during the year.

During last year's session of this Assembly, the defective character of the law relating to the rights and responsibilities of holders of inam villages and their tenants was brought to the notice of Government. Legislation has been undertaken authorising the introduction of survey and settlement into inam villages, if not less than three-fourths of the co-sharers agree to the measure. But as this will only partially solve the difficulties pointed out, Government have appointed a committee of officers and non-official gentlemen to consider the whole question and their recommendations will, it is hoped, enable Government to settle this vexed question in a satisfactory manner.

In December 1914, Government sanctioned a scheme for the creation of large landed estates; and details of blocks of lands available for the purpose in each district have been published for general information.

Revision settlement was introduced in the Tirthahalli Taluk of the Shimoga District. The average dry rate was unaffected by the revision, but the wet rate was increased by 12 per cent, and the garden rate was reduced by 8 per cent. The net result for the entire tract was an increase of 4·42 per cent over the revenue collected in 1909-10. Proposals for the revision settlement of the Maddagiri and Belur Taluks are under consideration.

The Excise revenue continues to increase. The gross receipts during 1914-15 amounted to Rs. 58,33,170 against Rs. 55,23,999 in 1913-14, giving an increase of more than 3 lakhs over the previous year's figure, which itself constituted a record at the time. The consumption of arrack, foreign liquor and ganja has declined during the year, and that of toddy and opium shows only an insignificant increase. Country beer is the only article in the consumption of which there has been some increase.

In connection with the expansion of the Excise revenue, some unfavourable criticism has been levelled against the policy of Government. But two important circumstances have to be borne in mind in this connection. The first is that the increased revenue has not been accompanied by a proportionate increase in consumption. The revenue has increased since 1911-12 by 28 per cent; while the incidence of consumption of arrack per head of population, which stood at 3·5 drams in 1911-12 has actually gone down to 3·3 drams in 1914-15. Again,

Government have steadily pursued measures calculated to check consumption as far as possible. The duty on arrack has been raised from Rs. 4-12-0 to Rs. 5-4-0 per gallon at which it stands at present and its strength has been reduced from 20° to 25° u. p. A further reduction in strength is under consideration. The tree tax has been raised to Rs. 2 in the case of date trees, and to Rs. 3 in the case of cocoanut trees. Ganja now pays a duty of Rs. 12-8-0 per seer. During the last ten years about 900 shops have been closed and a commencement has been made in restricting the hours of sale in the shops.

One outstanding feature of the working of the Forest Department during the year was the large reduction in the revenue from sandalwood owing to the dislocation of the European market. The quantity offered for sale was reduced to 1,314 tons, of which less than a third was sold for Rs. 3,42,258, leaving about 946½ tons unsold. The total revenue of the department under all heads was Rs. 22,22,320 as against Rs. 32,71,336 in the previous year, and the expenditure was Rs. 9,60,449.

Some activity was displayed in the economic exploitation of our forest resources during the year. A large quantity of sleepers required for the State Railways now under construction was prepared by the department. The officers placed on special duty for taking stock of the available raw material for the manufacture of paper pulp and matches have completed their investigations. The possibilities of supplying charcoal on a large scale for iron smelting from the Shimoga and Kadur Forests were examined, and experiments were conducted to ascertain the comparative results of preparing charcoal by the Brisbane retort and the methods now in vogue.

The abolition of the Munsiff's Court at Yedahalli (now Narasimharajapura) had led to some inconvenience and there were persistent representations for its revival.

Government have therefore sanctioned the re-establishment of the Court with effect from the 1st July 1915. An additional Munsiff has been posted to Tumkur since 24th May 1915. Sanction has been given to the formation of Bench Magistrates' Courts at Tumkur, Chikmagalur, Hassan and Shimoga. The scale of pay of the establishments of Civil Courts has been revised and the prospects of the subordinates have been improved, at an additional annual expenditure of over Rs. 23,000.

The sanctioned strength of the permanent Police force on the 30th June 1915 was 865 officers and 5,177 men. There was an increase in the less important class of offences, but the state of crime during the year was mostly normal. The Police Training School was re-organised during the year and a wholetime Principal and an additional Inspector were appointed. Provision has been made for a shooting range and other essential equipment.

The pay and status of the Infantry officers and men in the Military Department have been improved by the scheme for revision sanctioned by Government in August 1914.

Turning to the Medical and Public Health Departments, the Maternity at Robertsonpet, referred to in some of the previous Addresses, was opened on 7th October 1914. The Female Dispensary at Champion Reefs was at first absorbed in the new institution, but as its abolition was represented to be attended with inconvenience, the dispensary was re-opened on 4th March 1915. In order to meet the difficulty hitherto experienced in obtaining qualified candidates for the subordinate women medical service, more liberal stipends and salaries have been sanctioned. The school for the training of Sanitary Inspectors has been re-opened and will be maintained for a period of three years.

I now propose to deal with the activities of the State

under Education, Agriculture, Industries and Commerce and Co-operation.

Under the new scheme for opening more village elementary schools with the aid of the people, by offering a Government contribution of half the cost of each school, 1,100 grant-in-aid schools have been started, the liability incurred by Government being an annual maximum recurring charge of Rs. 84,000. An additional provision of Rs. 84,000 has been made in this year's budget for opening 1,000 more aided schools. One hundred and thirty new Government schools have been sanctioned at a recurring cost of Rs. 22,878 and also improvements to existing schools at a cost of Rs. 52,787. The scale of pay of village schoolmasters was revised at a cost of Rs. 84,000. With a view to encourage the study of English in rural areas, the rate of contribution, payable by the villagers concerned, for village English schools was reduced. One hundred adult night schools were sanctioned, though many of them could not be opened before the close of the year. A sum of 1½ lakhs of rupees was allotted for new village school buildings. The experiment of making itinerant teachers go round small villages situated close together to impart elementary instruction at intervals, is being tried in the taluks of Bangalore, Mysore and Tumkur.

The scheme for the introduction of compulsory education in selected centres has had a modest start. Out of 16,000 children of the "compulsory" age in the areas in question, 10,800 were attending school and facilities have been afforded for the education of about 1,200 more. It has been decided to extend the scheme to 12 new centres.

Sanction has been accorded to the establishment of three Kannada High or Upper Secondary schools for boys at Dodballapur, Hole-Narsipur and Tirthahalli, and two for girls at Tumkur and Bangalore.

Address to Dasara Representative Assembly.

A scheme has been sanctioned with the object of making vocational courses part of the secondary school curriculum, so as to give a more practical direction to education imparted in towns and villages. Forty centres have been selected and work has been started in a few schools. The department hopes to make substantial progress in the current year.

There was an increase in the number of candidates that graduated both from the Central College and the Maharaja's College, but the number is inadequate for the requirements of the State.

Female education is also making fair progress. The year's list of successful candidates for the public examinations included the names of two ladies who took the B.A. degree. The improvements in the Maharani's College and other institutions for the education of girls referred to in the last year's address have been carried out. A special provision of Rs. 7,000 has been made for the grant of scholarships and school-books to deserving girls in all the taluk and district schools.

A scheme for opening industrial schools at all the district head-quarter towns and for improving existing ones is under the consideration of Government. The Mechanical Engineering School at Bangalore and the Chamarajendra Technical Institute at Mysore have been doing useful work. A qualified Superintendent from England has just been appointed to take charge of the latter school.

Classes for the advanced or higher courses have been opened in the Bangalore Commercial School. A vernacular section has been organized in which instruction is given in the indigenous system of accounts, elements of banking, commercial geography, etc., through the medium of Kannada.

The improved arrangements for the normal training of

Address to Dasara Representative Assembly.

teachers explained in the last year's address were given effect to. The Normal Schools now working provide for the training of 500 teachers in all. The vacation classes held during last summer were attended by 120 teachers.

Owing to the large increase in the number of schools, the Inspectorate has been strengthened by the addition of 12 officers. An additional European Assistant Inspectress has been appointed for girls' schools. A scheme for the grant of foreign scholarships was sanctioned during the year. Eleven scholarships were awarded for the study of various technical subjects, such as paper manufacture, banking, systems of education, organic chemistry, mechanical engineering and actuarial science.

There has been an increase of expenditure on education of over three lakhs of rupees during the past three years. The total number of public and private institutions during these years has increased from 4,568 to 6,134 and their strength from 156,440 to 217,717. Of the total number of pupils in 1914-15, 179,866 were boys and 37,846 were girls. The corresponding figures in 1912-13 were 129,000 and 27,431, respectively. The percentage of male scholars to male population of school-going age was 29·8 in 1912-13. It rose to 35·7 in 1913-14 and to 41·6 in 1914-15. The percentage of female scholars to female population of school-going age which stood at 6·4 in 1912-13 rose to 7·9 in 1913-14 and to 8·9 in 1914-15. The percentages of the total number of pupils under instruction to the total population of school-going age during the three years 1912-13, 1913-14 and 1914-15 were, respectively, 18·0, 21·19 and 25·4.

The progress indicated by these figures is not confined to the lower grades of education only. The number of pupils receiving collegiate education during the three years in question rose from 619 to 930 and of those receiving secondary education from 41,481 to 46,855.

As regards distribution of schools, while on an average there was, in the year 1913-14, one public school for every 10 square miles, the area was reduced to 7 square miles, and including both public and private schools, to 5 square miles in 1914-15.

One of the most hopeful features in the situation is that the people are fully alive to the advantages of education and are evincing keen interest by coming forward with liberal contributions for maintaining teachers and constructing school houses.

His Highness' Government fully recognise that the educational system will be seriously defective without a local University, and necessary steps are being taken to prepare a working scheme. Government hope to be able to place the scheme before the public before very long.

The experimental and scientific work done by the Agricultural Department included further investigations into sandal spike and green bug on coffee. Implements were sold during the year of the value of Rs. 16,626 against Rs. 12,022 in the previous year. A large number of requisitions could not be complied with owing to the delay in the arrival of ploughs from abroad and the question of making arrangements for their manufacture in the local P. W. Workshop is under consideration.

The work of the Department of Industries and Commerce was somewhat hampered owing to the difficulty of getting machinery and dyes from abroad.

At the beginning of the year, 26 pumping and other plants were at work and 13 plants under erection. Thirty-two installations have been taken in hand. The Director has stated in his annual report that during the last 2½ years since this work was started, 71 installations have come into existence costing about 4½ lakhs of rupees and yielding probably a lakh of rupees a year as direct profit to their owners, and that, though, having regard to the area of the State and its population, the results may not be considered very remarkable, they afford evidence of some enterprise and of an increasing eagerness on the part of the people to adopt labour-saving appliances. Ten loans amounting to Rs. 43,750, and 16 hire purchases amounting to Rs. 41,480, were sanctioned, and a total sum of Rs. 13,281 was recovered on account of repayments.

A local syndicate at Tirthahalli has undertaken to construct a tile factory and the buildings and plant are in course of erection. Companies have also been formed at Channapatna and Tumkur for starting tile factories.

As the outbreak of the war had greatly reduced the demand for sandalwood, investigations were made into the possibilities of manufacturing oil on a profitable scale within the State. The result of the enquiries made in England having been satisfactory, it is intended to open a small experimental factory at a cost of about one lakh of rupees for sandalwood oil distillation.

The Co-operative movement in the State showed steady and continuous progress. During the year the number of societies rose from 530 to 725, the membership from 40,479 to 53,267, the working capital from Rs. 21,47,340 to Rs. 30,85,747, and the reserve fund from Rs. 56,238 to Rs. 96,669. The net profit earned is calculated at Rs. 1,61,521 and the saving in interest at Rs. 3,00,000. In the *malnad* also, there was a satisfactory increase in the number of societies, namely, from 50 to 90. The staff of the department has been considerably strengthened and it has therefore been possible to devote greater attention to the consolidation of the work of the societies.

One general Co-operative Conference, opened by the Yuvaraja of Mysore, and seventeen District and Taluk Conferences, were held during the year. It is difficult to over-estimate their value as an agent for educating the public in co-operative matters. The present year's State Conference which, as you are aware, held its sittings in this city between the 10th and 13th of this month, was graciously opened, as on former occasions, by the Yuvaraja, and was presided over by the Hon'ble Mr. Lallubhai Samaldas Mehta of Bombay.

I explained to you at some length last year the objects of the Economic Conference and the need for expenditure in preparing the people for economic progress. The cost of the Conference now amounts to nearly two lakhs of rupees a year. Though the Committees were not able to complete many schemes of a constructive character during the year, steady progress has been made in the investigation of a large number of subjects of economic interest and in the collection of useful information. The Conference held its annual session between the 21st and 26th June last and the proceedings of that assembly have been already published.

During the year, the Standing Committee met twice, and three Central Committees of Education, Agriculture, and Industries and Commerce, ten, eleven and nine times, respectively. Since the last session of the Conference, the Standing Committee and all the Central Committees are having monthly meetings on the same day. The enlarged Standing Committee, comprising all the three Committees, meets for about an hour with a view to take stock of progress and to ensure greater harmony and co-operation between all workers and all branches of the organization. At the Standing Committee meetings, the Chairmen of Committees explain the progress made on the subjects included in the programme and the plans of the Committees as regards work in the succeeding months.

The District Economic Superintendents, three of whom were appointed from non-officials, have proved themselves of great help to the Deputy Commissioners in work connected with economic improvement. Once in two months they meet the heads of departments concerned and the Secretaries of the Conference and the Committees, and in this way form a useful link between the work of the central bodies on the one hand and that of the local District and Taluk Progress Committees on the other.

The rules regarding the constitution and working of the Taluk and Town Progress Committees were revised during the year. The new rules are expected to make the work of these bodies more efficient. In accordance with the resolutions of the Conference, the Mysore Economic Journal was started in January 1915, for spreading useful information on economic subjects.

The most important subjects considered by the Education Committee during the year were the providing of further facilities for the education of the masses, the establishment of rural libraries, the training of teachers, the introduction of physical education and the employment of itinerant teachers for imparting education in villages too small to have schools of their own. A system of lectures for the education of adults was instituted and four travelling lecturers have been appointed. The Committee have organized Public Libraries in the cities of Bangalore and Mysore. A Conference was held under the auspices of the Committee to discuss the best methods of improving the Kannada language and literature. It was presided over by Rajamantrapravina Mr. H. V. Nanjundayya, C.I.E., and was attended also by delegates from the Madras and Bombay Presidencies.

The improvement of the sericultural industry engaged much of the attention of the Agricultural Committee. In accordance with a scheme for dairy farming prepared by the Committee, a private dairy has been established at

Bangalore for which a loan of Rs. 10,000 has been granted by Government. The Committee issued 20 English and 20 Kannada publications on various subjects. The Mysore Silk Association carried on experiments in throwing and preparing silk for the loom and is training boys and girls in these processes.

Investigations were made by the Industries and Commerce Committee in regard to the manufacture of matches, pencils, paper and soap and the establishment of a cotton mill.

With the object of ascertaining the subsidiary occupations which people in the State usually follow, and the scope which exists for their improvement, an officer was deputed for a survey of the various kinds of home industries and occupations in the cities of Bangalore and Mysore. His report has just been published.

Besides the establishment and promotion of industries, the Committee have investigated other questions intimately connected with the economic welfare of the people, such as the inauguration of a scheme of Life Insurance managed by the State and the opening of Village Savings Banks. They have also prepared schemes for offering facilities to merchants to travel abroad and for the appointment of commercial correspondents for the development of trade.

The total expenditure on Public Works from all sources, including Local Funds, amounted to about Rs. 70¼ lakhs, against Rs. 57½ lakhs in the preceding year. Of this amount, Rs. 39 lakhs were spent on irrigation works and Rs. 31¼ lakhs on Civil Works and Military Buildings.

Satisfactory progress has been made in the construction of the Cauvery Reservoir at Kannambadi. The dam has risen to a height of 51·50 feet in the river bed and 55 to 74 feet at the flanks. With the aid of scouring

Address to Dasara Representative Assembly.

sluices fixed in the dam, the discharge in the river, except during high floods, can be regulated according to requirements. The storage thus far secured will enable us not only to guarantee water to the existing power supply to the Kolar Gold Mines up to 9,321 h.p., but to provide, according to the new agreement with the Mining Companies, additional power to the extent of 5,000 h.p. The outlay on the construction of the dam during the year was Rs. 26,92,000, bringing the total expenditure up to the end of June 1915 to Rs. 71,45,000. A scheme for the generation of electric power, by utilising the head available in the reservoir, is under consideration.

Fair progress has also been made with the channel works undertaken for resettling the raiyats drowned out by the reservoir. Water was supplied for the irrigation of about 2,500 acres of new land under the Hemagiri and Mandagere channels as also for some distance down the Chamaraj South Bank Channel and the two low level canals. The expenditure on these channel works amounted to Rs. 5,39,000. Proposals for the extension of sugar-cane cultivation under existing channels are being matured.

The award of the Arbitration Committee appointed for settling the differences between the Government of Madras and this Government regarding the storage of the Cauvery waters is still under the consideration of the Government of India.

The results of the block system of irrigation introduced in connection with the Marikanave reservoir have so far proved encouraging. The area irrigated and the demand for irrigable land and canal water have been steadily increasing. There is also a noticeable improvement in the health of the canal villages. To facilitate the smooth working of the system, the rules have been revised in the light of recent experience. The canal area has begun to attract settlers from outside.

Address to Dasara Representative Assembly.

The question of the restoration and proper maintenance of minor tanks, on which the prosperity of the ryots so largely depends, was fully discussed at the last session of this Assembly. As a result, the old rules were revised, offering more liberal concessions than before, and additional *Maramat* establishment was sanctioned. Government trust that, with these facilities, the ryots will take more interest in the restoration of their tanks than they have evinced hitherto and enable the Deputy Commissioners to show greater progress in future.

The principal civil buildings under construction during the year were additions to the New Palace, improvements at the north and south gates of the Fort, the General Hospital and the Chamarajendra Technical Institute at Mysore; the extension of the Public Offices and the Public Works Workshop and Stores at Bangalore, and new Taluk Cutcherries at Sidlaghatta and Honnali. The construction of a travellers' bungalow and of quarters for Indian guests and the Representative Assembly members at Mysore, and of a large block for the Mechanical Engineering School at Bangalore and a new Taluk Cutcherry at Chikmagalur, were some of the other important works started during the year.

The principal items of work under the head of miscellaneous public improvements consisted of the construction of roads and drains in the Extensions, and improvements to the Cubbon Park, in the Bangalore City, the roofing in of the water service reservoir on the Kolar Gold Fields, the installation of a Jewell-Filter for improving the water supply of the Mysore City, the new water supply installations for the towns of Nanjangud and Davangere and certain improvements in connection with the Ghati Subramanyaswami temple in the Dodballapur Taluk.

To improve the prospects of Engineer officers, a new time scale of pay has been introduced with effect from

1st July of this year, in supersession of the one sanctioned in 1909. The recruitment to the Sub-Assistant Engineer class will be confined to graduates of distinction. The number of Executive Engineers has been increased from 10 to 14 on account of the increase of divisional charges.

The fourth Electric Installation works, which were undertaken to generate additional power to be supplied to the Mining Companies, were completed during the year and the machinery came into operation even before the date stipulated for the additional supply.

The capital outlay on the Cauvery Power Scheme during the year amounted to Rs. 28,000, and the total outlay to the end of June 1915 aggregated Rs. 84,88,053 exclusive of the expenditure of Rs. 18,72,350 incurred on the Fourth Installation works. The gross earnings during the year from the Cauvery Power Scheme amounted to Rs. 18,72,350 against Rs. 17,03,888 during the previous year, showing an increase of Rs. 1,68,462, which was due to an increase in the power supply to the mines. The working expenses amounted to Rs. 7,05,889, including a sum of Rs. 2,94,887 set apart for depreciation, and Rs. 37,762 spent in connection with the channels conservancy operations. The net profit, after deducting the interest charges of Rs. 2,78,598 at 4 per cent on the capital outlay of Rs. 84,88,053, was Rs. 8,73,857, which represents a return of 10·29 per cent on the total capital expenditure.

The rates for the supply of electric power to small consumers were further reduced in Bangalore and Mysore as a temporary measure for encouraging the growth of minor industries.

Government regret that the project for constructing an electric tramway service in Bangalore has, after many vicissitudes, been again held in abeyance owing to the difficulty of getting the required materials at reasonable rates on account of the war.

The year's results of the working of the State lines by the Madras and Southern Mahratta Railway Company show gross earnings amounting to Rs. 36,09,078 which is about Rs. 3 lakhs less than in the previous year. The decrease is mainly due to smaller movements of food grains, raw cotton and oil seeds and to a general falling off under coaching, due to war conditions. The expenses amounted to Rs. 20,36,742 or about Rs. 2 lakhs less than in 1913-14 and the net earnings to Rs. 14,98,355. The percentage of return on the total capital outlay of Rs. 2,58,03,840 works out to 5·81. After deducting from the net earnings the interest on the sterling loan of £1,200,000, the actual realisation from these lines amounted to Rs. 7,78,561, and this gives a net return of three per cent on the outlay. A portion of this return is, however, being spent annually on the railway itself, that is, on improvements to the open lines worked by the Company.

Fair progress was made on the Mysore-Arsikere Railway, which, it is expected, will be opened for traffic about the close of the year 1915-16. The Kolar-Srinivaspur section of the Kolar-Chikballapur loop is likely to be ready for traffic about December next. Work on the Lakkavalli-Narasimharajapura Tramway is in progress, and the line will be placed on a proper working basis during the current official year.

Surveys for the feeder railways in the Shimoga District were begun during the year. The projects for the Hassan-Chikmagalur, Chikmagalur-Kadur and Chikjajur-Chitaldrug lines are still under consideration.

The Kolar District Board Railway between Bowringpet and Kolar, the Yelahanka and Devanhalli section of the Bangalore-Chikballapur Light Railway and the

Tarikere-Lakkavalli section of the Tarikere-Narasimharajpura Tramway were working at the close of the year. The section between Devanhalli and Chikballapur of the Bangalore-Chikballapur Light Railway has also since been opened for traffic.

Among other lines under investigation by His Highness' Government may be mentioned the Bangalore-Hosur connection to link up with the Morappur-Hosur line and the Mysore-Coorg connection for which preliminary surveys have been sanctioned.

For a satisfactory development of the trade and commerce of the State, two main arterial connections are of vital importance. The metre gauge system in the State now terminates at Nanjangud and unless it is continued and connected with the same system in South India at a point near Erode, the Mysore railway system will remain incomplete. This question, which is of thirty years' standing, is again under correspondence with the Government of India.

A railway line is also urgently needed to connect the State railway system with a suitable port on the West Coast. A project for a line from Arsikere to Mangalore *via* Hassan has long been under consideration and His Highness' Government were at one time very keen about it. But fuller enquiries have damped our enthusiasm and we have had to reconsider our attitude.

In the first place, the port of Mangalore is not open to shipping for at least three months in the year and what the permanent interests of the State require is a port which would be open throughout the year. In the second place, the original project was for a narrow gauge line and, as our trunk lines are all on the metre gauge, its construction would have involved a break of gauge. A metre gauge connection to the West Coast down the Manjarabad ghat would cost the State over a crore of rupees and, in view of the altered conditions due to the war, we cannot afford this outlay. The narrow gauge line would not have answered the wants of our State because, at the Mysore end, there would have been a break of gauge and, at the West Coast end, an unsatisfactory port. I have no doubt any one who thoroughly examines the conditions and resources of the country will uphold the soundness of the final decision arrived at by the Durbar.

Investigations are on foot for an alternative line ending in a more satisfactory port. We have been in search of a connection to the West Coast for over 30 years, and even now our ability to construct one will depend, in a large measure, on the state of our resources in the near future.

I cannot conclude this portion of the address without referring to the services rendered by Mr. E. A. S. Bell, late Engineer-in-Chief and Secretary for Railways, to His Highness' Government. Mr. Bell had to organise and train a new staff and his high professional ability was of great advantage to the State in the economical construction of the new lines. His services were recalled in June last, but we are grateful to the Government of India for lending us the services of another high officer in his place.

Coming to the Department of Mines and Geology, the number of leases and licenses current during the year was 142 as against 184 in 1913-14. The output of gold from the Kolar Mines amounted to 568,847 ozs. of an approximate value of Rs. 327 lakhs, showing an increase in output of 9,015 ozs., valued at Rs. 3,22,785 over the results of the previous year. The royalty expected for the year is Rs. 18,95,740 against Rs. 18,95,018 in 1913-14.

With a view to the better utilisation of the mineral resources of the State, the Department of Geology was re-organised in February last. This department was started in 1894 with a definite programme for carrying out a complete geological survey of the State, publishing geological maps and bulletins, and training young men as geologists and mining engineers. This programme was tentative and after a careful consideration, a revised programme has now been sanctioned, with a view to ensure greater attention by the department to the investigation of questions having a direct economic interest. The production and manufacture of special metals, such as pig-iron and steel, ferro-manganese, ferro-chrome, etc., and the question of iron smelting, are some of the more important matters on which the department will concentrate attention in the near future.

To help the public to take a practical interest in the development of mineral resources, the department will shortly publish a brief bulletin, in English and Kannada, giving an account of the mineral resources and metallurgical possibilities of the State. Steps have also been taken to train a few young men as qualified geologists and mining engineers to meet the needs of the department as well as of private capitalists interested in mining.

The report of the Muzrai Committee referred to in last year's Address is still engaging the consideration of Government. Rules have been issued under Sections 13, 15 and 35 of the Muzrai Regulation, dealing with the maintenance of accounts in religious and charitable institutions, the conduct of business by Dharmadarsis and other cognate matters.

There was an increase in the outturn of work during the year both in the Central Press at Bangalore and the Branch Press at Mysore. The expenditure was Rs. 1,12,096 and Rs. 6,540 respectively against Rs. 1,05,484 and Rs. 6,048 in the previous year. The number of books and periodicals registered during the year was 124 as against 117 in the previous year. Copyright was taken for 50 new books.

As stated in my Address last year, a scheme of work has been laid down for the Archæological Department for the next three years, and additional establishment has been temporarily sanctioned in order that the programme may be carried out. The revision of the *Mysore Gazetteer*, which has been undertaken by this department, has made fair progress.

The question of improving the hill stations in the State has engaged the consideration of Government, and it has been decided that a beginning should be made with Nandidroog. The bungalows on the hill have been renovated and several conveniences have been provided for visitors. This hill possesses unique advantages of scenery and climate and it is to be hoped that the measures taken, synchronising as they do with the advent of the railway to the neighbourhood, will serve to revive the popularity which the place enjoyed in the days of the British Commission. The other hill stations, which will probably be taken up for improvement as funds become available, will be the Chamundi Hill near Mysore, the Devaroydrug near Tumkur, and Kalhathigiri on the Bababudans.

The number of Municipalities at the end of June 1915 was 89, of which 36 were governed by the Municipal Regulation. The income of all Municipalities in the State during the year amounted to Rs. 10,80,920, and the expenditure to Rs. 9,98,136. Including previous accumulations, there was a balance of Rs. 10,65,432 at the end of the year in favour of the Municipalities.

The Mysore Municipal Regulation was amended, so as to empower Municipalities, amongst other things, to raise loans, with the sanction of Government, for constructing works of a permanent nature.

The Bangalore City Improvement Committee, the formation of which was referred to in my last Address, submitted a preliminary report dealing with the more urgent requirements of the City. Government have recently passed orders approving generally of the Committee's proposals, and agreeing as funds become available to bear a substantial share of the cost of the improvements, if the Municipal Council are prepared to bear the remainder.

Government have also sanctioned certain proposals of the Mysore Improvement Trust Board for improvements to the Mysore City. The proposals include extensions to the Devaraj Market, re-laying the market square, construction of a new Municipal office and a scheme for housing the poor. In view of the increase in the number of works to be undertaken, the grant to the Trust Board has been temporarily raised to 3½ lakhs per annum.

The receipts under District Funds amounted to Rs. 13,23,503 and the expenditure to Rs. 11,18,846. The income and expenditure under Local Funds General were Rs. 2,06,470 and Rs. 1,58,400 respectively. In exercise of the power recently conferred on District Boards, a Railway cess was for the first time levied in the Kolar District which yielded a revenue of over Rs. 47,000. The District Boards of Tumkur and Chitaldrug have been authorised to collect a similar cess in their districts from 1st July last. The District Board of Shimoga are raising funds for the construction of railways in the interior of that district.

The question of introducing reforms in Local Self-Government in municipal and rural areas, with a view to placing it on a more popular basis, has been the subject of earnest consideration for some time past. To examine the subject from various points of view, Government appointed two Committees, one presided over by Mr. M. Kantaraj Urs, C.S.I., to deal with the constitution and functions of local bodies, and the other with Rajamantra Pravina Mr. C. Srinivasiengar, as Chairman, to consider the question of the improvement of their financial resources. The reports of the two Committees have been published for general information. Their recommendations were also discussed at the Local Boards and Municipal Conference held in Mysore in June last, under the presidency of Mr. K. P. Puttanna Chetty. It is worthy of note that this Conference owed its origin and success chiefly to non-official initiative.

It is generally admitted that Local Self-Government in Mysore has not progressed satisfactorily and that local bodies are not playing their legitimate *rôle* in the administration of the country. The apathy displayed by these bodies is attributed chiefly to a deficiency in the elected popular element and to the want of reasonable powers of control over their own funds. His Highness' Government have, therefore, come to the conclusion that steps should be taken to associate the representatives of the people more largely with the administration of local affairs.

The main lines on which Government propose to take action may be briefly referred to here.

In regard to Municipal Councils it is proposed to constitute three classes of Municipalities, *viz.*, "City," "Town" and "Minor," on the basis of population. The elected element will be not less than two-thirds in City, half in Town, and one-third in minor Municipalities. Presidents in selected cases, and Vice-Presidents more largely than now, may be elected in City and Town Municipal Councils. Larger powers will be conceded to the Councils as regards establishments, works and budget. The scrutiny of Government over budgets will be limited to a few specified points. The effect of these changes will be to increase very largely the popular character of the

Councils and the powers they can exercise within their areas.

As regards the constitution of the District and other rural Boards, the proportion of the elected element will be raised to at least two-thirds in the case of District Boards, and at least half in the case of Taluk Boards and Unions. It is proposed to sanction, with some modifications, the recommendations of the Local Self-Government Committee that the Taluk Boards and Unions should not be merely the agents of District Boards but should have a real corporate existence, independent funds and budget, and should be able to exercise within their own jurisdiction all the functions of the District Board. The powers of rural bodies with regard to establishment and budget will also be increased.

An important change is contemplated regarding the enlargement of the functions of these bodies. It is proposed to transfer tentatively the control over primary education, medical relief and veterinary dispensaries to selected local bodies and to invest the District and Taluk Boards with power to pass and submit resolutions for the consideration of Government in matters, which though not coming within the sphere of their ordinary duties, relate to local wants and grievances and the administration of the district or taluk generally.

The chief difficulty which hampers the progress of Local Bodies is the general unsatisfactory condition of their finances. The Local Finance Committee which dealt with this question has recommended that the Local Funds General and the Village School Fund should be abolished as distinct funds and made over to Local Boards and that the *mohatarfa* now credited to State Funds should also be assigned to Local Bodies. In addition to the assignment of these revenues, they were in favour of large grants-in-aid from Government. These recommendations involve considerable expenditure from State revenues and require further consideration before Government are able to accept them.

I have outlined a few of the salient features of the proposals which have tentatively commended themselves to Government, with a view to obtain the opinion of this Assembly in case the members desire to offer any suggestions.

The Efficiency Audit staff of the General Secretariat continued to devote attention to questions connected with the efficiency of the services. A further development in the lines of work has been lately sanctioned by making the services of the staff available to heads of departments and Deputy Commissioners for the investigation of irregularities, etc., in Government departments and offices.

Several measures have been undertaken for ensuring system and regularity in the various branches of the administration. As stated already, greater uniformity is being introduced in the work of the Secretariats. The departments are being re-organised and establishments revised, one by one, with a view to placing their working on an up-to-date basis. A set of sample rules has been issued in order to standardise office methods, and in the case of the larger offices requiring more elaborate instructions, the rules have been expanded into office manuals. Eight of these manuals have been recently prepared. Rules have been framed to secure prompt consideration of petitions, and the question of introducing a new system of correspondence and record arrangement in Government offices with a view to greater celerity and orderliness in the disposal of public business is engaging the consideration of Government. The systematic inspection of all offices at periodical intervals has been arranged for, and returns of business statistics have been prescribed in order that the state of inspection and office work of heads of Departments and Deputy Commissioners may come to the notice of Government.

The question of the personnel of the services also received considerable attention during the year. Certain suggestions indicating the standards of efficiency and conduct to which Government officers are expected to conform have been issued, and it is hoped that compliance with them, which is at present largely a matter of discipline, will soon become one of habit. A new system of qualification reports has been instituted in order to enable Government to obtain, from time to time, more detailed information than what has been hitherto available regarding the work and capacity of the several officers. A scheme for encouraging officers to visit foreign countries has been lately sanctioned.

The second examination under the new Civil Service Scheme will be held in November next. There were 45 applicants, of whom 27 have been admitted to the examination. Orders have been recently passed with a view to rendering the training of Probationary Assistant Commissioners more practical.

The rules governing the recruitment and promotion of subordinate officials have also been examined, and it is under contemplation to introduce some changes calculated to afford greater encouragement to men of high educational attainments and to eliminate irregularities in the exercise of patronage. No system of recruitment can be deemed sound unless it gives preference to merit rather than to seniority, and secures a fair representation of all communities, as far as possible, in the public service. The question of giving systematic training to subordinate officials in the technique and principles of their work and in the elements of public administration is also engaging attention.

With a view to ensure efficiency in the district

administration, and to take stock of progress made in the various special schemes, tours have been undertaken by the Members of Council and the Dewan, and during the year, 51 taluks and 5 sub-taluks were visited. The important wants and grievances of taluks have been catalogued, in order that continuous attention may be bestowed upon them both by the officers of Government and the people.

In addition to compilations of departmental interest, handbooks of general information have been prepared for all the districts and, with the exception of those for Kadur and Chitaldrug, have also been printed. Several taluk handbooks have been completed. Booklets giving essential facts have been published in respect of nearly twenty municipal towns. Compilations of this character will be useful to officials as well as the non-official public, and are intended to help people to think in definite figures instead of in vague generalities, when questions connected with improvements and expenditure come up for consideration.

In describing the operations of the several departments, I have already dealt with some of the special measures undertaken by Government. It might probably be an advantage to give here a prospective view of what is being done in two important directions, *viz.*, the development of the natural resources of the country and the improvement of the efficiency of the people.

Taking communications first, we have at present a road mileage of one mile for every 1,047 inhabitants and one mile per 5·5 square miles of country. Very few new roads have been constructed in recent years and more road mileage is needed in many tracts; but the work is retarded because District Boards have not the wherewithal to provide for the high cost of maintenance.

Address to Dasara Representative Assembly.

Owing to the cessation of all railway activity for over twelve years, the State lagged behind the rest of India in railway development. Till 1912, the progress on railroad construction was 1 mile for every 12,554 inhabitants while the corresponding figure for all India was 1 mile per 8,873. A Railway Construction Department was organised in 1912, and since then project estimates amounting to Rs. 96 lakhs have been sanctioned. I have already referred to the progress made in the construction of each of these projects. The system of levying a railway cess has greatly facilitated the construction of feeder railways. If the people of the districts who appear to be keen on railways raise the necessary capital locally, as some of them have already done, in addition to paying a cess, an ideal state of things will have been brought into existence for the extension of railways. When the new lines are completed and brought into working order, our railway system, besides affording occupations to the people and bringing the local producer and the manufacturer into closer touch with the markets of the world, will also form a remunerative investment bringing a steady annual revenue to the State.

There is increased demand for power supply and there is also scope for further extension of the Cauvery Power Scheme. Alternative projects for increasing the power supply are under investigation.

The first stage of the Cauvery Reservoir is expected to be completed in 1916-17. The storage already secured is sufficient to guarantee the stipulated power supply to the mines and the works have begun to earn an enhanced revenue of Rs. 6 to 8 lakhs per annum from July last. The construction of subsidiary works, intended mainly to bring under command land meant to be given in exchange for the area submerged in the bed of the reservoir, and to enable the drowned-out raiyats to settle down in the neighbourhood of their old villages, have been sanctioned at an aggregate cost of about Rs. 21½ lakhs. The works will also afford irrigation facilities to a large extent of land, already under private holding, and are expected to prove remunerative to Government.

I have referred elsewhere to the revision of the rules for the restoration of minor tanks sanctioned during the year in accordance with the understanding arrived at in this Assembly last year. The question of the restoration of the major tanks in the State is also receiving consideration. In future, the selection of these tanks for restoration or repairs will be more systematic, and will depend on the relative importance of the tanks in point of revenue or their special value to the raiyats of the localities concerned.

Another question requiring careful attention is as regards the measures necessary to make up for the loss in capacity due to the silting up of these reservoirs and to establish a closer correspondence between their capacity and the *atchkat* below. It is not intended to undertake immediately an extensive survey all over the State but such of the tanks, particularly in the Kolar District, as may have failed to answer the requirements of cultivation will be examined and suitable remedies adopted.

The normal forest revenue of the State may be taken at about Rs. 22 lakhs though, in the years immediately preceding the war, a very much larger revenue was being realised owing to the exceptionally good prices secured for sandalwood. We are advised that there are great possibilities of augmenting our forest revenues by developing communications and carrying operations into the interior of the forests. Lack of communications has been a great difficulty in working these forests on a com-

Address to Dasara Representative Assembly.

mercial scale. The construction of the Tarikere-Narasimharajapura Tramway is expected to greatly assist the department in exploiting forest areas hitherto untouched. The forest staff is being strengthened for the same purpose.

Our mineral resources await exploitation. There are possibilities in the iron deposits of the Bababudans and a profitable industry in iron and steel may be created if the problem of smelting iron ore with charcoal on a commercial scale is satisfactorily solved. Government recently engaged the services of an expert, Mr. C. P. Perin, Consulting Engineer to the Tata Iron and Steel Company, to examine and report on the prospects of an iron and steel industry and though his detailed report has not yet been received, his general opinion is understood to be favourable.

The chief agency for the improvement of the people is education. I have already dealt with this subject in another part of the Address. His Highness the Maharaja is anxious for the more rapid spread of education and provision of increased facilities for elementary and higher professional training. With the establishment of a University now under consideration, His Highness hopes to make the educational system in the State self-contained and better adapted to the needs of the country.

The operations of the Economic Conference have already been described. With the aid of this agency Government are doing all they can to spread sound and up-to-date ideas about economic improvement in the country, to make the people think and act for themselves and to help private industrial activities in various ways.

With a view to revive the old village communal spirit, schemes relating to village improvement, minor tanks, rural water-supply, village forests, village courts and tank panchayets, have been introduced.

Of these the one that is full of hopeful auguries for the future is the Village Improvement Scheme. During the two years it has been in operation, 7,745 village committees have been constituted for 13,360 villages or about 79 per cent of the total number of villages in the State. In 2,966 villages, the committees are reported to be holding weekly gatherings regularly for attending to works of improvement and sanitation in and around villages. In 2,659 villages, newspapers are being subscribed for, and 2,039 village committees have been holding weekly meetings for disseminating useful information. The value of works of permanent utility undertaken during the year is estimated at Rs. 2·75 lakhs, of which the villagers' voluntary contribution in cash or by labour amounted to Rs. 1·5 lakhs, the balance being met by Government. The actual amount spent by the committees during the year 1914-15 amounted to about Rs. 75,000.

It is gratifying to note that the advantages of the scheme have been fully realised by the villagers who are co-operating cordially with Government officers.

The scheme may be said to have passed the experimental stage and it is necessary to consider on what lines its further development may best be attempted. Some steps are necessary in the coming year to bring every village and hamlet in the State under the operations of the scheme. Hitherto, the committees have been working on a voluntary basis; but frequent representations have been made to Government officers that the provisions of the scheme may be placed on a statutory footing. Perhaps it may not be desirable at this stage for Government to make the scheme compulsory for every village. An alternative course would be to leave it to the villagers themselves to decide in favour of compulsion or otherwise.

Where not less than three-fourths of the inhabitants of any village vote for such a step, the scheme may be made obligatory. In that case, the villagers should be given the option to contribute labour or pay a cess in lieu of personal service, the amount of the cess and the exemptions to be granted being settled by the village committee. In every case the money collected will remain with the committee and will be spent by them. If there is sufficient support forthcoming from the public, Government will have no objection to undertake legislation on these or similar lines.

The other village schemes have only recently begun to work. One hundred and forty-three village courts have been established and many of them have begun to hear cases. The number of tank panchayets constituted is 65. Proposals are being received for the formation of village forests and are under consideration. A sum of rupees one lakh per annum has been set apart for an extensive programme of well works in villages, in addition to the amounts included for this purpose in the grant to the Village Improvement Scheme and the budgets of the District Boards.

A sum of Rs. 25,000 has been set apart in the current year's budget for town-planning work. The necessity for a Town-Planning Bill has been urged for the consideration of Government.

The scheme inaugurated in February 1914 for the sanitary and economic improvement of the *malnad* portions of the districts of Shimoga, Kadur and Hassan was in operation during the year. The measures, chiefly adopted on the recommendation of the committees, related to the shifting of villages from insanitary areas, provision of increased medical and maternity facilities—such as free distribution of quinine, appointment of more midwives and establishment of female hospitals in selected central places, removal of rank vegetation in and round villages, provision of better drinking water, popularising vaccination and spreading elementary education by increasing the number of schools. The committees have yet to work out plans for increasing communications, for relieving agricultural indebtedness, for better drainage in villages and for providing more occupations to the people, such as minor industries connected with forest produce. The problem of labour supply in the *malnad* is one of the most important subjects engaging the attention of the committees. The operations of the committees were greatly hampered at the beginning by the difficulty and delay in finding suitable subordinate staff for the executive work of the improvement scheme.

From the list of measures of improvement and reform which I have just enumerated, many people in this country may, perhaps, be inclined to the view that everything is all right with us, that we are attempting too much rather than too little and that there is small need for further effort. But this is not so. A closer view, you will see, reveals an unsatisfactory state of things.

The test of a country's condition must be based, after all, on its relative position with reference to more advanced countries in all the essentials that constitute progress. Let us see how we stand under this test in a few respects.

Taking education first, the literate population in Mysore numbered 6 per cent in 1911. It is, perhaps, 8 per cent now. In progressive countries, the proportion is over 80 per cent.

Occupation and production in the country are chiefly confined to the most primitive of professions in the world, *viz.*, agriculture. The total production in Mysore is valued at Rs. 31 per head. The corresponding figures for Canada and Australia are reported to be Rs. 1,110 and Rs. 621 respectively.

Recently, the Bureau of Standards of the New York Board of Estimate found, upon enquiry, that the lowest yearly income upon which an unskilled labourer's family of five in that city can maintain a standard of living, consistent with American ideals, was Rs. 2,520. This is equivalent to Rs. 504 per head or more than sixteen times the Mysore average.

The figures available for our local trade show that the yearly exports and imports together amount to Rs. 26 per head. The corresponding figures for Canada and Australia are Rs. 480 and Rs. 495, respectively, that is, about eighteen times that of Mysore.

We obtain nearly all the manufactured articles, which require science, skill and enterprise to produce, from foreign countries and pay for them by exporting from the country food and other raw products, in some years at the risk of underfeeding our local population.

Neither the abundant natural resources of the country nor the vast stores of brain energy of the people are properly cultivated and utilised to increase production and wealth in the country.

The country suffers from a low level of industry, a low level of education, a low standard of earning and living, a low capacity for co-operation and low ideals of aspiration and effort generally. There is no gainsaying the fact that a wide gulf divides us, from the more advanced people, in all that constitutes prosperity and enlightenment.

The present low standard of living, as past experience has shown, is a source of danger. It leaves no margin for bad times. Our rainfall is so uncertain that a break in the monsoon, such as we experienced in August last, keeps our population in a state of anxious suspense. A partial failure of rain is attended with much suffering and a severe drought may cause even loss of life. The poorer classes, who are sensitive to the calamities of the seasons, require training in diligence and thrift. By steady labour for three or four years, a working man can lay by enough money or grain, for himself and family, to tide over a couple of years of scarcity or distress. There is abundant demand for well-paid labour in the country at present and no honest labourer has any excuse for neglecting such an insurance against a year of scarcity. The people should get accustomed to work longer hours and take more largely to industries, manufactures and trade. If these conditions are fulfilled, famines would be as rare in this land as they have become rare, on account of similar precautions, in European countries.

I have placed the ideals of advanced countries before you, because it is safe for us to follow the well-trodden paths of people already in the van of progress. It may be that, on account of climatic and other conditions, we shall never be able to reach their level of efficiency and prosperity. But that is no reason why we should not strive for what is within our reach, namely, to raise our standards, and double or treble our earning capacity in the near future. The very low level at which we stand is itself a measure of the opportunities before the country, and an augury that our efforts will meet with a speedy reward.

Government are doing what little they can to promote the efficiency of the people; but their efforts will not avail much without an access of activity and enthusiasm on the part of the public themselves. It is our hope that the more enlightened representatives of the people will study the situation, realise the seriousness of it and endeavour to co-operate with Government in the execution of the various measures of reform and progress to which we have put our hand. The co-operation is needed both from the official and the non-official public, and it should be co-operation which suggests and asks for opportunities to make itself useful, instead of waiting for a call.

It is pleasing to observe that the co-operation we need has also begun to come. Last year, I acknowledged the services of about 60 members of this Assembly in connection with the Village Improvement Scheme, and this year, it is my privilege to thank some 200 influential persons throughout the State, many of whom are members of this Assembly, for help rendered in connection with the Economic Conference movement. After such a gratifying response, His Highness' Government have no doubt that, in the present and future years, more of this informal but invaluable assistance, will be forthcoming.

Gentlemen, you will agree that this Address would be incomplete if I failed to voice the widespread feeling of regret which His Highness the Maharaja and his subjects feel at the approaching termination of the beneficent Viceroyalty of His Excellency Lord Hardinge. His Excellency has been a sincere well-wisher and a warm-hearted friend in whose sympathy and sense of justice the Native States have learnt to place implicit confidence.

Also, I know you will feel much regret if I remind you that this will be, perhaps, the last occasion on which the Hon'ble Col. Sir Hugh Daly, our Resident, will attend this function. He came to us with a high reputation, and, during his term of office, the relations of the Durbar with the Residency have been exceedingly frank and cordial. He has been a true friend of the State and has worthily maintained the highest traditions of British statesmanship. He will carry with him, in his retirement, the warm regard of His Highness the Maharaja and the best wishes of the people of Mysore.

REPLY TO DASARA ADDRESSES.

19th Oct. 1915. [At the thirty-second session of the Dasara Representative Assembly, held on 19th October 1915, Dewan Sir M. Visvesvaraya received addresses from the representatives of the Kolar Gold Field Mining Board, the Central Mahomedan Association, the Koppa and Narasimharajapura Taluks, the North Mysore Planters' Association, the Tarikere Muslim Association and the members of the Representative Assembly. Sir M. Visvesvaraya, in his joint reply to them, said as follows:—]

Gentlemen,—On behalf of His Highness' Government, I wish to thank you for the several addresses which have been presented and for the general tone of satisfaction expressed therein in regard to the past year's administration. It is gratifying to Government that some of the more important measures of recent years are receiving a large measure of popular support.

I have already referred, in the opening address, to the co-operation which, in the small sphere permitted to us, we have been able to render to the Imperial Government in the present crisis. Government are glad to note, from the addresses, that the measures taken in this behalf have received enthusiastic public support in the State.

With regard to the representation of the Mining Board for the permanent re-transfer to the State of the jurisdiction over the Kolar Gold Field Branch Railway, you will be glad to learn that, subject to certain conditions, the Government of India have generously acceded to our request.

The question of extending the provisions of the Mines Regulation to the Branch Railway and the other points raised in the address of the Mining Board will receive the careful consideration of His Highness' Government.

Government are in full sympathy with the desire expressed, in the address from the representatives of the

Reply to Dasara Addresses.

Koppa and Narasimharajapura Taluks, for the spread of English education in rural areas; and they are taking the necessary measures to promote the object we all have in view.

I am glad to observe that the Mahomedan Association appreciates the special facilities given to that community in the matter of Mahomedan education. Any further expansion of this policy will be necessarily conditioned by the funds available and by the claims of other classes of His Highness' subjects similarly circumstanced. In some parts of British India, a tendency is noticeable on the part of Mahomedans to resort more and more to institutions meant for the general public, as they seem to realise that it is in this way, rather than in multiplying special institutions, that the permanent interests of the Mahomedan community will be best served.

Reference has also been made to the alleged increase of intemperance in the State. I have just explained in my address that, though there was an increase of revenue there has been no increase in the average consumption of intoxicants.

Several other subjects of local importance have been referred to in the addresses by the North Mysore Planters' Association and other bodies. These will receive due consideration.

I received only this morning a copy of the address by the representatives of a meeting of this Assembly held yesterday. Several important questions have been raised in that address. With your views on some of them, Government, as you may be aware, are in full sympathy. There are others in regard to which practical action is not immediately possible, though Government approve of the general objects which the members have in view. There are others, again, which require further consideration and discussion.

The more important of the questions which I have not specifically alluded to in this reply may, if necessary, be discussed within the next few days in the Assembly itself.

His Highness' Government much appreciate the graceful references, in the addresses, to the honour conferred by His Majesty the King-Emperor on His Highness the Yuvaraja of Mysore.

For your very appreciative reference to the various measures of reform and improvement undertaken by Government under His Highness' guidance, I return, on behalf of my colleagues and myself, our very sincere thanks. I am also grateful to you for your congratulations on the distinction conferred on me by the Imperial Government.

It will give me great pleasure, gentlemen, to communicate to His Highness the Maharaja the sentiments, conveyed in your addresses, of loyalty and attachment to his throne and person and your gratification at the many benefits you are enjoying under His Highness' benign rule.

SPEECH AT THE DASARA REPRESENTATIVE ASSEMBLY.

26th Oct. 1915. [The thirty-second session of the Dasara Representative Assembly closed its sittings on the 26th October 1915. In winding up the proceedings, Dewan Sir M. Visvesvaraya made the following speech :—]

Gentlemen,—The work of the session is over. We have considered in all about four hundred subjects, including those entered in the supplemental list furnished by the Assembly after the opening day of the session. Some twenty-five or thirty of these subjects being very important were fully discussed. I will now briefly indicate the views and present intentions of Government in regard to most of these.

I must premise my observations with an expression of regret for being obliged to curtail the discussion on some of the subjects. Had I not done so, it would not have been possible to complete our work to-day.

It was also a matter of much regret to me that, on account of financial exigencies, a great many of the requests of members, which involved additional expenditure, had to be refused.

The question of the relations between the *inamdars* and tenants, about which you made a representation last year, was considered by a committee and their report is already in your hands. But in the light of the further views now expressed by you, the subject will be again examined either by the same, or by an enlarged committee or commission.

In the matter of remuneration to village servants, *viz.*, *toties* and *talaries*, in the Nandidrug Division, Government have come to certain conclusions which they hope to announce shortly. The present idea, as suggested by some of the members themselves, is to collect *miras* at a rate based on the assessment payable by the raiyats.

The reduction of the irrigable area below tanks which have silted up will receive attention during the year. A beginning will be made by taking up a few selected tanks in the Kolar District for investigation. Our resources and establishment are not adequate to enable us to undertake this work on any very large scale at once.

In regard to Amrut Mahal Kavals, Government are willing to throw open for cultivation as much land as possible, after retaining enough for the requirements of the Department.

Speech at the Dasara Representative Assembly.

The question of the separation of the executive and judicial functions is one on which there is not much difference of opinion, on principle, between you and the Government. The Chief Judge is in favour of the proposal and we hope to make a beginning as soon as we see our way to provide the necessary funds.

The Rev. Mr. Gulliford enquired whether Government proposed to charge fees in primary schools. On the whole, I think, it is better to recover fees from children whose parents are able to bear the charge than forego the further expansion of education which such additional income would provide. During the past few years, Government expenditure on education has gone up by leaps and bounds, *i.e.*, from about Rs. 8 lakhs to over Rs. 20 lakhs. We want every available rupee for the further extension of education. It is true in certain other advanced countries, primary and even higher education is free. But we have not their resources. The expenditure on primary education in those countries bears, unlike in Mysore, a very small proportion to their total resources.

The difficulties connected with the School Final Examination appear to be very real and we learn from the papers that the Syndicate of the Madras University are themselves giving attention to the matter. The State will do what it can, in conjunction with the University, to minimise the hardships brought to notice.

The general wish of this Assembly was in favour of the retention of the scheme of religious instruction in our schools. Government have no desire to disturb existing arrangements. If possible, the present arrangements will be improved by providing for business education in addition.

We are actively investigating the question of a railway connection to a suitable port on the West Coast. As soon as the Mysore-Arsikere Railway is completed, other lines will be taken up, one by one, to expand our internal railway system. It is the desire of His Highness' Government to work the railways themselves and, as far as possible, with the aid of trained local men.

In the matter of railway thefts, I would suggest that every authenticated case may be brought to the notice of the Railway Secretary and the Inspector-General of Police. I feel sure that the higher officers of the Madras and Southern Mahratta Railway Company and the British Police will help to bring the offenders to book and remove this longstanding grievance of the Mysore public.

The specific proposal to extend medical relief into the interior of the taluks, which was recommended by so many members of this Assembly, will receive attention in the coming year.

There were two or three complaints in connection with the resettling of the raiyats drowned out by the Cauvery Reservoir. In working out a scheme of this magnitude, it is impossible to avoid stray cases of inconvenience or hardship. Any genuine individual grievance will receive immediate consideration from our officers, if brought to their notice.

The extension of the benefits of the State Life Insurance Scheme to the non-official public has been urged in this Assembly for several years past. You will be glad to learn that His Highness the Maharaja has been graciously pleased to sanction the extension, subject to reasonable limitations.

His Highness' Government are aware of the urgent need that exists for a proper piped water supply in several important towns in the State. They are prepared to give the usual help as soon as satisfactory proposals are received. They are also willing to stretch a point and give special aid to places like Chitaldrug where exceptional difficulties exist in this respect.

Speech at the Dasara Representative Assembly.

His Highness the Maharaja was pleased to state, at a recent function at Seringapatam, that his Government would give all reasonable help to improve that town. The wants of the town will be once more investigated with a view to give full effect to His Highness' wishes.

The subject of Local Self-Government has already been dealt with in my Address and active steps will be taken to introduce a scheme developed by the Committee presided over by Mr. M. Kantaraj Urs. Government trust that the public will heartily co-operate with them in giving practical effect to the scheme.

Government were gratified to receive the testimony of the members that the Malnad Improvement Scheme is making steady progress. There will always be defects and difficulties when a new scheme is started. We look to the representatives of the public to help us to remedy them.

As regards the Village Improvement Scheme, I have watched the progress made and the enthusiasm which the officers and the public have shown in furthering the intentions of Government. I have visited numerous villages; the many proofs of the capacity and enthusiasm which the people have shown in this work are gratifying in the highest degree.

Many of the members raised the question of the levy of a cess in lieu of personal service from recalcitrant villagers in connection with communal work due from them for half a day in the week. Government intimated last year that they wanted to work the scheme, for some time at least, on a voluntary basis relying on the enthusiasm of the people themselves. Although the proposal to levy a cess was approved by a majority of the members, Government are not in favour of introducing compulsion at once. The question will, however, receive reconsideration if the proposal meets with more unanimous support next year.

Speech at the Dasara Representative Assembly.

The requests made by members from the Hassan and Bangalore Districts for bridges over the Hemavati at Gorur and the Arkavati at Kankanhalli have been graciously sanctioned by His Highness the Maharaja. Both projects will, I hope, be put in hand in the coming year.

I have already informed you that Government are prepared in future sessions of this Assembly to consider twenty-five supplementary questions if they are of general public importance and put forward with the approval of a majority of the members of this Assembly.

You wanted a separate session for discussing the budget. The State Budget does not undergo any very appreciable variation from year to year. Any suggestions you may make now can be considered a few months hence, *i.e.*, about April next, when we begin to frame the budget for the following official year. Any minor suggestions involving variations in expenditure of Rs. 2 or 3 lakhs can be easily given effect to even after the budget is formally sanctioned. The necessary rules for the discussion of the budget in this Assembly will issue before the next session.

Our chief difficulties in arranging for a second session are the unwieldy character of the Assembly and the dislocation of public work which would ensue by withdrawing heads of departments and district officers from their duties a third time in the year.

The Assembly has been doing very good work in bringing deficiencies in the administration and grievances and wants of the people to notice. By long practice, it has learnt to do this work to perfection.

There are numerous other subjects touching vital matters in our civic and public life which require attention if our progress is to be more rapid. Some twenty of these have been brought to your notice. Their number might be easily increased to two hundred if only we had workers enough in the country to take them up. Economic subjects are placed in the forefront of our programme because the primary wants of the people claim our first attention. There are many other subjects awaiting suitable organization to deal with; subjects, for instance, like municipal government, town planning, encouragement of art and literature, improving discipline and social amenities in towns and villages. As no organization exists to make the people even to think about these subjects, it is no wonder that our earning power and working efficiency should be so low.

Government expect every citizen to be a worker. If, in addition to being this, he gives a portion of his time, energy or money for public work, either on behalf of the town or village in which he resides or of the State, as a whole, he will be making himself doubly useful. No subject of His Highness in this State should be content to remain a spectator.

It is also important that the members of this Assembly and the public should keep themselves well posted with public affairs and with the means and resources of Government. That is why we ask you to discuss the budget. If the representatives of the public know what requests are feasible and what are not and put forward well-considered proposals in which all aspects of a question have been previously considered, the work of compliance with them will be rendered easy.

You have placed before Government some four hundred subjects. Many of them require additional funds. You have not suggested any new taxation; there is no proposition in which you offer co-operation or help of any sort on behalf of the people. I may remind you that there are countries in which people hand over, in some shape or other, over 30 per cent of their net earnings to their

Governments to be spent on the public administration and the development work of their country.

The tendency of the public in the past has been to ask for a great deal more than Government can give. I hope, in future, there will be both give and take, and mutual trust and co-operation between the officials and the representatives of the non-official public. It is only when Government officers and the public begin to see eye to eye and supplement each other's efforts that good administration and the permanent prosperity of the country as a whole will be promoted.

SPEECH AT ST. JOHN AMBULANCE ASSOCIATION MEETING.

[A meeting of the St. John Ambulance Association was held at Bangalore on 19th January 1916. There was a large gathering of ladies and gentlemen present on the occasion under the presidency of the Hon'ble Col. Sir Hugh Daly, K.C.I.E., British Resident in Mysore. Sir M. Visvesvaraya, in addressing the gathering, made the following speech:—] 19th Jan. 1916.

Sir Hugh Daly, Ladies and Gentlemen,—I have been asked to make a few remarks on this occasion and it gives me much pleasure to associate myself with the very worthy object for which we have met here to-day.

Some years ago, I was present at a public meeting in this hall at which a high Military officer had to second a proposition which had been duly moved. The speech of that officer was remarkable for its brevity. He said "Mr. Chairman, I say ditto to speaker No. 3" and sat down.

Speech at St. John Ambulance Association Meeting.

After hearing what has been already said, I am tempted to follow the example of that gallant officer and content myself with saying ditto to what has fallen from our esteemed chairman.

The St. John Ambulance Association, as Col. Standage has told us, has been doing valuable work in peace time and it has shown a special access of vigour since the outbreak of the war. As far as I am aware, we have in the Mysore State and in the Civil and Military Station of Bangalore three distinct centres actively at work, *viz.*, the Bangalore District centre, the Mysore State centre and, if Col. Standage will permit me to say so, what is more important than either of them, the Bangalore Ladies' Branch.

The people at headquarters seem to have created a kind of friendly rivalry between the ladies and gentlemen by establishing the Ladies' Branch. The gentlemen have been content with giving some money and with that they feel their obligations discharged; but the ladies have not taken their responsibilities so lightly. They have had to give money and many of them have also had to work and prepare garments and hospital comforts with their own hands.

Several ladies have started smaller organizations of their own and have been collecting money and gifts of articles both in the Station and the City.

There are other funds, besides, to which the public are called upon to contribute, *viz.*, His Excellency the Viceroy's war relief fund, the Belgian relief fund, the Servian relief fund, and so on.

I learn that several prominent ladies in Bangalore have been untiring in their efforts in this good work—Lady Miller, Mrs. Chatterton and Mrs. Ormerod; also Mrs. Campbell and Mrs. Foulkes when they were here. Sir Hugh Daly and Col. Standage have borne testimony to the very valuable work done by the Honorary Secretaries, Mrs. Barton and Miss Govindarajulu.

The ladies of the Ursu community in Mysore have subscribed liberally and the ladies of the Seva Sedan and the Srinivasa Mandiram in the City have set an example, in however humble a way, which is worthy of all praise.

Sir Hugh Daly referred in enthusiastic terms to the work done by several ladies but he had not one word to say about the principal worker of them all, *viz.*, Lady Daly who, as President of the Ladies' Branch, has borne the brunt of the burden. Whether she went to Ootacamund or remained in Bangalore, she has had to receive and answer telegrams from Simla, organise working parties at the Residency and keep up an energetic campaign in the interests of the fund. When I asked her two or three days ago how she managed to do all this work, she said to me, "my husband has been helping me a little." So it comes about that both Sir Hugh and Lady Daly have taken a very substantial share in the work of the Ladies' Branch. They have always taken a keen interest in every important good work, whether in the Station or the City, during the time they have been in our midst. They have been a centre of concord and harmony among us and we have come to regard them as safe advisers and very valued friends. I feel that whenever the time comes for their departure, Mysore and Mysoreans will part from them with the sincerest regret.

You have in recent months witnessed the efforts that are being made in the Mysore State under the energetic guidance of His Highness the Yuvaraja, assisted by my friend, Mr. Kantaraj Urs, to provide gifts of comforts and conveniences to the Mysore Imperial Service Lancers at the front. This is the first time that the Mysore troops have gone out of India and, indeed, the first time for over a century, in which they have ever gone outside the State. There is much concern and sympathy for the men, who have been absent for over sixteen months, from our midst, and it is no wonder that there has been such a gratifying response to our appeal for funds on their behalf.

The St. John Ambulance Association, being in the interests of a wider community, I trust the people of Mysore will be able to spare some further small contributions for those who, to whatever country they may belong, have gone to fight for the British Empire.

As Col. Standage has told us, the Association has been doing its humanitarian work of relieving the sick and the wounded *without distinction of race, creed or colour*. We on our side should also take a broader view and see that charity in such cases extends beyond the home.

The troops fighting at the front number, perhaps, a million and a quarter, that is, well over six times the entire population of the Station and City of Bangalore put together. From all accounts, the fight is strenuous and the men are subjected to many privations and have to face the rigors of a northern winter.

Our work is intended to mitigate the sufferings and brighten the lives of the sick and the wounded among the many brave fellows who have gone to risk their lives. The sufferers need all our sympathy and tenderness. Their gratitude is worth having.

I have no doubt many of those present here to-day have already contributed to the funds of the Association and many are arranging to give more. There are numerous demands on our slender resources in these times. But even under such disadvantageous conditions, an organised appeal to the outside public cannot, I am sure, fail to meet with a cordial response.

The present is, perhaps, the most critical period in the course of the war. Any gifts, if sent at once, will be doubly useful both to the sufferers and also, in however small a way it may be, to the cause of the Allies. The need is pressing, help is required promptly and what we can give, we must give without delay.

ADDRESS TO MYSORE ENGINEERS.

[The ninth session of the Mysore Engineers' Association took place at the Association rooms, on 16th March 1916. In opening the proceedings, as a past President of the Association, Sir M. Visvesvaraya delivered the following address:—] 16th Mar. 1916.

Gentlemen, —I have the very pleasing function assigned to me on this occasion of welcoming the members of the Association and wishing this conference a successful session.

A most gratifying feature of this assembly is its representative character. The papers put down on the agenda represent nearly all brances of engineering—civil, including architectural and municipal, railway, mechanical, electrical and industrial. This is a guarantee that the application of science to local resources is under continuous study and that all branches of the engineering profession, however small may be the scale of operations in some of them, find a place in the public service of the country.

As a past President of your Association and the member of Government in close touch with the technical services, I am intensely interested in your work. Government want to see their engineers efficient and up-to-date. They want them to keep under investigation all large engineering problems calculated to add to the production of the country and promote the convenience and prosperity of the people.

As regards efficiency, the Association has been endeavouring to develop the scheme of special studies to make experts of some of our practising engineers. Some of our officers have taken to the study of selected branches of engineering and are improving themselves. Such officers will, by increasing the market value of their services benefit both Government and themselves in course of time.

The number of engineering questions and practical problems which await investigation is very large. Lists of these will be found in the various Secretariats. The work is limited only by the agency which we can find to undertake it.

The Public Works Department has been urged for some time past to bring into existence, by affording suitable encouragement, private engineers and architects, or firms, to take up designing and building work for the public.

I should be glad if, in the course of the discussion of departmental subjects, the President will kindly cause statements to be prepared showing progress made under the three heads I have mentioned and specifying the names of officers who have given time outside their regular duties to the study of special subjects or the solution of local engineering problems. I venture to suggest that programmes of work to be done in the coming year may be prepared in a similar form and copies furnished to Government.

It is a gratifying sign of the vitality of the Association that you have begun to issue a quarterly bulletin. I only hope you will be able to persevere and make it a success. Officers are full of enthusiasm at these annual gatherings and are liberal in making promises of what they are going to do; but I know some officers at least who think nothing more of their responsibility till within a few months of the next year's session. To help in organising these special studies, I suggested, at the last session, the formation of a vigilance committee of three officers and I should be glad to know whether any steps have been taken to form one and whether sufficient precautions are taken to enable performances to keep pace with promises.

There is one more point I wish to emphasise in the interests of general administration. Your work and my work are all intended for the public good. The permanent interests of the people are our concern and we exist for them. It is important that every department, nay every officer and subordinate of a department, should work in a spirit of harmonious co-operation both with one another and with other departments of Government and the general public. No Government department can long remain a watertight compartment without suffering in output of work and public estimation. In the office I have the honour to hold, I have frequent opportunities of gauging how often and how grievously public interests suffer through lack of adaptability and co-operation on the part of both the official and non-official public of this State. But I venture to think that things are improving, improving so rapidly as to give us hope that co-operation and spirit of responsibility for the public good may soon become a feature of our time.

I trust that when you take up departmental questions for discussion, within the next few days, all important defects of organization and procedure which clog progress will come under review; that when you go back to your respective spheres of work, you will bring fresh ideas to bear on it and that you will not be content with doing your duties merely according to custom and habit and tradition.

Gentlemen, I will not detain you any more. The year has been one in which, on the whole, engineering works of great magnitude and variety have been in progress in our small State. Deeds speak louder than words, and the engineers of this State, as a body, may look back with pride on the solid work they have done during the past twelve months. It is needless for me to caution you—at least the senior members of the services—that to maintain the existing fairly satisfactory state of things it is imperative that you should continue to put forth new vigour and initiative, and keep on making constant endeavours at higher efficiency and improvement.

INAUGURATION OF THE MYSORE CHAMBER OF COMMERCE.

8th May 1916.

[The inaugural meeting of the Mysore Chamber of Commerce took place at the Government High School, Bangalore, on the 8th May 1916. Over 500 merchants attended the meeting. The audience included the *élite* of Bangalore. Mr. W. C. Rose, Manager, Bank of Mysore and President-elect of the Chamber, made an interesting speech in which he referred to the local circumstances which called for the formation of a Chamber of Commerce. In inaugurating the Chamber, Sir M. Visvesvaraya, who occupied the chair, made the following speech :—]

Gentlemen,—We meet here to-day to inaugurate a Chamber of Commerce, the object of which is to safeguard and promote the special interests of trade and industry in Mysore. That those interests needed protection has long

Inauguration of the Mysore Chamber of Commerce.

been apparent and a proposal to start an organization for the purpose has been on the programme of the Economic Conference for over three years. During the past eighteen months, the question has received the special attention of the Industries and Commerce Committee. We owe it to that Committee and particularly to Mr. Chatterton, Mr. Rose, Mr. Garudachar, Mr. Vardhamaniah and Mr. Ranganatha Rao Saheb that all the preliminaries are completed and we are now in a position to announce the birth of the Chamber.

In his exhaustive and interesting address, Mr. Rose has drawn attention to the fact that the trade in grains and pulses, in piece-goods and cloth, in leather and skins, metals, oil-seeds, etc., has passed largely from local merchants into the hands of outsiders from distant Provinces. It is no fault of outsiders that they have come in and captured our trade. They have advantages which our local merchants have not had hitherto, namely, practical training in large business houses, capacity to work hard and under severe discipline, cheap capital and a powerful organization behind them. Whatever may be the external causes, the loss to the local merchants, which is deplorable, is attributed to the apathy of local merchants, their prejudice, lack of enterprise and unwillingness to move with the times.

It is no wonder that the trade conditions in Mysore should be so unsatisfactory. The bulk of the trade is carried on in the most primitive fashion. The outlook of our merchants is narrow. Their power of co-operation is feeble and their business methods are out of date. They are ignorant of trade statistics and, for lack of training, they are unable to adapt themselves to the rapidly changing conditions of the world trade.

It is, perhaps, the fault of circumstances that this is so. Every occupation requires study and apprenticeship. As in every other profession, merchants require training and guidance and these can be given by providing the necessary institutions and facilities calculated to broaden their outlook.

One of the first means to this end is the establishment of an association like this which would give them opportunities of personal service and of joint deliberation and action on large questions connected with industries and trade generally.

The work to be done by the Chamber is described in the address of Mr. Rose and also in detail in the draft prospectus. I need only emphasise a few sailent points.

The Chamber should bring the wants and grievances of men engaged in industry and trade to the notice of Government and of public service corporations like railway companies, municipal and other local bodies, bank, post and telegraph or other authorities whose operations affect them. The Chamber should do for its clients and to the trades what a lawyer does for the litigant public.

In the second place, it should maintain a continuous study of large commercial questions of local interest and constantly strive to strengthen the conditions under which trade and industries are carried on at present.

It should also focus and consolidate commercial opinion on current topics and publish the united judgment of representative merchants and business men regarding them for the information of the public.

Some of the earliest things which the Chamber of Commerce might put its hand to will be to undertake a compilation of trade statistics, a commercial survey of business houses, closer study of imports and exports and the publication of a trade directory.

It should promote co-operative enterprise and the establishment of business concerns on the partnership and the joint-stock company principle.

Inauguration of the Mysore Chamber of Commerce.

It should encourage the habit of travelling among merchants and introduce the system of commercial correspondents.

No individual or single groups of men can do the work which an organised association like the Chamber can accomplish.

The business portion of the public should be taught to recognise that whatever benefits the community benefits also the individual, sooner or later. By co-operation and joint action, the mercantile community may become a power in the land. An individual having a grievance may be snubbed, he may have to submit to unjust exactions; but no public authority can afford to ignore the joint representation of 500 merchants.

Mr. Rose has referred to the Economic Conference sitting in Paris where questions connected with the world commerce after the war are being discussed. There is no doubt that great attention will be paid to industry and commerce and that an era of large developments will follow at the end of the war.

Our first duty is to put our house in order, remove the disadvantages and strengthen the position of our merchants at home. We shall be contributing our share of effort, however humble it may be, to promote the commercial interests of the Empire, by studying what is going on in other parts of the Empire and by working in close association with similar bodies in British India.

One of the many ways in which a Chamber can make itself useful to the country is by interesting itself in the industrial and commercial education of the people, in qualifying them for practical pursuits and by making science popular among them.

The more urgent and essential directions in which the people of Mysore need training are:—

(1) in manufactures and building work,

(2) in commerce and business, and

(3) in science and applied chemistry.

It is aptly remarked that the day of the rule-of-thumb man is past, the day of the practical man is passing and the day of the scientific man is coming.

The Chamber should interest itself in spreading a knowledge of elementary science among the masses. It should see that a sufficient number of young men are kept under training in the schools and colleges to supply the future needs of business and trade in the country. It is our interest to induce a fair percentage of the best young men, the flower of the youth of the country, to take to industrial and business careers.

One of the first duties of the committee of the Chamber should be to appoint a section or sub-committee, whose chief function would be to induce as many merchants and manufacturers as possible to become members. The committee has to organise trade sections at headquarters and to start town committees or branch Chambers, commercial museums and enquiry offices, in eight or nine business centres within the State. May I express the hope that by the end of the first year, the Chamber will have on its rolls, at least 500 members, of whom perhaps 150 or 200 may be drawn from the cities of Bangalore and Mysore? You may be sure that merchants from the mofussil will not be indifferent to your appeal for co-operation. They will join if they feel they will get some return for their money or see a reasonable prospect of the same.

Before I close, I may be permitted to add a word or two regarding the work of your committee. I hear constant complaints of unpunctuality in the working of some of the local organizations but the composition of your committee is a guarantee that it will be an active body. No committee or association in the country should remain inactive even for a month, because some leading man or other connected with it has no time to participate in its work. When a member has no time for the work, he should be required to abdicate for the time being in favour of a substitute. I would suggest the formation of a vigilance committee, consisting of at least three high-class business men selected from the Chamber, whose duty it should be to see that the committee of the Chamber regularly prepares its annual and quarterly programmes beforehand and to respectfully remind the committee whenever its performances fall short of promises.

It is only when every member works and nobody shirks that the committee can keep itself continuously active and become an effective working force in the country.

Our best thanks are due to Mr. Rose, who is doing such excellent work in another sphere, for acceding to the request of the merchants to become the first Chairman of this new Chamber. His Highness' Government greatly value the co-operation of other members also, particularly of European gentlemen who have so readily come forward to help us. Thus piloted, the Chamber will be beginning its career of beneficent activity under the most favourable auspices.

Gentlemen, this association has been started with the gracious sanction of His Highness the Maharaja and nothing will be dearer to His Highness' heart than that all active elements in the State should work in unison to make the scheme a practical success. I will now conclude with what I know will be the fervent wish of everyone present here to-day, that this Chamber may fulfil all the expectations formed of it, that it may grow in utility and influence from year to year and that it may long remain the premier representative and guardian of the industrial and commercial interests of Mysore.

ADDRESS TO THE MYSORE ECONOMIC CONFERENCE.

9th June 1916.

[The seventh session of the Mysore Economic Conference was held at the Public Offices, Mysore, on June 9, 1916. Dewan Sir M. Visvesvaraya, President of the Conference, was in the chair. There was a large and representative gathering present on the occasion. In opening the session, Sir M. Visvesvaraya delivered the following address :—]

Gentlemen,—I belive that no important public meeting can be opened in any part of the British Empire at the present time without reference to the tragic death of Lord Kitchener during this critical time. Two years ago when Great Britain was faced with the great war, he was the man of the hour. He threw himself heart and soul into the task of organising the resources of the Empire against the enemy. He has succeeded in creating an army of five million soldiers. I had a long discussion with him on two occasions, and not one who met him failed to be impressed by his great personality, by his great grasp of details and his great organising power. The whole British Empire to-day feels the loss of the great soldier and eminent administrator. I think it our duty to add our praise to his work and record in silence our deep regret at the loss that the Empire has sustained by his death.

This day marks the beginning of the sixth year in the life of the Mysore Economic Conference. We meet at this annual session to discuss the more important economic questions which affect our State, to take stock of last year's progress and to prepare programmes of work for the coming year. If time permits, the organization of the Conference will be also examined from the standpoint of our experience during the past five years, with a view to introduce changes and improvements where necessary for the more effective fulfilment of its main functions.

Address to the Mysore Economic Conference.

A detailed account of the work done during the past year by the three Central Committees will be placed before you by the respective Chairmen. I will only refer to a few salient features of their activities.

As the Central Committees and the corresponding Departments of Government are intended to supplement each other's efforts, the work done by the Departments has also to be referred to in this connection.

In the Department of Industries and Commerce, about 24 installations of machinery and plant in different parts of the State were completed and 26 new ones were under erection. This brings the total number of installations completed to 76 and including those under erection to 102. A sandalwood oil factory has been started which is expected to give an appreciable revenue to Government. It is reported that the experimental factory already set up will be capable from next month of turning out oil valued at about Rs. 25,000 per month. Plant for a soap factory has been ordered. At present very good soap is being prepared in the Indian Institute of Science. Its manufacture on a commercial scale will become possible as soon as the machinery ordered is received and erected. Enquiries were in progress in connection with another cotton mill in Mysore, and investigations for starting iron and steel manufacture are making hopeful progress. The Industries and Commerce Committee, with the help of the Department, has been considering a variety of other subjects, such as paper-pulp manufacture, wood distillation, button manufacture, etc. A Home Industries Institute, proposed by the Committee, has been sanctioned tentatively for one year. It is proposed to develop industrial and commercial museums in different parts of the State and arrangements are being made to start the nucleus of one such in connection with the Dasara Exhibition. Commercial matters have not progressed very far but, as you are aware, a Chamber of Commerce has been recently started which will work independently of the Conference. The Bank of Mysore has increased its transactions from Rs. 40 lakhs to Rs. 53 lakhs during the year. The question of developing land and industrial banks has been receiving attention. Steps are being taken to encourage merchants to travel abroad. In addition to the compilation of statistics of rail-borne trade by the Department, preparations are being made to collect more complete industrial and commercial statistics in future for the whole State.

The Agricultural Committee has given special attention to the development of sericulture. The services of Signor W. Mari, who carried on preliminary investigations in 1914, have been re-engaged. The construction of a rearing school has been sanctioned at Channapatna where the Central Farm, which is the gift of a local merchant, will be developed to supply disease-free eggs on a large scale. The questions of fruit culture, extension of cultivation of commercial crops, improvement of agricultural stock and sheep-rearing and revision of forms for agricultural statistics have received some attention. Through the exertions of the Tumkur District Committee, an Agricultural School has been started at Chickanahalli, in the Sira Taluk, due mainly to the munificence of a private gentleman of the cultivator's class who bequeathed a building, with a small farm attached, and a substantial sum in cash, for charitable purposes.

The Director of Agriculture and his Assistants attended a large number of meetings of representative men and cultivators in the taluks and addressed them on agricultural matters. There has been a considerable extension of demonstration work. School courses were held for cultivators in Hebbal and Marthur. Oil-cake manure and agricultural implements were supplied on a large

Address to the Mysore Economic Conference.

scale. The Department also carried on the usual scientific work.

Coming to education, you are aware that preparations are well in hand for the inauguration of the new University of Mysore from 1st July next.

The Education Committee has further developed the public libraries in Bangalore and Mysore, and, at their instance, Government have sanctioned a scheme for rural libraries. Partly as a result of their recommendation for the improvement of industrial and commercial education, Government very recently sanctioned the conversion of the aided institutions at Hassan and Chitaldrug into Government Industrial Schools and the opening of four new Industrial Schools at Kolar, Tumkur, Chikmagalur and Shimoga. A beginning is being made for opening commercial classes at taluk stations. Arrangements have been made at the Maharani's College to give industrial training to girls and women. The formation of students' aid associations in large towns and cities has been taken up. Some of the other important schemes considered by the Committee were, opening special classes for training adults, improvements in normal training, school excursions, visual instruction, publication of books in Kanarese, etc. The Committee also prepared a comprehensive scheme for the collection and compilation of educational statistics, which has met with the approval of Government. The question of the education of the backward communities received some attention. The itinerant lecturers appointed at the instance of the Committee are reported to be doing useful work in spreading new ideas and enthusiasm among the people. A scheme of honorary supervisors has been approved, to enable taluk areas to provide themselves with agencies to help them in popularising sound ideas of economic improvement.

The Department started 776 aided village elementary

schools and 130 Government elementary schools during the year. One hundred and five adult schools and 418 village indigenous day and night schools have been started.

English education is being encouraged in rural tracts. Compulsory education is making satisfactory progress wherever it has been extended so far.

Industrial education is receiving attention both in the primary and secondary stages. A scheme for rural agricultural education has been recently sanctioned.

The Standing and the Central Committees gave special attention during the year to the subject of collecting and maintaining correct statistics. All available statistics have been incorporated in district and taluk handbooks already published and additional information and statistics of a technical nature are being compiled by the District Economic Superintendents.

With the co-operation of the Department of Industries and Commerce and the Registrar of Co-operative Societies, ten co-operative societies for crushing sugar-cane, manufacturing jaggery and hulling paddy, have been started and they have been financed by Government to the extent of Rs. 45,000. Agricultural co-operation is also being slowly developed and the co-operative credit societies have been instrumental in extending the use of improved implements, oil-cake manure and seed among raiyats.

The present disastrous war has interfered, to some extent, with our progress. Some of the projects which we may start at once are delayed for want of machinery. It is found difficult to procure the commonest machinery needed for the daily work of the country. The prices of imported articles, many of which we have come to look upon as necessaries, have been rising. The situation brought on by the war has opened the eyes of the people and revealed the helplessness of our position industrially, the result of our neglect and the increasing dependence placed on agriculture in the past. As a consequence, there is an awakening noticeable everywhere in India. The recent appointment of the Industries Commission is a proof of the solicitude of the Government of India for the industrial development of the country. But we must not shut our eyes to the fact that the war that is going on is partly an economic war due, in the words of Mr. Asquith, to the growing rivalry of the nations of the world. When it is over, the competition in trade and industries will go on as relentlessly as ever and, in this economic war of nation against nation, there will be no peace.

I will make a few general observations on the present economic situation in Mysore with a view to bring home to our people the urgent need that exists in the country for economic improvement.

A few weeks ago, we all read a Reuter's telegram which stated that the Commonwealth of Australia possessed property valued at £1,000,000,000 or Rs. 1,500 crores. Rough calculations indicate that the total value of property in Mysore, excluding the Gold Mines, amounts to about Rs. 125 crores. This disparity will seem particularly striking when it is remembered that the population of Australia is only five millions against our six millions in Mysore.

The value of farm produce calculated per head of population in Australia is estimated at Rs. 138, and, including dairying, pastoral produce, etc., at Rs. 351. In Mysore, the corresponding figure is Rs. 24. In industries and manufactures, Australia produces articles valued at Rs. 171 per head and Mysore only Rs. 7 per head. The value of the total production of Australia comes to Rs. 621

per head as against Rs. 31, or about twenty times that of Mysore.

In Australia, again, there are three acres of cultivated land per head of population against one acre per head in Mysore. Notwithstanding this, the Australians are not content with agriculture but are devoting special attention to the expansion of industries.

The estimated total trade of Mysore amounts to Rs. 26 per head and that of Australia to Rs. 495 per head.

Formerly, Mysore was fairly self-contained in regard to the small necessities of the people such as clothing, building materials, etc., but, owing to increase of communications and keen foreign competition, we get most of our supplies from outside at lower rates than we can manufacture locally with our crude hand labour. A large number of our people have, in consequence, lost their former occupations and been driven to agriculture.

If you take the figures for education, it will be seen, as I have so often said before, that the percentage of literate population in Mysore is about 8; in progressive countries, it is over 80. The calculated average duration of life of the people of Mysore is 25 years and that of the people of progressive countries 45. The low level of education is the cause, and the shortened lives the effect, of the low productive power and the low standard of living in the country.

There are other causes, no doubt, such as tradition and prejudices which obstruct progress but they are of a minor and subsidiary character and are sure to disappear if the main disability, namely, lack of education, general and vocational, is removed.

We must spread sound ideas of economic progress among our people. They should come to know that their economic vitality, if entirely dependent on agriculture, will always remain low, that local wants should be supplied as far as possible with local labour, and that the combination of agriculture and manufacture will make larger demands on the energy and skill of the people and will therefore contribute to the maintenance of a higher civilization.

Advanced countries copy one another's progressive methods and inventions, but our people are not yet fully awakened to follow their example. A persistent effort is needed to train the people to cultivate an enquiring turn of mind and alter their ideals and habits of thought from a fatalistic to an economic basis.

We must seek economic salvation through work,—skilled work and organised work. The prosperity of the country will reach its high water mark only when large numbers of people have begun to work in unison for mutual benefit, when their hours of daily toil approximate more closely to those of progressive people, when every one capable of earning is at work and the number of the inefficient and the idle is reduced to a minimum.

The entire working population of a country may be considered as coming roughly under three classes; an upper class, a middle class and the working classes. The upper class includes men at the top of every profession, leaders in politics and business, administrators, financiers, scientists, manufacturers, engineers, etc.

The middle class consists of persons who manage all the practical business of the country, as overseers of farms, foremen of factories, supervisors, accountants, managing agents, etc. Men of this class usually work under the superior direction of those of the upper class, and they employ and control large numbers of artisans and labourers belonging to the working-class population.

The working classes, again, may be said to fall under two divisions, one consisting of persons who possess a knowledge of the three R's and skill in some industry or profession and the other of unskilled workmen who have had no such education or training.

The manner in which a country's population is distributed in these three classes is an index of its civilization and prosperity. If we proceed to divide our working population in Mysore under the above classes, we find that the number of those who come under the upper class is small and even they have had only a literary or general education. The number of professional and technical experts is utterly insufficient for the needs of the country.

We have a fair number of persons who may be regarded as belonging to the lower middle class but these have not got the industry, application, business habits or the wide-awakeness of the corresponding classes in progressive countries.

The bulk of the Mysore population may be said to belong preponderatingly to the unlettered and unskilled section of the working classes.

We have now to take steps to train an adequate number of persons for the work of the country under each of the above three classes.

At least 8 to 10 boys should be under training in our vocational schools from each taluk, which means about 600 for the whole State. The bulk of these will be trained as accountants, maistries, etc., and a small number, say about 150, will be trained annually for the work of the upper and middle classes.

We ought not to be content with training boys in schools, for these would be useful for the work of the country only 10 or 12 years hence. Arrangements have to be made simultaneously to train corresponding numbers of grown-up persons, young men generally, engaged in some business or profession, and who have shown aptitude for practical work.

Address to the Mysore Economic Conference.

In addition to providing facilities for training in this way, arrangements are being made to select half a dozen to a dozen men in each taluk, town or city, who possess capacity, capital or skill for starting an industry, or promoting profitable agriculture. Each of these men will associate himself in turn with other capable men in his neighbourhood and form a syndicate or committee. These bodies may be entrusted with one or more items on the programme of the Progress Committees, and given expert advice, or financial or other help that may be considered reasonable, and allowed to develop practical schemes.

In this way, His Highness' Government hope to create conditions favourable to rapid economic development.

A most encouraging sign of the times is the willing help which the public, particularly in the mofussil, have been giving, and the alacrity with which officials and non-officials are responding to the call of duty.

The local press has begun to exhort the public to participate more actively in the work initiated by Government. His Highness' Government look upon the press as their valued coadjutors in the difficult but most promising work before them, and they cordially welcome this evidence of practical interest on their part.

As a result of our investigations and discussions, sound ideas of economic progress are gradually spreading. In addition to the three central committees, there were eight district committees and seventy-two taluk progress committees at work last year. Some at least have been active and the cumulative effect of the work of the seventy-two committees cannot be inappreciable. Some forty-eight taluk conferences were held for propagandist work and for educating the rural public. Bulletins are being issued and the Economic Journal, started in the previous year, is doing useful work. Towns have begun to wake up, some unwillingly and others with unmistakable enthusiasm. Officials and non-officials are meeting on a common platform to promote common objects. Some of the schemes we have started have been successful, others only partially so. A portion of our work may have been ineffective; a portion of our preaching may have fallen on deaf ears. These are but incidents in the natural process of development. We begin to do things imperfectly at first and then, by experience, learn to improve till the necessary level of efficiency is reached. There is no royal road to economic improvement. So long as our ideals are drawn from the experience of progressive countries and our operations are based on a correct appreciation of local conditions, so long as we are willing to learn and our methods are honest, the activities of this Conference cannot fail to make additions, from year to year, to the resources, efficiency and permanent well-being of the people of Mysore.

SPEECH AT THE MYSORE ECONOMIC CONFERENCE.

14th June 1916. [The seventh session of the Mysore Economic Conference concluded its sittings on 14th June 1916, after discussing for four days the propositions put before it. Dewan Sir M. Visvesvaraya, in winding up the proceedings, made the following speech :—]

Gentlemen,—During the four days of this session, we have passed a number of resolutions and taken notes of the suggestions made by members on a variety of subjects. These will receive the careful consideration of the respective committees who will examine and revise their programmes of work for the coming year in the light of these discussions.

In the course of their remarks on the report of the central committees, some members have made flattering references to the work done by the Economic Conference, particularly, Mr. K. P. Puttanna Chetty and Mr. M. Venkatakrishnayya. We have heard the opposite view also.

As a result of our deliberations, we see our way clear in many matters. Our arrangements, which were imperfect in the earlier years, are being improved and the organization is being perfected in many directions.

Progress in industries has been interrupted on account of the difficulty of getting machinery from foreign countries but there are several schemes ready, or nearly so, for practical action and we are adding to the number from time to time.

Some of our critics feel that we are dealing with too many subjects at one time. Members are aware that all these subjects come under one or other of three heads, *viz.*, practical schemes, investigation work and collecting and spreading information. We have to spread sound ideas of industrial progress in order to prepare the people. Special investigations must precede the preparation of practical schemes. This natural process is being systematically followed. Besides, we have agreed at a meeting of the Standing Committee that more than half of our time should be given to practical schemes, the remaining being about equally divided between investigation work and the work of collecting and spreading information of practical value. All the members of the committees who are engaged in our work and understand the details, are, I believe, satisfied with the share of attention we are giving to each of these classes of work.

We gave special attention during the past year to

improve the work of collecting and compiling statistics. We are preparing definite programmes of work at the commencement of each year. The object in both cases is to obtain a means of measuring the rate of our progress from year to year.

Much of the success of the year's work is due to the conscientious work done by the several Deputy Commissioners and Amildars. There is progress in every district and a great deal in some, particularly in Tumkur, the Deputy Commissioner of which, Mr. K. R. Srinivasiengar, deserves our highest commendation. We are receiving help from the Institute of Science in scientific investigations, chiefly due to the energy of Mr. Chatterton and the cordiality with which he works with the specialists of that Institute.

The Secretaries of the Conference and Committees, Mr. D'Souza, Mr. Ranganatha Rao Saheb and Mr. N. Rama Rao have been very active during the year. A word of commendation is necessary from us in appreciation of the very hard work done by them. I am sure the Conference will learn with regret that we will shortly be losing the services of Mr. C. Krishna Rao, the energetic Secretary of the Education Committee, but I am glad to state he will continue to work with us as a member of the Committee in future.

On the subject of education, we discussed a number of interesting propositions. The Rev. Mr. Thompson wanted to know whether the Education Committee was an executive or a deliberative body. Normally the Committees are deliberative bodies; but they are allowed to take up experimental work and the investigation or execution of practical schemes under the special orders of Government. This will be necessary only whenever heads of departments cannot see eye to eye with the Committee as to the utility or importance of any particular scheme. A proposition was moved advocating the levy of a cess or fees in primary schools but it was lost. Government have been spending very large sums of money on primary education in recent years but the provision is not sufficient. Taking the same population in advanced countries and in Mysore, there are ten literate persons in the former for every one such individual in our State. We have much leeway to make up and we look to the officers and leaders of the people to find funds and extend primary education through private effort to the fullest extent that the conditions of the country permit. In our large adult population, we have abundant material to work with for spreading a knowledge of the three R's.

Some suggestions were made concerning the education of the backward classes. The justice is admitted on all hands of giving these classes special educational facilities as well as facilities for obtaining an initial start in Government Service. For promotion and future prospects they must depend upon their own worth and work.

On the question of the new University, some very eloquent observations were made by the Rev. Mr. Thompson and Dr. Achyuta Rao. We are sensible of the defects and omissions in the scheme but they are inevitable at the outset. We have had the advice of the highest educational experts of the Government of India. The scope of the work has been deliberately limited with a view to confining our attention to the essential faculties only for a time till our equipment and staff are adequate. The question of adjusting our relations with the Madras University is under correspondence, and chiefly through the kindness and courtesy of His Excellency the Chancellor of the Madras University, the necessary negotiations are making satisfactory progress.

Under agriculture, the question of Amrut Mahal

Kavals, the need for well-boring tools and the subject of fuel and fodder reserves were discussed at some length. We have re-engaged the services of Signor Mari, who will devote attention to the two primary objects we have in view, *viz.*, increase of production of silk and training the people in modern methods of sericulture. I hope he will be able to show definite progress in these two directions. The economic distribution of water is another important question. The work already begun should receive the continuous attention of both Government Officers and the people. If existing irrigation facilities are properly utilised, we ought to be able to increase our farm produce from our irrigation works by about 30 per cent almost immediately. Another question raised was that of the labour supply. More working population is urgently needed in the *Malnad* and the preparation of a suitable scheme for attracting settlers to that region demands the serious attention of the Agricultual Committee.

Coming to the subject of industries, the cotton mill in Mysore is an important scheme and I hope that some practical work will be done within the next six months. The question of the manufacture of iron and steel has been under investigation and Dr. Smeeth, who so lucidly explained the present position to the Conference will, I hope, develop the project with the help of the Industries and Commerce Committee. The forest and mining industries should continue to receive attention. The scheme for a Land Bank should be further developed. We are anxious that the Chamber of Commerce should start Industrial guilds to bring together people who follow the same occupations. We want to see more joint-stock and partnership concerns springing up in the country for industrial purposes because that would be the only way in the present conditions of the country to obtain a large amount of capital for any industry or business. As regards help to industries, Government are ready to abide by the orders already issued and every promising scheme will receive their sympathetic consideration.

The chief economic defect of the country is its low productive power. This is due to lack of education among our people, lack of a correct knowledge among them of the world conditions and lack of practical skill in industrial and, professional pursuits. We have to equip our people with all these. His Highness the Maharaja has been pleased to direct that liberal provision should be made in the budget estimates for education. His Highness at the same time hopes that sufficient moral effort will be put forth by the officers and the leaders of the people to stimulate private enterprise and enlist private charity for the same object.

The programmes of the central committees are before you. The work entered in them after revision should, in the usual course, be divided between the departments on the one side and the committees on the other. The committees will distribute the work among sub-committees or individual members and the departments will do likewise among their most capable officers. Perhaps each of these might be able to enlist the co-operation of a dozen gentlemen or more, besides officials and non-officials from all parts of the State.

The departments concerned will doubtless take up the bulk of the executive work and the committees the work of investigation and preparation of schemes. The programmes should show very precisely how the work is distributed, within what time each item is expected to be ready and who is responsible for each. The conference is much indebted to the private gentlemen who have been doing pioneering work of this kind and who have already rendered much disinterested service in promoting its objects.

There have been several district and taluk conferences of late which have helped to rouse much interest and enthusiasm in economic work throughout the State.

Our education and tradition have hitherto had a tendency to discourage activity and initiative. Our education in the past has been receptive rather than productive. But times have changed and we see men of action are everywhere getting the better of men of contemplation. I would urge all persons connected with the Economic Conference to encourage initiative and activity wherever these qualities may be found, provided they are not of a mischievous character.

For organising economic activities, the entire work of the country may be distributed among 100 units comprising the three cities, 77 taluks and sub-taluks and 20 of the largest towns. Each unit should have its standard of activities as well as a definite number of local agricultural and industrial schemes and a separate self-contained organization for carrying on propagandist and other work.

The services of half a dozen or a dozen men who have sufficient capital, enterprise or enthusiasm in the unit area should be secured by each committee. Each of these gentlemen should associate himself in turn with some half a dozen other workers and form committees, societies or syndicates to give attention to individual items on the programme of the unit.

The economic future of the country lies, in a large measure, in our own hands. It may not be in our power to shape events; we may not be able to contol the monsoon or the harvest but we can train our people adequately till they are able to look after themselves. A large proportion of our peasant population live on one or two rupees a month, that is, live in abject poverty and misery because they have no conception of anything better. It will be the sacred duty of this Conference to equip them with knowledge and working power to enable them to rise to the full height of their opportunities.

SPEECH AT THE MYSORE LEGISLATIVE COUNCIL.

[A meeting of the Mysore Legislative Council was held at the Public Offices, Bangalore, on 29th June 1916, to consider among other subjects the Mysore University Bill. Besides the members, there were present a large number of visitors. The Bill evoked a warm and interesting debate. The speech of Dewan Sir M. Visvesvaraya printed below was made earlier in the debate. He said :—] 29th June 1916.

Gentlemen,—The bill to establish and incorporate a University in Mysore has been published and before it is formally presented to you, I wish to be permitted to make a few observations regarding the origin, object and scope of the proposed University. It is a small bill that we are dealing with to-day and I trust a non-contentious one, but it will be admitted that in the brief existence of this Council no more important measure was ever introduced.

A University for Mysore has been a long felt want, and in recent years the need has been pressed on the attention of Government in various ways, and particularly in the annual sessions of the Mysore Representative Assembly.

Speech at the Mysore Legislative Council.

The question has been actively engaging the attention of His Highness' Government for the past three years. Two educational officers of the State were deputed to foreign countries to make a study of University conditions there, with a view to suggesting measures for starting an institution best suited to our local conditions. Mr. C. R. Reddy, Professor, Maharaja's College, went out first and visited some of the principal Universities of England, America and Japan. A couple of years ago, Mr. Thomas Denham, Principal of the same College, visited Australia with the same object. Both these officers have furnished interesting reports which have already been before the public for some time.

A committee consisting of the Members of Government and the leading educational officers of the State began the investigation of the question in the month of July 1914. It sat at intervals for about six months. Rough proposals were prepared by the committee and they were placed before the Government of India with a brief memoradum in the month of July 1915. The Political and Educational officers of the Government of India interested themselves in our proposals and discussed them with Sir Hugh Daly, our late Resident, and myself. Shortly after this meeting, the Hon'ble Mr. Sharp, Educational Commissioner with the Government of India, furnished His Highness' Government with an important note criticising and suggesting various improvements in our scheme. His Highness' Government took full advantage of the suggestions and revised their proposals with the help of Mr. H. V. Nanjundayya, C.I.E., and Mr. Thomas Denham. The revised scheme was submitted for the consideration of the Government of India in February last.

Later in the same month, Sir Hugh Daly and myself had again the advantage of exchanging views personally with the officers of the Government of India who gave the matter their sympathetic consideration.

As the academic year usually begins on 1st July, His Highness' Government were anxious to start work on the new University from that date. If we did not so begin, we should have lost another full year. We, therefore, in the month of March last, appealed to the Government of India to permit us to start the University from 1st July next. The Government of India very kindly approved of the introduction of the scheme from the said date, subject to certain conditions respecting the adjustment of our future relations with the Madras University.

The negotiations with the Madras University are in progress. Through the courtesy of His Excellency the Chancellor of that University, an informal meeting was held at Ootacamund last month for a preliminary exchange of views, which was attended by the principal representatives of the Madras University, the Hon'ble the Resident and myself. We have every reason to hope that all necessary co-operation and support will be forthcoming from the authorities of that University.

No one present here can be unmindful of the debt of gratitude which generations of educated classes of this State owe to their *alma mater* the Madras University, since its establishment nearly sixty years ago. I trust that the mother University will, on her side, view, with pleasure and pride, the legitimate attempt of a daughter to set up a house of her own. It has always been the way of daughters, as they attain years of discretion, to look forward to the time when they could be mistress of an independent household.

As soon as the approval of the Government of India was obtained, a strong committee was appointed to take all necessary steps to give effect to the proposals. The scheme was published at about the same time and suggestions for its improvement were invited from the public. These have been received and reported upon by the University Committee, and the orders of His Highness' Government regarding the final shape of the scheme have been issued within the past few days.

It would not be correct to say that our work has all been plain sailing and that we have had no obstacles to face. The introduction of the scheme within a few months of its approval has entailed a considerable amount of work and the brunt of it has fallen on the University Committee.

When His Highness the Maharaja's decision to start a University in Mysore was first made known, the announcement was received with an outburst of delight from all parts of the State. On closer acquaintance with the scheme, however, many questions have been asked and many doubts raised, but most of them pertain to details. As to the soundness of the main features of the scheme itself, the suggestions received go to show that public opinion is singularly unanimous. We admit that in many points of detail such as, courses of study, rules regarding examinations, etc., there is room for improvement. Government have advisedly refrained from dealing with these questions finally, because they are essentially matters to be dealt with by expert bodies like the Senate and Boards of Studies, which will be called into existence, when the bill under consideration becomes law.

I may add that it is not through lack of vision that we have restricted the scope of the project. Provision is made for the bare essentials of a University for the present, and as the necessary equipment and staff become available—a matter of no small difficulty during this period of war—His Highness' Government propose, cautiously, to carry out the further developments needed from stage to stage.

Speech at the Mysore Legislative Council.

In a notable speech at Dacca in January 1912, the late Viceroy, His Excellency Lord Hardinge, stated that the Government of India were convinced that the more such Universities were multiplied and distributed all over India, the better it would be for the cause of Indian education and for the development of the moral character no less than of the intellectual ability of the students. Lord Hardinge advocated the establishment of small Universities, and I have satisfactory authority for stating that our University is in accordance with the latest views of the Government of India.

The population of Mysore being close upon six millions, the attempt to provide ourselves with a University cannot be regarded as ambitious. In the United Kingdom, there is one University for every 2½ millions of the population; in Canada and in Australia, there is one University for less than a million people. Our opportunities of benefiting from a University are not inferior to those of many of the existing Universities of Canada or Australia. We have nearly one thousand graduates engaged in various occupations in the State, nearly all of whom sympathise with the idea of a University and many of whom will actively work for it. It may be argued that although the population is large, the percentage of literate population in Mysore is comparatively very small. To my mind this is not a disqualification but an additional reason why we should have a University. Education promotes education and, without higher education, no appreciable expansion of secondary or elementary education can be looked for.

A University is required in the country because, with the growth of communications and the opening up of the country, we are passing from a rural life of few needs into an urban life of increasing wants, burdens and responsibilities. A University may be said to have a general object and certain specific aims depending on the state of the country's civilization and of material prosperity. The general object in the broadest sense is to encourage learning, to promote higher education, to create a centre of culture, to light a torch that would dispel the gloom of ignorance from the remotest corners of the country. The specific aims in Mysore should be what I stated, in support of the University idea at a public gathering of educationists in this city, over four years ago, namely, to develop the intellectual ability and executive power of our citizens and to afford the training necessary to "prepare future manufacturers, merchants, business-men, economists, lawyers, sanitarians, engineers, states-men, etc., for the country."

There is one more point I wish to refer to before I close. Government are at present providing the whole cost of this institution from public funds. They have also established a number of foreign scholarships, nearly all of which will be available in future for the *alumni* of the new University.

But in order to promote the many-sided activities of the new University we want more funds, particularly in the shape of endowments. This is an opportunity for every lover of education and every well-wisher of the State to endow prizes, medals, scholarships, lectureships and, if possible, also chairs for specific subjects. There are many people in the country who, we know, are able and willing to help, particularly the merchant classes, several of whom have already come forward with munificent offers to establish hostels in Bangalore and elsewhere for promoting education. I have no doubt it would be highly gratifying to this Council if one or more committees are formed, chiefly composed of non-official gentlemen, to collect funds for this purpose.

Before I close, I feel it a duty to refer to the sympathy

and support so generously accorded to the scheme by His Excellency Lord Hardinge as well as by our late Resident Colonel Sir Hugh Daly, to both of whom we owe our sincerest gratitude.

His Highness the Maharaja's keen interest in the progress of education is too well known to require mention. It is entirely due to His Highness' initiative and personal interest that the scheme has taken shape and is being pushed through so speedily. His Highness' subjects have hailed the measure with enthusiasm. The University is not meant only for to-day or for the next generation. It will be a permanent land-mark of His Highness' benign rule.

SPEECH AT THE MYSORE LEGISLATIVE COUNCIL.

[A meeting of the Mysore Legislative Council was held at the Public Offices, Bangalore, on 17th July 1916, to consider among other things the Mysore University Bill. After a long and interesting debate the motion that the Bill be passed into law was carried without a division. Speaking on the motion, Dewan Sir M. Visvesvaraya, as President of the Council, made the following speech :—] **17th July 1916.**

Gentlemen,—Before I put the motion to the vote, I need only make a few general observations on some of the more important points which have been raised in the course of this debate.

In the first place, I may be permitted to compliment the members of the Council on the ability with which they have discussed the various aspects of the University

Scheme, the depth and soundness of many of their observations and the searching character of their enquiries. My colleague Mr. Banerji also wishes to acknowledge the valuable help he received from the members of the Select Committee.

Of the several important points raised in the course of this debate, a good deal of controversy has centred on the question of the exclusive recognition of the Kannada language. I sympathise with the view that as far as possible the language of every community within the State should be represented in the curricula of the University. But, judged from a utilitarian point of view, you will agree that by having too many languages we will be placing an intellectual burden on the population. We shall be spending more time on language than on matter. We shall be dissipating the energies of our people and scattering our force. English is the language of civilization, Kannada is the language of the Court and of the great majority of the population. These two languages should suffice for our purpose. If we have more, it would mean that none of the Vernaculars will get a chance of rapid development.

As regards religious training, it would be difficult to satisfy all denominations and the attempt to help to develop religious sentiment through the University would, I fear, end in failure. Later on, Theology may form a separate Faculty if public opinion approves of it. The case of the Hindu University which has been referred to is different. It is professedly a denominational University.

Several minor amendments have been introduced into the Bill with a view to give the Vice-Chancellor a definite position and to retain with Government adequate power to watch over the work and the development of the University in its early stages. Our scheme provides for a new type of University of which the Colleges form an integral part. In the British Indian Universities, the Colleges are not directly under the University. They are a department supervised by Government. The Vice-Chancellor under our scheme will have duties and responsibilities towards the Senate and Council on the one side and towards Government on the other. Government have responsibilities to discharge in their relations with the Government of India and the neighbouring Universities and it is necessary that they should have an executive head who will be responsible to them.

Some remarks were made on the last occasion about the site selected for the University in the Mysore City. The site has been definitely fixed and the plans and estimates are nearly ready. The new University will be located round the existing College just on the outskirts of the City and as stated in the scheme the locality is considered an ideal one for the purpose. I have had the privilege of visiting numerous Universities in England, on the Continent as well as in America and Canada. The great majority of them are situated in populated areas. I do not believe in segregating the students and allowing them to grow up as it were in a cloistered life. They will be at a disadvantage when they come back to the hard realities of this work-a-day world. The aim of the University should be rather to train the character of the students under conditions not entirely different from those which they will have to encounter in later life.

Any scheme that we may devise will be necessarily imperfect at first. Developments should be attempted slowly and cautiously. The buildings must grow. We have to look out for more Professors, both European and Indian, men possessing lofty ideals and a high character. We begin with two Faculties at first and we will probably add Engineering and Commerce next; Agriculture, Law and Medicine may follow. Till the new Colleges

Speech at the Mysore Legislative Council.

are built and fully equipped, we may have to be content with granting diplomas or licenses or certificates to students. In the meantime, we may go on developing the bureaus of publication and extension work.

Since we published the University scheme, many criticisms have been levelled against it as regards the type, Faculties and other details. There may be several forms into which a University may be shaped. With the best will in the world, Government can choose but one form. If all the critics met and discussed each other's proposals and formed decisions by a vote of the majority, taking into account at the same time the present condition of education and the resources of the State, I am inclined to think that they would come to nearly the same conclusions that His Highness' Government have now placed before you.

I hope that the appeal made by me on the last occasion for endowments and gifts for the University will receive hearty support from the public.

It is His Highness the Maharaja's wish that this University should grow up into a high class institution and that all officers of Government and the leaders of the people should cordially co-operate to make it so. It is also His Highness' wish that under its fostering care all classes of His Highness' subjects should profit and that it should contribute to the uplift of all strata of society, the rich and the poor, the forward as well as the backward.

Now that we have decided on the form of the University and the scope of its work, may I express the hope that all controversies will be hushed till the sapling takes root? I know that all parties join us in the wish that the University should prove a blessing to the people and a credit to the State.

SPEECH AT THE MYSORE LEGISLATIVE COUNCIL.

[A meeting of the Mysore Legislative Council was held on 19th July 1916 at the Public Offices, Bangalore, to consider the State Budget. There was a warm and interesting debate on the Budget, several of the members making eloquent speeches touching on its different aspects. In winding up the debate, Dewan Sir M. Visvesvaraya, President of the Council, made the following speech :—] 19th July 1916.

Gentlemen,—My first duty on this occasion is to assure you that it will give me very great pleasure to convey to His Highness the Maharaja the loyal sentiments of gratitude, to which members gave expression in the course of this debate, for the several beneficent measures recently sanctioned by His Highness.

In his brief and graceful speech, His Highness the Yuvaraja has just remarked on the advantages of frank discussion in regard to the budget. I have no doubt we all appreciate those advantages. In his comprehensive reply this afternoon, our Financial Secretary likened the Mysore Finances to an ailing *purdahnashin* Sultana and he pointed out the difficulties under which the doctors formerly laboured whenever they wanted to understand the condition of the patient. Till a couple of years ago, the doctors could only diagnose the disease by examining the tongue shown through a slit in the *purdah*, or a hand thrust through a door chink. Now, however, the doctors have a free access to the patient to the fullest extent permitted by civilised medical etiquette.

My colleagues and myself have listened to the speeches, some of them very eloquent ones, as well as to the criticisms and observations of the members on the budget with the keenest interest. His Highness the Maharaja's

Speech at the Mysore Legislative Council.

Government have reason to be gratified at the spirit of enquiry which these budget debates have aroused and the high sense of responsibility with which, as a rule, members approach public questions in this Assembly.

I hope the members concerned did not mind my interrupting them yesterday in the midst of their addresses. In doing so, my only object was to correct wrong impressions which might have escaped notice and which, had I not interposed, might have been conveyed to the public. On a perusal of some of those statements, I fear any casual reader would conclude that the Mysore Government deliberately laid themselves out for multiplying blunders and irregularities.

I know how much time and labour members have bestowed on their work and at what sacrifice they are discharging this public duty. I gratefully acknowledge, on behalf of Government, the many valuable suggestions with which they have favoured us and I recognise that all honour is due to them for their unselfish and patriotic work.

The discussions opened yesterday with some severe strictures on certain supposed defects in the administration. I interfered and represented that the facts adduced did not warrant the inferences drawn from them. Mr. Venkatakrishnaiya, who has an honourable record of public service extending over thirty years, has all through his life been 'agin the Government.' He is, if anything, partial to the present administration but he cannot shake off his old habit. Has any one a grievance against Government? He supports the grievance and champions it impartially. He does not pause to enquire whether it is right or wrong. Is any irregularity hinted against a Government officer? His first impluse is to believe it to be true. Is there any increase of expenditure in a Government department? Then it must mean extravagance.

Speech at the Mysore Legislative Council.

When, however, the true state of things is brought to his notice, he is candid and generous enough to acknowledge, as he did yesterday, that the truth may be very different.

Some few other members also have thought fit to criticise the budget in the same strain and in many cases the facts adduced did not support the allegations made. What I demand is that when public men set out in this way to attack Government in cold blood, they must at least be sure of their facts.

Mr. K. P. Puttanna Chetty and Mr. B. V. Ramaswami Chetty had a few appreciative remarks to make of the work and the aims of Government. Mr. Krishnamurti Rao, who is usually our severest critic, seems to have relented and even the Economic Conference has passed through his hands unscathed on this occasion. Mr. Gulam Ahmed Kalami and Mr. Basavaiya have both spoken with eloquence and warmth and several other gentlemen, including Mr. B. Narasinga Rao and Mr. H. Narasinga Rao, have made impressive speeches. The official members of the Council effectively replied to most of the criticisms and Mr. Chakravarti has had quite a field day. After the replies which have been so ably given and the responsible statements of my colleagues, no apology is needed from me for confining my observations only to some of the larger issues connected with the budget.

The first question we have to ask ourselves is "Is the Budget satisfactory? Are our finances sound?" Some members have drawn attention to the fact that the expenditure is growing. That is a fact. Expenditure must grow in any administration which claims to be progressive. In last year's Budget debate, I referred to this aspect of the matter. Perhaps I had better quote the exact words used :—

"Now, gentlemen, I don't see why you should treat an increase of revenue and expenditure as if it were a calamity. If you look facts squarely in the face, you will find that in every civilised country, it is generally a sign of activity and prosperity. Increase of expenditure usually means increase of activitities, increase of production and increase of earning power. If you study the figures of foreign countries, you will see that, in the United Kingdom, the public expenditure has gone up in the past 20 years by 140 per cent ; in that luckless country, Belgium, it has gone up by 120 per cent ; in the Colony of Canada by 300 per cent ; in Japan by as much as 660 per cent ; whereas during the same period, the increase in Mysore has been only 60 per cent. To my mind, if there is to be any criticism, you must blame us for going slow."

From these figures you will see that the growth of expenditure in Mysore has not been abnormal. When you proceed to criticise a budget, you must go upon some standard. The standard which some of the members have adopted is to take the figures relating to expenditure in certain departments in previous years, and wherever there is an increase, to straightway conclude that there is extravagance. I told you the other day that we have spent over Rs. 2 crores on capital works within the past four or five years. That means that we have been creating an asset for the State which perhaps ten years hence will give Rs. 15 lakhs of additional income per annum and which has already begun to give over Rs. 6 lakhs.

Is there any danger threatening the finances in the future? Of course, there is the war, but we are recovering from the slight disturbance we experienced and at present there are no clouds in the horizon. We have taken additional precautions to reduce our capital expenditure from Rs. 66 lakhs last year to Rs. 40 lakhs in the current one and, at the same time, we have amply provided for all our ordinary wants.

Speech at the Mysore Legislative Council.

Comparing with conditions outside the State, you will notice that our financial statements are based on those of the Imperial Government. Even the nomenclature is nearly identical. The only difference is that on account of our geographical and political position, ours has all the characteristics of what may be called sub-national finance. Mr. C. Narasimhaiya wanted to know what indirect contribution the people of Mysore made to the customs and salt revenues of British India. The proportionate share which the Mysore population seems to contribute roughly works out to Rs. 24 lakhs and 12 lakhs, respectively, or a total of Rs. 36 lakhs. The recent addition of salt tax represents an increase of Rs. $1\frac{3}{4}$ lakhs. The sister State of Hyderabad gets something like Rs. 72 lakhs from customs and Travancore Rs. 12 lakhs. Mysore derives no revenue whatever from this source.

If we go outside India and compare ourselves with distant countries, you will see that, in Ceylon, for instance, the bulk of the receipts is from railways and customs. The land revenue is insignificant. In Australia again, the customs revenue represents about 60 per cent of the total receipts. If we want to increase our revenues in this State, our best course is to develop industrial and commercial enterprises such as, railways, hydro-electric works, large irrigation works, industrial factories, etc.

Another test of the soundness of our finances is the incidence of taxation. The actual taxes, as you know, amount to about Rs. 176 lakhs or Rs. 3 per head, after excluding non-tax revenues derived from railways, hydro-electric works, etc.

There is a further test which we may apply for this purpose. Some thirteen months ago, in the Economic Conference, we calculated that the total income of the Mysore people was Rs. 14 crores from agriculture and Rs. 4 crores from industrial and all other occupations.

Speech at the Mysore Legislative Council.

I have just stated that the revenue from taxes proper in the current year's budget comes to Rs. 176 lakhs. This represents a proportion between the Government demand and the income of the people of less than one-tenth. If we remember that, in other countries, the taxation occasionally goes up as high as 30 per cent of the net income of the people, ours must be considered a very moderate proportion. Test the budget how we may, the Council will see that it is a satisfactory one.

I now come to some of the individual criticisms of the members. As regards the charges for establishment in the Public Works Department, Mr. Chakravarti has explained how favourable the figures really are. I hope Mr. Garudachar is now satisfied that the Department is not over-manned as he feared it was.

As regards recent railway appointments, some overt hints were dropped that the department was top heavy. It is nothing of the kind. We have one officer at the head, who combines in himself three appointments. We have one Superintending Engineer for over 200 miles of construction work, and we have another Superintending Engineer for surveys, for which the people have been clamouring in several districts of the State. It is a remarkable testimony to the keenness of the demand that the people up till now have come forward to contribute an additional sum of nearly Rs. 15 lakhs for railway construction. This is a critical time in the history of our railways. Four years ago, we had only 410 miles and within another six months we shall have increased the mileage by about 50 per cent.

The Muzrai improvements question is receiving attention and orders will issue very shortly.

One member suggested the abolition of the Industries Department. I fully concur with my colleague to the left that it would be a retrograde step to abolish this useful department at a time when other Provinces in British India are creating new ones. A promising source of revenue from sandalwood oil has been created mainly through the exertions of Mr. Chatterton and the revenue expected from this industry alone will probably suffice to cover the cost of the department five or six times over.

As regards the Institute of Science, I must cordially acknowledge the valuable help which the present management have given to our Director in the laboratory work connected with the promotion of our chemical industries.

Coming to the request for a Budget Committee and the representation of non-officials on the Finance Committee, I find that even official members have expressed themselves in favour of the proposals. I can only say at this stage that the request will receive the best consideration of Government.

With reference to the Malnad Improvement Scheme, we have increased the budget provision by Rs. 50,000 in order to expedite progress.

The neglect of mofussil towns complained of is, I must admit, to some extent true but the fault is not all on our side. The real cause of delay is that people are accustomed to look to the central Government for everything, and the establishment in the Public Works Department is not adequate for preparing the necessary plans and estimates. If the Municipalities concerned consulted the local Public Works Officers or other technical experts and sent up projects in a final form together with a statement of the financial assistance needed, there would be no delay on the part of Government in coming to a decision.

As regards irrigation works, we have made ample provision for the development of minor tanks on the lines accepted by the Representative Assembly.

The irrigation major tanks are starved also because the

Public Works Department is shorthanded. Several important Public Works Department divisions are at present in the charge of very junior officers.

You will be glad to hear that the question of the separation of the judicial and executive functions is receiving consideration and my colleague, Mr. K. S. Chandrasekhara Aiyar, is giving the subject his special attention. In the current official year, we hope to take some substantial step forward to make a beginning.

As regards Mr. Ghulam Ahmed Kalami's request for help to Mahomedan education, Government will give their best attention if a brief statement of the requirements of his community mentioned yesterday is placed before Government. In any case, my colleagues and myself have agreed to recommend that sanction be accorded to the amount he mentioned, *viz.*, Rs. 6,000.

Coming to the Bangalore City Municipal improvements, Mr. K. P. Puttanna Chetty has made out a strong case. My colleagues and myself are willing to recommend that the annual grant of rupees one lakh already given to the Municipality be utilised on drainage and that the Municipality be permitted to begin work on the City Improvement Scheme by spending the Rs. 2 lakhs which they have in their possession on the understanding that Government will give them their promised share, as soon as they can conveniently do so. In the meantime, if necessary, they will pay interest if the Municipality chooses to borrow.

Proceeding to the question of provision for the backward classes, there appear to be two schools of thought represented by Mr. Basava Iya on the one side and Mr. H. Narasinga Rao on the other. It would be nothing short of a calamity to the country if the question gave occasion for any permanent cleavage of interests. No country can be said to progress satisfactorily so long as the great majority of its population, from whatever cause, continue to be classed as backward. If the backwardness is acknowledged, is it not the duty of the more enlightened classes to take their less fortunate brethren by the hand and lead them up to the front? We must take a broader view of our responsibilities. So far as Government are concerned, my colleagues and myself propose to recommend an addition of rupees one lakh for the education of the backward classes in the current official year. This amount, if sanctioned, will be utilised for giving scholarships in every taluk to members of the backward communities for primary and secondary education. Part of this sum will be expended on the education, both general and vocational, of the Panchama community also.

There are some general considerations to which I wish to invite attention before bringing these remarks to a close. It will be agreed that the public can have no reason to complain so long as the money taken from the people, or earned by the commercial enterprises of Government, is largely spent on the people for their benefit.

The objects on which public money could be most usefully spent are:—

(1) the improvement of natural resources, and

(2) the training of the people.

The former object is being carried out to the fullest extent permitted by public opinion and sometimes in spite of it. The development of resources will add substantially to our non-tax revenues. Even more important than this is the training and education of the people. We have increased the expenditure on education within the past four years by about Rs. 10 lakhs. Our energetic and much maligned Inspector-General of Education promised, in a scheme submitted a couple of years ago, that he would double the school-going population, that is, bring it up to 400,000 before the end of June 1917. He tells me that he has already reached 275,000 and that he will be able to produce the additional 125,000 in due course.

The best source of revenue in the long run comes of training the people: for, after all, we must depend on the intelligence and the executive ability of the people for any permanent progress in the State. To some representatives the additional expenditure of Rs. 10 lakhs on the education of the school-going population appears quite legitimate, but they stoutly oppose any outlay on the education of grown-up people. I have no doubt you all view with satisfaction the expenditure of about Rs. 15 lakhs on measures of development in various directions such as, grants to village improvements, rural water-supply, Malnad improvements, etc., included in the budget.

I make these observations because I want some of the gentlemen who hold the opinions I have set forth above, if possible, to change their view point and make up their minds to accept an increase of establishment and expenditure wherever necessary in order to stimulate activities, both rural and urban. It is large developments that pay. It is commercial activities that pay. Agricultural and irrigation improvements, banks, railways, large industries, factories, extension of electricity works, etc.,—it is such enterprises that will bring in large returns. On the other hand, if you effect a reduction of expenditure, if you stop the increase of appointments, the increase of salaries and travelling allowances, it only means stagnation or a cessation of activities. The large developments may earn you tens of lakhs of rupees, but the savings which accrue from curtailment of establishments will not exceed a few thousands. Even on the lower ground of increase of Governmnnt revenues only, it is the larger measures that will bring money to the coffers of the State, besides adding to the prosperity of the people.

If you will forgive my saying so, my complaint is that a few of our respected non-official critics take small views of things and are content with modest ideals when the condition of the people is loudly calling for activity and effort. Without meaning it, they are encouraging retrenchment and reaction. A few years ago they were complaining there were too many activities. Now the criticism is directed against establishment, travelling allowance and increase of expenditure in any shape or form. They do not know what a large amount of spade work is being done. They do not realise the prospective losses we shall suffer by adopting a policy of indifference and inaction at present. May I hope that our friends will reconsider their attitude? May I venture to invite them to leave their narrow groove of thought and aspiration and co-operate with Government to work on a higher level and a wider sphere?

I have said enough to show that all the refinements expected of a Government in dealing with the resources of the country are receiving attention. We do not pretend that there are no mistakes, and we are not by any means indisposed to accept well-considered suggestions for improvement from any quarter.

I may claim that our finances are in a sound condition. Happily, the war is progressing favourably and there is every chance of further improvement. With the success of the Allies, a new era of activity and prosperity will dawn on Great Britain and India, in which we shall also participate.

Gentlemen, we have reason to congratulate ourselves on the high level of efficiency on which our finances are administered. If you examine the budget results of previous years, you will find that the actuals are invariably better than the forecasts. Our Financial Secretary is the very embodiment of caution. I hope I am not revealing a State secret if I add that he practises caution to the verge of timidity. With so able and cautious an officer at the head, we may feel sure that no hazardous experiments will be permitted. I know you will all join me in congratulating Mr. Chakravarti on the successful completion of his labours for this session.

SPEECH AT THE MYTHIC SOCIETY.

7th Aug. 1916. [The sixth annual meeting of the Mythic Society, Bangalore, was held at the Government High School on August 7, 1916. The reading of the Annual Report and the election of the Committee and office-bearers for the year 1917 being over, Sir M. Visvesvaraya, who occupied the chair, made the following speech :—]

Mr. President, Ladies and Gentlemen,—The Mythic Society is a very learned body engaged in deep study and research. I feel one must possess an uncommon fund of erudition to presume to preside at any function connected with such an institution. I protested that I was not the right person and suggested other names, but Father Tabard would not take a refusal.

I can lay no claim to having worked in any of the various fields of activity in which this Society is engaged. I have only a distant acquaintance with archæological research, my recollections of ancient history have grown dim, I have never yet interested myself in ethnology or epigraphy or numismatics and I have long since forgotten the little philosophy I once knew.

Speech at the Mythic Society.

It is in accordance with the eternal unfitness of things that a person, labouring under so many disqualifications, should have been called upon to take the chair on this occasion.

The Secretary has read a satisfactory report and the President has treated us to an eloquent and inspiring speech.

Father Tabard makes a graceful reference to the help given by His Highness the Maharaja. Such help from His Highness has never failed for any worthy object for the good of his country or his people. His Highness has been giving liberal annual contributions and he has been pleased to authorise special grants for the new building both from public funds and His Highness' own privy-purse. Father Tabard has gratefully acknowledged the support the Society has received from His Highness the Yuvaraja and Col. Sir Hugh Daly. He has referred in generous terms to the contributions made to the literature of the society by the Reverends Messrs. Thompson and Slater, Mr. R. Narasimhachar, Mr. R. Shama Sastri, Mr. S. Krishnaswami Iyengar and other learned men.

Our President has also told us that he has secured a liberal supply of books and periodicals to form the nucleus of a fine library and he is justly proud of his new building scheme for which he has been able to collect subscriptions, both from within and outside the State, to supplement the Government grant.

When the Society gets a habitation of its own, we are offered the prospect of a sort of club life where Europeans and Indians will move intimately together and meet often to exchange ideas and carry on illuminating discussions connected with hoary Mysore and India of the past.

He rightly adds that the society will have deserved our sympathy and support if it did nothing more than promote intimacy of understanding between Europeans and Indians.

The work which the society is doing will not fail to raise Mysore in the estimation of the public. Mr. Sell makes an appeal for more members, for the regular payment of subscriptions, and for larger attendance at meetings I trust all these will be forthcoming and that the society will have enduring success and an ever widening circle of subscribers and supporters.

The proceedings of the society are in English and it is a blot on the fair name of Mysore that no connected original history has yet been written by a son of the soil in the language of the country. This defect will, I hope, be soon remedied. The vast majority of the population who should take a pride in the history of the country have at present no facilities to study its history and they have no conception of the excellent work that is being done by this society.

A suggestion has already been made to the learned head of our Government Department of Archæology that a small readable pamphlet containing an account of the more striking incidents in the history of Mysore, as revealed by Mr. Rice, by the Department of Archæology and the proceedings of this society, should issue in the Kannada language for the edification of the masses of the population.

Concerning the objects of the society, I am reminded of a couplet which described the work of a noted antiquary who lived at the beginning of the 18th century:

> "Quoth Time to Thomas Hearne,
> Whatever I forgot you learn."

The Mythic Society is trying to keep alive information which, but for its timely succour, is liable to be lost to the world. I take it that it seeks to piece together, for its edifice of true history, scraps of truths derived from books, inscriptions, folk-lore, palm leaves and other records which, if not utilized in good time, are likely to be "consigned to oblivion's uncatalogued library."

The objects of the society have been variously described on previous occasions. Thy are said to include the study of history, archæology, ethnology, philosophy and the religions of India. The President to-day brushes aside all qualifications and boldly asserts that the society's chief aim is to build up the history of Mysore and of South India and that all other studies merely subserve that prime object.

We all agree in this. Though many of us may lack opportunities or taste to take part in the actual studies, we are all intensely interested in the results of the Society's researches.

The President has referred incidentally to the interest which His Highness' Government are taking in improving the material and economic condition of the people.

It has been the constant wish of His Highness the Maharaja that all the beneficent activities of civilised countries should find a home in his own State. The work in which this society is deeply interested is one of them. We have a special Department of Government devoted to researches in Archæology. We want activities also in other directions, namely, the promotion of civic duties, of social service, the development of art, literature, science and morals.

We are aware that the number of enthusiasts for any field of activity are as yet too few compared to the needs of the country and there is a great deal of inertia to be overcome. The real problem of the hour is how profitably to distribute the limited energies of the people among the several activities which claim attention. Father Tabard rightly says that the studies of the Mythic

Society do not bring an extra rupee to the State or better in any material way the position of the lower classes but they contribute to the refinement of the mind and give the people the means of understanding the past history of their country.

I do not mind confessing that the term "Mythic" as applied to the society first repelled me and I have also noticed similar comments in other quarters. Whatever the original meaning may be, perhaps Father Tabard hopes to influence future lexicographers to change its significance by the character of the solid work done by this society. Thanks to his devoted labours, the Mythic Society to-day is no longer a myth but a concrete entity with a very real object and a great purpose, comprising a learned body of over 300 members with a patriarchal seer at its head.

One great defect in our past, in fact in India's past, has been the tendency to exaggerate and the inability to write correct history. Facts were mixed up with mythology and religion. If there was a good king, he was described as the greatest of the kings, comparable only to the gods; just as many a pious priest who worshipped at a shrine has after his death obtained a shrine for himself and eventually supplanted the original deity.

The Buddhist chroniclers in other countries have been more reliable. It was during a visit to Ceylon eighteen years ago that I first read in a small history of that colony that a prince of Mysore had gone there about the eighth century of the Christian era and ruled over that island for nearly thirty years.

A decade or two ago, any reference to the past history of Mysore would have been received with incredulity. We owe a debt of gratitute to Mr. Rice, the pioneer in Archæological researches in this State, to Father Tabard, Mr. Narasimhachar and others for redeeming ancient Mysore in the estimation of the world.

Speech at the Mythic Society.

Tradition has it that Mysore was the scene of some of the exploits depicted in the epic poems of Ramayana and Mahabharata. She has produced great preachers in religion and dynasties of kings who have wrought mighty deeds. The President last year referred to Mr. Rice's comparison of this country with Greece, Palestine, and other States inhabited by small but energetic nationalities.

That there was considerable activity in this country in the past in the fields of religion, art, literature and philosophy, is borne out by our great Sanskrit and Kannada works on religion and philosophy. That the people possessed a high degree of artistic skill and talent is evidenced by the superb specimens of sculptural art, such as, the rock temples at Halebid and Belur, the great stone statue at Sravanabelagola and the fine stone bull on the Chamundi Hill. These monuments of a by-gone age are the best of their kind and have no rivals in any other part of the world.

Father Tabard says "Mysoreans must study Mysore and they will love and understand Mysore all the more." I commend this advice to my countrymen. For great mountains, picturesque rivers, mighty waterfalls, superb scenery, Mysore is unsurpassed. Whether we consider tradition or history or the solid worth and beauty of the land, Mysore is a country which is, in every way, worthy of our devotion and love.

The President's erudition and industry have left their mark on the proceedings of this Society and his interest in Mysore and its traditions and his spirit of unselfish service in its cause must command our respect and admiration. With the help of Father Tabard and his cultured band of workers, let us hope historic research will find a permanent home in this State and that the Mysoreans will be awakened to a full conception of the past glory and greatness of their country.

ADDRESS TO DASARA REPRESENTATIVE ASSEMBLY.

7th Oct. 1916. [The thirty-third session of the Dasara Representative Assembly was held at the Public Offices, Mysore, on 7th October 1916. Besides many officers of Government and the members of the Assembly, there were present, the Hon'ble Mr. H. V. Cobb, C.S.I., C.I.E., British Resident in Mysore, and several visitors, European and Indian. Dewan Sir M. Visvesvaraya delivered the following address:—]

Gentlemen,—It is my privilege, under His Highness the Maharaja's commands, to extend a cordial welcome to you, the representatives of the people, to the thirty-third session of the Assembly, and, in accordance with precedent, to place before you an account of the administration of the State during the official year ended 30th June 1916.

The great war has entered upon the third year of its destructive career and its effects are visible in many directions on the trade and finances of the country. The activities which depend on the import of foreign machinery and tools are somewhat hampered and a strict watch has to be maintained over all departments of State expenditure.

We continue to receive favourable reports concerning the Mysore Imperial Service Regiment which has been on active service for the last two years. The regiment has distinguished itself in more than one encounter with the enemy and three of its officers have earned recognition, at the hands of the Government of India, for gallantry and distinguished conduct. The Imperial Service Transport Corps which has also been made available for active service will, we trust, acquit itself with equal credit. However small our contributions may seem when compared to the magnitude of the operations, they are the best practical expression we are able to give to the warmth of our devotion and our sense of Imperial obligation at this great crisis.

The seasonal conditions of the past year have been favourable. The rains were ample and timely in all the districts of the State except Tumkur, Shimoga and Kadur, and even in these three districts, agricultural operations were not materially affected by the shortage of rainfall. Save in the case of the coffee crop in the Kadur District, the produce throughout the State came up to the normal. No complaints were received of dearth of fodder or of drinking water from any part of the State.

The prospects during the current monsoon are, on the whole, good. The rainfall in the *maidan* districts has exceeded, in July and August, the average of the previous ten years, the excess in the Kolar District being as high as 8 inches. On the other hand, the rainfall in the *malnad* districts of Shimoga, Kadur and Hassan fell short of the average, the deficiency in the first two districts being 9 and 12 inches, respectively, in July. Most of the tanks are full, fodder is abundant, and although the ragi crop has suffered somewhat on account of excess of rain, the agricultural operations may be said to be progressing satisfactorily and the indications are all in favour of a good harvest and a prosperous year.

As announced at the last session, His Highness the Maharaja has been pleased to accord to the members of this Assembly the privilege of discussing the State budget. I have no doubt that the members have studied the budget as well as the rules of discussion. For the convenience of those who are not acquainted with English, abstracts of the budget have been prepared in Kannada and circulated.

Address to Dasara Representative Assembly.

Four hundred and fifteen subjects, in all, were discussed at the last session of the Assembly, out of which 279 have been finally disposed of and 136 are under consideration. Including the subjects of previous years, the number pending is 281.

The Legislative Council met five times during the year and considered 19 bills including the five pending from the previous year. The privilege of asking supplementary questions has been accorded to the members, and the total number of questions that may be asked at a single sitting has been raised from 12 to 20.

The seventh session of the Mysore Economic Conference was held in June 1916. The work done will be referred to in a future section of the Address.

Among the more important events of interest to our State, during the year, may be mentioned the confirmation by the Government of India, in March last, of the award of the Arbitration Committee appointed for settling the points of difference between the Government of Madras and the Government of His Highness the Maharaja, regarding the storage of the Cauvery waters. The final decision of the Government of India has enabled the Durbar to undertake the second stage of the reservoir project which, when completed, will bring under irrigation an additional extent of land of over 125,000 acres in the Mandya, Malvalli, Nagamangala and T.-Narasipur Taluks.

There appears to be considerable misconception, particularly among the inhabitants of the Cauvery delta in the Tanjore and Trichinopoly Districts, regarding the effect of this award. Statements have been made in the press and at public meetings that the decision has been too favourable to Mysore and injurious to the interests of Madras. This view probably found currency with the public, partly on account of the technical character of the points involved in the dispute and partly because, owing to the delicacy of the situation, it was not possible to contradict earlier the one-sided agitation that has been going on in the Madras Presidency.

At present the total area irrigated in the Cauvery valley within Mysore territory is 115,000 acres. The corresponding area in the lower reaches of the river within the Madras Presidency is 1,225,500 acres; that is to say, 92 per cent of the area irrigated by the river lies in the Madras Presidency, and only 8 per cent in Mysore.

Three-fourths of the total water-supply of the river passes through the Mysore territory, but, as stated above, the benefits derived by the State are wholly incommensurate with the high proportion of the total flow contributed by Mysore.

A large surplus flow in the river goes to waste into the sea, year after year, after meeting the needs of both Mysore and Madras irrigation. The Mysore project is intended to store only a small portion of this surplus.

While the Mysore reservoir is intended to hold a storage of a little over 40,000 million cubic feet, proposals have been matured by the Madras Government for constructing a reservoir of double this capacity practically from the same catchment at a point within the Madras Presidency just outside the Mysore boundary.

The extension of irrigation proposed within the Mysore State is only 150,000 acres. The Madras project, on the other hand, contemplated the extension of the already large irrigation in that Presidency by 320,000 acres, that is to say, by more than double the area which will be irrigated by the Mysore reservoir.

These two facts, *viz.*, that there is ample surplus water in the river and that the Madras Government had themselves proposed the construction of a storage reservoir of a capacity double that of ours and for the irrigation of more than double the area contemplated by us, afford unmistakable proof that, with suitable regulation of storage, the construction of our reservoir would in no way interfere with the existing irrigation. It is admitted on all hands that Madras is entitled only to as much water as is required to safeguard its existing irrigation.

The above bare statement of facts, from which legal and engineering technicalities are excluded, will perhaps suffice to show that we have not asked for, and certainly have not received, any special consideration in this matter. The construction of the reservoir will only enable us to utilise to a very moderate extent, the legitimate advantages to which Mysore is entitled by reason of its natural situation with reference to the river. This recognition of our rights, moreover, is accompanied by conditions which will be found to be very onerous as time goes on. For instance, we are required by the award to deliver a constant supply of 900 cubic feet per second regularly in the hot weather, while the natural river flow is on occasions as low as one-tenth of that discharge. It is true our main contentions have been conceded, but it is difficult to suppose that we have not paid a heavy price for success.

His Highness' Government are greatly indebted to the Government of India for having had this important question investigated and settled so promptly by an expert Committee.

According to the revised budget estimates, the total revenue for 1915-16 was Rs. 284·85 lakhs and the total ordinary service expenditure Rs. 260·98 lakhs, showing a surplus of Rs. 23·87 lakhs. Including an extraordinary outlay on capital account works of Rs. 60·31 lakhs, the total expenditure came to Rs. 321·29 lakhs, or Rs. 36·44 lakhs in excess of the revenue.

Address to Dasara Representative Assembly.

The State budget for 1916-17 was placed before the Legislative Council on the 29th June 1916 and discussed by that body on the 18th and 19th July last. As finally passed, it estimates for a revenue of Rs. 2,86,22,000, that is, Rs. 1,37,000 more than in the past year and provides for an expenditure amounting to Rs. 2,85,94,000 as against Rs. 2,60,98,000.

The expenditure of the State is regulated by means of triennial forecasts which are revised at the beginning of every year and which enable us to look ahead and calculate our resources and requirements three years in advance. The actual results compared with the forecasts have been uniformly favourable, showing that our estimates are usually conservative.

As I have stated on various other occasions, we shall soon have to face the problem of financing our public works programme. We have in recent years spent over two crores from our current revenues for creating property for the State which is already earning, or which will soon earn, much more than the ordinary rate of interest. A portion of this revenue may be well utilised for borrowing more money in order to complete with reasonable celerity the works of development necessary for the State. Such a course is followed in every civilised country as being not only safe but equitable, distributing as it does the burden of permanent and productive improvements over several generations who benefit from them. I revert to these considerations, not because Government want to borrow immediately—I think there is no likelihood of any large loan being contracted in the current year or even in the next—but because it is desirable that the public mind should become familiar with the idea that the construction of public works from loan funds is a legitimate means of advancing the permanent interests of the State and that failure to do so may reasonably bring on Government the accusation that it has not risen to its opportunities.

The land revenue collections of the year, including receipts from irrigation, amounted to about Rs. 1,04,50,000. The sorting and inspection of records have been receiving attention and a new system of registering and filing correspondence has been introduced in the offices of the Revenue Commissioner and of the Deputy Commissioners of Districts. The Village and Taluk Manuals have been completed and are being scrutinised. Revised rules have been recently prescribed for recruitment to the Amildari service. The rules provide, among other things, for giving equal chances to subordinate officials in the several departments of Government, and for showing special consideration to officials belonging to communities not hitherto sufficiently represented in the public service of the State.

With a view to stimulate interest in the work connected with public measures in the rural areas, the Deputy Commissioners and certain heads of departments arranged for conferences in various parts of the State at which questions connected with the Economic Conference, Village Improvements and Co-operative Societies, and the wants of the people generally were considered and discussed. In some cases, conferences were held also at the head-quarters of *hoblis*. In all, 95 conferences were held as noted below :—

Provincial	...	...	2
District	...	...	4
Taluk	...	...	83
Hobli	...	...	6

Of these, 56 were convened by the Revenue Department and the Taluk Progress Committees, 20 under the auspices of Co-operative Societies, 16 by the Agricultural Department and three more by other agencies. These conferences have an educative value and they help the district officers to ascertain and catalogue local wants and to focus the activities of the people on specific measures of improvement.

Revised rates of assessment were introduced in the Belur and Maddagiri Taluks. In the former the settlement operations resulted in a net increase of 7 per cent in the revenue on occupied land while in the case of the Maddagiri Taluk, the increase amounted to 13 per cent. Proposals for revision settlement have been received, or are nearly ready, for Tarikere and the late Gudibanda and Banavar Taluks. Arrangements are being made for expediting the re-survey and settlement work in the State and the additional staff required has been recently sanctioned.

The committee appointed for the consideration of certain questions relating to *inam* villages, to which I made reference in my Address last year, was strengthened by the addition of a few members representing the raiyats and the scope of its enquiries was enlarged. The report of the committee has just been received and is under consideration.

The gross receipts in the Excise Department during the year amounted to Rs. 58,32,195 as against Rs. 58,12,880 in 1914-15, showing an increase of Rs. 19,315.

With regard to the revision of the rules relating to *inamdars'* claims for excise revenue, draft rules have been published and orders will shortly issue.

The chief event of interest connected with the operations of the Forest Department was the revival of the market for sandalwood which had collapsed in the early days of the war. Altogether, more than 2,000 tons of wood were sold during the year and a sum of Rs. 16,91,452 was realised. Taking all the sources of revenue into consideration, the earnings of the Department amounted to nearly Rs. 32 lakhs and the expenditure was a little over Rs. 9 lakhs.

Owing to lack of communications and adequate staff, it has not been hitherto possible to work the interior forests of the *malnad* and of the Mysore District to their full capacity. The heavy district charges of Mysore and Shimoga have, therefore, been sub-divided and eleven new ranges have been formed in these and the Kadur District, the forest sub-divisions which formerly existed being abolished.

Among other events connected with the department may be mentioned, the deputation of an officer to America to make a special study of forest subjects, the revival of the appointment of a full time Forest Settlement Officer, the compilation of a commercial guide to the forest products of Mysore and the preparation of a provincial map showing the State Forests notified up to the end of the official year 1914-15.

There were 27 civil courts (excluding village munsiffs' courts) and 130 criminal courts working during the year. As stated in my Address last year, the Munsiff's Court at Narasimharajapura has been revived, and sanction has been accorded to the continuance of the Second Munsiff's Court at Tumkur up to May 1918.

The strength of the permanent Police force on the 30th June 1916 was 870 officers and 5,206 constables. The statistics of crime show that 7,970 cognizable cases were reported during the year as against 6,826 in the year 1914-15. But the increase occurred mostly under public nuisances and other minor offences. The cost of the department was about Rs. 10,61,000 against Rs. 10,84,000 in 1914-15.

The strength of the Cavalry and Infantry regiments and the Imperial Service Transport Corps at the end of the year 1915-16 was 1,300, 1,773 and 547, respectively, including officers and men. The work of the Military

Address to Dasara Representative Assembly.

Department was particularly heavy during the year in connection with the equipment of the forces for active service.

The number of medical institutions working at the end of the year was 165. Three semi-itinerant dispensaries were started in the Shimoga District and one itinerant dispensary in the Hassan District. The question of reorganising the Sanitary Department is receiving close attention and Government hope to arrive at a final decision very soon.

I observed in my Address last year that steps were being taken to prepare a working scheme for the Mysore University. The scheme has since been considered and adopted and the University has started work from 1st July 1916. The construction of the necessary buildings and the requisite equipment are receiving attention. University Entrance classes have been started under the scheme in the Government High Schools at Bangalore, Mysore and Tumkur, and, as soon as circumstances permit, it is proposed to start similar classes in the High School at Shimoga and the Maharani's College, Mysore.

The number of public institutions in the State increased from 4,278 to 5,436 during the year and their strength from 191,132 to 214,397 or by 23,265. The increase in strength occurred in almost all grades of schools, and particularly in primary schools, and was due to the large number of grant-in-aid, village indigenous and adult schools started during the year. The number of private schools was 1,822 and their strength 24,715. The total number of private and public institutions taken together was thus 7,258 with an attendance of 239,112 pupils as against 6,137 schools with 217,997 pupils at the close of the previous year. Of the total number of pupils, 198,077 were boys and 41,035 girls. The percentage of boys at school to the total male population of school age increased from 41·7 to 45·8 and that of the girls at school to the female population of school age from 8·9 to 9·7. The percentage of both boys and girls under instruction taken together to the total population of school age rose from 25·5 to 27·9. Classifying the pupils according to the several grades of education, there were 206,179 under primary, 26,371 under secondary, 934 under collegiate and 5,628 under special instruction.

Excluding 30 new schools sanctioned in connection with compulsory education, about 1,100 new primary schools were started during the year. The repair of village school buildings received special attention.

The compulsory education scheme was brought into operation in 12 new centres during the year, making up a total of 27 compulsory centres. Thirty new schools have been started in this area and about 3,600 boys of the compulsory age were induced to attend school. Comparatively little compulsion was used, notices of warning being served only in 82 cases where parents had failed to send their boys to school. Considering the eager desire for education evinced by the people and the number of applications received for the introduction of compulsory education, the scheme bids fair to be a success, its expansion being limited only by the rapidity with which the necessary funds and supply of teachers could be made available. Sanction has been given to the extension of the scheme to 41 new centres during the current year.

Advanced classes in commercial subjects were opened in the Government Commercial School, Bangalore, and evening classes in commercial subjects were held in Chikpet, Bangalore City, for the benefit of men engaged in business. His Highness' Government have recently sanctioned the opening of commercial classes in four other taluk head-quarter stations.

Address to Dasara Representative Assembly.

The opening of new Government industrial schools at all district head-quarters, except Mysore and Bangalore which have high grade institutions, was sanctioned during the year and preparations are well in hand for starting the schools. The Chamarajendra Technical Institute at Mysore and the Mechanical Engineering School at Bangalore, were further developed. The engineering section of the former was reorganised and the courses of study were revised on the model of the Upper subordinate classes of the Madras Engineering College.

Two additional district normal schools were started at Bangalore and Chitaldrug.

A donation of two lakhs and an annual recurring grant of Rs. 12,000 have been sanctioned for the Hindu University at Benares of which His Highness the Maharaja is the Chancellor.

The more important features of the work done by the Department of Agriculture during the year were the demonstration of improved methods and implements on lands belonging to raiyats, the distribution of large quantities of oil-cake as manure for sugar-cane, and the supply of several good varieties of sugar-cane and ragi seed. A scheme for imparting rural agricultural education in different centres throughout the State has been sanctioned and the details are under the consideration of Government.

Though the activities of the Department of Industries and Commerce were hampered by the difficulty in obtaining machinery and plant on account of the war, a fair amount of work has been turned out. Chiefly through the exertions of Mr. Alfred Chatterton, C.I.E., Director of the Department, a sandalwood oil factory was established at Bangalore during the year. It is working successfully and it is proposed to establish a larger factory at Mysore. The experiments in connection with the manufacture of soap were continued and the purchase of a plant to manufacture the article on a commercial scale has been ordered. A steam heating plant for making jaggery has been installed at Agaram.

The schemes under consideration include, among others, the opening of a cotton mill at Mysore and a small woollen mill in the Tumkur District, the preparation of charcoal by wood distillation and the establishment of an industrial workshop.

The erection of plant and machinery for private persons continued to receive attention. The number of new installations started during the year was 32 which, together with the number of those previously undertaken by the department, makes up a total of 103.

The financial assistance rendered by the department, for industrial undertakings, was the grant of 14 hire-purchase applications for Rs. 40,270 and of 16 loans amounting to Rs. 76,000.

The Director of Industries and Commerce and the Director of Mines and Geology have referred to the help rendered in various investigations pertaining to their respective departments by some of the members of the staff of the Indian Institute of Science. His Highness' Government wish cordially to associate themselves with the acknowledgments made by these officers.

One hundred and three new Co-operative societies were registered during the year and the registration of 28 societies was cancelled. The actual number of societies working at the end of the year was 800. The membership rose from 53,267 to 64,293, the share capital from Rs. 16,36,465 to Rs. 20,26,489, the working capital from Rs. 30,85,747 to Rs. 44,21,688, the total transactions from Rs. 1,31,13,546 to Rs. 1,72,53,813, the net profits from Rs. 1,61,521 to Rs. 2,17,976 and the reserve fund from Rs. 96,669 to Rs. 1,59,626.

Address to Dasara Representative Assembly.

The increase in the number of societies was not so great in the year under consideration as during the previous year. This was due to the fact that attention was concentrated on the consolidation of societies as evidenced by the large increase in the working capital, such numerical expansion as has taken place being spontaneous. The year is also noticeable for the increase in the number of industrial co-operative societies which rose from 19 in 1914-15 to 29 in 1915-16 and for the establishment of a new Provincial Bank.

In view of the increase of work in the department and in order to afford some relief to the Registrar, four districts have been constituted into a separate subordinate charge under the Assistant Registrar, and a Personal Assistant has been given to the Registrar to help him in office work.

The Standing Committee of the Economic Conference held nine meetings during the year at which the progress made by the Central Committees was reviewed and several important schemes were considered.

The District Committees met regularly and showed greater activity than in former years. The District Economic Superintendents were instrumental in enlisting the co-operation of the general public in the Conference work and helping them to start industries and agricultural developments. A mass of useful information and statistics relating to the districts were also collected by the Superintendents.

The formation of Progress Committees has been completed in all the taluks of the State and instructions defining their work have been issued.

A scheme for the appointment of Honorary Supervisors has been sanctioned in order to popularise Conference work in the taluks through non-official agency.

In my speech at the last session of the Conference, I

referred in detail to the activities of the three Central Committees of the Conference and it is unnecessary to go over the same ground again. I shall only touch on a few salient features of the work done by the committees.

Sericulture continued to receive the attention of the Agricultural Committee till the arrival of Signor Mari, when the work was placed directly under him. The committee devoted particular attention to the encouragement of fruit culture and the scheme submitted by them has been tentatively sanctioned.

The main questions which engaged the attention of the Education Committee were the preparation of a scheme for agricultural instruction in rural schools, the opening of commercial classes in taluk stations, the extension of the scheme of rural libraries and the development of the public libraries in Bangalore and Mysore. The committee have been entrusted with the work of starting special classes for industrial and other subjects with the aid of a special Government grant.

The Industries and Commerce Committee continued investigations regarding the manufacture of soap, tiles, paper pulp, wood distillation, etc. They also co-operated in the formation of a Chamber of Commerce, which has had a successful start under the guidance of Mr. W. C. Rose, its first President. A Home Industries Institute has been established and is working under the direction of the Chairman of the Education Committee.

In order that economic activities may be organised uniformly and on a more systematic basis, a scheme has been prepared under which the State is divided into 100 unit areas, consisting of the several taluks, the two cities of Mysore and Bangalore and certain important towns. The taluk units were required to select places and persons for carrying on individual items of work. Arrangements on these lines have been completed in respect of 62 units and steps are being taken to bring the remaining units shortly under the operation of the scheme.

The total expenditure on public works from all sources, including local funds, amounted to about Rs. 66½ lakhs during the year as against Rs. 70¼ lakhs in the preceding year. This expenditure is made up of Rs. 39¼ lakhs on ordinary public and local fund works and Rs. 27¼ lakhs on the Cauvery Reservoir and channels.

The Cauvery Reservoir dam has now risen to a height of 60 feet in the river bed and 75 feet at the flanks. The storage available at present is sufficient to guarantee the supply of 9,321 electric h.p. to the Kolar Gold Mines under the first three installations and of about 5,000 h.p. under the fourth installation. As a result of the construction of the dam, an additional revenue of Rs. 5,69,800 has been secured, partly on account of the higher rates charged for electric power in view of the guaranteed supply, and partly on account of additional supply of power made available with the aid of the reservoir. An annual expenditure of about Rs. 50,000 for conservancy operations in connection with the power works has been saved and the development of sugar-cane cultivation under the existing canals has been rendered possible. The outlay on the construction of the dam during the year was Rs. 20,93,170, the total expenditure up to the end of June 1916 being Rs. 92,39,373.

The investigations into loss of capacity of major tanks due to silting are proceeding. Measures for the scientific regulation and economic distribution of water have been introduced under eight selected tanks, one in each district, with results which are reported to be satisfactory.

In the workshop of the Public Works Department at Bangalore, a beginning was made during the year in the manufacture of agricultural implements and machinery for industrial concerns.

Address to Dasara Representative Assembly.

The fourth installation of the Cauvery Power Scheme, designed to meet the additional requirements of the mining companies under the new agreement, was completed during the year. Interruptions in the power and lighting service have been minimised by the erection of new overhead wires along the transmission line. To meet the growing demand for the supply of power, an estimate amounting to Rs. 3,63,188 for a fifth installation was sanctioned during the year for a 4,000 h.p. unit at Sivasamudram. When this work is completed, the total output of power will be 22,650 h.p.

The capital outlay on the Cauvery Power Scheme during the year amounted to Rs. 3,37,100 and the total outlay inclusive of the expenditure on the fourth installation, to end of June 1916, aggregated Rs. 1,06,87,000 in round figures. The gross earnings amounted to Rs. 24,28,100 against Rs. 18,58,300 during 1914-15, showing an increase of Rs. 5,69,800 which, as already stated, is due to the fact that the supply of power to the mines has been increased and guaranteed as a result of the construction of the Cauvery Reservoir. The working expenses, including a sum of Rs. 2,98,200 credited to the depreciation fund, amounted to Rs. 7,21,000. The balance which amounts to Rs. 11,37,200 (excluding the portion of the revenue due to the reservoir) represents a return of 10·64 per cent on the outlay as against 14·29 in the previous year.

The year's results of the working of the State lines by the Madras and Southern Mahratta Railway Company show that the gross earnings amounted to Rs. 38,28,883, which is about Rs. 2 lakhs more than in the previous year. The net return was Rs. 9,82,379 or 4 per cent on the outlay. As stated in my last year's Address, a portion of this return goes back to the railway itself, that is, for improvements to the open lines worked by the company.

The net result of the year's transactions for the State is a return of 2½ per cent on the outlay.

The construction work on the Mysore-Arsikere Railway has been progressing satisfactorily. Plate laying is being pushed on from both ends and the erection of girders on the Lakshmanthirtha bridge near Sagarkatte, which is the longest and highest on the line, will be started early. Owing to delay in getting the under frames and materials from England, and other unforeseen difficulties, the line could not be opened by the dates previously fixed. At the present rate of progress it may be possible to run through trains between Mysore and Arsikere by about June 1917.

The Kolar-Chintamani Section of the Kolar District Board Railway was opened for passenger traffic on the 6th March 1916. The portion from Chintamani to Chikballapur is expected to be ready for passenger traffic next month. The line from Tarikere has been completed up to Narasimharajapura. On account of heavy rains in the *malnad*, passenger traffic has been temporarily stopped but will, it is hoped, be resumed in December 1916, when the line will have been brought up to standard.

Preliminary investigations were made about the possibility of a harbour at Bhatkal and further detailed investigations are under consideration. A reconnaissance survey is being made for locating a railway line down the Kogaru Ghat to Bhatkal. The work will be continued next working season.

A preliminary survey for a line on the metre gauge to connect Coorg with the Mysore railway system has been carried out and four alternative routes were carefully investigated. One of the lines will be shortly selected for carrying out a detailed survey.

The results of the railway operations in the State may be summarised as follows:—

The total mileage open for traffic up to the end of 1911 was 411·17 miles and the capital cost of those lines was Rs. 2,51,64,185. Since then a Railway Department has been organised. The total length of lines taken up for construction is 231 miles and the outlay incurred thereon, up to the end of June 1916, was Rs. 85,72,401. The amount of money raised from the public for the smaller feeder lines is a little over Rs. 14 lakhs.

The following projects are ready for construction and their length and estimated cost are as noted below:—

Name of Railway		Length	Estimated cost
		Miles	Rs.
1. Chikjajur-Chitaldrug line	...	21	8·55 lakhs
2. Kadur-Chikmagalur line	...	28	16·60 ,,
3. Chikmagalur-Hassan line	...	37	17·48 ,,
4. Bangalore-Hosur line	...	30·69	12·75 ,,

The projects under investigation are the Mysore-Coorg connection, the Shimoga-Bhatkal and Mysore-Kakankote lines, the Narasimharajapura-Sringeri extension and the Thadasa-Hebbe tramway.

During the year, the offices of the Engineer-in-Chief and the Agent were combined with that of the Secretary for Railways. The Railway Board have kindly allowed Mr. G. Richards, Superintending Engineer, now employed in the investigation of railways to the West Coast ports, to work as our Consulting Engineer.

The reorganization scheme of the Department of Mines and Geology sanctioned in February 1915 came fully into effect during the year. Special attention was paid to the exploration and investigation of minerals of economic value. A bulletin on the geology of Mysore, with a map giving a summary of the results arrived at by the geological survey, was prepared and issued. Another bulletin on the mineral resources of the State, their modes

Address to Dasara Representative Assembly.

of occurrence, methods of mining and extraction and possibilities has also been published for the use of the local public interested in mining work. A Kannada edition of this bulletin will shortly be ready.

The output of bar gold during 1915-16 was 558,381 ounces of an approximate value of Rs. 3,11,32,760 as against 570,886 ounces of a value of Rs. 3,28,65,540 in 1914-15. The royalty for 1915-16 was approximately Rs. 18,69,931 against Rs. 19,15,803 in 1914-15.

The Efficiency Audit Branch of the Secretariat continued to devote attention to measures having for their object the systematization of work in Government offices and departments. Special attention was paid during the year to the Secretariats. A number of useful compilations of rules and standing orders have been prepared and a comprehensive scheme has been drawn up for ensuring the speedy preparation of manuals and for keeping them up-to-date. Considerable progress has been made in standardising inspections, preparing record rules, and in other directions. The officers of the Efficiency Audit Branch have also been employed, generally at the request of heads of departments and other senior officers concerned, for inspecting offices and investigating serious irregularities. Sanction has been given to the issue of a quarterly journal containing a summary of the more important Government orders and publications issued from time to time and furnishing information, on matters of departmental technique, etc., likely to be of use to officers in the discharge of their duties.

The proposals for improving the administration of the Muzrai Department were further considered during the year, and orders are expected to issue in a few weeks.

The income and expenditure of all municipalities in the State during the year amounted to about Rs. 12,96,800 and Rs. 12,56,100 respectively. The constitution of periodical municipalities has been sanctioned as a tentative measure in certain places in the Shimoga District where large annual *jatras* are held. In the Bangalore City, the number of *ex-officio* members on the municipal council was reduced from three to one. A non-official Vice-President was appointed for the Tumkur Municipal Council and a full time official Vice-President was appointed for the Shimoga Municipality.

The question of improving the water-supply of Chitaldrug by pumping water from the Katharahal tank, a distance of about eight miles from the town, has been approved. Government have promised a liberal contribution and arrangements have been made to finance the scheme by a loan to be raised, as far as possible, within the district itself.

The total income and expenditure under District Funds were approximately Rs. 12,27,618 and Rs. 9,78,266 respectively. The special features of the Local Boards administration during the year were the levy of a railway cess in the Tumkur and Chitaldrug Districts and the amendment of the Local Boards Regulation authorising the levy of shop tax in Unions.

In last year's address, I outlined the principal reforms in connection with municipalities and district boards then under contemplation and I also stated that the proposals involved a very appreciable contribution from State revenues, and required further consideration before Government were able to accept them. The question is now ripe for orders which Government hope to issue very shortly.

At the close of the last official year, 8,171 village committees were working in the several districts as shown below:—

Address to Dasara Representative Assembly.

Districts			No. of village committees
1. Mysore	...	...	1,580
2. Tumkur	...	...	1,249
3. Kolar	...	...	1,072
4. Bangalore	...	...	1,050
5. Hassan	...	...	999
6. Chitaldrug	...	...	853
7. Shimoga	...	...	846
8. Kadur	...	...	522
	Total	...	8,171

The population served by the committees was 4,514,244, or roughly three-fourths of the entire population of the State. The system of devoting half-a-day's labour every week for tidying up village sites and carrying out works of communal benefit has been followed by 3,825 committees representing a population of 2,069,453. Village libraries have been started or newspapers are being subscribed for, by 3,670 committees. The amount spent for works of permanent improvement such as wells, roads, etc., was Rs. 96,159 out of which a sum of Rs. 46,563 was sanctioned as Government grants-in-aid, the remainder being contributed by villagers either in cash or by labour. The improvement of village cart-tracks has received considerable attention and it is reported that a length of 750 miles has been laid out or repaired since the scheme came into operation. The progress made in this direction in the Bangalore District is particularly marked. Tree planting formed a special feature of the work done in the Chitaldrug District.

I made a special inspection of some parts of the districts of Tumkur, Mysore and Hassan to examine the working of the scheme and I noticed that everywhere a considerable amount of useful work was being done. It rests with the Deputy Commissioners and Amildars and the leaders of the people to see that the work done is consolidated and extended.

At the end of 1914-15, the total number of tank panchayets sanctioned was 53, and 20 panchayets were ordered to be constituted during the year 1915-16, of which 17 were in respect of tanks in the Tumkur District. The panchayets in the Kolar, Mysore and Kadur Districts are reported to be doing some practical work by attending to the annual repairs and regulating the distribution of water.

Nineteen village forests, covering an area of 9,487 acres, were formed during the year, and the constitution of 17 forests with an area of 8,149 acres has been since notified, making a total of 36 village forests covering an area of nearly 18,000 acres.

One hundred and twenty-eight Village Munsiffs' Courts commenced work during the year.

Six hundred and forty-seven tanks were taken up for restoration during the year and 186 were completed at an outlay of Rs. 86,130. Considering the large lapses in allotments, the progress made has been somewhat disappointing. Arrangements are being made to train educated villagers to enable them to undertake the construction of minor tanks and a manual of instructions has been prepared for their guidance.

To ensure better progress under the rural water-supply scheme inaugurated in January 1915, the purchase of a set of boring tools and the employment of a special staff consisting of one overseer and three or four maistries have been sanctioned for each district. The State grant of Rs. 1,00,000, and the contribution of half a lakh each from the village improvement fund and district fund respectively, are being continued. A set of instructions for sinking drinking water wells, together with type designs, has been circulated to all the District Boards.

Address to Dasara Representative Assembly.

The scheme for the improvement of the *malnad* was sanctioned in February 1914 and has been in operation for over two years. The progress achieved since the beginning may be summarised as follows :—

Rank vegetation has been cleared in 570 villages. The value of the work done under this head by the raiyats is estimated at Rs. 26,531, the contribution from Government being Rs. 3,042. Construction of wells has been proposed in 107 villages and 54 wells have already been completed. A beginning has been made in opening minor village roads. Greater facilities have been afforded to the people for obtaining sites and supplies of timber for building houses for themselves.

Large quantities of quinine tablets have been distributed to the people and it is reported that their use is becoming popular. The propaganda work included the distribution of leaflets on sanitation and hygiene and the exhibition of lantern slides depicting the health conditions of the *malnad* and the precautions to be taken by the people resident in the area. A disease survey has been commenced on a small scale in the Sagar Taluk. Increased facilities have been provided for affording medical relief.

In May 1916, a scheme was sanctioned for granting facilities to persons intending to settle down in the *malnad*. A commencement has been made in promoting industrial education in different centres. The adoption of measures on an adequate scale, for relieving the indebtedness of the *malnad* raiyats, is engaging the attention of Government.

With a view to popularise the scheme, Taluk Conferences were held during the year at Channagiri, Shikarpur, Sagar, Kallurkatte and Tirthahalli.

I have reviewed the routine work of the administration

and also referred to all the more outstanding questions of public interest which received attention during the past year. I will now briefly invite your attention to the existing circumstances of the country and to the reforms and developments demanded by the rapidly changing conditions of the present time.

In previous Addresses, particularly last year's, I drew attention to the low earning power, low standard of living and low ideals of aspiration and effort, which are such an unsatisfactory feature of the economic and social life of this country.

It is only by comparative study, by making an inventory of our resources in materials and men, that we shall know where we stand and realise our deficiencies. I am never tired of quoting statistics to show the relative position of our people economically, as compared with more progressive nations. I trust you will bear with me if I place before you a tabular statement giving this comparison.

No.	Main heads of progress	In advanced countries	In Mysore	Standard to aim at in Mysore in the near future
1	Percentage of literates to total population.	Over 80.	8	60
2	Percentage of pupils at school to total population.	United Kingdom ... 20 Canada ... 20 Australia ... 14·7 Japan ... 14·8	4	10
		Rs.	Rs.	Rs.
3	Production from agriculture—Value per head of population.	Canada ... 342 Australia (including pastoral, dairying.) 372	24	45
4	Annual income per head of population.	United Kingdom ... 720 Canada ... 555 Australia ... 495	81	60

Address to Dasara Representative Assembly.

No.	Main heads of progress	In advanced countries		In Mysore	Standard to aim at in Mysore in the near future
			Rs.	Rs.	Rs.
5	Estimated wealth per head of population.	United Kingdom ...	6,000	264	500
		France ...	4,875		
		Italy ...	1,986		
		Canada ...	4,440		
		Australia ...	3,960		
		Japan ...	1,087		
6	Total revenue per head of population.	United Kingdom ...	62	5	10
		Canada ...	50		
		Australia ...	66		
		Japan ...	18		
7	Savings Bank deposits per head of population.	Canada ...	40	1	10
		Australia ...	252		
		United States of America.	1,317		
8	Total trade per head of population.	United Kingdom ...	386	26	50
		France ...	232		
		Italy ...	106		
		Canada ...	480		
		Australia ...	495		
		Japan ...	40		

I have given in the last column of the table certain modest figures, under each head, to serve as standards to aim at in the near future. I call them standards with a view to place concrete ideals in some form before you, but it is open to the leading public men of the country to suggest alternative standards after carrying out the necessary investigations themselves. Till then, perhaps, these figures might be allowed to stand.

The table shows how poor the country is in all that the world prizes as material wealth. It shows, too, that, in point of capacity and skill, or what economists would call "personal wealth," the country is woefully deficient.

We know very clearly that lack of education, of science, of world knowledge, is answerable for the present condition of our people.

Address to Dasara Representative Assembly.

Priding, as we do, on our ancient civilization and past traditions, it hurts us no doubt to be told that we are very low in the scale of nations in point of capacity and prosperity. But the best proof we can give that we realise our position is to make an energetic effort to develop the country at least to the level of the standard figures indicated in the table.

The work before the country may be divided into three main heads, *viz.*, (1) developments in administration, (2) economic development, and (3) development of civic and social life. I will first deal with reforms in the sphere of public administration.

Improvements in the system of work in Government departments are receiving attention. I have already referred to the work of the Efficiency Audit Branch in the Secretariat which consists of a small staff whose duty, among other things, is to systematise the work of all departments and to help to correct anomalies and irregularities.

An attempt is being made, under what is known as organization and development work, to bring under investigation, with a view to ultimate practical action where necessary, the more important defects and needs of each department in the order of their urgency and importance.

In connection with Government departments and offices, a system of surprise inspections is contemplated, so that the work done may be seen in its normal condition and not as it is made up on receipt of notice of inspection.

Improvements are being effected in the *personnel* of the service. We have many capable officers and the general level of integrity is high. But their efficiency might be further improved if European business habits became more common among them and if the officers exercised more power of initiative and imbibed stricter habits of discipline.

Address to Dasara Representative Assembly.

In some of the departments, a beginning has been made to train officers to make original investigations and to specialise in the technical subjects connected with their duties. To broaden the outlook of officers, facilities are being afforded to encourage foreign travel.

There is an enormous increase of work in the Government departments, especially in connection with the expansion of railways, extension of Cauvery Irrigation Works, enlargement of the hydro-electric scheme, development of forest and mineral resources, new industries, improvement of tanks, etc. These have brought on new responsibilities on Government which they will be ill-prepared to discharge without a more efficient system of work, without additional establishment and greater public co-operation.

Referring to the co-operation of the public, the late Dewan, Mr. Rangacharlu, in his Dasara Address of 1882, spoke of the "crushing influence of officialdom" which, according to him, kept the population ignorant and denied it any power of initiative. Things have changed now and it is beginning to be recognised that one of the essential duties of every Government officer in a responsible position is to train the people, to make them more and more self-reliant and enlist their co-operation in public work. It is important that the people should be emancipated from the habit of petitioning Government for every small want and every petty grievance. The truism bears repetition that the efficiency of an administration depends, in the last resort, on the energy, capacity and vigilance of the people.

In the field of economic development, some substantial work, in the way of training the people and associating them in public work with Government officers has been begun through the agency of the Economic Conference and its committees. As our organization is improving in efficiency from year to year, my reference to developments under this head need only be very brief.

In respect of education, we look forward to further rapid expansion of primary education and to enlisting more public support for educating the adult population in the districts. Technical education also wants a great deal more attention than we have been able to give it hitherto. The work of the University recently started has to be consolidated. The extension and publication work has to be vigorously pushed through. It is pleasing to notice the keen interest which many leading men, both Europeans and Indians, are taking in developing the work of the new University.

Under agriculture, intensive cultivation, closer association between agriculture and science and development of rural industries have to be encouraged. The cultivators should be given an insight into modern conditions of business and encouraged to practise forethought and thrift. Agricultural credit must be more systematically organised.

Under industries and commerce, money has to be spent liberally to train the people and to give them financial and other help till they are better able to look after themselves. A few large industries will be pioneered by Government. The prosecution of smaller industries by co-operative effort, by partnership or joint-stock enterprise, should be specially encouraged.

The principal civic and social activities requiring attention may be considered to fall under the following heads:

(1) Public and municipal administration and social service.
(2) Social elevation.
(3) Science, literature, art, religion, morals.
(4) Raising standards of business conduct, thoroughness and finish in practical life.

Address to Dasara Representative Assembly.

A central committee for Bangalore or Mysore and at least one person for each town might be entrusted with the responsibility of developing each of these activities. In the work of investigation and enquiry, the duties of the central committee should be to maintain lists of leading workers interested in the subject, to gather and spread information, to collect funds, appoint lecturers, convene meetings and conferences, issue leaflets and publish a consolidated report of progress at the end of each year.

The general public should be encouraged to make a serious study of public and municipal administration. The duties of the Representative Assembly and the Legislative Council are growing. A revised scheme of Local Self-Government is expected to issue in a few weeks. A system of conferences has been inaugurated in the districts, taluks and even *hoblis* to ascertain the wants and wishes of the people and enlist their co-operation in public work.

We are now utilising the services of the rural population in a small way in village improvement work and in connection with minor tanks, water supply and other local works. The co-operation which the village people have shown is very creditable to their sense of public spirit; and, with a proper organization, many useful works can be carried out to promote public convenience and material prosperity in rural areas.

I referred to the necessity of civic and social progress in the Dasara Address of 1914, and I refer to it again here as part of a complete scheme of development work for the State. The subject of civic and social duties does not of course fall within the sphere of public administration. The work has to be done by the people themselves.

All these subjects which affect the prosperity and enlightenment of the country must come under investigation and enquiry by a few enthusiasts at first and a wider circle of workers afterwards.

Address to Dasara Representative Assembly.

The number of subjects which come under the domain of investigation is very vast. All persons competent and willing to co-operate should have work assigned to them according to their capacity and aptitude and kept thinking and working.

Investigation will gradually bring to light the defects which require remedy, improvements which demand attention and opportunities which can be availed of with profit.

These proposals in effect amount to a scheme of research, on a small scale, into all the principal activities of civilized life. If people are kept thinking, investigating and working on any subject, standards and ideals will be gradually evolved, leading ultimately to decisions and practical action.

A great economic change is impending in the world in consequence of the war and it is certain that industrial and trade competition will be very much keener after its close. It is stated, with authority, that His Majesty's Government are considering the outlines and the basis of a post-war policy, both social and industrial, and that a State scheme of assistance to scientific and industrial research is in course of creation. Our late Viceroy, Lord Curzon, recently stated that "to meet the situation, new schemes, new plans, new policies will have to be devised and a new adjustment will be called for of many of the basic principles upon which public life has hitherto rested." The same spirit is evinced in France, in Australia and in Canada.

When nations so incomparably richer than ourselves, who already possess a connected scheme of national life, are thinking of reconstruction, are we—who have no prosperity at all worth mentioning—to sit still? Shall we remain content with our low standard of life and work, or adopt a policy of development and progress? If the latter, are the standards I have indicated too ambitious in the present circumstances of the country, or, are they reasonable and practicable? If the answer to this question be also in the affirmative, you will agree that the present drift and traditional inaction should give place to a reasoned policy and a courageous initiative.

We must begin work at once with a changed outlook and new ideals. In these days of open-door, free communications, world competition, it would be unpardonable neglect on our part to omit to organise the resources and working power of our people in every walk of life.

REPLY TO DASARA ADDRESSES.

[At the thirty-second session of the Dasara Representative Assembly, held on 7th October 1916, at the Public Offices, Mysore, Dewan Sir M. Visvesvaraya received addresses from the representatives of the Kolar Gold Field Mining Board, the Central Mahomedan Association and the people of the Kadur District. Sir M. Visvesvaraya, replying collectively to these addresses, made the following speech :—] 7th Oct. 1916.

Gentlemen,—Permit me, on behalf of my colleagues and myself, to express to you the thanks of His Highness' Government for the appreciative references you have made, in the addresses just read, to the administration of the past year and generally to the policy followed by Government.

With reference to the principal request on behalf of the Mining Board, namely, extension of Sections 5 to 20 of the Mines Regulation to the Kolar Gold Field Railway, I may state that His Highness' Government are in communication with the Government of India on the subject.

The question of amending Section 17 of the Regulation and the proposal to augment the Police force stationed in the mining area are also under consideration.

The address on behalf of the Central Mahomedan Association urges the necessity of improving the pay and prospects of women teachers. Proposals in this respect are already before Government, who will give the matter their early and sympathetic attention.

As many of the subjects dealt with in the address from the members of the Kadur District are on the regular agenda of business, I do not propose to refer to those representations in detail.

The control of primary and secondary education by Local Bodies, referred to in the address from the Kadur District, will be dealt with in connection with the scheme of reforms in Local Self-Government which will shortly issue.

A project estimate for a railway from Kadur to Chikmagalur is reported to be ready and if, as suggested in the address, a railway cess is imposed, the all-important question of financing the scheme will be simplified and the early construction of the line will come within the region of practical politics. I am afraid Government cannot hold out any promise to convert the tramway from Tarikere to Narasimharajapura into a metre gauge line, as it involves a large addition to the outlay not warranted by the traffic expectations of the area.

Government fully realise the need for additional veterinary dispensaries and have under consideration a scheme of expansion which will be gradually brought into operation. The requirements of the Kadur District will, along with those of other parts of the State, receive careful consideration.

Speech at the Dasara Representative Assembly.

I wish once more to express to you my high appreciation of your friendly views and to say that it will give me great pleasure to convey to His Highness the Maharaja the sentiments of loyalty and gratitude to which the addresses have given such eloquent expression.

SPEECH AT THE DASARA REPRESENTATIVE ASSEMBLY.

[The thirty-second session of the Dasara Representative Assembly closed its sittings on 14th October 1916, after debating over 200 subjects put before it. In closing the session, Dewan Sir M. Visvesvaraya made the following speech:—] 14th Oct. 1916.

Gentlemen,—After five days' discussion, I find we have been able to dispose of 211 subjects, out of a total of 335. The 82 local and 21 supplementary subjects have been dealt with as also all important general subjects. We have agreed that the remaining 124 subjects, which are comparatively unimportant, may be taken up at the next session.

As on previous occasions, the discussions were conducted with ability and enthusiasm, although, in one or two instances, the language used by members was, as stated by Mr. A. Ramanna, more expressive than measured.

I have to express regret that, as the time at our disposal was limited, individual representations could not be given freer scope.

Coming now to the more important subjects discussed,

the regulation of water supply under tanks and canals has received some attention during the year. Government are anxious that the water distribution should be done scientifically instead of by rule of thumb. The Special Irrigation Engineer has been dealing with 8 tanks and a set of suitable rules giving practical hints on the subject has been drawn up for the information of the public.

As promised by me last year, the question of restricting the *atchkat* of tanks in proportion to the storage available is receiving attention. Five or six tanks are being surveyed. If the representatives of the people want more rapid progress, it will be necessary to put on additional establishment to expedite the work. The subject may be discussed again at the next session.

The subject of water rate on *inam* lands was argued with much ability. Following the precedent in other Provinces, we have sanctioned payment of commission at the rate of 12 per cent to the inamdar which ought to sufficiently compensate him. Government charge only 6 per cent for similar service when they take over the management of *inam* villages. New irrigation works are often commercial enterprises on which Government must realise a suitable return. No valid reason was put forward to show why Government should sell water at lower than its market rate to *inam* lands.

As regards the restoration of minor tanks, the share which the raiyats have to contribute was settled with your consent a couple of years ago. I am sorry to learn that full advantage has not yet been taken of the concession. Although it is too early to judge of the working of the rules, Government have no objection to authorise the Deputy Commissioners to recover the raiyats' contribution in instalments spread over from 3 to 5 years.

The increase of emoluments to Patels and Shanbhogs has been under discussion for a long time. The

Speech at the Dasara Representative Assembly.

Financial Department considers that the increase is inadmissible. Some few among you have stated that the appointments are coveted for the prestige attaching to them. The subject is beset with difficulties and must be kept under investigation till a proper solution is reached.

Government are anxious to deal with the settlement of inamdars' claims to toddy revenue within the next two or three months. They have definitely come to the conclusion that the tax on trees situated in *inam* villages should be paid to the privileged inamdars and that in Government villages to Government. The question as to how the claims already admitted should be dealt with is receiving consideration.

With regard to the contribution for building reading rooms in villages, I may say at once that, without increasing the total annual expenditure under this head, Government see no objection, at least for the present, to increase the grant in individual cases from one-third to one-half.

You brought to notice certain defects in the Muzrai administration. The whole question has been thoroughly investigated by a Committtee and the Muzrai Superintendent and certain conclusions have been arrived at, which, it is expected, will greatly improve the working of the Muzrai institutions in future. A Government order on the subject is expected to issue almost immediately.

Last year, you agreed to legislation for the enforcement of weekly labour in villages or the levy of a cess instead. This year, you have gone back on that decision. Every large improvement requires some measure of sacrifice or submission to discipline. Government consider that it will not be possible to keep up continuous interest or activity in the scheme without legislation.

The subject of the separation of executive and judicial

functions has given rise to sharp differences of opinion. It is, however, under active consideration and Government are anxious to reach a solution. The chief difficulty is one of cost.

In the matter of weights and measures, the Chamber of Commerce is being consulted. Government are willing to give facilities if private parties come forward to take up the work.

Government are aware of the strong feeling that exists about the delay in providing new telegraph offices in the State. We have made a representation to the Government of India. A meeting is to be held shortly in Bangalore to consider how our immediate requirements might be met.

In regard to the defects brought to notice in the administration of primary schools, Mr. Shama Rao has explained the difficulties of the Department on account of a large and sudden increase in the number of schools. In a matter like this, I must bespeak a little patience on the part of the public. Most of the difficulties are now removed and Government are doing all they can, by sanctioning additional inspecting staff and in other ways, to further improve matters.

The complaint as to want of seats in High Schools and Colleges has been met by the Inspector-General of Education who stated there was not a single case in which a qualified student was refused admission in the current year. He has been requested to see that troubles of this kind will not recur.

Many of you were present the other day when His Highness the Maharaja inaugurated the first meeting of the Mysore University Senate. I am sure you will all take a patriotic interest in the growth of our University and help its work by providing endowments, if necessary, for students coming from your own localities. At least ten students should be maintained at the University from each taluk.

Government are giving some facilities to encourage young men from the backward communities to take more largely to education and also to enable them to get admission into the public service in greater numbers than has been the case hitherto. It must be remembered that these classes have not yet acquired the habit of educating themselves and some temporary inducements are necessary. I have no doubt the public as a whole will commend the action taken by Government.

As regards railway development, Government are anxious to arrange for a connection to Bhatkal on the West Coast and to take up the Nanjangud-Erode link. For the rest, if any railways are brought near our borders, we may give connections from our railway system, if they are to our advantage. We can only build such lines as are calculated to promote the permanent interests of the State as a whole.

For the past forty years, the urban population of our State in proportion to the rural, has been going down, first on account of famine and then plague. We want more town population in order to carry on the higher work of civilization. Extensions should be marked out in every town, and building sites and sites for industrial suburbs should be kept ready. Settlers and industries may be slow in coming but, if the sites are there, the most formidable obstacle in the way of increase of population and business activities will have been removed.

I have drawn attention to the changing conditions of the times. Progress means work and work must be done by somebody, either by Government agency or by an organization of the people. There is no other short cut. I have, in my hand, a statement showing at least 20 cases in which you have asked for new schemes or new facilities in the interests of the public, which will cost many lakhs to comply with; but there is not a single suggestion for increase of revenue. You consider all increase of establishment as an unmitigated evil. You want many things. You do not pause to enquire how the cost is to be met. Now that you are going to discuss the budget in the next session, I trust you will take up a more practical attitude in future.

Whatever might have been the case in the past, there is no antagonism of interests between the officials and the non-officials at present. Many of the officers have to do their regular duties and also help in the new developments. They have risen splendidly to the occasion and been very zealously doing the people's work. We owe such officers a deep debt of gratitude.

In my opening address, I have explained that all the development activities of the country may be brought under three heads, *viz*:

(1) Developments in administration,
(2) Economic development, and
(3) Civic and social progress.

The first has to be attended to by the Government officers aided by the people, the second by the people aided by Government and the third exclusively by the people. In future, we want the people of each taluk, town and village to give up petitioning, and to take an increasing responsibility for supplying local needs themselves. You have local conferences at which you may ask for co-operation from officers. We are trying to fix standards of the level of development which taluks, towns and villages should aim at and we trust, in course of time, to have experts all over the country who would be able to survey each local area, and assess its percentage of efficiency.

I will mention an instance or two of how large improvements might be effected by local effort and organization. Government are desirous of giving power to local bodies to borrow money by guaranteeing interest with the aid of a cess raised in the localities themselves. Suppose, in a taluk like Tirthahalli, the Board was able to levy a cess which brought in an income of Rs. 15,000 to Rs. 20,000 annually; the Board will be able to borrow from the residents in the taluk itself a sum of over Rs. 3 lakhs and lend it to influential committees or other organizations to carry out tank improvements, roads, water-supply, drainage works, etc., within the taluk. The persons benefited will be able to repay in due course and till then the proceeds of the cess would go to meet interest charges. The restoration of old tanks and construction of new ones is a crying want. The tanks were originally constructed by local people and there is no reason why, with training and organization, the people of to-day should not take up similar responsibilities. If an organised attempt is made in this way, important works will be carried out in taluks, which fifty years of petitioning and dependence on Government will not effect. A similar attempt might be made for the improvement of the *malnad* region. There is money in the country, labour can be imported and a few years' training will give all the special skill required for developing the ordinary public works of the area.

Gentlemen, we are now agreed that the second session should be held in the fourth week of April and that it might last about four days. His Highness the Maharaja was graciously pleased to order this morning that the courtesy of granting *lava jama* to members should be extended to the second session also. As regards the discussion of the budget, facilities will be provided to members to obtain all reasonable information. If some of you specialise in different branches of administration, it will tend to raise the value of your suggestions and a time will come when Government may, of their own accord, seek your advice.

What is needed from the people is a change of outlook and enthusiastic co-operation with Government. We have Members of Government, all of whom have travelled abroad. Mr. Kantharaj Urs has, as you know, just returned from the Far East. His Highness the Yuvaraja has travelled both East and West and is taking the lead in many beneficent public movements in the country. His Highness the Maharaja is directing all large developments with an eye to the permanent interests of his people. If the great majority of the population give up their traditional apathy and work on new lines, developments will follow in rapid succession and we can face the future with confidence.

ADDRESS TO MYSORE ENGINEERS.

15th Mar. 1917.

[The tenth session of the Mysore Engineers' Conference was held in the rooms of the Mysore Engineers' Association, Bangalore, on 15th March 1917. Sir M. Visvesvaraya, in opening the session, made the following remarks:—]

Gentlemen,—Being a constant visitor at the annual sessions of this Conference, not many words are needed from me on this occasion. I am gratified to learn that there is an increase in the number of members since we last met. The engineering work of the State is growing in volume and variety and demands a vigilant attitude on the part of this Association. If the Association wishes to be sufficiently alert, it should be constantly employed in encouraging the study of new problems, stimulating original thinking and zealous work, and in helping members to be up to date in the respective branches of their profession.

Foremost among the larger engineering works which were in progress during the past year comes the reservoir on the Cauvery which, in future, will be known as the Krishnarajasagara after His Highness the Maharaja, to whose courage and constant support we owe the success of the enterprise. The Fourth Installation of the Cauvery Power Scheme is also now completed. Both these works have begun to earn a substantial revenue for the State. Some buildings of architectural importance, including those required for the new University, are springing up in Mysore and Bangalore. A few water-supply schemes are under construction and some more are under investigation. The Railway and Electrical Departments have been fairly active on new works and improvements.

These achievements, good as far as they go, represent, however, a continuation of the previous year's work. The past year was not by any means remarkable for initiative or enterprise on the part of our Engineers. Many questions of engineering interest have been brought to your notice and appeals have been made for continuous effort on your part. Progress on them means increase of production and prosperity for the country. There is, for instance, the question of the improvement of tanks, both major and minor. The work of restoration and reconstruction is not being pushed on with as much expedition as Government would wish. We are still on the fringe of the question of scientific regulation of water. The efforts so far made in the direction of town planning, drainage and water-supply have been spasmodic. Government have not stinted money for surveys or investigations but the work done during the past year in these respects is disappointing. As far as I can make out, progress on specialization studies has been inconsiderable. No wonder that instances of engineering research, forethought, initiative and enterprise are so few, and I have to complain of a conspicuous lack of organization and co-operative effort among you.

Altogether, I fear, the Association during the past year has not shown as much activity as we have a right to expect, if regard be had to the number of able men there are on its rolls and the opportunities which the country and the Government are affording at the present time. All honour, therefore, to the three or four men who have been carrying on the work of the Association amidst much of what seems like general apathy.

The profession presents many and varied opportunities for all of you to serve your country and through such service also to benefit yourselves. Government have improved the prospects of the Civil Engineers by granting them the time-scale of pay. They have also allowed them to fill positions of trust in departments outside the regular Public Works.

But it is disappointing to find the majority of engineers content with the routine work of their appointments. Work is taken up spasmodically and carried out without regard to system or method. Programmes and promises are soon forgotten instead of being treated as a debt of honour.

The Association, if properly utilised, should be a clearing house for new ideas and a tower of strength to the profession and to the technical departments of the State.

The new fields of public usefulness that are being opened up for your activities will bring you credit and profit. When you broaden your outlook and begin to think in terms of your State, of district, city, town and village, the country and the Government will also profit by your activities. No determined effort on the part of the Association to raise the standard of capacity, industry and character among the members of your profession will go unrewarded. The most capable and upright men among you have the highest prizes within your reach.

Is it, therefore, too much to ask you to prepare a very precise programme for the new year and treat it as a debt of honour and put forth your best efforts to give effect to it? By doing so, you will be raising the Association in the estimation of both the Government and the public. Every one of the members can add his "bit of work" according to his standing in the profession and capacity and opportunities.

SPEECH AT THE WAR LOAN MEETING.

[A meeting of the citizens of Bangalore was held on Saturday, 7th April 1917, in the Government High School Hall, Bangalore City, to encourage the people of the State to invest liberally in the new Government of India War Loan. Among those present were the Hon'ble Mr. H. V. Cobb, C.S.I., C.I.E., Resident in Mysore, the principal high officers of the State and numerous non-official gentlemen resident in the City. The meeting was largely attended and marked by enthusiasm throughout. Sir M. Visvesvaraya, in speaking on the principal resolution put before the meeting, said as follows:—] 7th April 1917.

Mr. Cobb and gentlemen,—We are met here to-day to encourage the citizens of Bangalore and the people of our State to invest liberally in the new Government of India War Loan. Meetings for popularising the loan have been held in all parts of India. Our own meeting we first intended to hold on the 26th March, but it had to be postponed pending a reply from the Government of India in regard to certain local proposals. Mr. Puttanna Chetty has anticipated my gratification that the Hon'ble Mr. Cobb has been able to attend our meeting. The presence of such a large number of high officers of Government and leading citizens shows that the cause has lost nothing by the postponement of the meeting.

The war which began over two and a half years ago has now developed into a titanic struggle among fourteen nations. All the resources of science have been pressed into service. All over the war area, attention is centred, for the moment, in the arts of destruction; production, unconnected with the war, is stopped or paralysed; food supplies are failing and vast numbers of people are put on short rations.

As a result of the piratical attacks of the enemy more than four million tons of shipping have been sent down to the bottom of the sea. The provinces which have come under the temporary domination of the enemy are suffering acute agony. Many of the neutral countries have also suffered heavily. The fight is carried on with such unprecedented savagery that even pacifist America has been goaded to enter the lists as a belligerent power.

In this struggle, England has taken the lead on the side of the *Entente* Powers and is fighting heroically. She has shouldered the burdens of the weaker nations and made untold sacrifices in men and money to uphold the cause of civilization. She has spent nearly Rs. 6,000 crores already and she is at present spending about 9 crores daily. She recently raised the greatest war loan in history amounting to £1,000,000,000. The struggle has now reached, perhaps, its acutest stage and the resources of the Empire have to be further mobilised before

Speech at the War Loan Meeting.

the power of the enemy is completely broken. England has never faltered in her determination to fight till victory is achieved as she knows that only a complete victory will pave the way for an abiding peace.

England wants men, munitions and money and it is our duty to go to her aid in her hour of need. The Government of India and the people of this country have promised a contribution of Rs. 150 crores towards the expenses of the war. The Indian Government have agreed to raise by additional taxation a sum of 9 crores annually to meet the charges for interest and sinking fund. What is now wanted is hard cash to fulfil this national obligation. Hitherto, we were contributing for the relief of the sick and the wounded and for providing comforts for the troops at the front. The present is quite a different proposition. We are not asked to make a free gift but to contribute towards a loan carrying a handsome rate of interest for prosecuting the war.

The extraordinary self-sacrifice and tenacity of purpose shown by England compels our warmest admiration. It has always been so with the British Nation. A friend has drawn my attention to what the late Amir of Afghanistan has said, in his autobiography, concerning the English and their methods of warfare. The late Amir recalls the words of Napoleon, who said, "It can never be known when the English are beaten." "This was because," he goes on to say, "the British subjects are so devoted and loyal that, no matter how many times the British army meets with reverses, their spirit of loyalty and enthusiasm and support of their Government, mingled with the desire to crush the enemy, continues to increase. This feeling is not confined to the British Isles alone. It extends to every one of her colonies. . . . . . . The whole population of the British Empire, which is ten times more in number than that of

Speech at the War Loan Meeting.

England, can be calculated upon as forming a reserve force to call up, or who will voluntarily come forward to form part of the British army in time of war. The English could thus continue a war for which they have plenty of money, arms and men till at last the enemy's resources for providing for her army are exhausted and the victory would fall to the English, as has always been the case in every great battle that England has fought against her foes."

In the same connection, I would ask your leave to quote a passage from a private letter I received about a month ago from Mr. Sydney Fisher, an ex-Minister of the Dominion of Canada, whose acquaintance I made during my last visit to that country. Writes Mr. Fisher:—

"I am sure you will understand that at the present time we in Canada are absorbed in the war questions. You in India will appreciate this, for how magnificently the people of India have responded to the call of Empire and in what glorious manner they have contributed for the rights of the world in the struggle! It is the proudest evidence that the English, whatever may be their faults and omissions, are still a great, just and free people and ready to sacrifice everything for justice and freedom, and the Indian people recognise this and show their appreciation in their contribution . . . . The common people of Canada have contributed freely in their money and the young men have shed their blood without stint and without shrinking . . . . I fear there is still more to do and we will have to stimulate our people to further sacrifice, for the war must end in victory, complete enough to secure the objects for which it is being waged."

Mr. Sydney Fisher's letter also emphasises one of the most pleasing experiences of the war, namely, the increase of mutual respect and friendly feeling between

Great Britain, India and the self-governing colonies as a result of their close association in the presence of a common danger.

As I said before, the war has entered upon a critical stage and our duty and self-interest alike demand that we should actively co-operate with the rest of the Empire in all the measures calculated to ensure a speedy triumph for the Allies. Any weakening at the present moment will probably lead to an unstable peace which may at no distant date bring on again the horrors of a second war.

What we can spare, we should give quickly. Every small payment is so much help to hasten the success of the Allies. Newspapers tell us how from day to day Bombay and Calcutta have been vieing with each other as to which should contribute more. The Hon'ble Mr. Cobb has expressed a hope that there may be a similar friendly rivalry, locally, between the Civil and Military Station and the City.

At the last war loan meeting in the Civil and Military Station, Mr. Cobb referred in eloquent terms to the liberal help in men and money—liberal within the limits of our resources—given by His Highness the Maharaja. His Highness has now decided to contribute a sum of nearly Rs. 33⅓ lakhs or one-third of a crore to the war loan, and His Highness earnestly hopes that our appeal this evening for individual subscriptions will meet with a prompt and liberal response from his people.

Never before has it been our privilege to help in a cause of such world-wide importance. Every citizen of our State who contributes to the loan will play a part, however humble it may be, in raising the good name of Mysore, in helping India to fulfil her national obligations at this juncture and in aiding the Allies to shorten the war and restore peace and good will among mankind.

ADDRESS AT THE SECOND SESSION OF THE REPRESENTATIVE ASSEMBLY.

23rd April 1917.

[The first auxiliary session of the Mysore Representative Assembly was held, in obedience to His Highness the Maharaja's Rescript of 9th October 1916, at the Public Offices, Mysore, on 23rd April 1917. In opening the proceedings of the session, Sir M. Visvesvaraya delivered the following address:—]

Gentlemen,—We meet for the first time in a supplementary session to-day in obedience to His Highness the Maharaja's gracious Rescript of 9th October last.

You have come to the capital at the height of the season, at much self-sacrifice, to discharge your honorary duties as citizens of the State. Public business is also interrupted to some extent by the withdrawal of the officers from their normal duties. But the holding of a second session is sufficient recompense, since it helps to fulfil His Highness' resolve to educate and elevate his people, and your own cherished desire for closer association with Government.

The number of subjects brought over from the Dasara session is 124, and 113 new subjects have been added, making a total of 237 subjects for consideration at this session.

Some of the subjects on the agenda are of special interest. There are others which Government would like to see discussed and in regard to which they would welcome an expression of your views. It is proposed to select from both these classes a few important subjects for discussion by the whole Assembly. If you agree, we may, as a preliminary step, appoint small committees of members, in the course of this afternoon, to study the subjects and submit recommendations by twelve noon on the third day of the session. It may be an advantage to associate officers of Government with the committees to supply facts and figures and help them in their deliberations.

One of the principal items of work of the session is the consideration of the State Budget. Last year, it came before you after it had been approved by Government. That was because sanction could not be delayed beyond 1st July, and the Assembly could not meet earlier than October. This year, however, the budget is placed before you, even before it is considered by the Legislative Council.

From the rough detailed estimates for 1917-18, already furnished, you will have noticed that the main heads of receipts and expenditure, as now altered, correspond more closely to the actual operations of the administration and that the new budget has undergone important changes in the manner of presentation.

One of these changes is in respect of the financial policy of the State. At present, grants for the development of departments are not made on any definite principle. Sometimes, in the absence of a recognised policy, the most insistent departments get all they want, while others, more modest but whose need may perhaps be greater, fail to obtain what is necessary for bare maintenance. Grants are liable to lapse if they are not spent before the close of the official year. There is frequently a rush of expenditure towards the end of the year on schemes that have not been fully matured. Government have, therefore, adopted, on the advice of the Special Financial Officer, Mr. Datta, a scheme of financial settlement for the State which is calculated to remove many of these disadvantages.

The new system will enable administrative officers to take increased interest in improving the efficiency of the departments in their charge. It will also enable Government to pay attention to the needs of all departments in the order of their urgency and importance. Each department will have its due share of the benefits arising from the prosperity of the State. The creation of special reserves is another feature of the scheme. It will provide for extraordinary contingencies like famine and for the discharge of all loans incurred for the construction of productive public works.

Another welcome innovation is the issue of the estimates of the two important spending departments, *viz.*, Public Works and Railways, simultaneously with the State budget.

I do not propose to weary you with a lengthy address but my preliminary observations will not be complete without a passing reference to some of the topics which are engaging public attention at the present moment.

The great world war has reached an acute stage. The accession of the United States of America to the side of the Allies and the recent successes of the British arms, on the western front and in Mesopotamia, are indications that the end of the mighty struggle cannot be long delayed.

You are aware that the Government of India are raising a loan for the purpose of making a suitable contribution towards the expenses of the war. His Highness the Maharaja has been pleased to contribute, towards the loan, Rs. 33⅓ lakhs from State Funds and His Highness hopes that the leaders of the public will loyally co-operate with the officers of Government in securing as large an amount of loan as possible so that the aggregate contribution may be worthy of our State.

Since the last session of the Assembly, a comprehensive order has issued dealing generally with all questions relating to Local Self-Government. The details necessary for practical action are being worked out and the drafting of the needed legislative measures is nearing completion. Government hope to be able to introduce the scheme from 1st July 1917. Effect has already been given to the financial portions of the order, in the budget for the coming official year, by the transfer of the *mohatarfa* and the Local Funds General, to District Boards.

The systematic improvement of towns has also a claim on the attention of Government. Every town should have a plan indicating its future extensions and rough schemes should be maintained for water-supply and drainage, graduated according to local resources. The economic needs of the towns, *viz.*, provision of facilities for education, multiplying occupations, formation of banks and co-operative societies, maintenance of information bureaus, museums, conveniences to travellers, etc., also require special attention.

As regards taluk development, Government attach great importance to the provision made in the order which enables the inhabitants of every taluk to finance local projects, such as, tanks, roads, rural water-supply works, etc. This provision will afford scope for leading men of enterprise and capacity to develop the economic resources of the local areas in which they may be specially interested.

The Village Improvement Scheme is making very fair progress. During my tour in the Chitaldrug District at the beginning of this month, I noticed that many villages have shown commendable enthusiasm in undertaking works of permanent improvement under the guidance of local officers. Considerable attention is paid to the sanitation of the villages; the system of voluntary weekly labour is meeting with increasing favour; and school-houses, wells, roads, *chavadies*, etc., are springing up rapidly. During the last five years, the number of pupils receiving instruction in that district has doubled, and the district officers hope to further raise the number by about 25 per cent in the course of the current year.

I have received numerous representations urging that legislation may be undertaken to compel villagers either to contribute labour once a week, or to pay a cess instead. Wherever a few refractory people make their influence felt, the willing majority are rendered helpless and the even progress of improvement is checked. The advisability of undertaking legislation to remedy this defect has been discussed during the last two sessions of this Assembly and the question will be brought up again during the present session.

Side by side with the increase of schools for the school-going population, Government are anxious to push on with the education of adults. A sum of about Rs. 50,000 is now spent for this purpose and Government will have no objection to double the grant, if the Deputy Commissioners of districts will continue to take the primary responsibility for increasing adult schools. For some time to come it should be possible to add about 100 adult schools in each district every year.

Another question which has often been discussed in this Assembly is that of the respective rights and obligations of inamdars and their tenants. Certain specific points raised in this connection have been considered by two Committees constituted by Government. Their opinions will be placed before you and Government will be glad to have your recommendations before they come to a decision.

The systematic restoration of major and minor tanks has been receiving the anxious consideration of Government. The question as regards minor tanks was discussed here more than once and orders have issued in conformity with the wishes of this Assembly. The rules were recently revised after they had been in force for about a year.

In connection with major tanks, an Irrigation Division, for the purpose of developing the scientific side of the work, was constituted in 1913. The tanks under which the regulation of water is being controlled by the Irrigation Division are reported to be working satisfactorily. It is stated that, in the case of nearly every one of these, the area under irrigation has increased and the lands, which formerly suffered from deficient waterings are receiving a regular supply at present.

The investigation of new projects, the examination of *atchkats* in relation to the storage of tanks, the systematic collection of hydraulic data, are some of the questions which claim further attention, and special steps are being taken to strengthen the Irrigation Department for the purpose.

At the last session of the Assembly I stated that measures were in progress to investigate the possibility of a harbour at Bhatkal. The investigations are still proceeding and I am therefore not in a position to make any definite pronouncement. But it seems necessary to correct certain erroneous impressions which have found their way to the press in respect of the main features of the scheme.

You will see from the map that the seaboard near Bhatkal is only about ten miles from the State frontier. Other circumstances being equal, you will agree that, when you are seeking access to the coast, the most natural thing for any State to do is to select a point nearest to its boundary. You are aware that Government have arranged for an extension of the railway line from Shimoga to the top of the ghats for opening up the forests and the *malnad* area. Some money has actually been collected for the line from the people of the district. The distance to Bhatkal from the terminus of the new railway will be less than fifty miles. The length of additional railway needed to join the seaboard at this point is much shorter, and the descent from the top of the ghats to the coast much easier, than it would be if we selected any other objective.

His Highness' Government are anxious to work in cordial co-operation with all interests both within and outside the State except where, as in the present case, the co-operation involves grave disadvantages and disproportionate cost to the State.

As regards the suitability of Bhatkal for a harbour, all I need say at present is that the investigations carried out go to show that the project is very promising. It is unnecessary to assure you that Government will not commit themselves to the project unless it is found to be quite satisfactory both financially and from an engineering point of view.

The port is in British territory and the execution of the project depends entirely on the sympathy and support of the Government of India.

There is also another matter in regard to which the press has been prematurely inquisitive; namely, the proposal to manufacture iron within the State. I can make no precise statement as yet, but a brief explanation seems necessary at this stage to prevent the circulation of exaggerated reports. The lack of coal has hitherto been in the way of our working the rich iron ore deposits of the Bababudan Hills. The question of manufacturing pig iron on a small scale, with the aid of charcoal fuel, was investigated by Mr. C. P. Perin, the expert of the Tata Iron and Steel Company, Limited, of Sakchi, who has furnished a detailed report in the matter. After careful consideration, His Highness' Government have decided to instal a wood distillation plant to manufacture charcoal and a blast furnace for smelting iron. The scheme will be financed by Government, and the Tata Iron and Steel Company, Limited, have kindly undertaken to manage the technical portion of the business, *viz.*, the manufacture of charcoal with its bye-products and the actual smelting of iron. This agency will work in accordance with the terms of a special agreement and under the general supervision of a board of management. The rest of the work will be conducted under the direct supervision of Government for the present. The scheme is expected to yield a fair return on the capital outlay, besides helping in the development of the *malnad* area and affording valuable industrial training to the people of the State.

Before I close, you will, perhaps, allow me to say a word or two respecting the permanent work of this Assembly, and its relations to Government in the altered conditions under which we meet to-day. If you go to work on the time-honoured lines, without any further thought than submitting representations to Government, you will soon begin to suffer either from *ennui* or discontent, whereas the country's interests demand that you should take a sustained interest in your duties and work with hope and confidence for the future.

From our previous sessions, we now know more or less precisely the magnitude and character of the work before the country. After the demands of the daily administration are satisfied, our first aim should be to spread education and enlightenment among the masses, and our next step to increase production both from agriculture and under industries and occupations.

Broadly speaking, the subjects on which the Government and the people can work in close association may be considered to fall under three classes, according as they pertain to local areas, districts or the State as a whole. Subjects of local interest in the taluks will be dealt with by the subordinate officers of the Revenue and other departments of Government under the supervision of the Deputy Commissioner. Those which affect the district as a whole will be attended to by the Deputy Commissioner, assisted by the district officers.

From the commencement of this official year, the holding of district and taluk conferences has become obligatory. They are usually presided over by the Deputy Commissioner. The local wants are examined and attended to, according to a well-understood procedure, by the joint exertions of the officers of Government and the leading representatives of the locality.

It is only subjects which affect the State as a whole, which relate to policy or principle which affect large interests or involve heavy expenditure of public money, that have a claim on the attention of this Assembly.

It is not enough that you should discuss the needs of the country in this Assembly and form sound decisions or make recommendations. We shall have done nothing to give practical effect to them, unless, on one side, the staff employed by Government is strengthened and, on the other, the members themselves participate in the work of development, either in conjunction with the central Government or with the officials of the local areas concerned.

There is, in the public mind, a prejudice against increase of Government establishment in any shape or form. The present scale of establishment in the higher grades of the public service was fixed at a time when the work and revenues of the country were about one-half of what they are at present. Additional work requires more staff to cope with it. We may make a few mistakes in

Address at the Second Session of the Representative Assembly.

choosing recruits; occasionally the remuneration may be unequal; but if regard be had to the importance of the additional work to the country, the results will far outweigh the expenditure involved.

We have hitherto been able to secure the co-operation of private persons chiefly in village improvement work and in activities connected with economic progress, and I am in a position to bear testimony to the large amount of useful work that is being attempted in the districts in these directions. The attempt is novel but the genuine enthusiasm with which large bodies of people, including not a few of the members of this Assembly, are participating in the work is in the highest degree creditable to the public spirit of the country.

What is now desired is a wider co-operation on the same lines, in order to give practical effect to the decisions and recommendations of this Assembly.

It is the duty of every citizen to give a portion of his money, time or energy for the good of the country, even if his interest went no further than the taluk, town or village to which he may belong. In all advanced countries, taxation is comparatively heavy and the leaders of the people give their time freely for public work. In times of war well-to-do persons, in countries like England and Japan, have been obliged to hand over to their Government as much as one-third of their net income in the shape of taxes. No such demand has ever been made upon you. If you want to see a rise in the general level of prosperity around you, you must be prepared to make sacrifices. You must be prepared to seek it through your own exertions or those of the general public whom you represent.

SPEECH AT THE SECOND SESSION OF THE REPRESENTATIVE ASSEMBLY.

27th April 1917.

[The auxiliary session of the Mysore Representative Assembly came to a close on 27th April 1917. In winding up the proceedings of the session, Sir M. Visvesvaraya made the following speech:—]

Gentlemen,—You must be weary working continuously for the past five days, and I have no wish to detain you by any lengthy remarks.

My first duty is to assure you that it will give me great pleasure to convey, as requested, your loyal and respectful acknowledgments to His Highness the Maharaja for granting you the privilege of a second session.

We have discussed many subjects and in regard to most of these, I can but indicate the opinion of Government only in a general way. Most of the subjects have to be considered by my colleagues and myself with the aid of all available information and then submitted to His Highness before a final decision is reached.

In connection with the Village Improvement Scheme, I notice that the gentlemen who constituted the committee are not in favour of legislation to enforce the system of weekly labour or payment of a cess instead. At the beginning of this month I personally visited nearly fifty villages in the Chitaldrug District, and both in the villages and at meetings of representatives at the headquarters of taluks, the opinion was unanimous that some such measure was necessary.

The complaints of the cultivators under the Cauvery channels below the Krishnarajasagara have been brought to our notice with much ability by Mr. B. Narasinga Rao, who pleaded for letting things alone. Only one side of the case was placed before you. If sugar-cane is allowed to be cultivated wherever the raiyats choose, the whole area will get water-logged, and with heavy manure the country is sure to become unhealthy with the result that, in the end, the cultivation itself will suffer. The new rules are intended for the orderly growth of sugar-cane cultivation. It is no pleasure to us to impose restrictions. Besides, water has been stored in the Krishnarajasagara at an expenditure of over a crore of rupees and a reasonable additional rate has to be levied for the supply. The representations will be investigated by a Committee and Government will give their decision on receipt of the Committee's recommendations.

Turning to forest grievances, nothing that the members have said has gone to show that the general principles of our forest policy are in any way unsound. But I am willing to concede there may be individual grievances arising out of the practical application of the orders. These will be rectified if the gentlemen who complained will kindly send up a brief statement of such instances to Government.

We are all agreed that the system of irrigation under our large tanks is far from perfect but some improvement is noticeable wherever the Tank Panchayet Regulation has been working. It is hoped that people will take fuller advantage of the Panchayet system and endeavour to improve irrigation under all the larger tanks and channels. If it is demonstrated that the system itself requires improvement, Government will readily revise the measures.

As regards increased postal and telegraph facilities, the officers of the Government of India have kindly given an assurance that special attention will be given, in future, to the wants of our State. We cannot expect any extension of telegraph lines till the war is over, but some immediate relief in respect of post offices has been promised. The public who have any recommendations to make may address the Financial Secretary to Government in the matter.

Government have recently issued, after much consideration, an important order sanctioning certain reforms which have for their object the better supervision and management of temples and other Muzrai institutions. Those who are interested in the work of the department will, I hope, help to give practical effect to the reforms sanctioned by Government.

The question of throwing open Amrut Mahal and date reserves for cultivation was discussed at some length. The departments concerned are quite willing to surrender the lands not absolutely required for their immediate use and a Committee is now sitting to consider how such, transfers might be effected. Time is required for arranging preliminaries but it may be possible to complete the arrangements in the course of the current year.

The question of the separation of judicial and executive functions has been advocated with much earnestness. All I can say at present is that it is mainly one of cost and that it is receiving active consideration at the hands of Government.

In the discussions relating to the Excise Department, stress was laid on the importance of reducing drunkenness within the State. You have heard it from the Excise Commissioner himself that he is prepared to enforce the principle of local option. If, in any locality, the opinion in favour of the abolition of an existing shop is unanimous, he is willing to give effect to local wishes. A beginning has been already made. Government are prepared to face some loss of revenue, although they do not think it would be appreciable.

The recommendations made by the Committee regarding the increase of remuneration to *shanbhogs* and *patels* will receive early consideration.

The question of the relation between inamdars and tenants is, as you may have noticed, a highly contentious one. It requires careful handling and will receive further attention.

As money is wanted for so many purposes, I cannot hold out any hope that the *supari* cess will be abolished. But every effort will be made to utilise the money realised in the best interests of the locality in which it is raised.

The most important work of this session has been the discussion of the budget.

Mr. Venkatakrishnayya and Mr. Krishna Sastry were in favour of raising loans for the construction of productive public works. I welcome this statement, since it marks a great advance over the views held till recently by the leading public men of the State on this question.

The question of labour supply is being agitated with much enthusiasm and vigour by Mr. Hosakoppa Krishna Rao. Government appreciate his efforts and they hope he will persevere till a remedy is found.

Several Mahomedan members, led by Mr. Abbas Khan, spoke warmly on certain wants relating to Hindustani schools. The Inspector-General has made an effective reply. Government are prepared to further consider any reasonable representation that may be made on the subject.

I was glad to hear from the representatives of the Mulbagal Taluk that they are willing to contribute half the cost of a railway line from Kolar to Mulbagal. If an application is submitted through the district authorities, with necessary particulars, it will receive the best consideration of Government.

Speech at the Second Session of the Representative Assembly.

Several important innovations have been introduced into this year's budget all of which make for the financial stability of the State and I am glad that they have met with your approval.

The total expenditure on productive public works since the Rendition comes to about 6¼ crores of rupees, of which quite 2½ crores have been spent on railways, irrigation and hydro-electric works within the past five years. While maintaining the finances in a sound condition, Government have been creating valuable property which is already bringing in additional non-tax revenues to the State.

The second session is chiefly intended to provide an opportunity for the discussion of the budget. I am sorry that the debate had to be curtailed to some extent. Probably, next year, we might be more fortunate and be able to spare more time.

You have kindly undertaken to form yourselves into committees for the investigation of a number of subjects before the next session. I am hoping that your labours may prove helpful to Government. It is not enough for you to say that, because Government officers are paid, they alone should do such work. You will also have to give a portion of your time to study public questions and give effect to the recommendations of this Assembly. It is easy to ask questions but you will agree that to attempt to solve them yourselves is even better, as it will enable you to appreciate more fully the difficulties of Government.

It would be good for the country if you specialised and became experts in the several branches of the public administration. In this work, there is no antagonism of interests, but there may be healthy rivalry between the officials and yourselves. The attempt will inspire confidence and increase your sense of responsibility. You will then, perhaps, more readily pay taxes and make sacrifices. To the extent you do this will depend your influence with Government and the people.

ADDRESS TO THE CIVIC AND SOCIAL CONFERENCE.

[The first Mysore Civic and Social Conference opened its session at the Rangacharlu Memorial Hall, Mysore, on 3rd June 1917. There was a large and representative gathering of ladies and gentlemen present on the occasion. The proceedings were opened by H. H. the Yuvaraja. Sir M. Visvesvaraya then delivered the following address :—] 3rd June 1917.

Ladies and Gentlemen,—In a comprehensive programme of the country's work placed before the Representative Assembly last year, the duty of promoting civic and social activities was appropriately left to private initiative. When I was asked to address this assembly, I readily consented, as I understood it would make no demands on Government sympathy and support.

Government are expected to maintain an attitude of benevolent neutrality in regard to such questions, and I am sure my friends will recognise that whatever I say on this occasion will be my own personal views, and that I bring with me no authority, in any shape or form, on account of my official position.

The first requisite of society is a stable and well-organised administration. As people advance in civilization and capacity, they are accorded a voice in the government of their country. In actual practice, it is not possible to utilise the thoughts and suggestions of every cultured private citizen. So a few chosen leaders are returned to represent the interests of our large population both in the Representative Assembly and the Legislative Council. Under His Highness the Maharaja's watchful care, the association of the people with the officers of Government in the administration of the country has been making very satisfactory progress.

Next to administration comes the economic safety and development of the country in regard to which, compared to more advanced countries, we occupy, as I have so often reminded the public, a position of marked inferiority. We have now a special organization, known as the Economic Conference, started in 1911 under the orders of His Highness the Maharaja, to watch and promote our economic welfare. As this organization will be much in evidence during the next few days, no special reference to its work is needed on this occasion.

All the remaining activities of the country may be classed under the head "Civic and Social." Civic activities comprise the duties of a citizen to the fellow residents of his town or village and to his countrymen of the State as a whole. The social activities of the country may be viewed in relation to the daily life of the people, their home or family habits and their mutual association for business, pleasure or amenities of life.

The thinking and working power of the people should be brought to bear on all the three classes of activities, *viz.*, administrative, economic, and civic and social. As this thinking and working power is limited, we would do well for the present to concentrate attention on essentials only, that is, on spheres of work which promise the largest and speediest results.

Every citizen owes it to himself and his neighbours

Address to the Civic and Social Conference.

that he maintains his house and surroundings clean, that he is free from debt, that he educates the members of his family and keeps as many of them as possible engaged in gainful occupations. If he does this, he will be helping the State to keep down the number of the idle and the inefficient in our midst.

Besides paying rates and attending to other obligations imposed by law, he is expected, as a resident of his town or village, to return capable representatives to the local corporation, watch its work through the agency of rate-payers' association or vigilance committee and, in other ways, help in organising charities, medical relief, etc. A town planning or improvement committee should be constantly engaged in projecting schemes of improvement. Every town or village should be able to show some improvement as a result of its activities from year to year.

A citizen is also interested in the economic improvement of his town, that is to say, in the provision of facilities for education, travelling conveniences for visitors, creation of industries, increase of occupations, encouragement of thrift, reduction of indebtedness, establishment of co-operative societies, trade associations, etc.

The citizen has duties to the State analogous to those which he owes to the town but in a wider sphere. These duties include loyal co-operation with his fellow citizens in promoting all beneficent activities, love of country and spirit of self-sacrifice. He is expected to participate in all enterprises calculated to benefit the State as a whole, such as the spread of science, literature, art, etc., in the country.

The civic virtues which the country most needs are a capacity for hard work, business punctuality, the habit to carry on appointed work without supervision, the willingness to subordinate personal interests in some measure to those of the municipal area or the State. We have learnt the virtues of subordination and humility. What we have yet to acquire is capacity for co-operation, for working in harmony in large numbers, and for controlling large bodies of people. This must come with opportunities and by practice.

Another quality which we lack is the spirit of appreciating good work in others. The country is very poor in initiative and public spirit, partly because ungenerous criticism keeps away many otherwise willing citizens from the public cause.

These qualities require to be systematically cultivated and encouraged by special instruction in schools, by means of public lectures and by insisting on approved standard practices in all the business transactions of public bodies.

Efforts have to be made to modify or remove some of our habits and prejudices which act as a bar to social advancement.

The caste system, which is responsible for a great many of our disabilities, has left an appreciable portion of the population in a state of permanent degradation. The condition of the people belonging to what is known as the depressed classes is not creditable to the community. It is a long standing evil for which reparation is due to those classes. Their condition can be improved first by placing education within easy reach of these classes, and next, by forming humanitarian associations to wean them from objectionable habits and to place correct ideals of conduct and behaviour before them.

Our marriage customs are also a hindrance. Early marriages are responsible for much avoidable mortality among infants every year, and the restriction of marriage within a limited circle can only result in feeble progeny.

It should be possible to further popularise marriages between members of allied castes. This will widen the field of choice of suitable partners and help to stop, in some measure, the ruinous practice of demanding dowries. The obstacles in the way of widow marriage, particularly in the case of girl widows, should be gradually removed, and the cruel custom of disfiguring young widows stopped without delay.

Another serious evil is the extravagant expenditure incurred on marriage and other obligatory ceremonies. Many a person starts life with the encumbrance of a debt contracted for his marriage which he is never able to shake off on this side of the grave. The curtailment of expenses on account of these religious and social ceremonies should find a prominent place in our programme of reforms.

It would be a boon to many a family if this association can lay down schedules for all ordinary social ceremonies restricting the expenditure to very moderate sums. In many people, the temptation to play the rich man even for a day is very great, and society should educate public opinion to discountenance such extravagance and social vanity.

Our women require training in modern methods of housekeeping, and in the cultivation of the fine arts such as, music, painting, etc. We keep them too much in the background and deprive them of self-reliance, a quality of inestimable value to them in the struggle for existence, especially in the case of those who in later life may chance to lose their male protector.

The social life of the people, in a Western sense, is so much neglected that a mixed social gathering of men and women is still a rare phenomenon. The poorer classes have more freedom in this respect.

If an Englishman's house is his castle, an Indian's

house is very often a woman's prison. Under the *purdha* system, we know that, in parts of Northern India, grown-up men and women, even of the same family, rarely meet. I have known a person who confessed he would not have been able to identify his own sister-in-law if he met her, say, at a railway station.

In addition to instruction in house management, a good proportion of our women, belonging to the middle and poorer classes, should be given training in some industrial pursuit appropriate to their condition and capacity. The war has disclosed unsuspected capacities among women, and it would be a great loss not to develop and utilise, to the best advantage, the varied gifts which they possess for the work of the home and the community.

The discipline enforced by religion is a great moral force in every community. Places of worship require to be kept scrupulously neat and clean, and only persons of the highest moral character should be entrusted with the control of such institutions.

It is a matter for congratulation that restrictions against sea voyage and in regard to food and drink are being relaxed. A large number of young men, belonging to the higher castes, who had gone abroad for study or training, have returned and been welcomed back to their homes and society. His Highness' Government have indirectly done a great deal to promote this desirable reform by instituting scholarships for study in foreign countries. In the years to come, we should like to see more and more of our officers and merchants and other citizens visit Western countries for study, business or pleasure.

In a great many other directions, changes and improvements are needed in our society and it is by constant investigation, and determined effort at the proper time, that we can effect reforms. The idea that time will

Address to the Civic and Social Conference.

somehow bring about improvements is a mischievous and suicidal fallacy.

Attempts have been made in this State from time to time to advance the cause of civic and social progress. The Christian Missionaries have shown laudable enterprise in this respect. It is to their credit that their philanthropic endeavours have been concentrated largely on the improvement of the most neglected sections of the community. The cause of female education, which has been seriously taken up within the past thirty years, has made some progress, chiefly on account of the interest taken by the Royal Family. The Widows' Home at Mysore owes its existence to the self-less labours of that ardent supporter of female education, Rao Bahadur A. Narasim Iyengar. The Depressed Classes Mission at Mysore, with which Mr. V. N. Narasimiengar, Mr. M. Venkatakrishnaiya and other public men of this city are associated, the Social Service League started by Mrs. Whitehead at Bangalore, and several less well-known organizations have been engaged on this work. In recent years, a movement has come into existence among the Vokkaliga community in the *malnad* to reduce the expenses of marriage and spread temperance. These are all isolated efforts and it is necessary to see that their work is properly co-ordinated and directed to their proper purposes with the increased vigour which they will derive by co-operation.

The Civic and Social Progress Association, started last year, of which His Highness the Yuvaraja is the President, owes its origin to the enthusiasm of a few earnest workers like Mr. K. P. Puttanna Chetty, Mr. M. Venkatakrishnaiya, Mr. V. N. Narasimiengar, Mr. M. Chengiah Chetty, and about a dozen other gentlemen.

At the time of its formation last year, His Highness

the Maharaja showed his sympathy with the movement by making a substantial contribution towards its initial expenses. His Highness the Yuvaraja, who is at the forefront of every reform movement, is the Patron of the Bangalore Social Service League, of which Sirdar M. Kantaraj Urs is the President.

Civic and social progress movements in this country have hitherto been shortlived and ineffectual chiefly owing to absence of business methods, sufficient funds and devoted workers and associates. In order to guard against a repetition of this experience, I would suggest, for your consideration, a few essential precautions to ensure uninterrupted progress of work in the coming years :—

(1) A Central Bureau or Committee should be established at Bangalore or Mysore as the recognised headquarters of the organization.

(2) Local Committees, affiliated to the Central Organization, should be formed to carry out detailed work in each unit area, that is, city, town or taluk.

(3) Funds should be collected for carrying on the work of the central and local organizations (details should be settled if possible at this Conference).

(4) An accurate printed record should be maintained of the names of the gentlemen interested in civic and social work throughout the State.

(5) An office should be started and an energetic paid Secretary or Joint or Assistant Secretary appointed.

(6) Efficient arrangements should be made for intercommunication and prompt response between each unit area and headquarters.

(7) A detailed programme of work for each year should be drawn up in advance, *i.e.*, before the commencement of the year.

(8) A survey should be made of the existing agencies

employed in civic and social work with a view (after examining their utility and financial stability) to co-ordinate their work with that of the Association.

(9) A record should be maintained of each year's work and of the names of all persons who have contributed to it, in however small a degree.

(10) A vigilance officer or Committee should be appointed to watch the progress and bring defects and slackness to notice from time to time.

If the press identifies itself with the ideals and objects of the association and co-operates with the leading public men, it can render much useful aid to the cause of civic and social reform. The local press has already shown sympathy with the movement.

Some legislative measures have been enacted in the past for raising the marriageable age of girls and promoting other reforms. In recent months, we have heard of legislation of a far-reaching character for similar objects attempted in Baroda and Indore. How far such legislation is necessary or useful is a subject which we would do well to investigate, with due regard to local feeling and local conditions. It is true that legislation can only sanction what public opinion demands, but there can be no objection to make a detailed enquiry.

It requires the patient labour of many years to realise the ideals we have in view. I have discussed our future plan of work with the leading men associated with the movement and, with your permission, I will briefly indicate a tentative programme for the coming year.

Civic Activities.

(1) The formation of Citizen Bodies in the principal towns to induce individual householders to attend to the

two primary requisites of house sanitation, *viz.*, the proper disposal of liquid sewage and of solid refuse ; and to collectively organise measures for maintaining a whole street or ward, in which they have their abode, clean.

(2) Preparation of standard rules of conduct and behaviour for the higher, middle and common classes of people so as to ensure the cultivation of those qualities in which as a nation we are particularly deficient.

(3) Town planning and village planning to ensure the orderly development of habited areas and the beautification of villages.

(4) Provision of wholesome accommodation in all residential areas to the working classes and the poor generally.

(5) Relief of indebtedness among the poorer classes, particularly agriculturists.

(6) Reduction of litigation and establishment of arbitration courts.

Social Activities.

(1) Measures for the elevation of the depressed classes.

(2) Curtailment of expenses on account of marriages, funerals, and other religious ceremonies.

(3) Preparing public opinion for raising the marriageable age of girls to 14 years, and that of boys till they are able to earn their living.

(4) Promoting social intercourse and harmony between the various communities in every grade of the social scale.

(5) Promotion of indigenous methods of physical culture and of habits of temperance.

(6) Investigations into the question of the necessity or otherwise of further social legislation.

I have only touched the fringe of a vast subject.

Address to the Civic and Social Conference.

In the Economic Conference, we have already got an economic framework for the State. This organization will provide what may be termed a civic and social framework. The problem is nothing less than the regulation of the collective energy, the adjustment of the aggregate working power of our population, to the needs of the country.

The worst curse of the country is passivity, slackness, a fatalistic outlook on life. The lesson of ages is that we should attempt to mould circumstances to our own ends. The task is irksome. In any individual attempt we may succeed or we may fail. But the attempt itself is worth making. By learning to make the attempt we place ourselves under the influence of a great moral impulse.

If only we try, it is well within our power to carry out the reforms we have in view. Their adoption puts no strain on our faith in the true tenets of our religion or the accepted moral standards of the civilised world. We have only to make the attempt with the requisite vigour and earnestness. And to be successful, the attempt should be collective and continuous.

Ladies and gentlemen, I will not detain you further. I earnestly hope we are beginning a movement of much future promise. I trust many enthusiastic workers will join your standard and that your association will give a good account of itself in grappling with the great task that lies before it.

ADDRESS TO THE MYSORE ECONOMIC CONFERENCE.

5th June 1917. [The eighth session of the Mysore Economic Conference was held at the Public Offices, Mysore, on 5th June 1917. In opening the proceedings of the Conference, Sir M. Visvesvaraya, in his capacity as President of the Conference, delivered the following address :—]

Gentlemen,—This meeting marks the close of the sixth year of the Mysore Economic Conference. The object of the Conference is to promote the economic prosperity of the people of this State by giving them the necessary training and familiarising them with the modern conditions of material progress.

The work began with the initial handicap of an untrained population, unaccustomed to the usages and discipline of Western business life. For three out of six years the Conference has been in existence, trade conditions have been abnormal due to the world war, markets have become disorganised and the supply of machinery practically stopped. Notwithstanding all these disadvantages, the movement has been gaining ground, some few results are already placed to its credit and many more may be expected with the efflux of time.

The reports of work done by the several committees and departments have already been placed before you, and it is not necessary for me to give here more than a brief outline.

The Conference organization has worked with greater smoothness and harmony than in previous years. All the committees have been following approved programmes with the co-operation of the heads of departments concerned. Sub-Committees and individual members gave material help in carrying on important investigations and in formulating practical schemes. The organization for bringing taluk areas into close touch with the central agencies is being perfected. In every unit area, groups of workers have been appointed to deal with the more urgent local problems. This system is undergoing expansion so as to provide opportunities for every citizen with capacity for public work to contribute his share towards the development of the area with which he is directly concerned.

Government have proposals ready for the reorganization of the Industries and Commerce Department based upon the experience of its working during the past few years. Special steps are being taken to strengthen the commercial side of the department. In view of the rapid expansion of its work, the Education Department also needs, and is receiving, special attention.

The Education Committee finally dealt with 54 schemes during the year. The most important subjects which engaged their attention were, proposals for the improvement of libraries of which 98 were started during the year, receiving a total grant of Rs. 10,000, the encouragement of the education of, and grant of scholarships to, backward classes, the spread of scientific knowledge and preparation of easy books on science, the systematization of scholarships and elementary technical education for the masses. Schemes have also been prepared for imparting general moral instruction in civic, business and social ethics and for remodelling the system of female education in the State. A large number of notes on various educational subjects were contributed by the members. Some of them co-operated with the University Council in the preparation of advanced engineering and commercial courses for the University.

In addition to investigation and deliberative work, the

Education Committee have been entrusted with the working of several special schemes such as the Home Industries Institute, Home Education Classes, the Public Libraries at Bangalore and Mysore, and district and rural libraries. The Committee have also appointed itinerant lecturers in the cities of Bangalore and Mysore in addition to the existing lecturers in the districts.

The expenditure on the Education Department has risen from Rs. 23,07,289 to Rs. 27,85,328 which represents about 8 per cent of the total expenditure of the State. The number of elementary schools, both Government and aided, has risen from 4,930 to 5,423 during the year, and the number of pupils under instruction in the elementary grade from 1,29,728 to 2,01,728 in the case of boys and from 28,430 to 43,230 in the case of girls. The number of pupils under instruction in all grades of education has doubled during the past five years.

The proportion of male pupils under instruction to the school-going population is as yet only 45·8 per cent and of girls 9·7 per cent. Female education is particularly backward. The proportion of girls that go from the primary to the secondary stage is 4·25 and to the high school stage, only 0·22 per cent. The education of adults requires further effort. At present, there are only 924 adult schools. As arrangements can be made for the instruction of adults in almost every village school at a comparatively moderate cost, the field for the expansion of adult education is practically unlimited.

The work of the Agricultural Committee is being carried on in close co-operation with that of the Agricultural Department. Proposals for starting and working manure depôts, conjointly by the Departments of Agriculture and Co-operative Societies, have been worked out and a few

Address to the Mysore Economic Conference.

depôts have been opened. Special attention is being devoted to the encouragement of agricultural co-operation. The Committee have done much useful work in connection with the development of fruit culture and the improvement of agricultural stock, and Government have sanctioned at their instance, the establishment of a sheep-rearing farm. A scheme has been prepared for imparting vernacular instruction in agriculture and improving the short courses for the raiyats. As regards commercial crops, special attention is being devoted to the extension of cultivation of sugar-cane and mulberry and the improvement of coffee. Rules have been framed for granting assistance to people who intend starting cattle and pony-breeding farms. Some half a dozen large landed estates were sanctioned during the year. Steps have been taken to collect information regarding the economic condition and subsidiary occupations of raiyats. The Committee have prepared estimates of production for the whole State. They have taken part in organising several agricultural demonstrations and exhibitions and have issued a number of bulletins on useful subjects.

The work of the Agricultural Department was carried on on the usual lines. A great deal of attention was paid during the year to the introduction of improved implements, the popularisation of the use of manures and the development of commercial crops. For experimental and demonstration purposes, work on two more farms was started during the year, one at Babbur for dealing with cotton and other crops suited to the Marikanave tract and the other under the Krishnarajasagara Reservoir for sugar-cane. The progress of agriculture in the State is greatly handicapped for want of a sufficient number of trained men and the subject is engaging the special attention of Government. The first vernacular agricultural school in the mofussil was opened at Chikanahalli in the

Tumkur District to train sons of raiyats, and proposals for opening similar schools, with the help of private endowments, are under consideration.

Signor Washington Mari, who was appointed Director of Sericulture for a term of one year, has just completed his engagement. He has prepared a detailed scheme of organization for the department and for developing a central sericultural school with connected popular taluk schools. He has also done some experimental work.

The work of the Industries and Commerce Committee has been closely associated with that of the Department from the very commencement. Among the large industries taken up for special investigation by the Committee may be mentioned, a paper pulp factory, the manufacture of cyanamide and the starting of cotton mills. The Committee also considered the question of granting concessions for starting pencil manufacture, the development of the granite industry, the manufacture of paints, the starting of an up-to-date furniture factory, the establishment of a Central Industrial and Commercial Museum and of district museums, the improvement of the Arts and Crafts Depôt and the extension of the Art-Litho Press. Owing to the difficulty of getting machinery under the present war conditions, practical work on most of the schemes has had to be suspended till the end of the war, but in the meanwhile every effort is being made to have detailed schemes ready.

The Committee have taken the necessary steps for starting up-to-date hotels in the cities of Bangalore and Mysore and in some of the district head-quarters. At the instance of the Committee, a proposal for the grant of loans for the development of small industries has been sanctioned. Schemes have also been worked out for starting industrial suburbs in Bangalore and Mysore.

The Chamber of Commerce, which was started last

year, has been doing useful work, the number of members at present being 213. It publishes a weekly trade bulletin, and branches have been formed at Tumkur, Tiptur, Davangere and Chikmagalur.

Information of value to merchants is now supplied by the commercial correspondents at Bombay and Madras and it is proposed to organise an information bureau in connection with the Central Commercial and Industrial Museum in Mysore. Half a dozen merchants visited Japan during the year to study the conditions of industry and trade in that country.

As stated already, the operations of the Industries and Commerce Department were greatly handicapped by the difficulty of getting machinery. The Sandalwood Oil Factory has now been placed on a commercial basis and the manufacture of oil is likely to be started in the Mysore Factory before very long. The department has under consideration the development of the manufacture of soap and buttons, and the preparation of dyes in connection with which a great deal of preliminary work has been done. A scheme for a Central Industrial Workshop, with branches at each district head-quarter town, has also been worked out. The erection of about 33 pumping and other installations was taken in hand by the department during the year, making a total of 118 from the commencement. Among the larger projects that Government have in view, may be mentioned the scheme for the manufacture of iron in connection with which the necessary preliminaries are receiving attention.

The Co-operative movement is making steady progress. The number of credit societies and societies of other forms has raisen from 800 to 934. The total amount of transactions carried on by Co-operative Societies has risen from Rs. 1,72,00,000 to Rs. 1,87,00,000. Arrangements have been made to carry on a debt survey with a view to devise measures for reducing indebtedness in the *malnad* area.

The District and Taluk Progress Committees have undertaken much useful work in connection with the Economic Conference. In order to enable them to enlist a large group of workers, lists were prepared of small individual items of work which might be undertaken in each unit area and the work distributed among various groups of workers in that area. It is understood that the services of local men of influence, at the rate of about 50 for each taluk, have been enlisted in this way for carrying on both practical and propaganda work.

The most marked results of this organization in the districts are noticeable in the development of education. As many as 1,239 new elementary aided schools were opened during the current year as against 729 in the previous year. Arrangements have been made for the construction of 53 school houses. A sum of Rs. 1,20,489 was contributed by the people during the year for educational purposes. In addition to this, the District and Taluk Progress Committees have interested themselves in starting 59 practical instruction and 7 home education and home industries classes, in granting scholarships and arranging for the industrial and agricultural training of a number of pupils from the taluks.

Preliminary investigations for starting a number of factories such as rice, sugar-cane, oil and flour mills pumping installations, tile, bone meal and ginning factories, were carried on as usual in all the districts, and some degree of special attention was given to the improvement of rural industries.

Under the auspices of the Revenue officers and District Committees, District and Taluk Conferences have been held in all the taluks and at all district head-quarters to consider the economic and other needs of the areas concerned and to take stock of work done. In many places, agricultural and industrial exhibitions were organised simultaneously. In a few cases, these exhibitions have led to the establishment of permanent district museums.

All the District Committees are endeavouring to collect funds for carrying on economic work within their respective areas. The Mysore District Committee have made a good beginning by collecting a sum of nearly Rs. 12,000, and similar funds are being formed in the Tumkur, Kolar, Hassan and Chitaldrug Districts.

The Bangalore District Committee have started under their auspices a fortnightly journal to deal with questions of economic interest in that district. The District Committees of Tumkur and Shimoga have been instrumental in starting similar Kannada weekly newspapers in those districts.

The District Committees, with the help of the Economic Superintendents, have published "Essential Statistics" for all the districts.

The main lines of our work are well understood, and our chief aim in the near future should be to consolidate what has been begun without, at the same time, losing sight of further developments or new features which promise early results or which are calculated to strengthen the organization. In what follows, I shall briefly refer to a few of the latter to which attention will be invited in the coming year.

Statistics.—The need of special effort to revise and improve the present methods of compiling statistics has been repeatedly pressed upon the attention of the departments and the committees concerned.

All available statistical information relating to the State has been collected and issued in a Statistical Abstract, in the District and Taluk Handbooks, and in the compilations known as "Essential Statistics." Arrangements have been made to issue the educational statistics in a complete form. The season and crop report has also been revised, but the statistics of agricultural production are still far from satisfactory. The statistics available for industries and trade are incomplete and unreliable, but arrangements have been made to collect and compile detailed figures for one district, to begin with, as an experimental measure.

Research Bureau.—At present, research work and experiments in industries are being carried on, in a small way, with the help of the Indian Institute of Science. A Research Bureau should be started with an organising Secretary to put into active service the expert and scientific knowledge available in the country for the practical work of industrial development. The Bureau may advise the Central Committees and the Departments of Industries and Agriculture, initiate experiments and provide the proper atmosphere and equipment for young men to carry on scientific work connected with the chemical and mineral industries of the State.

The existing laboratory accommodation should be fully utilised and, if necessary, extended and the scattered technical libraries brought into one place and stocked with the latest trade journals and technical magazines.

Forest Exploitation.—Our forests offer a new field for industrial enterprise. If we train a sufficient number of chemists to exploit the forest materials on scientific lines, a new source of wealth will be created for the country, and the population living near or around forests will benefit from them in the same way that people along the seaboard do from the sea.

Model Taluks.—Much interest attaches to the proposal of the Standing Committee to develop a model taluk for each district by what may be termed hot-house culture, *i.e.*, by taking special steps to raise its level of education, of farm production and industries and trade. The necessary outlay should be incurred and the proposals given a fair trial.

Standards of development.—His Highness' Government attach much importance to the preparation of quantitative estimates of progress under education and production from year to year. Recently an attempt was made to collect particulars of the existing condition as regards education, agriculture, industries and trade of each unit area and to lay down certain standards of development to be attained during the next five years. Estimates of what might be achieved in that period were prepared for the whole State by the Central Committees, and it was sought from their figures to distribute the responsibility for the work and lay down standards of progress for guidance in each unit area or taluk.

Standards for village, town and taluk.—In order to increase the percentage of literacy among the population, the outturn of agricultural produce and the output of industrial concerns, it is necessary to place before the public a few specific standards or ideals to afford quantitative tests, in a rough way, of the improvements effected from year to year.

The *village* is the smallest unit and attempts at improvement should begin here. In every self-respecting village, the following minimum results should be insisted on:—

(1) At least 10 per cent of the population should be at school. If there is no school in the village itself, the pupils should attend one in the neighbourhood.

(2) There should be a school, or other arrangement, for imparting a knowledge of the three R's to the adult population of the village.

(3) The economic efficiency of every village should

be examined annually by preparing rough estimates of production, and no village, where the annual output is less than, say, Rs. 33 per head of population, should be considered economically safe.

(4) There should be at least one trained blacksmith and one carpenter in every village having a population of 300 and more.

(5) Every agricultural family should have some subsidiary occupation to supplement its income from the land. Roughly speaking, there should be one minor or subsidiary industry practised in a village for every 250 inhabitants.

(6) Every raiyat should be induced to store at least two years' supply of food grains to provide against the calamities of the seasons. The tendency to contract debts, except for productive purposes, should be severely discouraged.

In *towns* again, we should have at least 15 per cent of the population under instruction. There should be a fair proportion of pupils undergoing High School, University and professional education, say, at the rate of 1 in every 200 of the population in the High School, 1 in 500 in the University and 1 in 1,000 in the higher professional institutions.

In the case of all towns, an occupation survey should be carried out with a view to adopt constructive measures to reduce unemployment.

For *taluk* areas, the lines of development will be somewhat similar to those of the village. Our first aim should be to obtain an accurate idea of the economic condition of the taluk as a whole; and here a detailed survey of occupations and the maintenance of correct estimates of agricultural and other production are indispensable.

As regards education, at least 1 in every 10 of the entire population should be in the primary schools, 1 in every 500 undergoing technical education, and 1 in 3,000 High School and University education. An attempt should be made to increase agricultural production by at least 50 per cent. Two or three large industries and a dozen rural and cottage industries should be fostered in every taluk. There should be, at the taluk head-quarters, a well-equipped library and reading room, a commercial and industrial museum and enquiry office, and a sufficient number of banks and co-operative societies to finance local trade and agriculture.

I have already exceeded the usual length of the President's address on such occasions. I have explained the working of the organization during the year and given details of work done or attempted and of some of the work requiring attention in the immediate future. This is a time for consolidating what is already begun. The machine is at work; we have to feed it with fuel and water, oil the joints and screw up the nuts from time to time.

We are working under the shadow of a great war, in which the Empire has been forced to take part, in which she is fighting with unprecedented valour and determination and for which she is making extraordinary sacrifices. It is scarcely necessary to add that our hope of progress in this as in every other department of activity depends on the early and successful termination of the war.

With reference to the Conference organization, we have practically outlived all the opposition and difficulties under which His Highness' Government started it in 1911. The public have come to realise that what we are attempting is based on past experience, tha our methods are honest, that we are as willing to learn as anxious to remove misapprehensions, and that we are as ready to correct existing defects as we are eager to explore new realms of thought or experiment with new processes of manufacture. We are working in close association with the people. In most decisions we carry with us the Committees on which are represented high officials and leading representatives of the people.

It only remains for me, on behalf of His Highness' Government, to appeal to every one connected with the organization to be punctilious in fulfilling his share of responsibility, for the coming year's programme, to the best of his ability and opportunities.

SPEECH AT THE MYSORE ECONOMIC CONFERENCE.

8th June 1917.

[The eighth session of the Mysore Economic Conference closed its sittings on 8th June 1917. Sir M. Visvesvaraya, in winding up the proceedings of the Conference, made the following speech :—]

Gentlemen,—I have no doubt you will welcome this new feature in to-day's proceedings, namely a review, by the chairmen of the three central committees, of the work for which they are responsible. This materially lightens my burden. The number of subjects brought up for discussion was very large and you all agreed that it was impossible to go through the whole programme. We hope next year it may be possible to appoint a subjects committee for the selection of subjects and considering the order of their discussion. The general level of discussions was very high and several members have contributed able and lucid speeches.

I shall now hurriedly go over a few of the more im-

Speech at the Mysore Economic Conference.

portant subjects discussed. Taking education first, I believe everybody will agree to the transfer of elementary education to the local boards and to the constitution of separate school boards for the purpose. This subject will receive attention as soon as the Local Self-Government scheme is introduced.

The proposal for starting a school for training boys and men from the taluks in some practical occupation or other, such as, house building, carpentry, rural industries and, if possible, also agriculture, has to be considered in conjunction with the existing industrial schools and the proposed district workshops.

The question of instruction in science, business morals, account keeping and some industry including agriculture, in all elementary schools, requires early attention.

We have listened with much interest to the criticisms of the Revd. Mr. Thompson on the Home Industries Institute and home education classes. The institution has come into existence within the past one year and I thought it would have been more appropriate to discuss the details first in the Education Committee. Mr. K. R. Srinivasiengar was, on the other hand, equally emphatic that the institution was young, and defects, wherever they existed, were being remedied. Until the explanations on both sides have been thoroughly examined, it is difficult to see exactly how matters stand. But we welcome Mr. Thompson's assurance that he will co-operate with the chairman and other members of the committee in any permanent measures calculated to place these institutions on a satisfactory working basis.

I have followed the discussion on the question of girls' education with much interest. The proper compulsory period for girls seems to be between tbe ages of 7 and 10, and I am also in favour of separate curricula for the education of girls and women.

Speech at the Mysore Economic Conference.

It is a pity that Mr. Venkatakrishnayya's proposal to raise a cess for education did not come up for discussion. We also overlooked the necessity of appointing a lady member on the Education Committee. I hope the omission will be supplied ere long.

Speaking of education as a whole, the volume of work has increased very considerably and there is, in consequence, a lack of proportion in some of the operations and staff of the department. It is also necessary to maintain a proper proportion in regard to the number of young men under training in each grade of general, practical and professional education. These matters will receive the earnest attention of Government in the coming year.

Coming to agriculture, Dr. Coleman was understood to say that if sufficient supply of manure could be procured, the agricultural output of the country might be doubled, particularly in the case of irrigated crops. I know, from personal experience in other parts of India, that sugar-cane can yield as much as Rs. 1,000 per acre.

The proposal that bonuses should be granted for the extension of commercial crops was thrown out but I trust that in the coming year, the committee will consider some alternative method of stimulating the expansion of these crops.

In the matter of sericulture, there is at present no technical head for the department and the Silk Association, on the confession of Mr. Abdul Quddus, seems to be in a moribund condition. In addition to the subjects engaging consideration, the question of re-reeling and twisting the silk locally and the establishment of a silk mill also require special attention in the coming year.

The subject of horticulture is, thanks to the efforts of Mr. M. Subbaiya, being taken up enthusiastically.

The establishment of rural co-operative stores, like

those found in almost every town in Italy, deserves special attention.

The question of land banks was explained, in an enthusiastic speech, by Mr. Ranganatha Rao Saheb, but fears were expressed that it might interfere with the growth of Co-operative Societies and that it might increase, instead of reducing, indebtedness by placing cheap money at the disposal of the raiyats.

The question of labour supply was another subject which is being warmly agitated by Mr. Hosakoppa Krishna Rao. As to the need of an organization, there is no difference of opinion. It is also plain that a private organization by itself will not meet the case and that private initiative should be supported by Government. The essential point to be ascertained is whether the landholders concerned are willing to bear the greater part of the cost involved. I have no doubt that this important subject will receive the special attention of the Agricultural Committee with an eye to practical action.

Several interesting questions were discussed in connection with the work of the Industries and Commerce Committee and Department.

We have at present commercial agents in Bombay and Madras. The proposal to extend the system seems worthy of support.

Mr. H. Subba Rao gave us his experience regarding the employment of a commercial traveller by his firm. The system of groups of merchants sending out such travellers deserves every encouragement.

Commercial surveys might be usefully taken up by the local bodies, *viz.*, town progress committees and municipalities. After examining the results of the survey in progress in the Bangalore District, the question of legislation in connection with a Census of Production Act will receive attention.

Speech at the Mysore Economic Conference.

Mr. Vardhamaniah brought to notice certain difficulties in the existing procedure for granting aid to industries. We are anxious to have more practical proposals or Government help from the committees. No reasonable proposal has hitherto been refused.

Proposals are under consideration for giving more staff and attention for developing the commerce of the State.

Among other questions discussed, the proposals to legislate for the abolition of mendicancy received warm support.

The question of fuel supply for local needs, largely affected by exports and demand for Government works, received much attention. It is for the District Committees to consider whether, having regard to local conditions and requirements, the additional supply should be obtained from forests or whether new plantations should e started.

On many of the subjects discussed, I felt that the non-official members were not in possession of full information. In all such matters, the discussions are likely to lead to practical results if the members applied beforehand to the Secretary for information.

The subject of co-ordination of the work of the committees and the several agencies came up for discussion and there was a feeling that too many things were being attempted.

The work of organization and .development must necessarily involve the investigation of most of the connected questions. The work is divided under three heads:—

(1) Practical action,

(2) Investigation, and

(3) Collecting and spreading information.

Although under the third head, any subject might be included, the work under the first two heads may be made definite by taking up not more than a dozen important subjects at a time. The District and Taluk Committees will, in addition, have numerous other minor subjects and local questions and matters of detail under their consideration.

Mr. D'Souza has already read to you the names of gentlemen who have done useful work for the Conference or contributed to the public work connected with it. There has been closer co-operation between the committees and departments and the harmony with which work was carried on is due to the ability and tact of my colleagues, Mr. Kantaraj Urs and Mr. Banerji, and also Mr. Chakravarti, the Chairman of the Education Committee. I have in my mind two or three Deputy Commissioners who have been working energetically to advance Conference work but it would be invidious to mention names where all have worked so loyally. We are indebted to Mr. Rose and Mr. Barton for developing work in the Chamber of Commerce. Mr. Humza Hussain has helped in extending libraries within the State. Mr. Navinam Ramanujachar's munificent gift of Rs. 30,000 to the University is worthy of special mention. Mrs. K. S. Chandrasekhara Aiyer is doing very valuable work to advance women's education in Bangalore. Mr. Venkatakrishnayya has been giving much of his time and attention to the work of the Conference and his co-operation has been of great use to us. Mr. K. P. Puttanna Chetty, in the midst of his many other activities, has helped to start a printing press and a tile factory in Bangalore.

The work of the Economic Conference is not the work of to-day. We can only see the full value of it when we reap the results in the next decade or generation. It is a work of silent preparation and is beset with difficulties. Of opportunities, we have many. We might engage ourselves in mining work, build tanks, start cotton mills, oil mills, etc. It is not difficult to find money or even experts. What we lack is a sufficient number of leading men to take the responsibility to advance such projects. This is why we have been cautious in sanctioning new schemes.

There is considerable disinclination to spend money on productive or other public works. That is a very necessary outlay. I received by the last mail from an old and tried friend of Mysore, Col. Sir Hugh Daly, our former Resident, a newspaper article on what is described as the "neglected art of expenditure." We must know how to spend money in order to earn money.

It is unnecessary to add that we owe all our beneficent activities to the progressive policy and courage, to the inspiration and example, of His Highness the Maharaja who is ever watching over our interests and stimulating our work and outlook.

SPEECH AT THE MYSORE LEGISLATIVE COUNCIL.

29th June 1917. [A meeting of the Mysore Legislative Council took place at the Public Offices, Bangalore, on the 29th June 1917, to consider the State Budget for 1917-18. The sitting continued for two days and many interesting speeches were delivered by the official and non-official members. In winding up the debate, Sir M. Visvesvaraya, the President, made the following speech :—]

Gentlemen,—I wish to associate myself, with my two colleagues, in their cordial appreciation of the favourable reception which the Council have given to the Budget. The debate was lively and interesting, and, as remarked by Mr. Banerji, it is in marked contrast to what we have been accustomed to listen in previous years. It at one time looked as if we, that is, the members of this Council and of Government, were never going to agree. This is what I said in closing the Budget discussion in 1915:—

"Some members took a very gloomy view of the condition of our finances. They spoke of the present 'crisis,' 'embarrassing situation,' and so forth. The circumstances, in my opinion, do not warrant any such assumption. If you go closely into the question you will find that the truth is very different. Our financial position to-day is stronger than it ever was in the history of the State except during the past two years."

It is gratifying to see that there is substantial agreement between us on this occasion and that my optimism of previous years was fully justified.

On the Government side, much has been done to place the accounts on a correct and sound basis and to develop a stable and consistent financial policy. The Budget has been in your hands for over two months and I am glad to be in a position to acknowledge the general fairness of your criticisms which are based on a close study of our resources.

It will be very gratifying to His Highness the Maharaja to hear how satisfactorily the privilege of discussing the Budget, conceded four years ago, is being utilised to promote the interests of the State.

I may claim that financial reform has been a special feature of Government activities during this year. We have had the advantage of securing, for this work, the services of Mr. Datta, a retired Government of India officer, of considerable financial experience and reputation. Mr. Chakravarti, who has paid a generous tribute to

Mr. Datta's worth and work, and Mr. M. N. Krishna Rao, our Comptroller, have both cordially co-operated with him in this work.

The new classification in the budget is different in many respects from that of previous years. It is specially adapted to exhibit in their true relations the requirements of the different Government departments and the demands of the moral and material progress of the country.

For the first time the Budget includes the detailed estimates of the Public Works Department also. Special grants are made for strengthening and improving the efficiency of the public services and for a liberal programme of productive public works. Special reserves have been created with an eye to secure financial stability. There is the mining revenue capitalisation fund, sinking fund for loans, reserve for interest on capital expenditure, an increased famine insurance grant and a special reserve for non-recurring expenditure.

The need for all these reserves, intended to ensure the stability of the State finances, is fully explained in the Financial Secretary's memorandum. The reserves, I may tell you, are not meant for hoarding. The major part will be invested in productive public works, as is done in all progressive administrations.

The criticisms of members have been replied to in several able speeches, first by heads of departments, then by Mr. Chakravarti and finally by my colleagues. From the large mass of subjects, I can only pick out a few for special comment.

As regards the percentage of working charges in the Public Works Department, Government will be glad to furnish fuller details to enable Mr. Garudachar to get to the bottom of the matter. In the meantime, he may accept my assurance that the charges are not excessive.

Mr. Basavaiya referred to the inadequate expenditure on technical and industrial education in the districts. There is much difficulty in finding proper men for the work. A number of schemes are ready but for lack of trained staff there is delay in bringing them into operation. The importance of extending the Malnad Improvement Scheme to the taluks of Heggaddevankote and Hunsur, suggested by Mr. Narasimhaiya, deserves consideration. His suggestion that some part of the revenue from sandal trees should be given to owners of private holdings is worth noting.

Mr. Ramaswamy Chetty referred to the importance of providing a good water-supply for all municipal towns. Several water-supply schemes are held up for want of pipes and machinery. His suggestion that instruction should be given in their hereditary occupations to artificers and artisans is worthy of attention.

Mr. Krishnamurthi Rao made a telling reference to the excessive travelling by officers. There may be a few exceptions, but it need hardly be said that the generality of our officers are honourable men who do not travel merely for the sake of allowances. We must not forget that the maintenance of a car is costly and every one who owns a car knows that it is not possible to make any profit from this source.

On the question of the separation of executive and judicial functions, Mr. Kantaraj Urs has already given you an encouraging answer.

I was gratified to find that Mr. Venkata Shamanna recognised that expenditure on education was a productive investment.

Mr. Chengiah Chetty drew attention to the need of consolidating work in the Education Department.

Speech at the Mysore Legislative Council.

Considering how little of literacy there is in the country, it is important to expand education, even if it involved some little sacrifice of efficiency.

Mr. Gulam Ahmed Kalami has brought to notice certain defects in the education of the Mahomedan community, and these have been noticed by the Inspector-General of Education. Mr. Puttanna Chetty spoke with much enthusiasm of the importance of proceeding with the Krishnaraja Sagara works and the scheme for a sea-port for Mysore.

Mr. Venkatakrishnaiya referred to the delay in sanctioning extensions in the Mysore City. Government have already given administrative sanction to the proposals. It now remains for the local officers to work out details without delay.

Turning to criticisms of a general character, I noticed that the members and the Excise Commissioner have been exchanging courtesies. The one advocated an increase of salaries to the subordinate staff and the other offered to surrender a portion of the excise revenue to the Municipalities.

The Inspector-General of Police also received much deserved support to his proposals for the amelioration of the Police force.

On account of its rapid expansion, the Department of Education presents many opportunities for criticism, but if we take into account the rapid expansion of work and the many-sided activities for which that department is responsible, few will deny that the Inspector-General of Education deserves much credit for vigorous progress in various directions.

I was glad that the iron scheme as well as the Bhatkal harbour were referred to with so much enthusiasm and appreciation by members. Both are under active consideration.

Speech at the Mysore Legislative Council.

There was a touch of bitterness in some of the statements made by Mr. Basavaiya and Mr. Kàlami in connection with certain controversial questions. I do not wish to go into the merits of those questions, for Government have an open mind and they want to see the right thing done. Surely, situated as we are, it should be possible to arrive at a satisfactory understanding by mutual discussion. I would appeal to the members with all the earnestness I can command not to utilise these occasions for creating differences. There are so few workers in the country that lack of harmony among these few would be a calamity. This is a time when co-ordination of effort and harmony of feeling and action are most wanted. At such a time, to encourage differences is like sowing lantana in a fruit garden. Disunion grows fast, much faster than harmony, and when the weed grows, let me assure you, it will be an unhappy day for you and me and the people of our State.

A few remarks may not be out of place to show how the resources of the State are utilised to promote the three main objects of Government, *viz.*:—

(1) Ordinary administration;

(2) Developments of natural resources; and

(3) Training and improvement of the people.

The budget provides for the ordinary wants of the administration, including special grants needed for strengthening the establishments of the General Secretariat, Land Revenue Department, Forests, Police and Registration Departments. This is necessitated by the growth of activities and growth of work, which, in the General and Revenue Secretariat alone, has risen within the past five years by nearly 50 per cent.

The allegation commonly made that Government are eager to push on special schemes and are not particular about routine administration is entirely void of foundation. Within the past three years, many irregularities have been detected and suitable action taken. These do not come to the notice of the public. No one who is anxious to effect improvements will allow existing defects to lie unremedied. The special grants made in the budget are intended to improve the efficiency of the departments and also to increase public revenues where possible.

Under development of natural resources, the works projected, or in hand, fall under five classes :—

(1) Railways ;
(2) Hydro-electric works ;
(3) Cauvery reservoir works ;
(4) Other irrigation works ; and
(5) Industrial undertakings.

One of the members was of opinion that we were spending too much on productive public works. I for my part do not see why any limit should be placed, apart from considerations of our resources and capacity, on expenditure which creates property or assets for the future. Another member objected to the appointment of a new Chief Engineer for Irrigation. This appointment, I may explain, is in the place of the late Chief Engineer, transferred to the Railway Department. We badly want an officer of wide experience to vigorously deal with questions connected with major tanks and other irrigation works.

We have also made liberal provision in the budget for the training and improvement of the people, under education, agriculture and industries and commerce. We have increased expenditure under these heads from Rs. 23 lakhs to about Rs. 41 lakhs. We have largely added to the school-going population. The Economic Conference work is intended to train the adult population. It is closely associated with the creation of a business atmosphere in our country. The main object is to equip the people with skill and knowledge, so as to increase individual earning power and the total production of the country.

We are arranging to invest as much money as we can get in productive public works, and in this respect we are only following the example of British India and the progressive countries of the West.

I was gratified to see several members advocate borrowing for productive public works. Borrowing has an unsavoury significance for us, because private persons in this country resort to it on the smallest pretext. But a national debt stands in a different category. It is so universal in advanced countries that it has been described as the first stage of a nation towards civilisation. Five years ago, I recorded these words in a minute: "In a State like Mysore, I should never advocate a debt for unproductive purposes, which stands on a different footing, but it is permissible to carry out productive works which bring revenues to the State and occupation and food to the population by means of loans, if we cannot do so from surplus revenues." This is still the policy of His Highness' Government.

We have something substantial to show in two directions as a result of our new activities. As stated at the Representative Assembly, we have spent Rs. 2½ crores on capital account works during the past five years. From these works, we have begun to derive, as the budget shows, a direct annual revenue of Rs. 11 lakhs. It is unusual that works should begin to yield a return so early. Including indirect results, the gain to the State revenues from these undertakings cannot be less than Rs. 20 lakhs. In other words, the State will, in the course of a few years, have a permanent non-tax revenue of Rs. 20 lakhs from this source. One important consideration which we are apt to forget in this connection is that, for every lakh of addition to State revenues, the value of the increase of production or wealth to the country is often tenfold.

Another notable result is that we have doubled the number of school-going children within the past five years. As improvements go in this country, these two results cannot but be regarded as satisfactory.

There was, till last year, a misapprehension in certain quarters, which was reflected in these annual budget discussions, that we were spending money on chimerical projects and living beyond our means. To this charge the present budget and the precautions it embodies are the best answer. The debate has shown that the members themselves no longer labour under any such misapprehension.

There are still left other critics who tell us that because we are attempting a few new things and making the people think, we are going too fast. Progress and change, they say, should be slow and steady, whatever that may mean. We are told that we should slacken the pace or be for ever lost. I know this assembly will not be disposed to endorse such a view. If our critics think that the feeble attempts we are making in this respect are premature or superfluous, I wonder what they would say to the advice which Mr. Lloyd George gave the other day to the representatives of the Labour Party who waited on him. This is what the Prime Minister of England said :—

"Think out new ways; think out new methods; think out even new ways in dealing with old problems. Don't always be thinking of getting back to where you were before the war; get a really new world."

Speech at the Mysore Legislative Council.

We in Mysore are not seeking a new world. We are not seeking a place in the sun. We are attempting, in a small way, the educational and economic reconstruction of the country so long overdue. We find that 92 per cent of the people are illiterate and nearly 75 per cent are dependent entirely on a single industry, *viz.*, agriculture. The earning power of the people is not enough to support a decent existence. If we look round to take stock, we find many wasted resources and neglected opportunities. All we are attempting is to awaken the people to a true sense of their position and the danger of continued lethargy on their part.

In the pursuit of these modest aims, I have no doubt, we have behind us the full sympathy of the public and the unanimous support of this Council.

INDEX.

A

B

C

D

E

G

H

L

M